Reading George Steiner

THE JOHNS HOPKINS

READING GEORGE STEINER

EDITED BY

Nathan A. Scott, Jr.,

and Ronald A. Sharp

UNIVERSITY PRESS ◊ *Baltimore and London*

© 1994 The Johns Hopkins University Press
All rights reserved. Published 1994
Printed in the United States of America on acid-free paper
03 02 01 00 99 98 97 96 95 94   5 4 3 2 1

The Johns Hopkins University Press
2715 North Charles Street
Baltimore, Maryland 21218–4319
The Johns Hopkins Press Ltd., London

ISBN 0-8018-4832-6 (alk. paper)
ISBN 0-8018-4888-1 (pbk.)

Library of Congress Cataloging-in-Publication Data will be found at
the end of this book.
A catalog record for this book is available from
the British Library.

Contents

Preface

G E O R G E   S T E I N E R, born in Paris to Viennese parents in 1929, was brought by his family to the United States in 1940, just before the barbarities of Nazism descended upon France. Thus, much of his early education was received under American auspices. But after receiving his B.A. from the University of Chicago in 1948 and an M.A. from Harvard in 1950, he took up residence in Oxford, where he was awarded a D. Phil. in 1955. Apart from various brief appointments in the States (New York University, Princeton, Stanford, et al.), the setting of his academic career has been mainly English and Swiss: from 1961 to 1969 he was a Fellow of Churchill College, Cambridge, and, since 1969, he has served at once as Extraordinary Fellow of Churchill and as Professor of English and Comparative Literature at the University of Geneva.

In 1959, as a young man of but thirty years of age, Steiner burst upon the literary scene with the appearance of his first book, *Tolstoy or Dostoevsky*. The subtitle he bestowed on this volume—*An Essay in the Old Criticism*—was intended to announce his rejection of the kind of formalist hermeneutic sponsored by the New Criticism of the 1950s, which sought to fence literature off from the subjectivity of the author, as well as from its historical milieu and from the realms of morality, politics, and systematic ideas. All his subsequent work has expressed a profound consciousness of how inseparable a literary text is from the inwardness of its author and of how deeply it is shaped and conditioned by the weathers of history. Indeed, it is just this sense of the complexity of the matrix from which literature springs that has committed Steiner to so wide-ranging an inquiry into not only the nature and forms of literary art but also the larger backgrounds of its entanglements with the history of ideas and culture. Moreover, his unquellable shock at the Holocaust's revelation of how human speech can be used "both to bless, to love, to build, to forgive and also to torture, to hate, to destroy and to annihilate" has prompted him again and again—in books such as *Language and Silence, In Bluebeard's Castle,* and *The Portage to San Cristóbal of A.H.*—to probe the labyrinthine mysteries of language and to ask how the *word* may be at once the "force and medium of creation" and the instrument of brutality and annihilation.

Whether he was trying to get a serious hearing for Marshall McLuhan or Paul Celan or introducing Lévi-Strauss to the non-anthropological world, as he did long ago in the *Times Literary Supplement,* Steiner has spent nearly forty years bridging fields. Whether writing about Lukács, Benjamin, Adorno, and others (as he was thirty years ago) who have recently been attracting attention, or doing pioneering work in his early essays on subjects that became fashionable only years later (pornography, semiotics, Heidegger and poetics, the inhumanity of high culture), Steiner has taken up the challenge of new ideas with a cosmopolitan breadth and literary-intellectual range that are unmatched in our era.

It is this breadth of interest and his unrelenting quest for a "poetics of meaning" that have given Steiner's work a density and richness that make his readers occasionally feel that his writing, with its eloquence and passionate seriousness, belongs not to that canon of the secondary which usually embraces literary criticism as such, but to some more primary order of expression (as we may sometimes presume to be the case, say, with a writer such as Walter Benjamin). Steiner himself would not, of course, be happy were we to press this point, for he has put into the record his own impatience with that hubris whereby some current theorists deny the validity of the old "hierarchical cut between primary and secondary texts" and regard the poem or the novel as merely a pre-text for critical exegesis.

In his "Responsion" to the essays in this book, Steiner refers to "the instrumental collusion between the genres in my [own] work" and to the possible emergence of a new form "located at the confluence of philosophic discourse and the imaginary." Steiner's most recent collection of fiction, *Proofs and Three Parables* (1993), does indeed seem to move in this direction. But all general assessments of his work must confront something like the problem that Sterne faced in *Tristram Shandy*: his corpus will not sit still! As this book goes to press, Steiner is completing for publication his revisions of the 1990 Gifford Lectures and delivering a series of lectures at the Collège de France. By the time *Reading George Steiner* is actually published, these new books by Steiner will also undoubtedly be out. And this is to say nothing of the dozens of recent pieces in the *New Yorker*, *Times Literary Supplement*, *London Sunday Times*, *Salmagundi*, and numerous other journals.

Surely this veritable priest of reading deserves to be read with a patience and punctiliousness very much greater than what he is sometimes accorded in this way in the English-speaking world. And it is to that end that we have prepared this volume.

N. A. S., Jr.
and
R. A. S.

Reading George Steiner

NATHAN A. SCOTT, JR.

Steiner on Interpretation

OF THE MAJOR literary critics of our period there may be, apart
from Northrop Frye, few others whose work requires us to reach
toward such a term as *greatness*, yet surely preeminent among these is
George Steiner. The shocking massiveness of his learning, which extends across the entire gamut of humanistic studies; the prodigiousness
of his competence in the major Western languages; the speculative
power of his hermeneutical reflections; the brilliance of his textual
commentary; the piercing eloquence of his prose—all this helps to
make *Tolstoy or Dostoevsky*, *The Death of Tragedy*, *Language and Silence*,
In Bluebeard's Castle, *Extraterritorial*, *After Babel*, *Antigones*, and his various other books form a kind of *oeuvre* that, in its puissant majesty, is
virtually without parallel. Yet an enormous amount of ill will toward
him is harbored within the Anglo-American university community.
As one of his friendlier critics remarked a few years ago, "he can seem
too vehement, hortatory, overbearing; he raises his voice in public."
Moreover, beyond the special kind of intensity and earnestness that
belong to his public persona, conventional academicians cannot forgive his polymathic virtuosity, and thus—of this chap who writes on
chess and mountain-walking and philosophy and imaginative litera-

ture and poetics and various other adjacent subjects—they ask dismiss-ively, "But what is his field?"

So, expectably, captiousness and animadversion and rancor have frequently shaped the reception of his work. But the integrity that belongs to his vision of the hermeneutical enterprise is undauntable, and it has been a privilege over the past thirty years to watch that vision consolidate itself in the many remarkable books he has produced. Yet, though he is commonly thought to be committed to linguistics and cultural criticism and theoretical poetics and intellectual history and philosophical anthropology, it is curious that his reflections on the religious tendency of the literary imagination have rarely been seen to have a kind of exemplarity deserving of careful advertence. In *Extra-territorial* (1971), he lays it down that "most of serious literature from the jubilant close of Pindar's Third Pythian Ode to Eluard's *dur désir de durer*, and underlying a coherent response to that literature, is a gamble on transcendence" (161). Or, again, in his "Introduction" to *George Steiner: A Reader* he declares that most of the great literature of the West expresses "a more or less articulate consciousness of the presence or absence of God in and from human affairs" (8). From his very first book (*Tolstoy or Dostoevsky*, 1959) on, so constantly has such an in-sistence been a part of his fundamental testimony that he makes us feel that he is very doubtful indeed about the possibility in any strict sense of a secular poetics. For, as he would say, whether one turns to the *Oresteia* or to Dante's *Commedia*, to the poetry of Hölderlin or Montale or Paul Celan, to *The Brothers Karamazov* or *Light in August*, what we are finally by way of encountering is a *mysterium tremendum* that, like that armchair torso of Apollo in Rilke's famous poem, bids us to "change your life."

Steiner, in other words, is not inclined in any degree at all to treat with that "Byzantine acrobatics" whereby the "deconstructive" mode of poststructuralist hermeneutics radically dissociates literary art from its circumambient world and exhibits it as without any specifiable stability of meaning or any capacity for reference and predication. As he says in his recent book *Real Presences*, "where it is consequent, deconstruction rules that the very concept of *meaning-fulness*, of a con-gruence, even problematic, between the signifier and the signified, is theological or onto-theological" (119). In this one particular he wants resoundingly to register his assent to contemporary skepticism, for what has come to be with him a matter of primary principle is that "any coherent account of the capacity of human speech to communicate meaning and feeling is, in the final analysis, underwritten by the assumption of God's presence" (3). In short, a logocentric universe is not for him the odious specter that it is for Jacques Derrida, for he conceives it to be precisely the immanence of the *Logos* within the world order (requiring, as it does, a "transcendent metaphysics") that has guaranteed the possibility of that covenant between word and world which forms the basis of the entire cultural project of the Western tradition, the whole sense so deeply endemic to our mode of civility that reality is "sayable."

This "deed of semantic trust" (91) has, of course, been radically impugned by many of the foremost strategists of modernity. Already in the late years of the nineteenth century Mallarmé was insisting that the essential genius of language lies in its self-reflexiveness, in its nonreferentiality, in its absolute separation from any kind of phenomenality. And in due course his poetic presentiment was in various ways to be given systematic form by that line of *Sprachphilosophie* reaching from Fritz Mauthner to Saussure and on to Wittgenstein and Frege and Quine and Kripke. The latest chapter in this developing history of *Sprachkritik* is that being currently written by deconstructionist ideology of the present time which asserts that literary texts can tell us nothing at all about anything outside the world of textuality itself. Indeed, as the new savants would have it, the signifiers that compose all discourse only bear upon themselves the traces of still other signifiers, so that the very distinction between the signifier and the signified proves in the end to be an utter delusion. To seek the meaning of any given signifier is only to be confronted with an alternative signifier, and thus any kind of terminal meaning is forever scattered and "not yet," so much so that even the reality of one's own selfhood must be found to be something thoroughly insubstantial and vaporous. This is to say that our condemnation is to "the prison-house of language." "*It is,*" says Steiner (and the italics are his), "*this break of the covenant between word and world which constitutes one of the very few genuine revolutions of spirit in Western history and which defines modernity itself*" (93).

In this late time of "the 'after-word,' " when *logos* and cosmos are no longer considered to meet and when "the very concept and realizability of reference, nomination, predication . . . are put in question" (102), Steiner refuses any simple optimism about the possibility of subverting deconstructionist ideology. As he says, "*On its own terms and planes of argument*. . . the challenge of deconstruction does seem to me irrefutable" (132). This is by no means for him to concede that there are no grounds, substantial grounds indeed, for rebuttal. But he chooses not to waste time on polemic: because what Paul Ricoeur calls "the dismantled fortress of consciousness" is not to be "restored or made stormproof by replacing this or that fallen brick" (133), Steiner wants instead to register a passionate plea that we risk "a wager on transcendence." He sees with absolute clarity that the most essential repudiation lying at the heart of the whole deconstructive enterprise is a theological repudiation, and thus, as he feels, the one kind of faith (in unfaith) may be countered only by another kind of faith. Indeed, that he for the title of his book of 1989 should have borrowed from the lexicon of eucharistic theology the term ("real presence") that speaks of the habitancy of the body and blood of Christ within the two species of the Christian sacrament was on his part a carefully considered tactic (though one wonders why "presence" is pluralized), for what he wants most principally to suggest is that, ultimately, the predicative power that hermeneutics has traditionally attributed to human discourse is underwritten by a theological guarantee, by a radical faith in the immanence of God, this immanence itself in turn making possible significant junctures between word and world.

Contemporary nihilism, after Nietzsche and Foucault and Derrida, declares that our metaphysical situation is that of living amidst absolute nullity, at what the late Roland Barthes liked to call *le degré zéro*. So it says that language lies, insofar as it persuades the innocent that it offers access to anything other than itself: it says that "the games of meaning cannot be won. No prize of transcendence, no surety, awaits even the most skilful, inspired player" (127), because "language inevitably undoes the figures of possible, momentary sense which emerge, like ephemeral and mendacious bubbles, from the process of articulation" (123). But Steiner's rejoinder says, no, our metaphysical situation is defined by the habitancy, the immanence, within our world of a transcendent otherness, which, as in myriad ways it touches human existence, makes us know that the foundations of the house of being are in no way at all of our making. It is this otherness that calls forth those rites of recognition that are enacted by the kind of language we call "literature." "For poets," says Steiner, "these matters are straightforward: over and over, a Dante, a Hölderlin, a Montale tell us of what poetry is saying when, exactly when, words fail it. So does the light at the Vermeer casement. And all great music" (216). By which he does indeed mean to say, shockingly indecorous as it may seem in our phase of civility, that all truly serious poiesis, that everything in literature and the arts that we find to be of compelling stature, is of a religious inspiration and intends one or another kind of religious reference. He puts it in this way:

Referral and self-referral to a transcendent dimension, to that which is felt to reside either explicitly—this is to say ritually, theologically, by force of revelation—or implicitly, outside immanent and purely secular reach, does underwrite created forms from Homer and the *Oresteia* to *The Brothers Karamazov* and Kafka. It informs art from the caves at Lascaux to Rembrandt and to Kandinsky. Music and the metaphysical . . . have been virtually inseparable. It is in and through music that we are most immediately in the presence . . . of the verbally inexpressible but wholly palpable energy in being that communicates to our senses and to our reflection what little we can grasp of the naked wonder of life.

. . . Western painting, sculpture and much of what is incarnate in architecture, have, until the Enlightenment, been religious and, more specifically, Scriptural, both in motivation and representational content. Epic poetry and tragic drama . . . are altogether inseparable from the postulate of "more things in heaven and earth." Tragedy, in particular—and it may be, until now, the most eloquent, concentratedly questioning of all aesthetic genres—is God-haunted from Aeschylus to Claudel. . . . There is, as Socrates hints, a corollary in the *tristia* of high comedy. The gods are most present in their hiddenness when they smile. (216–19)

So Steiner's conclusion is that "it is the enterprise and privilege of the aesthetic to quicken into lit presence the continuum between temporality and eternity, between matter and spirit, between man and 'the other'" (227). It belongs, in other words, to the essential gravity of major art to remind us that the metaphysical situation to which we are ultimately committed is one established by ours being a world indwelt by a Presence that calls us into something like what Martin Buber spoke of as the relation between I and Thou. True, the literature of our vexed modernity is sometimes to be found insisting (as in the manner of a Kafka or a Beckett) on the *absence* of God, but, even amid the density of that absence, Steiner, by no mere dialectical pirouette, suggests that we will be struck by an "edge of presence" (229).

One cannot but be struck by the tack Steiner takes in the interesting argument he put forward in a great essay he issued in 1979 in *New*

Literary History, "'Critic'/'Reader'" (also available in *George Steiner: A Reader*), where he in effect treats the hermeneutical situation itself as bearing an analogical relationship to the metaphysical situation, because it, too, as one enters the world of a text, involves an encounter between presence and presence, between the presence of the reader and that *présence transcendante* which is the "jinnee" in "the well-wrought urn" of the poem or the novel.

In the 1940s and 50s, when the pieties and shibboleths of the New Criticism held sway in the critical forum, one used to hear young disciples of Cleanth Brooks and Allen Tate pridefully declaring their aim to be that of "taking the text apart and putting it back together again," whereas today those who have received their tutelage from Paul De Man and Derrida and Stanley Fish are likely to congratulate themselves simply on their deftness in taking texts apart. But, in either case, from the perspective of Steiner this view of the literary text as merely a neutral object awaiting dissection and mastery, far from representing any sort of bracing rigor, appears to bespeak only a kind of brash philistinism. For, as he urges, "the letter is the vessel . . . of the spirit" (*R*, 95), and thus I am certain that he would want to subscribe to the line that was being taken a generation ago in a brilliant essay by Fr. Walter Ong, "The Jinnee in the Well Wrought Urn," which appeared in *Essays in Criticism* (4, no. 3—reissued in Ong's *The Barbarian Within*). Here, Fr. Ong calls into question that modern theory of the poem-as-object, with its emphasis on the work of art *as such*, the whole notion that "it is neither the potter who made it nor the people, real or fictional, to whose lives it is tangent, but the well-wrought urn itself which counts" (*BW*, 15). And he wants to declare his own sense of how imperfect is the justice done the actuality of aesthetic experience by this modern idolatry of the art object. Fr. Ong is careful to acknowledge that the artistic situation does itself claim for the work of art a certain measure of autonomy: he knows it to be the case that the poem bids for an intransitive kind of attention. But he contends that, precisely in the degree to which the object is taken with ultimate seriousness, our contemplation of it inevitably involves us in a very profound disappointment. For, given the essentially personal orientation of our humanity, we cannot finally perform a genuinely intransitive act of attention before anything less than a person. Contemplation of this sort requires that someone else be *there*, for it involves love—which cannot

be "projected into an unpeopled void." Yet, curiously, the end of the
aesthetic transaction is not psychological disaster, for, as he maintains,
"in proportion as the object of art pretends to be serious," it drives us to
the point of considering it, indeed, as "a surrogate for a person"—as a
surrogate not (as I take him to mean) for the actual scribe who wrote
the sonnet or the story but for him whom Wayne Booth in *The Rhetoric
of Fiction* calls "the implied author" (71–76) and whose real profile is to
be found not in the biography of the historical person but in the texts
that he created. "In proportion as the work of art is capable of being
taken in full seriousness," says Fr. Ong, "it moves further and further
along an asymptote to the curve of personality" (*BW*, 24)—or at least
of a person behaving "enough like one to betray the bias of the human
heart" (25). The world of literary experience is a personalist universe, a
world of dialogue—where the poem is a word spoken and a word
heard, this speaking and hearing enabling us to reach the interior not of
an "object" but of a personal vision of reality.

So, this being the case, Steiner wants to remind us that, when we are
face to face with the *donné* presented by the poem, we do not (or ought
not) *attack* it as if it were merely an object to be dismembered for
inspection, for the real question is how it is to be granted entrance into
the narrows of the heart. "We light the lamp at the window" (*RP*, 149),
when a guest approaches our threshold. "We lay a clean cloth on the
table." And he argues that we must indeed summon the chivalric spirit
of a most scrupulous *cortesia*, if "the living significations of the aesthetic
[are to] seek [us] out [and find us]" (147): we must give true welcome to
the poem when it calls at our door. The "critic" will, of course, take a
step backward from that which is before him: he will "externalize" it as
he tries to decide how to "grasp" it. And, if he is honest, he will in no
way at all attempt to conceal the particular angle—whether it be histor-
icist or psychoanalytic or formalist or some other—from which he
views the text. Moreover, he will not only undertake to achieve an
"ordering sight" (*R*, 69) of, or "objectivity" of perspective on, what he
faces: he will also try to decide how to rank his text, because, "however
eminent, however theoretic in bias, [he] assigns and ascribes valuations
every time he views and designates. . . . He marks down . . . Milton,
and marks up Donne. He 'rates' Hölderlin above, say, Mörike; he
underwrites new issues, such as the modernist movement, as . . . offering a higher yield to attention and sensibility than the late Romantics

or Georgians" (73–74)—and so on and so on. As he "selects and 'prices,'" the "critic" tends to establish a "syllabus," which instructs us regarding those texts that will be found to be most richly rewarding.

The "reader," on the other hand, situates himself in relation to the text quite differently: he does not objectivize it into any sort of datum, because for him its otherness is that not of an object but of a "real presence": so his relationship to it cannot be that "of reification, of competition, and, by logical extension, of supersedure" (86). Because his aim is deeply to internalize the text, he strives to obliterate the distance from it that the critic would actualize, sometimes undertaking indeed to commit it to memory, to learn it *by heart*, thus permitting it to become an agency in his own consciousness and to "generate a shaping reciprocity" between itself and his own deepest selfhood. In this way he seeks to be a shepherd and servant to the texts he treasures.

Among the actual clerisy in the field of *litterae humaniores*, some will incline more to the one than to the other type of study, but Steiner makes us feel that he regards a "criticism" unpenetrated by "reading" as ultimately destined for a sad kind of dryness and infertility, because it is only by way of "reading" that we are led to subscribe to that "contract of implicit presence" (95) which comports with the sort of loving trusteeship of the canon that constitutes the profoundest obligation of a truly humane criticism. Always the interpreter needs to solicit that tact of mind and heart which *cortesia* would accord to the presence incarnate within the text. As Steiner says,

There are questions we do not ask of our "caller," of the summoner's presence in the poem or the music, lest they diminish both the object of our questioning and ourselves. There are cardinal discretions in any fruitful encounter with the offering of form and of sense . . . Maturity of mind and of sensibility in the face of the aesthetic demands "negative capability" (Keats). It allows us to inhabit the tentative. . . . The philological space . . . is that of the expectant, of the risks of trust taken in the decision to open a door. (*RP*, 176–77)

Indeed, we might say that for Steiner the hermeneutical moment occurs when that presence which is incarnate within the text comes knocking at our door to bid for reception and to seek tenancy within the house of our being. Just what is it that would take up residence within us? Steiner's answer to this question can be come by only as close attention is paid to his way of reckoning with the prior question as to why it is that there should be poetry or painting or music at all. To which his answer is that the motive animating artistic creation

is radically agonistic. It is rival. In all substantive art-acts there beats an angry gaiety. . . . The human maker rages at his coming *after*, at being, forever, second to the original and originating mystery of the forming of form. The more intense, the more maturely considered the fiction, the painting, the architectural project, the more palpable inside it will be the tranquil fury of secondarity. The more sensible will be the master maker's thrust towards a rivalling totality. The mortal artist would beget, . . . he would encompass, he would make an articulate *summa* of the world, as the unnamable rival, the "other craftsman" (Picasso's expression) did in those six days. The most concise of *haikus*, the briefest of Webern's studies, an early Kandinsky of a rider in a nightwood, so concentrated in scale that we must bend close, can do just that. They create a counter-world so entire, so imprinted with the mark of their craftsman's hand . . . that we in turn give it echo, sanctuary of remembrance, by discovering in it a habitation for our most intimate needs and recognitions. (204)

The poet's *mundus contra mundum* is not, of course, wrought *ex nihilo*. "Fictions and formal imaginings do select, recombine from among the world's warehouse." But the novelist or poet or dramatist does produce a second creation, which, as it reenacts the fiat of the original creation, becomes a means of epiphany, for it brings us into the neighborhood of that "out of which, inexplicably, have come the self and the world into which we are cast" (215). In short, when we enter into transaction with the work of art, what seeks tenancy within us is the "radiant opacity" of that transcendent Otherness of which Rilke's "angels" bring him news in the *Duino Elegies*. This is why, as Steiner would argue, the logic of poetics can never be, wholly and without remainder, a logic of immanence, for poiesis does in the nature of the case bring us into contact with "possibilities of meaning and of truth that lie outside empirical seizure or proof" (225). "Can there be an understanding of that which engenders 'texts' and which makes their reception possible which is not underwritten by a postulate of transcendence?" (223). To this question he wants resoundingly to propose a negative answer.

So, given his view of the unique kind of nourishment offered the soul by the arts of the word (as well as by the plastic and musical arts), it is not surprising that Steiner gives such short shrift to that new mystique invented by the deconstructionists which declares the work of the commentator and exegete to have a status equal to and perhaps even superior to that of the primary text. In the symposium "Literary Theory in the University," published in *New Literary History* (14, no. 2 [Winter 1983]), he said, "I regard as pretentious absurdity current claims for the equivalence in importance or specific gravity of text and commentary" (445). Ours is, of course, a time in which there seems to be no end to commentary. "Books of literary interpretation and criticism . . . are about previous books on the same or closely cognate themes. Essay speaks to essay, article chatters to article in an endless gallery of querulous echo" (*RP*, 39). The secondary and tertiary are so much the great narcotic of the age that they are often by way of seducing us into forgetfulness of the primary fact that the poem, the novel, the drama is "the literal 'ground and rationale of being' of the interpretations and judgments which it elicits." When the new theorists undertake indeed to argue in effect that the work of art is merely the accidental and subordinate " 'pretext' of all subsequent . . . 'textualities,' 'inter-textualities' . . . and 'counter-textualities' " (151), they are not only trivializing the source texts but also seeking to "domesticate . . . [and] secularize the mystery and summons of creation" (39). So Steiner absolutely refuses to assist in any way at all in the burial of the original source text by exegesis. "The poem comes before the commentary. The construct precedes the deconstruction" (150). And it, therefore, has right of way.

Steiner's whole structure of thought—which it has been possible only partially to review in this brief essay—is profoundly antithetical to those styles of doctrine and expression that are currently modish in the forums of hermeneutical theory. He continues to believe, for example, what he said in his first book, *Tolstoy or Dostoevsky*, that "no man is more wholly wrought in God's image or more inevitably His challenger than the poet" (7). And, in a period when the human subject is considered to be but a cipher at the behest of the norms and protocols governing his linguistic culture, Steiner's unabashed romanticism will to many seem to be vatic and obscurantist in the extreme. Nor will the intransigent skepticism with which he faces "the carnival and saturnalia of post-structuralism" be readily forgiven, nor his equally intransigent loyalty to the great humanistic tradition, the tradition of Augustine and Dante, of Hegel and Hölderlin and Coleridge, of Humboldt and Benjamin and Heidegger. Moreover, despite his immense distaste for anything resembling "vulgar" Marxism, his sympathy for the effort of such critics as Lukács and Adorno to situate literature and the arts within the matrix of history and his belief that this effort holds forth significant lessons for the liberal imagination have often aroused misgiving and suspicion. There are not a few for whom it is nettling that, by dint of the circumstances of his upbringing, he can find his own polyglot background to be "circumscribed by Leningrad, Odessa, Prague and Vienna on the one side, and by Frankfurt, Milan and Paris on the other" (*R*, 13). So his hectoring eloquence, with its occasional Latinate prolixity, is resisted and has sometimes provoked ugly charges of "pomposity" and "theatricality" and "egotism": in this late, bad time it is sometimes thought to be a breach of the decorums for a man (in the manner of a Lionel Trilling or an Erich Heller) to address himself to the generality of cultivated people and to abjure the brutal, barbarous jargon that is today deemed to be the requisite parlance for criticism.

That which seems often to make Steiner's critics most nervous is his habit of driving hermeneutical questions into a theological dimension. Surely, *surely*, says Ihab Hassan, for example, "Steiner is too much part of our secular, agnostic, vaguely rationalist, uneasily humanist, community of letters to evince an unseemly preoccupation with transcendence."[1] But it is clear that Steiner's sense of what is seemly and unseemly does not comport with Hassan's, for his is a hermeneutic that never ceases to insist upon the ultimately religious import of literary art. Yet Steiner's argument dances round the whole question of transcendence in ever so gingerly a way: so chary an argument is it indeed that it never quite becomes a true argument, never quite manages to be more than a matter of sheer assertion. Although he conceives it to be the primary principle of hermeneutics that the possibility of junction between word and world is guaranteed by the immanence of the Transcendent, he never undertakes to set forth what it really means to speak of the world as indwelt by God. The affidavit that he offers in this connection is sometimes deeply moving, but it never rises above the level of personal testimony, whereas the role it plays in his discourse does require a systematic elaboration of the grounds on which his testimony is based.

Coleridge spent the period between the early spring and late summer of 1815 setting down those reflections that form the *Biographia Literaria*, and they record, of course, in part the sense by this point he had won as a literary theorist of how blighting for his age had been the whole legacy of neoclassical rationalism. The empiricist tradition of Locke and Hume had been so scornful of those versions of experience offered by literary art that it had bullied the literary community into supposing (as evidenced, say, by the Addison of the *Spectator* papers) that, far from recasting his inherited language and in the process reconstituting the world, the poet could legitimately elect only the role of copyist who reproduces the natural order as faithfully as possible. Thus the vision of the literary enterprise as involving an act of poiesis had been displaced by a primitive kind of mimeticism. But it is precisely the doctrine of poiesis that Coleridge in the *Biographia Literaria* is declaring it to be his intention to reinstate by way of a theory of imagination. However, because the creativity of the artist was in his view but an instance of the creativity displayed in all man's basic transactions with the world, by 1815 he knew that what he had to do was not merely to produce a reinterpretation of the poetic act but also to call into question the whole system of British empiricist philosophy, which took the mind to be nothing more than the passive recipient of sense data. So the kind of metaphysical enterprise to which he thereafter committed himself in *The Friend* (1818), the *Philosophical Lectures* (1819), *Aids to Reflection* (1825), and the three volumes of papers now known as the *Opus Maximum* was by him felt to be a matter of obligation.

It is a part of George Steiner's distinction to be, after Walter Benjamin, perhaps the only other major literary theorist since Coleridge whose literary reflections do in effect ask for completion by a metaphysical and theological project. It is our inability to discern in his publications to date what the contours of this project might be expected to entail that accounts for the special kind of discontent with which his hermeneutical theory leaves us. Indeed, it is this discontent that prompts a great eagerness for his Gifford Lectures, which he delivered in the spring of 1990, for one remembers, of course, that Lord Gifford, who died in 1887, in that section of his will that endowed the lectures (to be delivered in the four Scottish universities—Edinburgh, Glasgow, Aberdeen, and Saint Andrews), laid it down that the lecturers shall take "Natural Theology" as their subject. When Karl Barth took this platform at Aberdeen in 1937 and 1938, because he conceived natural theology to be the work of the Devil, he elected as his subject "The Knowledge of God and the Service of God according to the Teaching of the Reformation," and a few of his successors have at times also found one or another way of dodging Lord Gifford's challenge.

But, because Steiner's scrupulousness in this matter is to be taken for granted and because if he keeps faith with the founder's intention he will be by way of doing precisely what his work to date invites him to do, the publication of his own Gifford Lectures is to be awaited with very considerable interest.

Note

1. Ihab Hassan, "The Whole Mystery of Babel: On George Steiner," *Salmagundi*, nos. 70–71 (Spring-Summer 1986): 331.

This essay originally appeared in *Religion and Literature* 22, nos. 2–3 (Summer-Autumn 1990), and is issued here with the permission of the editors.

Works Cited

Barth, Karl. *The Knowledge of God and the Service of God according to the Teaching of the Reformation*. Translated by J. L. M. Haire and Ian Henderson. New York: Charles Scribners Sons, 1939.

Barthes, Roland. *Writing Degree Zero*. Translated by Annette Lavers and Colin Smith. New York: Hill and Wang, 1968.

Booth, Wayne C. *The Rhetoric of Fiction*. Chicago: University of Chicago Press, 1961.

Ong, Walter J., S.J., *The Barbarian Within*. New York: Macmillan, 1962.

Steiner, George. *Tolstoy or Dostoevsky: An Essay in the Old Criticism*. New York: Alfred A. Knopf, 1959.

———. *The Death of Tragedy*. New York: Alfred A. Knopf, 1961.

———. *Language and Silence: Essays on Language, Literature, and the Inhuman*. New York: Atheneum, 1967.

———. *In Bluebeard's Castle: Some Notes towards the Redefinition of Culture*. New Haven: Yale University Press, 1971.

———. *Extra-Territorial: Papers on Literature and the Language Revolution*. New York: Atheneum, 1971.

———. *After Babel: Aspects of Language and Translation*. New York: Oxford University Press, 1975.

———. *Antigones: How the Antigone Legend Has Endured in Western Literature and Thought*. New York: Oxford University Press, 1984.

———. *George Steiner: A Reader*. New York: Oxford University Press, 1984.

———. *Real Presences*. Chicago: University of Chicago Press, 1989.

"Literary Theory in the University," *New Literary History* 14, no. 2 (Winter 1983): 411–51. Steiner was one of thirty-nine contributors who prepared brief statements for this symposium.

ROBERT BOYERS

Steiner as Cultural Critic: Confronting America

GEORGE STEINER'S views of the United States are not easy to sort out. Although often accused of a Eurocentric bias, he obviously knows a great deal about American culture and has spent considerable time teaching and lecturing at American universities. Educated at the University of Chicago and at Harvard—where he won the Bell Prize in American Literature—he won a Rhodes Scholarship from Illinois and is a member of the American Academy of Arts and Sciences. He often writes on American themes for leading magazines, and though he devotes considerably more attention to European writing and ideas than to American topics, he is clearly comfortable with the work of Updike and Penn Warren, Plath and Doctorow. Sharply critical of American education, he is also deeply respectful of American scholarship and has gone out of his way to support, explain, or contend seriously with the work of leading American intellectuals. Sometimes dismissive of American ideals, he is clearly troubled by the implications of his inveterate resistance to things American and thoughtful about issues that many of his contemporaries refuse to acknowledge. Rightly convinced that his own obsessive regard for genius and for the best that has been thought and said "will strike the vast majority of *educated* Americans as effete or even (politically, socially) dangerous nonsense," he persists in carrying the argument into the literate American heartland, absorbing one rebuke after another.

Of course the American theme in Steiner is ordinarily subordinated to broader themes. He has never devoted an entire book to American culture, and the overwhelming majority of the nearly two hundred articles and reviews he has written for the *New Yorker*—to cite just one important venue—are on European topics. If Steiner had more fully developed his views of the United States, we would no doubt find it easier to sort them out. What to some readers seems gratuitously provocative in Steiner's formulations might then seem not only more plausible but also necessary. When Steiner asserts that American philosophy is "of a distinctly secondary order," his readers would probably be rather more tolerant if he had devoted more than a few paragraphs to the subject. When he dismisses out of hand the American "creative writing centers" and "poetry workshops," he would no doubt receive a different response if he grappled with what actually goes on under such auspices and demonstrated that compelling art and ideas are not generated in those precincts. No one doubts Steiner's courage, his willingness to provoke and to open debate. But his work on American themes especially has failed to elicit from most American intellectuals the respectful attention accorded to his far more substantial writings on literary, linguistic, and philosophic issues.

Some would no doubt contend that, for all his large Arnoldian ambition, Steiner is not at his best when he operates as a cultural critic. The thinness of his writing on the American theme would then be accounted part of a broader failure. This is a tempting notion, but clearly it will persuade only those for whom Steiner's provocations are mostly fruitless. Others, for whom a briskly essayistic book such as *In Bluebeard's Castle* continues to speak with telling cogency, will simply prefer to wish for fuller substantiation. Such readers will regard Steiner's scattered observations on America as refreshingly free of cant and will note the degree to which his arguments have informed subsequent critiques of American culture that are at once more detailed and less consistently suggestive.

Noting that Steiner's characteristic mode as a cultural critic is not brash assertion but nimble speculation, many say of his criticism— quite as Raymond Williams once noted of Edmund Burke's—that it is "an articulated experience, and as such it has a validity that can survive even the demolition of its general conclusions." What proportion of those "general conclusions" one would deny is of course open to question, but just as it is clear that Steiner often avoids full substantiation of important insights, it is also clear that his speculations are the product of extraordinarily wide reading and a grasp of diverse particulars. Unlike many of those who casually dismiss his cultural criticism, Steiner names names, pronounces firm judgments, constructs intricately ramifying arguments. The "articulated experience" of which Williams wrote is in Steiner a reflection of total commitment to the life of culture. That commitment, in turn, rests upon deep investment in particular loved objects, traditions, artists, thinkers, and agencies of renewal. That there are important limitations in Steiner's cultural criticism no one will doubt; that these limitations are largely disabling, or have principally to do with the relative proportion of assertion to evidence, will hardly seem credible to careful students of the work.

The resistance to Steiner's work on the United States has some relationship to a political and theoretical attack on cultural criticism which has lately held sway in parts of the American academy. Theodor Adorno, himself one of the century's most brilliant cultural critics, raised objections to "the notion of culture as such," and particularly to the fetishization of culture and other "isolated categories such as mind, life, and the individual." Making the case for an alternative "dialectical criticism," Adorno saw in what he took to be the more venerable mode features sometimes cited in attacks on Steiner. "The cultural critic," Adorno writes, "can hardly avoid the imputation that he has the culture which culture lacks." Thus the "arrogance" of a criticism that presumes to pass judgment from a perspective that "exempts itself from evaluation" and speaks as from "a higher historical stage." Fatally tempting to practitioners of this criticism, Adorno argues, is to take up a "position" within the established "culture industry" and, while ostentatiously refusing to make a "commodity" of themselves, to "reproduce the socially prevalent categories." The consequence of such practice is the debasement of culture to "cultural goods" and the promotion of that "hideous philosophical rationalization" which is "cultural values," with all that implies of a willingness to "place culture at the will of the market" or to pretend an escape from the market by a turn "towards the past."

Adorno's probing of cultural criticism nonetheless issues in an appreciation of its indispensable significance, even as he presses for its subsumption by a "dialectical" criticism less susceptible to the dangers he catalogues. Rejecting a fashionable "theory" that "knows the place of every phenomenon and the essence of none," he avows the need for a cultural criticism—like Steiner's—that can maintain "a spontaneous relation to the object." Here, in Adorno's treacherously elusive presentation, one finds the negation of the polemical negation to which his critique had seemingly been bound. That sort of dialectical turn is of course largely absent from the work of Steiner's critics, who see in him only what is "reactionary" or "arrogant." Whereas Adorno grasps the relationship between strengths and limitations in the most bracing criticism, refusing to be dominated by categories such as "reactionary" or "elitist" yet reflecting upon them, American academics are often misled by such terms. To say of Steiner that his views are elitist is to say what is untrue, namely, that he writes from a fixed ideological position, which he promotes with single-minded determination. To say of his work on American culture that it is arrogant because its tone is occasionally aggressive is not to see that the fatal arrogance is only present where the mind of the critic truly "exempts itself from evaluation" and accepts more or less unconsciously that the important questions have been answered. Cultural criticism as anatomized by Adorno is infinitely more various and unpredictable than the caricature of Arnoldianism pilloried by most "advanced" critics today. But the climate in which that caricature has taken hold is generally inimical to thinking clearly about the actual merits and deficiencies of someone such as Steiner.

In one of its primary aspects, Steiner's work on American themes, like his cultural criticism generally, is frankly a part of the classic Arnoldian project. As a reviewer and practical critic, he has tried to see the objects of his attention as they really are and, in so doing, to identify the major work produced in his own time. More ambitiously, in books and essays, he has sought—in Arnold's words—"to make an intellectual situation of which the creative power can profitably avail itself," and in this he has seen criticism as a useful though entirely secondary enterprise. More willfully provocative than Arnold, and decidedly less

sanguine about the effectuality of sweetness and reasonableness, he has
been no less obsessed than Arnold by the prospect of "living by ideas"
and exercising "the free play of the mind upon all subjects." More open
to the anomalous and eccentric, he has also been less inclined than
Arnold to disparage the polemical and the immoderate. Reluctant to
accept Arnold's "central standard" and "the application of principles"
as essential to the business of judgment, Steiner is more frankly committed to intuition and vehement speculation, at once more abrasively
contentious and more willing to be corrected. His observations on
American culture are "Arnoldian" in the sense that they proceed from a
concern for the health of culture and a belief in the continuing validity
of distinctions between high and low, serious and frivolous, enduring
and transitory. But Steiner is very much his own man, and few Western
writers have offered so thoughtful a welcome to different kinds of
twentieth-century art and thought, from Heidegger to Gershom
Scholem, from Nabokov to Montale. The notion that, in rejecting
American rock music and other expressions of "popular" culture,
Steiner shows that he is hopelessly stuck in an outworn Arnoldian
posture is no more credible than the same notion when applied—as it
has been—to Adorno.

When Steiner returns, again and again, to such themes as the decay
of literacy, and speaks with revulsion of the new "leveling," he invites
the charge that he presumes to have "the culture which culture lacks."
To some, this presumption seems not only offensive but also a mark of
Steiner's distance from the egalitarian civilization he wishes to study
and address. *In Bluebeard's Castle*, far more than other books by Steiner,
is marked by his assertion that high accomplishment is the province of
"the gifted few," that there cannot be "value without hierarchy," that
in the United States especially primary and secondary education are
committed to an "organized amnesia," which has made it ever more
difficult for the sophisticated mandarinate to perform its higher functions. Those without a proper grasp of "physics, astronomy and alge-
braic analysis," Steiner asserts, can hope to read seventeenth- and
eighteenth-century literature "only at the surface." The literary tradition, in which one work echoes, mirrors, alludes to another, "is now
passing quickly out of reach" as "glossaries lengthen, . . . footnotes
become more elementary and didactic, . . . marvelous spontaneities of
enacted feeling become 'literary' and twice-removed." In calling atten-

tion to these conditions, Steiner hopes to sound an alarm. His critics are turned off by the hyperbole.

Adorno cautioned against the idea that the cultural critic could transcend by sheer force of will the conditions he deplored. To this caution Steiner offers a compelling if not wholly persuasive response. First, while it is true that a total "transcendence" is neither possible nor desirable for the cultural critic, he can surely propose an alternative model and embody it so fiercely in the very tone and sinew of his prose as to compel acknowledgment of difference. Steiner knows as well as Adorno did how hard it is to resist the encroachment of mass culture into every area of life. Adorno's pained attention to Tin Pan Alley and to American jazz is matched by Steiner's more circumspect treatment of rock music and the technologies of the mass media. But far more important is Steiner's insistent evocation of the alternative self that alone can in any sense resist the culture that is studied. Although in Steiner there is argument, even brash polemic, one is struck more forcefully by the sheer *presence* of an unfamiliar personal vehemence, passion, obsessiveness. Steiner's language enacts resistance in its very disregard of the decorums that mandate caution, impeccable generosity of sentiment, at all costs moderation. Steiner speaks with the driving fullness of one possessed by feelings increasingly unfamiliar to contemporary intellectuals. His capacity to evoke his otherness, his willingness to see himself as "hunter," his unembarrassed identification with those "for whom a great poem, a philosophic design, a theorem, are, in the final reckoning, the supreme value"—these features of Steiner's work embody difference and make Adorno's caution about transcendence irrelevant here. Steiner need not pretend to transcend the culture he describes. While participating in it, he obviously does not belong to it in any way that would make his limitations typical or symptomatic.

Steiner also responds—again implicitly—to Adorno's caution by evoking the power of contemporary culture, its ability to effect massive transformations in every domain of experience. Nothing is more alien to Steiner than the posture of the drawing-room critic holding himself aloof from the changes taking place just outside his window. Steiner's engagement with his culture is aggressive. The very speed of his sentences as they follow hard on one another, the voracity with which he grabs now at one vivid item, then another: these represent to us not only Steiner's singularity but also his indomitable curiosity, the visceral satisfaction he takes in immersion without submission. With sometimes hammering insistence, Steiner dwells upon changes inevitably taking place in our "central habits of consciousness." He argues that it is the vision of the contemporary sciences, *their* energy and "forward dreams," that increasingly "define us." This is not the observation of one who hopes to transcend his own cultural moment. When Steiner speaks of "our reduced condition," when he worries over the degree to which "we are in metamorphosis," he does not exempt himself or anyone else from these conditions. Like very few other critics, Steiner registers the fact of change, tests it on his pulses, responds with sometimes ferocious, never detached fascination. Nor is there anything merely conventional in Steiner's speaking of "our" condition as a common fate. For all of his resistance to much that he describes, he acknowledges that there is no viable way to transcend modernity. One can opt out only by willfully blinding oneself to what is central in our experience. For one who wishes above all to see, neither mystic withdrawal nor aristocratic disdain will serve.

What of the charge that Steiner "presumes to have the culture which culture lacks"? Is it not the case that Steiner declares himself privileged in ways remote from most others? Does he not associate himself all too readily with "a small number, a conscious élite"? The charge is in one sense impossible to answer. To accuse a culture of deliberately denying or tearing down hierarchies of value is obviously to assume that one is in touch with cultural imperatives in the name of which the accusation is leveled. To furnish vivid examples of declining literacy is of course to imply that the critic himself suffers no such debility. But if this seems offensive, then those offended must ask themselves why a forthright assault on recent developments in the culture should seem so unsavory. If the critic only pretended to have the culture that culture lacks, then indeed he would seem presumptuous. But if the very terms in which he indicts the culture seem cogent, the facts more or less unassailable, why then so grave a discomfort with his speaking truthfully?

We have learned to be suspicious of anyone's claim to be simply telling the truth. Steiner makes no such claim. He offers instead a strenuous discourse on various themes in which sometimes tendentious, sometimes unimpeachable observations inform an attempt "to get certain perplexities into focus." That is the heart of Steiner's cultural criticism. Is it grandiose for him to declare his willingness to "press home the debate with the unknown"? The objection has little validity if it reflects only a collision of different intellectual styles, what Irving Howe has called "the Anglo-Saxon" rejecting "the Continental." Beyond that, a serious objection would need to demonstrate that Steiner is not genuinely engaged with the unknown, that he does not ask hard questions for which there are as yet no reliable answers. When he reflects on the relationship between political tyranny and the specific density of certain works of imagination, can any reader feel certain that the relationship is not worth pondering? When he asks whether particular taboos, discernible in American academic life especially, do not portend proscriptions on political, genetic, or theological research, is it clear that he is simply making interesting noises? Intelligent readers in many countries believe that it is necessary to ask such questions, and many wonder why so few writers are willing to ask them. In part it is the burden of Steiner's criticism to ask that question as well and to offer various plausible reasons, which have stimulated debate throughout Western Europe and even in the United States.

The fact that numerous seminars at major universities have been devoted to—or built around—discussion of Steiner's cultural criticism is hardly proof that it is of enduring value or even of serious ephemeral interest. Adorno might well see in the fact nothing more than Steiner's success in making himself a spokesman for the culture industry and brilliantly reproducing the cultural values of a dominant elite. But the very existence of a coherent elite is today more than ever open to question, and one can only wonder who might be said to belong to it. Academics? Poets? Museum directors? Editors of quarterly magazines? However one draws the ranks, it is clear that an elite is today more than ever a dubious fiction and that even the once useful concept of a culture industry invites such confusion and imprecision as to be quite dangerous. If Steiner's cultural criticism has had some resonance —it has surely attracted loud and violent detraction—that cannot be because he has articulated values held by a powerful establishment. Few of the best known cultural figures in the country share Steiner's views on most matters. Leading literary intellectuals in the United States surely do not regard Steiner as a representative voice, and, however much he is admired by many writers, only rarely is he mentioned in their periodicals of choice. Although in England Steiner has certainly remained "visible" in leading magazines such as the *Times Literary Supplement* and *Granta*, he has never achieved among intellectuals the venerable status of an Isaiah Berlin or a Frank Kermode. Even in France, where his works have been warmly received, no one would claim for him a "representative" status. More important, the cultural establishment in these countries is so much a matter of competing factions as to resist any sort of representative voice.

Of course the values informing Steiner's cultural criticism were once central to intellectual elites in Europe, and even to some extent in the United States. So much Steiner himself contends. But those values were then upheld with a confidence no longer conceivable. Steiner, after all, must now take those values to be under assault not from "philistines," but from the very intellectual class whose convictions they were once thought to express. That fact rightly suggests that the values themselves have undergone important changes. What were once elite establishment values are now truly minority values and are in process of being repudiated by many who know quite as much as Steiner does about the formation of cultural elites. Whereas for Arnold a "classic" spoke with an accent sure to be recognized by decently educated readers, for Steiner there can be no "classic" without the accompanying apparatus of argument designed to challenge a general resistance to "perfection" and "tradition." Whereas for Arnold the "value" of great works had something to do with their enabling sweetness and light, Steiner denies that "value" is likely to have any relation to humane virtues. Whereas Arnold could believe that, in speaking for himself, he was speaking for others, Steiner must know that he fights a rear-guard action in a culture for which the rear has been pushed to the margins.

If Steiner's cultural criticism is proof against Adorno's sharpest strictures, it is nonetheless built upon a suspect concept of "culture." For Steiner, "a culture 'lived' is one that draws for continuous, indispensable sustenance on the great works of the past, on the truths and beauties achieved in the tradition." In such a culture, some constituents at least will be willing to "gamble on transcendence" (though not the "transcendence" indicted by Adorno). The gamble can only be sustained by a conviction that certain things are immeasurably more important to our civilization than other things, that the fulfillment of identity is tied to participation in a still living tradition: only the tradition, with all it entails of past glories and forward dreams, can free and make vital what Pindar called "the divinity that is busy within my mind." Adorno feared that such investment in culture, such concern

with "divinity" and "transcendence," would inevitably distract attention from "the true horrors," the exclusions and injustices everywhere
present in the domain of culture. For Steiner to argue on behalf of "the
gamble" must, in Adorno's terms, only ensure that "culture" remain
the domain of the few, as it has been. To pursue the "concrete judgments" that can as yet only be reached by the few must further embed
one's criticism in the very society from which one would stand apart.
For Adorno, the danger to which cultural critics such as Steiner must
succumb is that of supposing culture to be an autonomous realm.
Adorno argues that culture, as an autonomous realm, is deprived of
"the ferment which is its very truth—negation." Insofar as Steiner
purports to encompass culture, to assume that it is a realm of sufficien-
cy constituted by the vitally sufficient judgments and creations of a
traditionally informed elite, he cannot see culture as he should: as a
necessarily indeterminate object "not yet illuminated by reason."

   In defense of Steiner, it might here be objected that no Continental
or American cultural critic would be exempt from Adorno's condemnation. In calling for a dialectical criticism, Adorno demands that cultural criticism refine itself out of existence. Then culture would no
longer be an idea offering comfort by reminding adherents of the
unbridgeable divorce between high and low. The necessary critic, it
follows, must not be content with the "superficial" satisfaction of exposing the philistinism or shallowness of those passing before him.
What the critic would then do to promote the desired "negation" is
nowhere clearly articulated by Adorno, but his primary demands do
surely call into question certain assumptions to which Steiner sub-
scribes. Although Steiner's writing on American themes is but an
aspect of his cultural criticism, it is surely useful here to look at that
work with Adorno's demands in view. For perhaps Steiner's cultural
criticism is, in ways Adorno himself would have appreciated, a good
deal closer to the ideal than his opponents would allow.

   Consider Steiner's most sustained, and notorious, essay on American culture, the long piece "The Archives of Eden," which appeared in
the quarterly *Salmagundi* in 1980. The centerpiece of the magazine's
special issue "Art and Intellect in America," the piece was there subjected to mostly hostile criticism by such writers as Cynthia Ozick,
Susan Sontag, Leslie Fiedler, Dwight Macdonald, and Christopher

Lasch. Subsequent responses, printed in the "Letters" pages of the magazine, showed considerable support for Steiner's arguments among European readers, but something less than approval among most Americans. As in other controversies focused on Steiner's cultural criticism, his harshest critics complain that his speculations are largely without foundation. Others complain that the implications of his "position" are unsavory and that he should know better than to let them stand. Still others complain about the tone of the essay, its arrogance and stridency. Defenders of the piece, and of others like it, generally have little to say of the tone or manner of presentation, preferring to argue the broad merits of Steiner's case, citing the impressive thoroughness with which he assembles the materials of a very complex argument. Accepting that Steiner could not have provided substantiating detail for all of the contentions he makes in such an essay, many respondents are grateful to have the lineaments of the argument and the various "leads" Steiner provides. Those familiar with his earlier work note his continuing emphasis on themes developed in previous books and essays.

Steiner's essay opens with a quotation from a Puritan text on the Great Migration to America, and it cites other contemporaneous speculations on "whether the establishment of the New England polity was not a signal of the end of secular time, for this was the *ne plus ultra* of mundane innovation." He goes on in the opening paragraph to refer to "the reign of everlastingness as foretold in Revelation," of exceeding "terrestrial possibilities," of "ambiguities in the trope of final renovation." Steiner's language is charged with the intensity and hope of those whose vision he records. Elsewhere, things are rather less strenuously energetic, but the overall coloration of the writing is vivid; the temper, vehement. Steiner often selects for quotation the most dramatic formulations he can find, and his own prose shows his fondness for words such as "antinomian," "prodigality," and "infection." His rhetorical questions typically pose very large issues and genuinely challenge the reader in a way not often associated with the milder uses to which that accessible device is often turned. When Steiner asks "can it be an accident that" or "is American culture not precisely what" or "How much" does this or that "matter," he means us to feel that our serious response is urgently required. Even if we have not the information to proceed confidently—so the tone and persistence of the questioning would suggest—we cannot but feel that our thinking on these matters may not be put off and should follow in the general courses Steiner has set down.

Whereas in other writers tentativeness often bespeaks a retreat to calm reflection and stock-taking, in Steiner the statement that "one is bound to get magnitudes and relations wrong" simply concedes that, though one may make mistakes, there is much to be said for aggressively following one's hunches and inviting correction or debate. If a part of the landscape one is covering "is strewn with critical hyperbole and modishness," one ought still to move vigorously forward: to be forewarned is not to be forestalled or intimidated. In his cultural criticism, the rhetoric of Steiner is often one of thrust and thrust. There is little parry and counterthrust, however often Steiner notes potential objections to his line of inquiry. For all of his obviously genuine desire to get things right by consulting every conceivably relevant source and alternative opinion, he moves with a relentless determination toward the fullness of his argument. He has a marked fondness for conclusive insights that permit him to use such terms as "indisputable," "preeminent," and "decisive." Although Steiner routinely questions his own formulations and wonders aloud whether "there is anything but ignorance or short-sightedness" to them, the driving insistence of his writing makes it difficult to think of him as a modest fellow. Tentativeness in Steiner is part of an aggressive rhetorical posture.

There is no law that requires of the cultural critic a becoming modesty. Of course a number of Steiner's best-known predecessors would hardly have seemed modest to their respective audiences. For all of the occasional sweetness and light of Arnold, he purported to know what was what, and he used his touchstones to arrive at literary judgments that were remarkably inflexible by any standard. When Arnold presumes in *Culture and Anarchy* to speak for "Culture" and asks his reader to "consider these people [philistines], then, their way of life, their habits, their manners, the very tones of their voice . . . the things which give them pleasure . . . the thoughts which make the furniture of their minds," and goes on to ask "would any amount of wealth be worth having with the condition that one was to be just like these people by having it?," he is here speaking immodestly, with the untroubled conviction of being right. When Clement Greenberg in "Avant Garde and Kitsch" argues that "the urban masses set up a pressure on society to provide them with a kind of culture fit for their own consumption," he does not apologize for suggesting what may seem offensive or mistaken. He knows that the culture of "the urban masses" feeds an appetite for kitsch and other kinds of junk. Even Adorno is not at all beyond arrogant and inflexible reflections on matters that might have seemed open to legitimate dispute. Jazz fans, for example, seem to Adorno to contribute to "the disintegration of culture" by helping to erase "the distinction between autonomous 'high' and commercial 'light' art." Adorno claims that glorifying "a highly rationalized section of mass production" is "philistine": "Anyone who allows the growing respectability of mass culture to seduce him into equating a popular song with modern art because of a few false notes squeaked by a clarinet; anyone who mistakes a triad studded with 'dirty notes' for atonality, has already capitulated to barbarism." Clearly, Steiner's brashness and his attraction to decisive formulations and ringing judgments are very much in the grain of the cultural criticism practiced by many distinguished forebears. Although one would be loath to designate these as constitutive features of cultural criticism, it is clear that a liberal distaste for such elements ought itself to be subjected to further scrutiny.

Steiner's "Archives of Eden" is also marked by another characteristic feature of his cultural criticism, namely, an attempt to "think the contradictions" of an argument. Throughout the essay Steiner not only concedes that he may be in error but also forcefully undercuts some of his most "decisive" charges. This has nothing to do with self-contradiction. When Steiner indicts the American counterculture he does so with a consistency that is nowhere diminished by confusion. When he associates an authentic culture with "the transmission forward of the best that reason and imagination have brought forth in the past and are producing now," he does not muddy the argument by allowing for exceptions that would invalidate his own emphatic preferences. Steiner's position on most matters is about as coherent as an intelligent position can be. To think the contradictions is for him to acknowledge perspectives radically different from his own. This he does in a spirit of considerable generosity and tolerance. "Liberalism" is not for him the enemy; it is another perspective, different from his own. It entails decencies that he admires, that he would embrace insofar as they are compatible with other imperatives to which he feels at least comparable allegiance. It is reasonable, he feels, for a liberal to oppose elites, though he himself can oppose them only to the extent that he need not thereby renounce his convictions about the way that

culture is transmitted. Thinking the contradictions here involves trying to establish what are and are not compatible ideas. At its most
severe it involves an attack on those who not only "want it both ways"
but are unwilling to concede that the most appealing values often
conflict with one another and entail painful choices. Thinking the contradictions can be for Steiner the practice of exposing "puerile hypocrisy" or an ever more contagious confusion. It is also a part of the
ongoing quest to establish hierarchies of value by questioning the nature of first- and second-order priorities.

That thinking the contradictions is not in Steiner quite what Adorno
meant by dialectical thinking is clear. Steiner is not intent upon doing
away with the large contradictions and incompatibilities to which he
pays attention. His sense is that such antinomies necessarily persist
and that culture expresses them without ever really knowing how to
eradicate them. Efforts to think beyond the contradictions, though
sometimes exhilarating, are too often undertaken by overtly coercive
regimes. The very different prospect envisioned by Adorno, of a dialectical thinking that would install negation at the heart of a culture's
sense of itself, does not for Steiner offer a sufficiently coherent view of
culture. Neither does negation as a presiding principle offer an adequate underpinning for a common experience in which human beings
drink deeply from, and are regularly nourished by, the things they
love. Steiner is too much the obsessed servant of particular loved texts,
musical scores, metaphysical proofs, theorems, to be as comfortable as
Adorno with a dialectical thinking that is largely theoretical and consistently geared to avoiding any kind of domination. To be "dominated"
by a great painting is not for Steiner an experience one should wish to
renounce or overcome—much though he believes that possession at
best entails an aggressive component, a *taking* possession in which the
work is itself transformed, no longer the object that at first confidently
imposed itself. Although Adorno warned against the infatuation of
theory, his fear of "enthrallment in the cultural object" makes his
criticism quite different from Steiner's, for which self-possession is
fully enabled by the loved objects that take permanent root in the mind.

The "contradiction" central to "Archives of Eden" turns on the
professed desire of Americans to extend culture to everyone and what
Steiner takes to be the consequent "disaster" of American "pseudo-
literacy," "the awful state of intellectual affairs" in the United States.
The essay is not in the main an attack on institutions but on self-

deceptions and lies that affect American education and in turn perpetu-
ate myths about the great American experiment. The self-deceptions
are discernible in many kinds of American "promotional" discourse.
Often they are most vivid in the practice and rationalization of the
American professoriate, which can routinely "trivialize" and "water
down" what it teaches while pretending to have sacrificed nothing of
consequence. Or they are vivid in the claim that one can "educate" a
person without asking him to read much or to master a range of
intellectual disciplines. In exposing these self-deceptions, Steiner is not
at great pains to provide documentation, believing that the evidence is
fully available and widely accepted. Although many will disagree with
what he makes of these matters, the *fact* that trivialization and watering
down take place seems to him unanswerable. So, too, with the fact that
many in the American educational establishment express contempt or
indifference to "content-oriented" courses and profess instead simply
to teach students how to think—as if thinking could be taught at a
university level to people who typically have almost nothing to think
about. Although Steiner offers here and there an anecdote or a reference, the force of the argument is largely dependent upon his willingness to speak truthfully about what others also see, however accustomed they may be to denying it. If some American readers utterly
reject the argument, that may reflect their continuing refusal to acknowledge the facts or their feeling that Steiner makes more of those
facts than is warranted.

Another significant contradiction has to do with the gap between
American "custodial" achievement and the relative indifference of
most Americans to high culture. The United States has been for some
time preeminent for "the scope, generosity, technical brilliance and
public prestige" of its cultural enterprise. So Steiner contends. The
"didactic energies" and curatorial achievements of the American museum world are remarkable. So are the "scale" and "pitch of quality"
of American musical performance, the organization and activity of
American libraries, the resourcefulness and thoroughness of the country's archives. Although it is possible, Steiner says, that in some domains the United States "will not produce first-rate contributions," it
is clear that in some areas at least the culture has already produced
works of "classic occasion."

If all this is so, Steiner goes on, why do works of the first magnitude
matter so little in the United States? Why the "contradiction" between

a culture brilliantly organized to preserve and present the best that has been thought and said and a society utterly unable to view a rich cultural tradition as the principal source of its strength? Steiner knows that this question, like others growing out of it, may well rest upon "oversimplification." But such questions are central to his thinking on the vicissitudes of liberal culture, and the American instance seems to him particularly troubling, given the manifest strengths of the culture and the diversity of its intellectual and artistic elite.

Two elements come together in the argument about the United States as "the archives of Eden," and it is not always as clear as Steiner assumes that they belong together. On the one hand, there is the contention that the American genius tends to organization, coherence, preservation: it is committed to culture as a "thing out there," something to be packaged—willfully, professionally, efficiently prepared and disseminated. On the other hand, Steiner contends that Americans tend not to take to heart the works of spirit and beauty that are routinely made accessible to them. Inclined, conditioned, to regard great works of thought and imagination as "adjunct" to real life, as "artifact" or "monument," Americans typically are reluctant to let themselves go in the presence of the real thing or to regard an obsession with a powerful work as anything but remediable affliction. The American citizen at his best is inclined to "have" culture as a "something" potentially valuable, perhaps even in some way indispensable, but in no way intrinsic to his intimate sense of self or his valuation of the society in which he lives.

Steiner clearly believes that the one issue is, in important respects, essential to a grasp of the other, but it may also be that neither can be tested without treating it independently. Take the argument about the intrinsic character of the American genius. In suggesting that the national genius is more inclined to organization than to "organic" creativity, Steiner places primary emphasis on the country's institutional achievements. This is inevitable. As long as Steiner can point to the extraordinary investment Americans have made in their cultural institutions, he can speak persuasively about a major dimension of their ambition. The number and quality of their symphony orchestras, the acquisitive reach and largesse of their museums, and other manifestations do surely help to make Steiner's point. Americans are not only good at preservation and presentation but also throw themselves into these enterprises with perhaps unrivalled conviction and efficiency.

What of the other side of Steiner's assertion, that Americans are more inclined or suited to organization than to organic creativity? The one aspect of the assertion is of meager polemical interest without the other, and the other is, to say the least, not only provocative but highly questionable. Not many will deny that culture is packaged and sometimes watered down and conspicuously consumed in the United States. But many will deny that Steiner can mean what he says when he suggests that, "in some cardinal domains at least, America will not produce first-rate contributions." Steiner is quite right to admit that in undertaking a broad assault on all of American culture he is necessarily reduced to an "intuitively vague, partial account," that there is nothing for him but to "generalize and drop names in an impressionistic register of guesswork and prejudice." And yes, such an inquiry may surely elicit fruitful debate and rebuttal. But what makes Steiner's vagueness or partiality acceptable whereas another's would be irresponsible? What makes Steiner's "prejudice" worth contending with, his name-dropping more than a facile ploy?

First, and most obviously, there are the important concessions and exceptions built into Steiner's argument. We note his attempt to make a case for the "authority" of the American novel and observe him grappling with the dominance of American painting in the mid-1950s. However briefly he handles these matters, he does clearly see the weaknesses in his thesis. Just so does he acknowledge "innovative" genius in American dance and architecture and wonder whether it is his "incompetence" in mathematics that leads him to doubt the validity of American claims there. These doubts, acknowledgments, and concessions are telling signs of good faith in an argument so willfully provocative as to need as many signs of this order as it can muster.

Yet the persistence in vagueness and partiality remains troubling. For Steiner to conclude the generalizing and merely suggestive name-dropping with a statement such as "this is not an overwhelming harvest" is peremptory almost to the point of arbitrariness. One cannot say, after all, that a culture with considerable claims to contemporary preeminence in literature, the visual arts, dance, mathematics, and the sciences is nonetheless deficient in creativity. Nor is it tenable to assert that the creativity that does exist is not organically related to nurturant factors in American life and institutions. Perhaps it is true, as Steiner contends, that no American painter will "emerge as possessing a stature, an innovative or recreative strength," to match that of a Duchamp or Picasso (the example of Duchamp is itself highly dubious). But perhaps—and here one confronts the limits of this kind of speculation —it is *not* true. Perhaps, moreover, the "overwhelming harvest" Steiner wishes to see has already been realized in a degree his own "prejudice" cannot allow. Suppose that he is right when, in citing the "authority" of the American novel, he asserts that "the summits are *not* American." Is there any reason to go on from that to deny that there has anyway been an "overwhelming harvest" in twentieth-century American literature, from Dos Passos, Hemingway, Faulkner, O'Connor, Ellison, and Bellow in fiction to Eliot, Pound, Stevens, Bishop, Frost, and Lowell in poetry, or Mailer, Baldwin, Trilling, Gass, and Wilson in the essay? The vagueness in Steiner's argument is troubling largely because it leaves important parts of the relevant questions not only unanswered but also unformulated.

Steiner hopes that, in asking "unappetizing" and sometimes even "indefensible" questions, he will elicit the "fertile instigation to understanding" which is "No, but." The hope is often repeated in the body of his cultural criticisms, and he does surely believe that some of what he proposes will be shown to require revision. But, we ask again, What makes the largely unsupported generalizations and hunches worth attending to? First, the assertions are not wholly unsupported. To drop names is a kind of support. To set up comparisons is another: Steiner does not merely state that Faulkner and Hemingway are not the summits of modern prose fiction; he offers in "evidence" the names of Mann, Kafka, Joyce, and Proust. We are free to disagree, but not to deny that a comparative framework may be useful. Part of the American provinciality that Steiner indicts is the reluctance to accept the validity of such contexts, with all they imply of hierarchy and ranking. But Steiner is as good as his word in insisting again and again that there can be no judgment and no understanding without frameworks for comparison. Although he rarely pursues the comparisons in his cultural criticism—where he has other purposes to fulfill—he does so with enormous care and shrewdness in his literary and philosophical criticism. In works such as "Archives of Eden," the generalizations and hunches stir us in the degree that we can sense the pressure of a careful and shaping reflection just behind them. If indeed audacity is required to make in passing the kinds of sweeping judgment Steiner makes, that is not to deny that the judgments are cogent and that the logic of the argument is usually unassailable.

The best reason for attending to Steiner's sometimes unsupported generalizations is that they furnish and enable an argument that is really more important than its parts. One can reject his statement that in the United States there has not been "a major philosophic presence with the possible exception . . . of C. S. Peirce" and still take very seriously indeed his broader charge that in the United States even educated people have never been deeply persuaded "that abstract thought is the true motor of felt life." Ought Steiner, then, to have seen how unnecessary was the statement about "a major philosophic presence" and omitted it? Some of his critics would surely say so. But the statement, if not essential to the broader argument, does have a good deal to do with it, and it does in itself not only provoke but also raise a legitimate issue rarely accredited today. The larger argument does not depend on the collateral issue because the linkage is suggestive, not a matter for conclusive determination.

So Steiner asks us to accept that certain propositions are usefully arguable. "The climate of American feeling," he says, is resistant to ontological thinking. This *may* be a consequence of the failure of the country to have produced "a major philosophic presence." The major philosopher "is one whose discourse, as it were, successive generations carry on their person." In Europe—think of the public stature of a Sartre, a Gramsci—philosophic debate is an "emphatic" element "of political and generational identity," as it cannot be in the United States. And so on. Some say this business of making things usefully arguable cannot be a sufficient goal for so palpably extensive an enterprise. After all, it is argued, we do not need Steiner to propose what we are able to consider without him, such as the possible connection between the intrinsic merit of a work and the long-term effects it may have. But the intervention of Steiner may well seem critical in a way his critics do not acknowledge—in reminding us, for example, that these are not merely academic issues, that observations on the state of philosophic thinking may bear heavily on much else, that the willingness of educated people to take seriously matters vital to the life of their culture is very much in doubt. A number of the American writers who expressed disdain for Steiner's attacks on cultural disorder and blithe academicism in the 1970s showed themselves quite ready twenty years later to sound their own alarms. Among these are two of the most accomplished American cultural critics, Irving Howe and David Bromwich, both men of the liberal Left, both once sharply critical of Steiner's work. To see how far such writers have come, one need only note that in his 1991 essay "The Value of the Canon," Howe finds himself having to cite for support Georg Lukács, Leon Trotsky, and Antonio Gramsci in order to make the point that "students should read great books." Obvious? No doubt, says Howe, but necessary, given "where we are." Looking back, it may well seem to many of his critics that Steiner saw first where American education and intellectual life were headed and that the tone of feverish urgency one finds in his cultural criticism is not at all excessive.

So let us consider again Steiner's contention that the very character of "a community of rational men and women" is involved in their willingness to "think being" and to feel its experience "pervaded by explicit philosophic argument." In citing what he takes to be vulnerabilities in the philosophic record of the United States, Steiner vividly calls our attention to a problematic dimension of the national character. In saying that there is no American "enquirer into the meaning of meaning to set beside Heidegger or Wittgenstein or Sartre," he presses us to accept as valid—as full of implication—the relationship between one thing and another ordinarily seen as distinct. For Steiner—and this is what he truly hopes to make "usefully arguable"— educated people for whom there is no point in making comparisons, for whom it is not important whether American philosophy may rightly be said to have merely an academic interest, do in fact tell us a great deal about "America." The many educated Americans for whom these are not usefully arguable issues help us to see that Steiner has long been on to questions few other critics have been willing to address.

Steiner's work as cultural critic has often borne on the character of the intellectual and artistic elites that help determine the direction of a culture. His writing on things American is in this sense characteristic. What Steiner takes to be central to American culture has much to do with the attitudes of its cultural elites. If in his view American music "has been of an essentially provincial character," this has much to do with continuing ideas of "newness" and innovation which move American composers to operate outside "formal and substantive" continuities more usually embraced elsewhere, even by bold spirits. In his cultural criticism Steiner often follows the implications of ideas— newness, frankness—that routinely exercise artists and intellectuals. What benefits, he wonders, follow from a culture's insistence that "fairness" predominate in its organization of educational priorities? What indispensable strengths are there in works of imagination which hope to "make it new" by denying their relationship to previous works? How clear are the distortions and spiritual deficits, the intellectual weaknesses and delusions, consequent upon those predominating ideas and commitments? Even those uncomfortable with Steiner's sense that the health of a culture can be gauged in its attitude toward an elite minority will agree that an elite does influence the temper of a culture. If members of that elite deny that it is their business to exert cultural influence, or that their interests are in any way different from those of other citizens, that denial is surely of significance to the cultural critic. So Steiner would have us understand.

No doubt, Steiner's constant circling back to the idea of an elite minority is hard for most American readers to stomach. Accustomed to thinking well of people who speak frankly, many of these readers are nonetheless unable to forgive Steiner for believing that most of us do not amount to much and that "it is a Socrates, a Mozart, a Gauss or a Galileo who, in some degree, compensate for man." Those—"the vast majority of educated Americans"—who regard this kind of thinking as "dangerous nonsense" are likewise convinced that there is nothing so special in the numerous lesser members of Steiner's elite who attempt to transmit insight and beauty, in the classroom or in works of secondary "paraphrase." To his critics, the elite of Steiner is typically self-important and out of touch with much that lifts the spirit of most thoughtful people. For Steiner, the elite figure is to be understood as "infected with the leprosy of abstract thought," an "obsessed servant" of texts, "a loving, a clairvoyant parasite" living on, passing on a feeling for ultimate things. Such a figure "abides," as others cannot, "the hideous fact that hundreds of thousands could be fed on the price a museum pays for one Raphael or Picasso." On the other hand, the critics of Steiner, feeling a decent revulsion at the "hideous fact," as at his confident enunciation of priorities, often dismiss his concerns as "effete," his instincts as so willfully mandarin as to separate him from all but a handful of his contemporaries.

What does Steiner see as the proper relation between his elite and the culture? On the American scene the proper relation is at present only a remote ideal, and it must remain so for as long as the intelligentsia refuses to behave like a responsible elite. So Steiner contends. Citing Julien Benda and "The Treason of the Clerics," Steiner refers to those who have "sought pardon" for their gifts and advantages "by seeking to strip themselves of their own calling," going in for a "masochist exhibitionism" and "seeking to howl with the wolves of the so-called counter culture." In practice, this stripping and howling have amounted to protestations of solidarity with the oppressed, the young, the disaffected, even with groups in the Third World who openly express contempt for the intellectual traditions and institutions of the West. The posturing of many academic intellectuals especially has had the effect of generating an "apologetic" and "defensive" attitude in the intelligentsia, which knows that people without feeling for the intrinsic benefits of higher education are often deeply resentful of intellectual elites. To reach those who are skeptical or downright contemptuous toward the very disciplines and traditions they represent, many believe it is necessary and good to stress their primary commitment to equality, gregariousness, pluralism, and openness.

Steiner regards the preference expressed in such commitments as "thoroughly justifiable." The person who genuinely believes in the merits of an open society and in his own primary responsibility to work to enhance the pride of formerly oppressed peoples, to spread ideas of distributive and social justice, and to deny the validity of hierarchy, and who "makes this choice and lives accordingly deserves nothing but attentive respect." Steiner instead condemns those—"and they have been legion in American academe or the media—who want it both ways." He condemns, that is to say, "the puerile hypocrisy and opportunism" of those "who profess to experience, to value, to transmit authentically the contagious mystery of great intellect and art while they are in fact dismembering it." The academic who professes to teach "literature" while offering students an easily digestible and patently mediocre work on the grounds that it contains acceptably humane sentiments and liberally accredited identity images is such a hypocrite. The hip, ever so sophisticated literary journalist who professes to find in a rock lyric as telling an expression of the modern condition as any to be found in Joseph Skvorecky or Thomas Bernhard is another. So, too, the intellectual who wants to know who gave anyone "the right" to "invalidate" the tastes of others by presuming to set in place evaluative contexts to which even "popular" art may be submitted. In these instances Steiner sees treason or betrayal: principally, on the part of those who "espouse—a justly sacramental verb—" a commitment to great art and thought, "while seeking to deny the conditions of person and of society from which they have come to us, from which they continue to come."

The most obvious rejoinder to Steiner would ask why we should not wish to have it "both ways." Americans often believe, quite as Steiner has shown, that the pursuit of happiness is compatible with just about any other worthwhile goal and that the ordinary is not a "despotism" but a perspective useful for undercutting disproportionate attention to the rare and pretentious. Why should American academics desist from teaching in the name of democratic and liberal values if only those values, worn prominently on every sleeve, will win for them the hearing they crave? Why should a robust feeling for the contemporaneous and immediate interfere with a sober interest in the past, or disable the effort to make it seem relevant? Why should a distaste for the consecration of culture to the discovery of "genius" be absolutely inimical to the study or appreciation of important art? To put these and other such questions in this way is clearly to move toward an answer. Those who want things both ways ought at least to see what they can do, and Steiner would be foolish to deny that some have already enjoyed considerable success in their efforts. Steiner has no fully persuasive evidence that "the correlations between extreme creativity . . . and political justice are, to a significant degree at least, negative." His sense of the past is such that he is necessarily inclined to read the correlations as negative, but—as any American would surely remind him—*that* was *then*, and *this* is *now*. If, as he says, "the flowering of the humanities is not worth the circumstances of the inhuman"—or the unjust?—then it not only makes sense to regard that flowering as a secondary priority but also to try to make the humanities flower under very different auspices. Many artists and intellectuals have sought to have it both ways, and not simply by trying to promote in their works a respect for social justice. Many, after all, have harnessed their creative obsessions to the achievement of personal advantage or comfort. Steiner's language of infection does not always do justice to the creative experience even of artists and thinkers he admires. That language of extremity may also distort our understanding of the appetites underlying the devoted transmission of culture. So Steiner's critics contend.

Just as there is no fully persuasive reason why people should not try to have things "both ways," there is also no denying that Steiner is right to speak of hypocrisy and shallowness in American culture. Given the enormous numbers enrolled in American colleges and universities, it is astonishing how slight in the United States are the sales of serious fiction and poetry, how little first-rate theater can be sustained in

American cities, how small a proportion of Americans can speak or read even a single foreign language, how few are the daily newspapers that carry "hard" news and adult commentary, how entirely even the leading professional schools in the arts and sciences are content to be vocational training grounds whose students are in the broad sense uneducated, how even reputable institutions routinely graduate students who have read little and are not able to compose coherent papers. To be sure, there is a wide public response to blockbuster museum shows, the success of American musical training, the international prestige of American medicine, and so on. No one denies that the United States has accomplished a great deal. But Steiner rightly points to so many fundamental deficiencies in American culture that his attack cannot be easily dismissed. Neither should anyone too readily dismiss what he says of the "sheer dishonesty" involved in the promotion of American open-admission universities or programs. The absence of academic standards in many of these institutions is no secret. We are learning, moreover, that most of these colleges and universities not only fail to teach very much college-level material but also do not succeed in creating the kind of pride and commitment to growth that might otherwise be said to "compensate" for academic deficiencies. If the "populist ideal of general education" for all is not "totally superficial and mendacious," it has yet failed to achieve generally satisfactory results. The hypocrisy of those who claim success and refuse to address the deteriorating state of the culture is obvious. Here Steiner has for many years touched upon a sensitive and critical issue.

The shallowness of American culture is an elusive matter. Many have taken it on, none with greater cogency than Tocqueville. Philip Rieff's observations on "The Triumph of the Therapeutic" were similarly instructive. So, too, the testimony of leading poets and novelists. Consider Randall Jarrell, who wrote in "A Girl in a Library" of a nineteen-year-old college student who—"very human"—dozes over her books or, awake, "studies" to get ahead. Jarrell's girl passively insinuates herself into the poet's mind, which "shrinks from its object" and concludes that "this is a waist the spirit breaks its arm on." Steiner's reflections on American culture are very much in this vein, not quite so ironically playful, but comparably fierce and, even in their generous moments, unforgiving. Like Steiner and others confronted with the numbing common sense, "the sovereign candour of American philistinism," Jarrell in his poem calls as witness not an American friend but a

European—specifically, in Jarrell's poem, Pushkin's Tatyana Larina—
so that together they may agree that when "the Angel comes," it is
"better to squawk like a chicken / Than to say with Truth, 'But I'm a
good girl.'" In his own calls to Pushkin, Kierkegaard, Wittgenstein, and
Heidegger, Steiner has seemed routinely to invoke the European spirit
as witness against the pervasive shallowness of American cultural life.
So he reminds us that in the standard American version, "a psychiatric
social worker waits on Oedipus, . . . a family counselling service at-
tends on Lear," and Dostoevsky is reassured that there are "cures for
epilepsy." Caricature, to be sure, but telling caricature, and by now
familiar among critics of the United States, though Steiner was among
the first of his generation to frame the case in these terms.

Steiner's critique of American culture does not lead on to programmatic recommendations. For one thing, Steiner insists that the culture
is too diverse to be neatly contained within any single formula. For
another, the choices and circumstances that have made the United
States what it is have much to be said for them: Steiner is perfectly
serious when he repeats that the so-called American way is "thoroughly justifiable." His admiration for particular American achievements is
considerable. When his critics complain about the absence of persuasive judgments or recommendations in Steiner's work on the United
States, they usually say that it is finally hopeless to judge by looking
back or consulting European models. Also hopeless is Steiner's idea
that one can judge by drawing comparisons between the American
experience and the experience of oppressive societies. Few of Steiner's
assertions have met with as much resistance as his contention that great
art and thought are more likely to come from politically repressive
circumstances than from relatively open societies. Although Steiner
cites Borges—"Censorship is the mother of metaphor"—and Joyce—
"we artists are olives; squeeze us"—he is routinely accused of building
a theory on what is in others merely a vagrant suggestion. Steiner, it is
said, cannot expect to do justice to the American condition armed with
notions taken over from cultural settings that will not transfer to distant shores. His refusal of programmatic overtures is therefore often
regarded as evasion, even by academic intellectuals who would never
dream of demanding from other cultural critics a practical program.

What must be stressed, of course, is that Steiner does not expect
Americans to quit their ways and take up his urgencies. His task is to
point out the cultural consequences of particular assumptions and to

see the United States as a peculiar, in some ways exemplary, phenomenon in the history of the West. In citing Borges and Joyce, he does not recommend that American writers find ways to labor under censorship or tyranny. His view of exigency does not lead him to deny the first-rate work that is produced in pleasant circumstances. Although he persistently applies to American culture standards taken over from other precincts, he most strenuously judges the United States by its own high claims. It is not only the candor but also the aggressive contemporaneity of American intellectuals that Steiner anatomizes and seeks to understand. His oppositional critique is everywhere a response to inflated or misleading claims, as well as to the betrayal of promises Americans themselves have often made.

There is no use in trying to defend Steiner against recent proponents of so-called cultural studies. People who believe that a university curriculum should be principally built on the interests and demands of the population at large may have a valid case to make, but there is no way that they can seriously confront Steiner without finding a way to take seriously once again the idea of culture that informs his stance. Academics who automatically sneer at "humanists" who "imagine that the general progress of civilization has something to do with appreciating great art"—here I quote a prominent postmodern thinker—are themselves an important part of the problem Steiner confronts. So also are those for whom the idea of an elite minority is said to be reprehensible and disgusting, though they are themselves frequently contemptuous of generalist intellectuals such as Steiner, Irving Howe, and John Bayley, who write not solely for a professional literary class but for a common reader. Although Steiner has aggressively locked horns with many of those who casually consign "humanists" to the dustbin of history, it is unlikely that at present he will carry the day in the American academy.

Of course there are many kinds of readers, and even in the American academy substantial numbers continue to regard Steiner as a model of intellectual range and brilliance, whose cultural criticism on the whole is deeply stirring. Those who would make a case for the cultural criticism obviously follow some of his own procedures so as to place him where he belongs. This seems fair, and helpful. When one says that he belongs with Adorno, or Arnold, one is aware that the points of legitimate comparison are partial at best. Place him alongside other cultural critics and the impression of disparity remains. Yet at his best—and he is often at his best—Steiner does often call to mind other prominent cultural critics. Is there a single model against which to measure his achievement? Probably not; no two writers could be as different from each other as Adorno and Arnold, and other such figures are no less singular. At the same time, one does often have the sense that cultural criticism is an enterprise characterized by a particular sentiment. That sentiment, one feels, would underwrite and enable the work of a writer in such a way as to make it useful or inspiriting to his contemporaries at least. Steiner's posture might not be—in this sense—so eccentric as to prevent his doing the essential work of the cultural critic.

What posture? What work, exactly? Elias Canetti, speaking in 1936 of Hermann Broch, describes the true writer as "the thrall of his time," one who "sticks his damp nose into everything," who is "insatiable," "unintimidated by any single task," attentive always to the "diversity of the world." Canetti also demands that the writer "stand against his time, . . . not merely against this or that," but against the very "law" of his time. This opposition, Canetti goes on, "should be loud," and the writer will thus have to "kick and scream like an infant," though "no milk of the world, not even from the kindest breast, may quench his opposition and lull him to sleep. If he forgets his opposition, he has become an apostate."

Canetti's profile was not intended to describe the cultural critic, but a certain kind of exemplary writer. That much is clear. So, too, is it obvious that, as in any typology, individual particulars may not apply in every relevant instance. Yet, taken together, the qualities cited by Canetti say a great deal about our experience of the best cultural critics, and of Steiner's work most especially. Which critics in our day have so consistently and lucidly opposed the "law" of their time? Which have been so "insatiable" and "loud" while managing to hold a very broad and serious readership? If Canetti's profile helps us to identify the sentiment underlying cultural criticism, it surely helps us to see what Steiner is about.

So, too, do elements in the profile trouble us. Can a writer who invokes the tradition as Steiner does be said to be "the thrall of his time"? Can one who rejects so much be genuinely and openly attentive to "diversity"? Is the demand for a radically "oppositional" stance not an encouragement to iconoclasm and posturing? These are useful cautionary questions, to be sure. But Steiner would seem proof against the objections they convey.

For one thing, Steiner is compulsively engaged with the thought and main currents of his time. He writes about not only new books and theories but also basic changes in the culture, from the impact of rock music to recent developments in sexual practice. The easy notion of the traditionalist as one who buries himself in the past to avoid having to confront the terrors of the present is totally inapplicable to Steiner. His hostility to aspects of contemporary culture is matched by his exhilaration in taking on fresh ideas. Just so, though his work is everywhere informed by a furious moral earnestness, he is deeply curious about everything and willing to look closely at things from which others fastidiously recoil.

In the 1960s Steiner took seriously the long-term implications of pornography, sexual candor, and sexual license in a way that ostensibly liberated critics were then unwilling to follow. Later he carefully considered the relation between racism and art and made a case for writers such as Céline, whose noxious views are everywhere implicated in their writings. In the 1980s he launched an outspoken assault against the Israeli betrayal of the Zionist dream, against Israel's adoption of a "Bismarckian nationalism" in which other human beings are made "disinherited," "wretched," and "homeless"—with the consequence that "Judaism has become homeless to itself." More recently he has considered the curious rebirth of religious perspectives in advanced Western precincts from which it was thought that religion had been permanently eviscerated. In all, an abundant harvest, a record of extraordinary candor and sustained engagement. The polemical uses to which the concept of diversity has lately been put should not obscure the genuine diversity of the passions of Steiner and his openness to issues others are reluctant to tackle.

The oppositional dimension in Steiner's work is hardly a manifestation of unbridled compulsiveness or negativism. Steiner has found much to praise. He has also found ways to be generous to opponents, and he typically has selected for strenuous criticism the most brilliant, audacious, and well-armed adversaries. Consider that Steiner has taken on, at the height of their influence, such figures as Leavis, Chomsky, and Derrida. If his attack on selected aspects of the culture has sometimes seemed intransigent, his insatiable appetite for positive models and his instinct for precise discriminations are no less apparent. Those who find him overbearing, relentless, and unembarrassed by the aura of learning and avidity he conveys might again think to place Steiner within the tradition of largely European cultural criticism to which he belongs—a tradition to which numerous Americans have themselves made notable contributions. Having done that, they will perhaps reflect more scrupulously on Steiner's connections with the Elias Canetti to whom Susan Sontag, in an essay exemplary for its sympathy, attributes such qualities as self-confidence, insolence, impatience, ambition, and passion. "I try to imagine someone saying to Shakespeare, 'Relax!'" says Canetti. Of Steiner's cultural criticism, we may well say what Sontag writes of Canetti's: "His work eloquently defends tension, exertion, moral and amoral seriousness."

Steiner's Literary Journalism:
"The Heart of the Maze"

LET US SAY IT at once. George Steiner is the best generalist reviewer of books since Edmund Wilson. Some of his intellectual contemporaries begrudge Steiner this distinction, and he himself, with his
contempt for book-chat journalism, would no doubt prefer to be
praised in other terms. But the distinction is real. In a period that has
witnessed the nearly total supersession of the generalist man of letters
by the academic literary specialist, Steiner is unsurpassed in his range
and in his hospitality to genius in all its cultural expressions.

In an interview Steiner described himself in these terms: "I never
considered myself chiefly as a literary critic, but rather as a critic of
culture in general. I have always thought that literary criticism is linked
to broader cultural issues and spiritual viewpoints."[1] I want to save
those "spiritual viewpoints" for later consideration in order, at the
start, to concentrate on Steiner the "critic of culture in general." As a
critic of culture, Steiner has entered into conversation with older figures such as T. S. Eliot and with contemporaries, most recently with
Jacques Derrida. He has carried on a mode of critique he has himself
celebrated in essays on German-language writers such as Walter Ben-

jamin. But he differs from all of these in the sheer variety of cultural topics he has canvassed: historians, painters, chess masters, and philosophers, as well as specifically literary figures from all over Europe. He has written about the classics (separate essays on Homer, Sophocles, Dante, and Shakespeare); the tradition of tragic drama (books on *The Death of Tragedy* and the transformations of the Antigone theme); the Russian novel (*Tolstoy or Dostoevsky: An Essay in the Old Criticism*); issues in language and translation (*After Babel* and *On Difficulty and Other Essays*); even an essay on children's games.

Can there be a center to all this? Or does Steiner come to us all in pieces, as against other critics who seem all of a piece? The answer is not simple. Steiner does indeed have the restless curiosity of the born journalist. But his variousness is in the service of a moral seriousness and purposefulness that are anything but journalistic. The seriousness is seen in Steiner's culturally conservative attachment to the best that has been thought and said. No contemporary critic is as attached to the old Romantic notion of genius or to the idea of the masterpiece.

In the United States today there are several influential critics who combine a taste for advanced theory with a rear-guard loyalty to the traditional canon. But in a critic such as, say, Hillis Miller or Stanley Fish, the attraction to the canonical lacks the passion, or perhaps the obsessiveness, of Steiner's fascination. It is a fascination especially with all that is difficult about the classical, and it appears in paradigmatic form in his short essay on chess, "A Death of Kings." Steiner focuses here on the "specialized, freakish quality" of the chess master's skill, a cerebral delirium captured in Nabokov's early Russian novel *The Luzhin Defence*.[2] Steiner writes a great deal about the humanities in relation to humanity but, unlike most American critics who have worried this question, makes no concessions to democratic sentimentality. What matters—in art, sport, military affairs—is singularity, no matter how obsessional or even mad. Just as when Steiner writes about the novel or poetry it is only about the greatest instances, when he writes about actors in history it is about world conquerors such as Alexander the Great and Hitler.

The taste that determines these selections is mandarin. Steiner brings to criticism a spirit of connoisseurship, which is mainly absent in American cultural commentary. Indeed, his choice for greatness disposes him to a familiar European disdain for the accommodations of American high culture. Not surprisingly, American intellectuals typically respond to these mandarin gestures with irritation. Provocation (Steiner's essay "The Archives of Eden") and response (Cynthia Ozick and others) are on view in the *Salmagundi* special issue (nos. 50–51 [Fall 1980]) "Art and Intellect in America."

However much Steiner may sound at times like an old New York intellectual fretting about mass culture or like a Yale professor of literature mourning the passing of a text-centered public, he is not one of us. True, he studied in the United States and has written fondly of his undergraduate career at the University of Chicago under Robert Hutchins ("An Examined Life," *New Yorker*, 23 October 1989). Moreover, he wrote his first book, *Tolstoy or Dostoevsky*, at the Institute for Advanced Study in Princeton. But very little that we think of as characteristically American rubbed off. On the contrary, it may be argued that Hutchins's University of Chicago and R. P. Blackmur's circle at Princeton were two of the most singular, uncharacteristic American institutions of their time. In any case, Steiner appears to acknowledge his distance from the United States by writing very infrequently about American books, even in the *New Yorker*, which has been publishing him for twenty years. The *New Yorker* pieces compose a larger body of work than that Steiner has published in any European journal or literary paper.

Steiner writes as the last European, as "a kind of survivor." That tag was intended to stand for his sense of himself as a central European Jew who was alive only because of luck and his father's good sense in leaving Vienna in 1924, five years before his own birth. He is the survivor of a lost world of Jewish culture bounded by Prague, Vienna, Budapest, and Frankfurt, between roughly 1870 and 1940. "A Kind of Survivor," like many of the essays I shall cite, is reprinted in *George Steiner: A Reader* (1984). That essay recalls us to the forepart of our century, to Freud, Schoenberg, Kafka, Adorno, Mahler, Lukács, Broch, and Benjamin, among others. All of these were secular Jewish artists and intellectuals, instances of a type the historian Isaac Deutscher called "the non-Jewish Jew." Lost to Judaism, then, Steiner nevertheless accepts an archetypal Jewish role for himself, as the son-survivor who has taken on the responsibility of remembering the dead father.

There are many dead fathers to pray for: Marx, Heine, Wittgenstein, Bergson, Hoffmansthal, Proust. Half-Jews, members of families that had converted to Christianity, Frenchmen, central Europeans who did their work in England, such as the art historian Aby Warburg. The boundaries of Steiner's piety are fluid. The point is to suggest what emancipated Jews accomplished in the little more than a century between Napoleon and Hitler and to suggest the dimensions of the loss. But it is not only German-Jewish culture that Steiner laments, for which his career provides what he calls an "afterword" or "epilogue," following "the retreat from the word." The writers he celebrates and mourns were mainly assimilated; they were continuators of a great tradition of central European humanism that was through most of its history explicitly Christian and in more recent times secularized without dissolving older Christian patterns of value and feeling. It is a case of the dyer's hand being permanently stained by the materials of his craft. So with Steiner a lifelong devotion to the classic texts of European humanism has produced a personal culture that is as much Christian as it is Jewish. So this Jewish survivor has been led by the logic of his defense of old Europe close to the edge of a specifically Christian affirmation. His book *Real Presences* does not seem to me a clear-cut statement of belief of any kind, except perhaps in the sacrality of great masterworks of art. But to the extent that it is "religious," it is as much Christian as Jewish in its implication.

I have been saying that Steiner's writing has an integrity and coherence despite the colossal diversity of his subjects. His single great theme has been the status of language and the humanities in the wake of the political bestiality of our century. His "spiritual viewpoints" have led him to a kind of incarnationist aesthetic that affirms the presence of God in great works of art, just as the medieval Church had affirmed the "real presence" of Christ's body and blood in the wafer and wine of the Eucharist. Now I want to reverse course and argue that Steiner is at his best in his reviews and occasional essays rather than in his full-length studies, and that the superiority of the short pieces is owing to their diversity when taken as a whole. Steiner's main themes work together to form a whole, but as a critical personality he is very diverse. That personality is on better display in the variety of the review-articles taken all together than in books, which of necessity require a narrower focus.

There is a kind of writing, such as Wordsworth's, that is bound up with a particular place. But there is another kind, which we associate with exiles and émigrés, that has as its provenience no particular place but only the unbounded mind of its producer. Steiner is an instance of such extraterritorialism. Consider the scenes of his instruction and pedagogy. Although his origins are in the upper-middle-class world of assimilated German-speaking Jews, these scenes have been mainly West European and American: France, where he attended lycées and received his first baccalaureate; the University of Chicago, where he took a year to earn a B.A.; Harvard, for the M.A.; Balliol College, Oxford, as a Rhodes Scholar; the Institute of Advanced Study at Princeton; teaching stints at Williams College and Stanford and a Fulbright professorship in Austria; Churchill College, Cambridge, where he is still a fellow; and, his longest sojourn, the University of Geneva, where he is professor of English and Comparative Literature. This is an incomplete listing, but it suggests why Steiner can describe himself as a Jew of the Diaspora for whom the only homeland is the text.

Steiner's intellectual cosmopolitanism is of a piece with this history of wandering. So is his abstractness, one of many elements in his makeup which dispose him to prefer the urban intellectual Dostoevsky to the landed aristocrat Tolstoy. His cosmopolitanism implies, on the one hand, a detestation of all nationalisms, including Israel's, and, on the other, a fascination with those arcane forms of scholarship and thought that are most removed from the quotidian life of *l'homme moyen sensuel.* Steiner's mandarin fastidiousness makes it all the more paradoxical that some of his most effective writing has appeared in a magazine, the *New Yorker,* which has never been notable for an intellectual tone.

Steiner's *New Yorker* reviews are typically printed in narrow columns often bordered on both sides by advertisements for expensive gifts, real estate, and other goods of upscale consumer culture. It is not a culture for which Steiner has a high regard. Yet that culture includes a sensitive, well-educated minority that has the highest regard for him. That nonspecialist American readership is probably larger than Steiner's readership in England, France, Germany, and Switzerland combined.

There is nothing sinister about Steiner's warm reception among American readers. These readers are mainly the kind of people who regularly read Edmund Wilson's *New Yorker* reviews because Wilson introduced to it so many new books and interests. This audience also includes the kind of people, the educated liberal middle class, who had once looked to Lionel Trilling for guidance. Steiner combines Wilson's range and Trilling's moral urgency, and, like his American precursors, he is a superb teacher and brilliant popularizer. His value as a cultural critic is not limited to these roles, but amidst the great prestige of the academic literary "theorist" his gifts seem all the more rare and deserving of acknowledgment.

I call attention to the reviews and occasional essays because Steiner has published more than a hundred such pieces, in the *New Yorker*, *Times Literary Supplement*, and elsewhere, that he has never reprinted. Whereas John Updike, his fellow reviewer at the *New Yorker*, gathers everything he has written (except perhaps for his grocery lists) in book form, Steiner the mandarin purist seems to regard only his most ambitious projects as truly valuable. That seems to me a misjudgment. His sheer love of learning for its own sake and his pleasure in sharing his knowledge make his magazine writing very different from American cultural commentary, which is often just barely disguised political-ideological argument. Steiner is the closest we now have to the Victorian sage. In turning now to the texts themselves, I shall quote at length in order to illustrate his temper and tone.

I have said that Steiner's great theme has been the fate of language and literacy in an age of political inhumanity. He announced this theme in a number of essays in his first, and up to now only, collection of reviews and essays: *Language and Silence: Essays on Language, Literature, and the Inhuman* (1967). Steiner mainly approached this theme in philosophically informed discursive pieces such as "The Retreat from the Word" and "To Civilize Our Gentlemen." A decade later he published a number of interim studies, or "working papers," as he called them, in the small book *On Difficulty and Other Essays* (1978). The large questions Steiner was worrying require large speculative discourse. At the same time, however, he was writing other short pieces in which he revealed an intuitive sense of individual character and personality. Thus the excellent brief biographical studies that began with his 1960 essay "Georg Lukács and His Devil's Pact" and continued with pieces in the *New Yorker* on such figures as Arthur Koestler, Walter Benjamin, Karl Kraus, and Aby Warburg. Even pieces that are not biographically oriented, such as those on the philosopher Stanley Cavell and historians like Foucault and John Boswell of Yale, rarely limited themselves to aesthetic analysis and philosophical critique. Steiner was always alert to personal motive, especially the flaw or weakness that energized the career.

These notations on personality remind us that Steiner began not as a philosopher of culture, but as a poet and novelist. The three novellas collected in *Anno Domini* (1964) are Dostoevskian in combining attention to individual psychology with broad intellectual-ideological preoccupations. The book jacket of *Language and Silence* announces another fiction in progress, "'a very personal book,' part fiction and part political essay." This work never appeared. Or perhaps it did, very much changed and more than a decade later, as the novel *The Portage to San Cristóbal of A.H.* (1981), Steiner's controversial imagination of Hitler. From the beginning, then, Steiner has brought a novelist's eye to the work of cultural analysis.

The essay of his that best combines daring historical-philosophical speculation with speculation about character and motive is "The Cleric of Treason."[3] Perhaps because its speculation is contained within a structure of actual historical events, this essay is more effective than any of Steiner's fictions. It also has the merit for my purpose of taking us directly to Steiner's great obsession with the moral ambiguities of the scholar-intellectual in an age of political depravity, that is, in our own time. As early as 1960, in his essay on Lukács, Steiner had emphasized the self-betrayals of the intellectual corrupted by politics: "In the twentieth century it is not easy for an honest man to be a literary critic."[4] Steiner has refined and complicated that perception in the three decades that have followed. At what he calls "the heart of the maze," we find the heart—perverted, divided, turned to stone—of the scholar-critic-intellectual. Many of Steiner's essays about modern intellectuals could be subtitled "The Devil's Pact." The old myth of Dr. Faustus, and Thomas Mann's modern retelling, are at the heart of Steiner's maze.[5]

The cleric of treason is Anthony Blunt, the distinguished art historian who was also guardian and surveyor of the art treasures of the British royal family. In November 1979 British Prime Minister Margaret Thatcher revealed to the British public that this much-honored pillar of the establishment had for many years been simultaneously a member of the intelligence branch of the British Secret Service and a spy for the Soviet Union. Just when Blunt's treason began was unclear—it may have been as early as 1940, when he joined the Secret Service. Neither was it clear in the public revelations when his betrayal of England ceased. According to one version of the story, Blunt had confessed to treason in 1964 in return for a promise that his crimes would not be publicly divulged and that he would not be prosecuted.

The details of Blunt's involvement in the escape from England of his fellow spies Guy Burgess and Donald Maclean, and of his relations with yet another Soviet spy, Kim Philby, were withheld from the public. But some things were certain: the austere art scholar had blood on his hands. Blunt had been, as Steiner says, "a K.G.B. minion whose treason over thirty years or more almost certainly did grave damage to his own country and may well have sent other men—Polish and Czech exiles, fellow intelligence agents—to abject death" (191).

We are on well-worn terrain here. British journalists had anguished at length about the treachery of some of England's most gifted and privileged intellectuals; and Graham Greene and John le Carré had dealt in fiction with the motives for espionage. Steiner himself had previously brought together, in his novella "Sweet Mars," themes of sexuality and social class in the context of British involvement in World War II. In the present essay Steiner asks the question Britain's intellectuals were frequently asking themselves in the postwar period: Why had Blunt (or Philby or others) done it?

It was not political ideology, Steiner says, although he grants that as a young art historian Blunt might well have felt contempt for a capitalist social order in which great works of art were owned privately and were not available for the pleasure and edification of ordinary people. Steiner also asserts the appeal to Blunt of totalitarianism as such, adducing essays in which Blunt praised Hitler's Germany as well as the Soviet Union as societies in which painting, sculpture, and architecture are encouraged by a strong central authority. Acknowledging these possibilities, Steiner follows his master Dostoevsky, in preferring explanations that appeal to motives not so easily available to rational consciousness.

Hence his speculations on the relation between Blunt's duplicity and his homosexuality. It is not homosexuality as a private sexual preference that interests Steiner, but homosexuality as an aspect of the cultural attitude of Blunt's social circle at Cambridge in the late 1920s and later in London. Something of the outsider's coolness—a mixture perhaps of envy and disdain—colors Steiner's account of "the freemasonry of golden lads" (197), the pervasive homoeroticism of the British public schools and "the shared enchanted setting of Cambridge cloisters and gardens" (195). For the privileged inheritors of England's legacy, loyalty to school chums might count for more than loyalty to nation.

It is with Steiner's third explanation that we arrive at "the heart of the maze." That explanation locates the source of betrayal not in the scholar's political or sexual preferences, but in scholarship as a vocation. For Steiner the challenge is to understand how a scholar who is in his professional work the quintessence of scrupulous integrity can yet have been a creature of infinite duplicity. The question concerns "the nature of intellectual-academic obsession" (191). Steiner proposes the riddle of "a man who in the morning teaches his students that a false attribution of a Watteau drawing or an inaccurate transcription of a fourteenth-century epigraph is a sin against the spirit and in the afternoon or evening transmits to the agents of Soviet intelligence classified, perhaps vital information given to him in sworn trust by his countrymen and intimate colleagues" (191). In *Language and Silence* Steiner had wondered how a cultivated German might read Rilke or listen to Mozart, then go off to gas prisoners or operate the crematoria of a Nazi concentration camp. Steiner's account of the paradox in Blunt's career is isomorphic with his account of a similar paradox in the depravity of Nazi murderers who had grown up on the humanistic tradition of Goethe and Schiller, the most advanced cultural tradition in Europe.

We say that Steiner has been concerned with the relation between the humanities and the inhuman. We could just as accurately say that Steiner has been most centrally concerned with the scholar-intellectual as a modern social or spiritual type. When he writes about fascism, it is not about Nazi thugs but about the most cultivated Germans, people such as Heidegger, who offered no resistance to nazism and sometimes actively collaborated. The case of Heidegger is cause of special anguish to Steiner inasmuch as he has shared Hannah Arendt's view of Heidegger as the master of modern European thought. The question Steiner raises, then, is not one of the abstract relations between European humanistic civilization and barbarity, but of the way such ideas have coexisted within the hearts of Western scholars, those entrusted with the transmission of their great legacy.

The rottenness, it appears, is latent in the fairest flowers of high civilization. If lilies that fester smell worse than weeds, it may be that lilies contain within themselves the seeds of their own corruption. The scholar is not the unambiguous seeker after truth and beauty of his own idealized self-image. Rather, the scholar is driven by an obsession that may be at odds with faith, friendship, and common decency. The "true scholar," the "scholar absolute," to use Steiner's own terms, is driven by a quest for perfection that makes him indifferent to the public good and even to his own welfare: "The archivist, the monographer, the antiquarian, the specialist consumed by fires of esoteric fascination may be indifferent also to the distracting claims of social justice, of familial affection, of political awareness, and of run-of-the-mill humanity. . . . To the utmost scholar, sleep is a puzzle of wasted time, and flesh a piece of torn luggage that the spirit must drag after it" (198).

Most American professors, when they think of "the scholar," do not think of the archivist, the antiquarian, or other connoisseurs of the rich and strange whom Steiner adduces. What have our sunlit quadrangles to do with the Gothic melodrama he puts before us, of "obsessed, sacrificial, self-devouring lives . . . at the sharpest edge of autistic engagement? . . . The numismatician labouring to identify archaic coinage, the musicologist deciphering medieval notations, the philologist at his corrupt codex, or the art historian who is endeavouring to catalogue minor baroque or rococo eighteenth-century drawings" (198). In the United States we do not usually think of scholarship as a madness. We are children of Emerson, whose "American Scholar" is not a scholar at all from Steiner's European point of view. The Emersonian scholar tries to make new, to usher in a fresh, golden day. He strives in his own imagining to escape the influence of books, of traditions. He runs the risk, of course, of ignorance and a windy populism. Steiner's Faustian "utmost scholar" runs very different risks. Even if he does not lose his soul altogether in his devil's pact, that scholar is prey to "hermetic addiction," Mallarmé, say, rather than Whitman.

Steiner is his generation's great pathologist of the bitterness and perversity of the humanist intellectual in a posthumanist age. This is not at all to say that he is himself a model of Olympian equanimity, as in our idealizing image of Goethe. Steiner takes his stand as a belated continuator of the central tradition of European humanism, but his writing is most alive when it is most eccentric. Scholarship as he practices it—reading deep into the most intimate motives of his subjects, without self-protective distancing[6]—is "indeed a haunting and haunted business." I have borrowed from Steiner's early work on Dostoevsky in suggesting the analogy between his own, so very un-English intensity and Gothic melodrama. But what genre might be more appropriate for a write• struggling to be answerable to the cries of the millions of restless dead?

To set off what I am calling Steiner's Europeanness, we might compare him with another highly eccentric defender of canonical Western literature: Harold Bloom. Bloom is the great instance in our time of the Emersonian scholar. As such he is committed, as Steiner is not, to radical originality. But both critics de-idealize the intellectual, exposing the violence beneath the surface; both dramatize their own inevitable estrangement from the great traditions they celebrate, their isolation and singularity; both reject progressive politics and wonder at the confluence of great art and retrograde social attitudes; both define the Jew in terms of text-centeredness, rather than religious belief or partisanship with Israel. Yet, finally, these exemplary critics belong to different worlds, in Bloom's case the High Romanticism of Carlyle and Emerson, in Steiner's a late phase of German-Jewish modernism. The model for Steiner would seem to be Walter Benjamin the connoisseur, collector, and theorist-exemplar of the "destructive Character."

Steiner's idea of the scholar as destructive character emphasizes the "autistic" quality of some types of intellectual work. Steiner's account of the fall of Anthony Blunt opens out in "The Cleric of Treason" into a quasi-novelistic reflection on the scholar as a creature consumed by *ressentiment*: "The practice of devoting one's waking hours to the collation of a manuscript, to the recension of watermarks on old drawings, the discipline of investing one's dreams in the always vulnerable elucidation of abstruse problems accessible only to a handful of prying and rival colleagues can secrete a rare venom into the spirit" (199). This is a conception worthy of Dostoevsky: a paragon of self-abnegating scruple is corrupted by the purity of his own motive. His asceticism and detachment from common life breed cruelty and a desire to act out fantasies of sadistic destruction that betrayal of one's country uniquely makes possible. The violence in most scholar mandarins remains formal, says Steiner; "not so, one supposes, in Professor Blunt" (200).

It is not possible to exaggerate the dialectical power of Steiner's portrait of the scholar as spy. There is surely something strained, "Gothic," in his imagination of "solicitations of violence, which bubble like marsh gas from the deeps of abstruse thought and erudition." But this is not simply fantasy. Steiner displays a Dostoevskian vigor of intellect as well:

Here the hair-fine exactitudes of scholarship found compensation or parodistic counter-statement—for there are sensibilities both strong and obscurely lamed which demand some kind of mocking self-subversion, which find it compelling to deride something central to their own being, as one's tongue exasperates an aching tooth—in the lies and corruptions of the mole. Here the ascetic scruple of the pedagogue who instructed generations of disciples in the merciless code of documentary truth was counterpoised by the long mastery of falsehood and of forgery. (200)

The "parodistic counter-statement" is the latent possibility threatening any attempt to sum up Steiner in any simple formulation. Americans not used to studying dialectic—whether in Hegelian, Marxist, or other versions—need especially to be cautious. In an essay on Emmanuel Levinas, Steiner writes: "To Levinas, as to Adorno, a totality is, by definition, a falsehood."[7] We might add: to Steiner as well. That is why the reviews and other short pieces are valuable, in giving us facets rather than totalities. The titles of superb essay collections by two of Steiner's precursors point to their own sense of truth coming in flashes and fragments: Benjamin's *Illuminations* and Adorno's *Prisms*.

In "A Kind of Survivor" Steiner has written about the European Jewish intellectuals he counted as his living models. He said that in all of them—Arendt, Ernst Bloch, Adorno, Erich Kahler, Lévi-Strauss—"you will hear a common note as of desolation." But they are the most authentically contemporary voices, "whose work and context of reference are indispensable to an understanding of the philosophic, political, aesthetic roots of the inhuman."[8] Walter Benjamin once proposed the idea of a critical work that would include only quotations. No one has accepted the challenge, although Susan Sontag approaches this ideal in her most Benjamin-inspired work, *On Photography*. I shall close now with some passages from brief essays by Steiner on exemplary Jewish writers. Each of the pieces was published in the *New Yorker* and has not been reprinted.

There is a sense in which Arthur Koestler is more than the sum of his writings. There are in epochs and societies men and women who bear essential witness, in whose private sensibility and individual existence the larger meanings of the age are concentrated and made visible. In this black century, the Central European Jew has, more perhaps than any other tribe, borne the enormity of enforced vision and experience. . . . Koestler's cards of identity, genuine and forged, the stamps and visas in his passports, his address books and desk diaries, make up the map and itinerary of the hunted in our century. (11 June 1984, 121)

With signal exceptions, the noon and the darkness of the late Austro-Hungarian era, the incandescent energies and the crises of the Vienna-Budapest galaxy, are those of emancipated Judaism. To speak of the work and heritage of Freud or of Wittgenstein, of Kafka or of Broch, of Mahler or of Schoenberg is to speak of the most creative and tragic chapter in the history of post-exilic Judaism. . . . Are there not ways, subterranean but all the more determinant, in which the destruction of European Judaism, the era of the death camps, and the taste of bile it has brought even to those innocent and far away relate to that which was destroyed? Was the critical, deconstructive power of Central European Jewish thought, music, literature wholly without responsibility for that which it (partly) foresaw? The area of actual concentration, of the kinship between Jewish radiance, Jewish self-hatred—a phenomenon particularly well represented in Vienna—and mounting anti-Semitism, was too dense. Precisely as in an atomic pile, the mass had gone critical. The cool and liberal threshold had been crossed. Reading Kafka's parables and Kraus's "The Last Days of Mankind," listening to Schoenberg's Second Quartet, seeking to grasp the poetics of silence in Wittgenstein's "Tractatus" and Hoffmansthal's "Letter of Lord Chandos," looking at Kokoschka's portraits and gyring landscapes, one asks oneself, inevitably: What were the links with the night to come? When is clairvoyance also responsibility? (28 January 1985, 92)

The collapse of Germany and of the old Europe during the First World War triggered a major mental crisis. [Aby] Warburg's breakdown lasted from 1918 to 1923. . . . Even at the best of times, moreover, dark shadows pressed on Warburg's mind. But it was just this vulnerability that attuned his insights and his research so aptly to the esoteric, systematically irrational material crucial to the mysterious and visionary components of art. The demonic figures, the superstitions, and the archetypal insinuations that Warburg discovered in the cellarage, as it were, of High Renaissance and modern aesthetic forms were closely akin to those compulsions toward fear, toward an almost hallucinatory intimation of dissolution, that blackened his own spirit. (2 February 1987, 97–98)

It may well be that the most celebrated of [Karl] Kraus's brevities is also the most controversial: "Concerning Hitler, I can think of nothing to say," or "nothing occurs to me" ("Mir fällt zu Hitler nichts ein"). The prophet stood speechless before the nightmare realization of his own worst apprehensions. Set down in the late spring or early summer of 1933, this abstention from discourse, this valediction to eloquence, tells of a terrible weariness. . . . In front of Hitler, an anti-master of the word more ruthless than he was—an actor, mountebank, declaimer more mesmerizing—Kraus fell silent. At some very deep level of half-consciousness, he may have sensed in Hitler the monstrously distorted but also parodistic image of his own talents. He now found himself between crystal ball and mirror and was struck dumb. (21 July 1986, 91–92)

Over and over, [Paul] Celan put his terrible question: In the "no-oneness" of God, who "shall bear witness for the witness?" Celan and Primo Levi, before their elected deaths, came nearest to bringing human language to bear on that which no tongue ought ever to have known or articulated—on that which should, since it is morally and rationally unspeakable, terminate man's primordial contract with the wonder and "wording" (Emerson's term) of the world. That these poems exist is at once a kind of miracle of ultimate need and a kind of grievous indecency. Celan was self-laceratingly possessed of this contradiction, of the intuition that his own genius was active in the denial of the nothingness of speech and metaphor which should have followed on the Holocaust. (Why, indeed, have art and poetry not gone on strike?) But from the deeps of his incensed sorrow came, undeniably, the counterpoint of creative mastery, the conviction that

tree-
high thought
tunes in to light's pitch: there are
still songs to be sung on the other side
of mankind.   (28 August 1989, 95)

Notes

1. Gabriel Moked, "An Informal Conversation with George Steiner," *Tel Aviv Review* 3 (Winter 1991): 28.

2. George Steiner, "A Death of Kings," in *George Steiner: A Reader* (New York: Oxford University Press, 1984), 177.

3. George Steiner, "The Cleric of Treason," *New Yorker*, 8 December 1980; reprinted in *George Steiner: A Reader*, 178–204.

4. George Steiner, "Georg Lukács and His Devil's Pact," in *Language and Silence: Essays on Language, Literature, and the Inhuman* (New York: Atheneum, 1967), 339.

5. Mann, perhaps even more than Dostoevsky, is the philosophical novelist who has most influenced Steiner's thought and imagination. One of his earliest essays (1963) is on Mann's last, parodic novel, *Confessions of Felix Krull*.

Steiner finds precedents for it in Goethe's *Faust*. In the mid-1970s Steiner was involved in a polemical exchange about Mann in the pages of the *Times Literary Supplement*.

6. It may be that Steiner is a great reader rather than a great critic. For his reflection on these very different activities, see "'Critic'/'Reader,'" which first appeared in the journal *New Literary History* 10 (Spring 1979): 423–52. It is reprinted in *George Steiner: A Reader*.

7. George Steiner, "Levinas," *Cross Currents: Religion and Intellectual Life* 41 (Summer 1991): 245.

8. Steiner, *Language and Silence*, 149.

GUIDO ALMANSI

The Triumph of the Hedgehog

I SUSPECT that there are two George Steiners, though one was quite enough already. I also believe that the first is rather wary of the second, and the second is intolerant of the first. This conflict creates the sort of dramatic tension in which the genius of Steiner the critic blossoms.

Twisting slightly the cultural myth that underlies the fox-hedgehog dichotomy, I intend to call the first Steiner the fox and the second Steiner the hedgehog. At the fount we have a fragment by Archilochus: "The fox knows many things, but the hedgehog knows one big thing."[1] In his essay "The Fox and the Hedgehog," Isaiah Berlin used the Archilochean opposition as a touchstone wherewith to divide writers, artists, musicians, thinkers, and perhaps mankind into two categories. On the one side the centrifugal fox, who follows "many ends, often unrelated or even contradictory"; on the other the centripetal hedgehog, who subordinates each action and thought "to a central vision."[2] According to Berlin, the arch-hedgehog would be Dante (surely not for me, for I see Dante as both a great fox and a great hedgehog; and I guess Steiner, author of "Dante Now: The Gossip of Eternity,"[3] a masterly essay that parallels Dante and Proust, would agree with me); whereas the arch-fox would be Dante's eternal antagonist, Shakespeare.

In Russian literature, the fox *par excellence* is Pushkin, and the hedgehog is Dostoevsky. As for Tolstoy, Berlin solves the crux with a sleight of hand: "Tolstoy was by nature a fox but believed in being a hedgehog";[4] the conflict between what he was and what he thought he was is most obvious in his conception of history, to which the rest of Berlin's essay is dedicated.

Berlin's paradox on Tolstoy is actually a brilliant variation of Apollinaire's musing about Picasso in *Les peintres cubistes*. Apollinaire also starts from a dichotomy between two types of artists. Some are dominated or guided by a muse or an unknown entity who uses them as instruments of creation. They produce effortlessly, spontaneously; they do not have to use the filter of their intelligence: art just gushes out from them naturally. The others, who are not inspired but obsessed by solitude and the craving to express themselves, strive by trial and error to stammer something new. And Picasso? Apollinaire says Picasso belongs to the first category but tried to move to the other, and "il n'y a jamais eu de spectacle aussi fantastique que cette métamorphose qu'il a subie en devenant un artiste come les seconds."[5]

To come back to Steiner, I think he is an arch-fox among critics who tries to become a hedgehog. The transformation is almost complete in his recent book *Real Presences*. Steiner the fox is "the fastest reader in the West." During my youth, in Italy, it was generally understood that the most learned man in the country was Benedetto Croce, who had read every book with disastrous results. Today the most learned man in the Western world, the one who can quote with the greatest ease *any* poem in the Western tradition, from Mirtides of Antidone to Paul Celan, is certainly Steiner, an awesome phenomenon who assimilates with portentous immediacy anything he reads. And he has read *everything*. This excess of culture encumbers him, like the character in Borges's story "Funes el memorioso" who is condemned by his implacable memory. In Steiner's case, all recollected emotions, intuitions, and insights that authors from the past have delegated to his prodigiously retentive memory crowd upon him, haunt his writing, and often spoil the witty, formulaic density of his style. Suppose you came across the following sentence: "Whether in Hesiod, Humboldt or J. Monod, we find the implicit or enunciated supposition that the evolution of human speech is concomitant, generated by, or creative of trans-individual societal behaviour."[6] The concept is difficult enough, and the style is self-evidently heavy; but even before we are allowed to think about the connection between speech and society (or about the common denominator between the one poet and the two scientists), Steiner forces us, mercilessly, to make a number of adjustments in order to summon whatever we know about Hesiod, Humboldt, and J. Monod. The fact that Steiner drops these names in the same breath means that we cannot keep up with him. Hence he has failed in his role as a writer and as an educator.

Of course, this consideration is born out of envy. How would it be possible, for any man concerned with *litterae humaniores*, not to be envious of this monster who knows everything and has no difficulty in expounding his ideas about *all* the main works of Western literature? So, as a line of defense, I claim the right to be impressed but never fully convinced by Steiner the fox, that is, by Steiner the encyclopedist. His learning and reading, which are immense, are there, of course; and they are astounding. But Steiner wears his vertiginous knowledge with a wee bit of exhibitionism, without the nonchalance of the genuine polymath (Goethe would have been more modest). His "Hesiods" and "Humboldts" are often meant to hit and hurt rather than help.

But there is Steiner the hedgehog, unstained by the ink of the odd thousands of books he has read or skimmed or perused, a Doppelgänger perhaps not much liked by the first, who—notwithstanding his immense knowledge—"gets down to the roots," that is, to the questions that lie at the basis of all knowledge, to the premises of our intellective efforts, with an immodest and brutal directness that hits the reader where it most hurts, in the solar plexus of his guilty conscience. In most of his books there are passages where Steiner is able to divest himself of the awesome pageantry of learning and achieve a sort of blessed ignorance in which you are only faced by radical issues. Unrelentingly for more than thirty years, Steiner has kept asking the fundamental questions about the connection between ethics and aesthetics; and this does not require a *particular* erudition (Wittgenstein *docet*: the problem with him is certainly not "how much he knows"). To have seen one picture or one thousand pictures is ultimately the same if all you want to examine is the Pascalian problem of the vanity of painting: whether a picture is ethically justifiable. It is my assumption in this essay that Steiner the hedgehog is winning and that *Real Presences*[7] is the final triumph of the hedgehog over the fox. But this requires some arguing.

Steiner has been haunting me as an avatar of my bad conscience since 1971, when I heard him deliver the Eliot Lectures at my college at the University of Kent in Canterbury.[8] In the last twenty years I have led what is described in academic terms as "a full and productive life" (I blush at the awful commercial twang of the adjective "productive"), writing dozens of learned articles and books, which, together with the great bulk of all academic criticism, are "totally ephemeral . . . soon out of print and sepulchred in the decent dust of deposit libraries."[9] Each time, literally or metaphorically, I submitted my brainchild to Steiner, he shook his head disapprovingly. In the last years I have dealt with parody, erotic literature, comic writing, irony, writers of fantasy; and every time I was aware that Steiner thought (or would have thought if he had read it): "No, that's not it." My book or article did not pass his severe test: it did not face *his* important issues. Then came the final lesson of *Real Presences*. As a critic, as a teacher of literature, as an intellectual connected with the current debates and variations on the problems of art and culture, I am a denizen of the "secondary" world. Stealing the words from Steiner himself, "How could I not know and acknowledge this to be so?" (*RP*, 23). My whole professional life has been spent under the sign of the parasitic: I am a critic, therefore I am a moth fluttering around the radiant light of the work of art. *Real Presences* is a brutal and offensively efficient reminder of this fact. This is the last blow in the dismantling operation Steiner has unwittingly perpetrated against me in his persona of "father" or "father confessor" (therefore object of my awe and hatred). But I think this is his role in Western culture: to be the bad conscience of intellectuals, in a tragically grandiose and morally disturbing effort to get down to brass tacks: How can we conciliate the close links between high culture and twentieth-century barbarism? How can we explain the role of Hitler, not only historically, but on a meta-historical level? Why Babel and the multiplicity of languages? What caused the "energy of reiteration" of Greek culture? How can we transform the occasional visitations of great works of art into a lasting tenancy, unless we are ready to make a wager on transcendence?

The books I have alluded to are easily recognizable, and each of them is a sledgehammer blow against frivolous complacency. There is something of a Savonarola in Steiner, something that forbids us to relish our culture too much, that batters and humiliates any Barthesian *jouissance* —even though the *jouissance*, apparently banished, finds its way back in the subtlety and acuity of his textual readings. Steiner, a voracious and insatiable reader, is afflicted with not only cultural bulimia but also literary satyriasis. He always tries to possess the text twice, in a double and perhaps perverse congress: a sensual foreplay with the tongue, then an attempt at intellectual bondage through the ethno-cultural data. But this cerebral stage sometimes destroys the defensive line of irony. I shall come back to this point.

This program means that Steiner must perforce write "unattractive books." I still remember the dismay of the audience in Canterbury when Steiner, at the beginning of his first Eliot lecture, referred to *Notes towards a Definition of Culture* by T. S. Eliot as "not an attractive book."[10] What he meant was that Eliot, in 1948, after the numerous signs of barbarism in the history of our century, after the Shoah and massacres of two world wars, in a book that was still "gray with the shock of recent barbarism" (*BC*, 13), could still appeal to a Christian order, to the continuity of the great religious myths of former centuries without any explicit mention of the colossal letdown marked by the twentieth century. Each single work of Steiner could be described as "not an attractive book" for the opposite reason: the author does not allow us to forget. And forgetfulness is always "attractive."

Let us dwell a little longer on this book, *In Bluebeard's Castle*. According to Voltaire, in Steiner's words, "with the decline in strength of religious creeds, there would follow a concomitant decline in human hatreds, in the urge to destroy another man because he is the embodiment of evil and falsehood" (43). This faith in a progress that was to be not only scientific and technological but also ethical and civic is a myth present in the whole nineteenth century, an "imagined garden of liberal culture" (14) which foretold, with various modulations in each nation, a bright and progressive future. But this dynamic optimism was accompanied by an alternative static pessimism which took the form of ennui, of Baudelairean spleen. Théophile Gautier exclaimed "plutôt la barbarie que l'ennui" (and his wishes have been fulfilled beyond expectation). While progressive forces were boiling over with enthusiasm, the gray mist of boredom was spreading over Europe. "The 'anti-heroes,' the spleen-ridden dandies in the world of Stendhal, Musset, Byron and Pushkin [moved] through the bourgeois city like *condottieri* out of work. Or worse, like *condottieri* meagrely pensioned before their first battle" (22). (I still remember this sentence by heart after twenty years).

And today? What general theory of culture can we offer after the horrors of the last ninety years? The close links between higher culture and the most murderous sources of twentieth-century barbarism, in the vicinity of concentration camps, in the bosom of the great German universities, hinder any clear thinking when we profess our faith in culture, in art, in liberal education. Why should we hand over culture to the next generations if culture is useless?

We find the same line of speculation in Steiner's novel, *The Portage to San Cristóbal of A.H.*[11] Despite the atrocious evidence of a nation of great humanist tradition giving birth to Nazi barbarism, Steiner keeps defending the moral function of higher culture (almost all his books, and in particular *Antigones: How the Antigone Legend Has Endured in Western Literature, Art, and Thought,*[12] are variations on this theme). In this first novel, Steiner compares the moral responsibilities of the Nazi and the Jew in the crisis of our century and in the vaster parable of Western history. *The Portage to San Cristóbal of A.H.* is a fiction about Israeli commandos who find Hitler, now ninety years old, in the remote marshes of Brazil and attempt to bring him back in order to try him for his crimes.

In the last chapter, of great ethical and stylistic tension, Hitler bases his own defense on the paradox of the Great Inquisitor in *The Brothers Karamazov*. In Dostoevsky's novel the Inquisitor declares that, if Christ were to come back, the Church would be forced to suppress him in defense of Christian doctrine. In Steiner's novel Hitler claims to be the Messiah who made possible the birth of the State of Israel through the bloody offering of the Shoah. Hitler himself may have been a Jew, and it was his mission to lay bare the ambition of his brethren throughout history: the Nazi dictator only imitated his Jewish masters, giving his own interpretation of historical transcendence. His anti-Semitic racism is just a new version of the Jews' own pro-Semitic racism, as expressed in particular in the Old Testament.[13] The millennium of the Third Reich is but a pale imitation of the eternity of Zion.

The speech of the delirious old man is an extraordinary tour de force and a virtuoso piece of stylistic parody, because Hitler's rhetoric in his self-portrait as the Messiah is a pastiche of Dostoevsky and Hitler himself, who paints history with broad, sublime strokes in a fresco where the fate of the individual and of whole communities is canceled by the megalomaniac grandiosity of the scheme.

The greatest contrast between the two different facets of Steiner's personality is to be found in *After Babel: Aspects of Language and Tradition* (1975).[14] In this book, the ostentation of cultural encyclopedism is at its strongest, and some critics have been ungenerous, picking on minutiae in the wealth of linguistic and literary quotations offered by the text and notes. This aspect has somewhat obfuscated the lineaments of Steiner the hedgehog, who deals once more with an absolute problem, reminding us of something we have always known and always ignored: Why the Tower of Babel? Why the five thousand odd languages spoken around the world?

In the human animal, the digestive system does not vary within the species; its biochemical structure and genetic potential remain almost the same in its various types; the creases of the cortex are analogous in all people and in all stages of their social and cultural evolution. But this physiological unity is counterbalanced by an extravagant linguistic multiplicity. Why this unlikely variety of languages? Why this enormous waste of neologistic invention, this antieconomic proliferation of incommunicability? Darwin's discourse on the multiplicity of animal species rests on the economy of the mechanisms of adaptation; but we cannot find its parallel in the wonders and feats of the various languages, because there is no evident correlation between idiom and social, ecological, climatic, and other conditions. The death of a language is not a phenomenon of natural selection, for some dead languages appear to have generated the most sublime products in human culture. Some destitute tribes use idioms of incredible refinement, and "starving bands of Amazonian Indians may lavish on their condition more verb tenses than could Plato."[15] This is a mind-boggling idea.

Any summary of *After Babel* is perforce a brutal simplification: of the five hundred intense pages that tackle the most complex knots of linguistic methodology, a good half are written by Steiner the fox. But the mere fact that the book brings to our awareness the significant issues connected with the Tower of Babel (and this is the work of Steiner the hedgehog) is enough to make it a landmark in political and social reflection. Besides, *After Babel* reminds us that translation is not a mere interlinguistic phenomenon. Any thorough reading of any text of the past, from Leviticus to last year's bestseller, whether written in our own tongue or in another language, involves a complex process.

Translation is a concern both of the Foreign Department and of Internal Affairs; it takes place between different languages and within the same language. Civilization does indeed consist in our capacity to translate from language to language and from period to period, through space and time. Consequently Steiner offers an ideology of the translator: man is man because he keeps translating and retranslating the linguistic signs of his present and of his past.

Even in *Antigones* (1989), the exhibition, sometimes ostentatious, of cultural information (as, e.g., the readings of Sophocles's *Antigone* offered by the Danish Hegelians of the 1870s!) (54) is awesome, but the passionate tension of the main argument is such that the hedgehog manages to control the vainglorious whims of the fox. Why the uninterrupted authority of an odd dozen Greek myths, why their unique and unrivaled attraction (300) for us, whereas other parts of the world (Amazonia, Australia) offer a much more varied canon of traditional stories? This is the fundamental question asked in *Antigones*. "Even before Joyce . . . our peregrinations and homecomings were Odysseus'. The incensed hurt of women continues to find voice via Medea. The Trojan Women speak our lament over war. The drug culture and flower-child looked to the Bacchae. Oedipus, Narcissus are enlisted to dignify, in fact to define our complexes" (129).

Starting from this incredibly lasting fecundity of Greek myths, Steiner explores several wider issues of Western civilization: Why the "tyranny of Greece over the Western mind," whereas other cultures "exhibit no comparable energy of reiteration?" (122). Is it so difficult to invent new "stories"? It is as if "the nerve of symbolic invention, of compelling metaphor [had died] with Athens" (123). We can only invent a new myth every five hundred years. (Perhaps Don Giovanni is the only genuine addition to the repertory of Western mythological characters: he does not belong to the canons of Greek psychology, though Jove had a similar physiological disposition.) In more than twenty centuries, from the decline of classical Greece to our own day, European culture has not invented a single new grammatical form: "The gamut of past and future tenses, of optatives and subjunctives, which empower remembrance and expectation, which allow hope and counter-factual supposition to create room for the spirit in the midst of the crowding imperatives of the biological, are organized along Greek lines" (134). So is our capacity to articulate experience in a grammatical form, "the syntax of deduction and of inference, of proof and of negation, which are the alphabet of rational thought" (134–35). We have inherited from the Greeks, says Steiner, "the radical wonder of knowing" (125) (though we have transformed it into simple "knowingness").

In this wide exploration of the relations between Greek myths and our forms of thought, Steiner starts from a focal point, Sophocles' *Antigone*, which, between the end of the eighteenth century and the beginning of the 1900s, was considered throughout European culture as the most miraculous among the works of art created by the human mind. Later, after 1905, through the influence of the Freudian reading, the emphasis shifts to *Oedipus Rex*. In the nineteenth century the stress is laid on sisterly love, which is both ambiguous (Antigone, as the daughter of Oedipus, cannot escape the suspicion of incest) and the purest of all (in her total dedication to the duty of burying her brother Polyneices, killed while fighting against Thebes, his own city). In our century this ideal is replaced by the awareness of libido. Counterexamples immediately come to mind ("And now that I think of it, I have never heard any man mention his brother. The subject seems distasteful to most men," says Gwendolen in Wilde's *The Importance of Being Earnest*);[16] but generalization is unavoidable when dealing with problems so huge.

Less gigantic issues do not interest Steiner. His intellectual *jouissance* seems to spring exclusively from the immensity of the considered issue. Steiner always wrestles with the *massimi sistemi*: the core questions of the Russian novel (*Tolstoy or Dostoevsky: An Essay in the Old Criticism*);[17] the nineteenth-century leitmotiv of ennui and its consequences (*In Bluebeard's Castle*); the crux of difficulty in poetry (*On Difficulty*). However, his immense erudition and his capacity to tackle the most complex issues do not serve a mere theoretical project, but are used to delve deeper into the burning issue of artistic morality. Steiner does not intend to forget fundamental problems, even if they can never be fully resolved. In *Antigones*, for instance, Steiner's analysis of the Sophoclean heroine and of her countless reincarnations in the works of the philosophers, playwrights, and poets who have elaborated on this theme in the last twenty-five hundred years aims at exploring the sense that we can find in Shelley's declaration that "we are all Greeks."[18]

In contrast with the stratospheric themes of his books, Steiner, one of the greatest readers, takes his examples from concrete passages of the text. See, for instance, his penetrating analysis of the use of the dual form in the third verse of the first scene of the tragedy, where the grammatical observation illuminates "the unspeakable cohesions of kinship in the House of Laius."[19] But Steiner is at his best when he discusses poetic passages dealing with the clash between high principles. Steiner as critic is like Blake as prophet, who saw "a World in a grain of sand, / And a Heaven in a wild flower." In the first great clash between Antigone and Creon, perhaps one of the most sublime passages in Greek literature, Steiner finds a concentration of "all the principal constants of conflict in the condition of man":[20] man and woman, the old and the young, individual and society, the living and the dead, human beings and gods. Only Creon and Antigone show in a unique moment, with such intensity, these five fundamental confrontations that embrace the whole problematics of human life. It is at this vertiginous level that the discourse of Steiner penetrates us and suffuses our most intimate problems—even though we cannot always share his conclusions.

The book in which the hedgehog wins the long-drawn battle with the fox is *Real Presences*. Here, all the resources of his learning and rhetoric are at the service of an idea, of an obsession, of a creed. The struggle between the hedgehog and the fox is not bloodless: in his *pars destruens*, aimed at the academic establishment *tout court*, Steiner the hedgehog seems intolerant of any cultural endeavor that is not meant to preserve the burning contact with the radiance of the text.

As in Alexandria, contemporary culture is debased and dominated by secondary writing: "A perpetual hum of aesthetic commentary, of on-the-minute judgements, of pre-packaged pontifications crowds the air."[21] The great bulk of what is being published nowadays in arts faculties is not only useless but also ridiculously, grotesquely so. What about the loving philological editing devoted to the preservation of a correct text? But we are well aware that all fundamental works have already been egregiously edited; the rest serve the career of mediocre dons. In a grim parody of Talmudic studies, but without the total faith in the primary value of the text that fired the exegetes of the Torah, the commentary on former commentaries on former commentaries replaces direct contact with the original.

Nowadays in Western culture the contact with the text, the painting, the musical work is always mediate. Robert Hughes writes in *Nothing if Not Critical: Selected Essays on Art and Artists* that the American student of art history feeds on a diet of slides and reproductions,[22] like a battery chicken. But the reproduction stands to the work of art as a dirty phone call to actual sex. In the humanities, "essay speaks to essay, article chatters on article in an endless gallery of querulous echo . . . and Polonius is master" (39–40), comments Steiner. But he is too generous: most of our exegetes are far more measly than Polonius, though they share his vanity and self-righteousness. The disproportion between secondary discourse and its object has become grotesque, but the motive is easy to spot: we are frightened by the mystery of the great work, and the simplest defense against its threat is to reduce the text to a pretext.

Arts faculties justify their existence by advertising the panacea of theory. But, as we know, the use of the word *theory* in literature is at best a limited metaphor, at worst a trick to hide emptiness. The High Priests of theory, in full garb, celebrate their esoteric rituals in vain. In his condemnation of the presumptions of theory, Steiner is extremely harsh and, I think, absolutely right: "Two indispensable criteria must be satisfied by theory: verifiability or falsifiability by means of experience and predictive application. There are in art and poetics no crucial experiments, no litmus-paper tests. There can be no verifiable or falsifiable deductions entailing predictable consequences in the very concrete sense in which a scientific theory carries predictive force" (75). I would personally add that any theory of literature is at best like a textbook on eroticism, a *Kamasutra* meant to titillate our imagination in our love-relation to the text. We do not discover anything new, but in the happiest cases we "enjoy" a variation of Barthes' *jouissance*.

How can we go back to the text, to the radiance of the original work that smites us and burns us? How can we recover this lost treasure today, when the indictment of language "has made naked our modernity?" (110). In the chapter "The Broken Contract," Steiner examines the main stages of this severance between word and world. Up to the nineteenth century, classical skepticism, from Pyrrhonism onward, did not question the legitimacy of expounding in an articulate form its radical doubts about the existence of any absolute truth. Exceptions in which this doubt was extended to language itself were scarce. I have always been haunted by Feste's declaration in *Twelfth Night*: "Words have grown so false I am loathe to prove reason with them,"[23] which sounds like a vertiginous anticipation of our present linguistic crisis. But between 1830 and 1870, with Nietzsche, Rimbaud, and Mallarmé, the conviction emerges that there is "no external Archimedean point"[24] outside discourse with reference to which we can verify or falsify the assertions we make. Thus the covenant between word and world is broken, in "one of the very few genuine revolutions of spirit in Western history and [one] which defines modernity itself" (93). In order to reach a poetics of absence, according to Mallarmé, the words of the tribe must be freed from their representational bondage and purged from the utilitarian lies, imprecisions, and dross of this servitude. The provocative antitheological assertion by Rimbaud that "Je est un autre" pulverizes any psychological coherence and destroys the Cartesian certitude, whose classical formulation is reversed into "I think . . . , therefore I am not I" (100), as Steiner puts it. For Kafka, "it is the inevitable passage of language through our consciousness and acts, and the consequent 'bending of the light' by the lies, hypocrisies, cruelties, bureaucratic emptiness, with which their usage by fallen man infects words, which makes inconceivable or imperceptible . . . the coming of the messianic" (113–14). But unfortunately Kafka's linguistic pessimism produced a strange breed. Today we witness the triumph of the professional "realists of entropy and overbrimming emptiness, the rhetoricians of simulation and infinite mockery," as Botho Strauss puts it in his postface to the German edition of *Real Presences*.[25]

I believe things could have been different. The trend of parody and self-parody in contemporary art and criticism might have led us to a merrier world. Think of Stravinsky and his ironic versions of other musicians of the past; or of Picasso, so great an artist that he could turn against himself his immense *vis parodica*; or, among critics, Roland Barthes, whose semiotic acid tests are at times self-referential.

The many artists, writers, and musicians and the handful of critics who believed in parody and self-parody have been overthrown by the grim bureaucrats of nihilism, punctiliously monitoring dissolution and nothingness. In a lecture already entitled "Real Presences," but delivered four years before the publication of the book, Steiner attacked one of the leaders of deconstructionism for saying that "it is more interesting to read Derrida on Rousseau than to read Rousseau," and he commented that this statement was "a perversion not only of the calling of the teacher, but of common sense, where common sense is a lucid, concentrated expression of moral imagining."[26] For Steiner, it is a matter of what Aristotle called *apaideusis*, "an indecency of spirit and understanding" (231). I know of an Italian professor of the history of criticism who told his students at the beginning of the academic year that it was more important to attend his lectures than to read the assigned texts. This is certainly another form of "indecency of spirit," but it also marks the confluence of personal and collective stupidity. At an individual level, this professor is stupid because he is stupid; but there is also a kind of group stupidity, based on the common arrogant claim of "theorists" to scientific formulation, hence to a final truth superior to the simple intuitions that can be found in Chaucer, Dante, or Shakespeare.

This is, in a debased form, an instance of the aping of the exact sciences by the humanities, with their aspiration to "rigorous" analysis and judgment. Below the subtler practitioners of deconstruction, whose dance before the Ark of meaning is "instinct with sadness, for the dancers know that the Ark is empty" (122), we have those whom Botho Strauss calls "the guardians of a Thersites-culture . . . that contains no spark of vision, no power of renewal or change."[27] Among the academic epigones in particular, the great bulk of deconstructionist plodders are recognizable by their "repulsive jargon . . . contrived obscurantism and specious pretensions to technicality."[28]

What is the answer to their negativism?

The situation is particularly awkward in my country, Italy, where culture is deeply impregnated with the nineteenth-century highfalutin histrionism of the sublime wonder and terror elicited by masterpieces. We are more wary than our colleagues in the rest of Europe and in the United States of the trembling and passionate acceptance of the work of art, which we associate with the worst in our former national tradition. Twentieth-century irony saved us from the swamp of sentimentalism, and we are not ready to abandon it so easily. For us, "playing it cool" is a vital necessity. I have always been true to this ironic, cool culture—even when enthusiasm burned underneath. Steiner asks me to cancel not only thirty years of university teaching but also a half-century of experience as a reading and cultural animal. I cannot accept this easily.

Yet on many points I find myself in perfect agreement with him. Indeed, the best interpretation of art is art itself; the greatest critic of Velázquez is Picasso, and Steiner offers us a marvelous anecdote about Schumann, who, on being requested to explain a difficult étude, sat at the piano and played it again. I can also follow *Real Presences* in its general indictment of criticism (coming from one of the greatest critics alive) and in its advocacy of *cortesia* in our approach to a work of art or literature. Two aphorisms usefully illustrate Steiner's position. The first is from Schopenhauer: "With the masterpieces of art we ought to behave as we do with important personalities: be quiet next to them and wait to be spoken to." The second is from Karl Heinrich Waggerl: "Art is a grand lady. Don't be rude and wait for her to address you." To quote Steiner, who quotes Coleridge, who quotes Boehme's rephrasing of Saint Augustine:[29] "I warn all inquirers into this hard point to *wait*—not only not to plunge forward before the Word is *given* them, but not even to paw the ground with impatience. For in a deep stillness only can this truth be apprehended."[30] We must welcome the work of art as an unexpected guest, not assault it, bang it on the head, lay it on the table, and start anatomizing it in order to discover its secret, "in some brutal rhetoric or hermeneutic of total penetration and subjection" (176). Even in their apparent playfulness, there are elements of this violence in structuralist and deconstructionist analyses such as Barthes' *S/Z*.

For Steiner, without this fundamental *cortesia*, without the recognition of the absolute priority of the work of art over secondary discourse, all aesthetic *jouissance* is reduced to an empty titillation. This *cortesia* implies some risks: we may be disappointed or hurt by our guest. But if we are not ready to take those risks, there will be no real encounter. At this point, Steiner makes a quantum leap. He aggressively and perturbingly links the "real presence" calling on us in all great art with the concept of transcendence. Although I am convinced of the nobility, the sincerity, and even the "greatness" of the emotion elicited by high poetry, art, and music, for such an agnostic as I am this is an aggressive and deeply disturbing move.

Real Presences is a wager (in both the Cartesian and Pascalian senses) on transcendence or, as Steiner puts it, "on the informing pressure of a real presence in the semantic markers that generate" (215) great works of art. The word *presence* frightens me and makes me cringe. We may be close neighbors to the transcendent, but we need not share the same house. As long as transcendence remains an hypothesis, a metaphorical key to our struggle with the angel, I can keep encountering the work of art in pain and delight, without being forced to profess a creed. But Steiner would impose upon me a total immersion, which would mean giving up the distance, the irony that is the living nerve of my aesthetic sensibility (the style of the critic is influencing the style of the critic's critic!). I can shiver with delight at the touch of some supreme lines in Dante because they harbor a modicum of irony. If I were to give myself up totally to the monstrous fascination of those lines, this would not be an aesthetic experience, but an act of faith.

Yeats said: "No man can create as did Shakespeare, Homer, Sophocles, who does not believe, with all his blood and nerve, that man's soul is immortal" (228). Steiner offers a variation on this sentence as his profession of faith: "No man can read fully, can answer answeringly to the aesthetic, whose 'nerve and blood' are at peace in sceptical rationality, are now at home in immanence and verification. We must read *as if*" (229). We Italians are all too familiar with the "as-if" aesthetics, because we are used since school to read Dante "as if" we were believers. But this is not enough. A distinction must be made between "being at home in immanence" and "being at home in transcendence." I am aware that this is not what Steiner requests of us, but his impatience with the meanness, the limited vision of the man of immanence makes him hostile to any distanciation, circuitousness, masking, travesty, in short to all those theatrical processes that allow us to survive in the otherwise lethal contact with the sublime.

I would therefore offer my own emendation to Steiner: "We must read *as if*, and at the same time we must be ironically aware of the hypothetical element in this *as if*, and perhaps even of the unreality of this hypothesis." For me, as agnostic, there is no salvation outside irony.

Notes

1. Archilochus, frag. 201, in *Iambi et Elegi Graeci ante Alexandrum cantati*, ed. M. L. West, 2 vols. (Oxford: Clarendon Press, 1971), vol. 1.

2. Isaiah Berlin, "The Hedgehog and the Fox," in *Russian Thinkers* (London: Hogarth Press, 1979), 22.

3. George Steiner, *On Difficulty and Other Essays* (New York: Oxford University Press, 1978), 164–85.

4. Berlin, "The Hedgehog and the Fox," 26.

5. Guillaume Apollinaire, *Les peintres cubistes*, ed. L. C. Breunig and J.-Cl. Chevalier (1965; reprint, Paris: Hermann, 1980), 78.

6. Steiner, *On Difficulty and Other Essays*, 62–63.

7. George Steiner, *Real Presences* (Chicago: University of Chicago Press, 1989).

8. The lectures were later published in book form as *In Bluebeard's Castle: Some Notes towards the Redefinition of Culture* (1971; reprint, London: Faber and Faber, 1974).

9. Steiner, *Real Presences*, 23.

10. Steiner, *In Bluebeard's Castle*, 13.

11. George Steiner, *The Portage to San Cristóbal of A.H.* (London: Faber and Faber, 1981). The novel had already appeared in the *Kenyon Review*, n.s., vol. 1, no. 2 (Spring 1979): 1–120.

12. George Steiner, *Antigones: How the Antigone Legend Has Endured in Western Literature, Art, and Thought* (New York: Oxford University Press, 1986).

13. In a lecture, Steiner went even further; reflecting about the paradox of the refusal of Christ as the Messiah by the Jews, he says: "In the black light of the Shoah, one is almost tempted to define Christianity as Jewish self-hatred. . . . There is, between Golgotha and Auschwitz, a parodistic symmetry nearly unbearable to understanding. By refusing God's *kenosis* in the person of Jesus, Judaism judged spurious, contrary to reason, the divinity of a man. At Auschwitz. . . the butchers and torturers . . . bestialized humanity, in the person, in the flesh of those who had denied the literal divinity of the flesh in Jesus the Jew. Metaphors can kill" ("Two Cocks," a lecture delivered in Munich in November 1991, as yet unpublished in English.)

14. George Steiner, *After Babel: Aspects of Language and Translation* (New York: Oxford University Press, 1975).

15. Ibid., 55.

16. Act 2. The play was first performed in 1895.

17. George Steiner, *Tolstoy or Dostoevsky: An Essay in the Old Criticism* (1959; reprint, Chicago: University of Chicago Press, 1985).

18. Quoted in Steiner, *Antigones*, 135.

19. Steiner, *Antigones*, 211.

20. Ibid., 231.

21. Steiner, *Real Presences*, 24.

22. Robert Hughes, *Nothing if Not Critical: Selected Essays on Art and Artists* (New York: Knopf, 1990), 12.

23. *Twelfth Night* 3.1.24–25.

24. Steiner, *Real Presences*, 95.

25. Botho Strauss, "Der Aufstand gegen die sekulare Weit—Bemerkungen zu einer Astheitk der Anwesenheit" [The Revolt against a Secular World—Notes towards an Aesthetics of Presence], in George Steiner, *Von realer Gegenwart* (Munich: Carl Hanser Verlag, 1990), 313–14.

26. George Steiner, *Real Presences: The Leslie Stephen Memorial Lecture.* Delivered before Cambridge University on 1 November 1985 (Cambridge: Cambridge University Press, 1986), 16.

27. Strauss, "Der Aufstand gegen die sekulare Weit," 313–14.

28. Steiner, *Real Presences*, 116.

29. This is clearly the triumph of the secondary. Or perhaps we should quote André Gide's dictum: "Toutes choses sont déjà dites; mais comme personne n'écoute, il faut tounours recommencer."

30. Steiner, *Real Presences*, 224.

Tolstoy and Dostoevsky:
Seductions of the Old Criticism

GEORGE STEINER wrote his major contribution to Russian literary studies, *Tolstoy or Dostoevsky: An Essay in the Old Criticism*, in the late 1950s.[1] At the time, academic critics in the West felt much closer to nineteenth-century Russian culture than to any literary product of that forbidding and well-sealed monolith, the Soviet state—even though, paradoxically, our regnant New Criticism recalled in many particulars the spirit of Russian Formalism from the Soviet 1920s. Now over thirty years old, *Tolstoy or Dostoevsky* still renders exemplary service to those two great Russian novelists. But the book casts unexpected light on our own current critical debates as well.

Steiner opens his essay with a defense of his "old" critical approach. Its primary purpose, he tells us, is to serve the text "subjectively." Thus its starting point must be a positive, almost an electrical, contact between an artwork of genius and its admiring and energized reader. In Steiner's words, "when the work of art invades our consciousness, something within us catches flame. What we do thereafter is to refine and make articulate the original leap of recognition" (45). This quasi-mystical mission—which, one suspects, only Steiner's astonishing erudition could bring to heel and down to earth in our secular age—is then pointedly contrasted with the spirit of the New Criticism: "Quizzical, captious, immensely aware of its philosophic ancestry and complex instruments, it often comes to bury rather than to praise" (4). Indeed. In retrospect Steiner is perhaps too harsh on the New Critics, whose captiousness is but a minnow to the leviathan of later, postmodernist burials of the world's great literature. Still, he sees ample evidence of a falling away from earlier, more radiant modes of reading. The unhappy vogue of "objective criticism," he claims, has made us uncertain of our great books and suspicious of tradition. "We grow wary of our inheritance," he writes. "We have become relativists" (4).

Three decades ago, then, Steiner had come out in defense of a literary canon and the reader's unmediated primary contact with it. As *Real Presences* indicates, this commitment has not changed. But what, precisely, is primary contact? It need not mean immersion in the native language of the literary text (in his dealings with Tolstoy and Dostoevsky, Steiner apologizes for his ignorance of Russian—but the deficiency hinders him much less than he fears); nor does it mandate a meticulous, insider's knowledge of the political or cultural background of every world-class text. Primary contact, for Steiner, is both more modest and more risk-laden. It requires from the reader less an intellectual than an *aesthetic* commitment, a willingness to "tune oneself" to the artwork and thus to become part of the text's glorious problem rather than its solution. In short, we have come into primary contact when, one way or another, we fall in love with a piece of art and are moved to expand on its value in ways that expose our own vulnerabilities before it. "Literary criticism should arise out of a debt of love," Steiner writes (3). From this love relation, apparently, there are no merely scientific or "secondary" ways out.

In our current age of suspicious interrogations, all this sounds very, very old. But what takes us by surprise, in rereading *Tolstoy or Dostoevsky*, is its high degree of theoretical sophistication. The number of potent critical ideas that Steiner eases directly out of primary texts (and it goes without saying that Russian scholarship has a vast "secondary" industry on each of these novelists, but Steiner is not and cannot be in thrall to it) is simply exhilarating. His resulting thesis is so expertly cobbled together from the bottom up, out of the wide-ranging and integral world views of the novels themselves, that it easily survives the language barrier and the passage of time. To reconstruct and extend that thirty-year-old thesis, with an eye to some intervening critical developments, will be the major task of this essay.

The brunt of Steiner's thesis is reducible to a topic sentence: that Tolstoy's art revives the traditions of Homeric epic, whereas Dostoevsky's reenacts, in novelistic garb, ancient tragic drama. One is immediately struck, of course, by the derivative nature of the whole dichotomy—by its apparent indifference to the manifest "novelness" of the novel, which has been justly celebrated as the most non-Aristotelian of genres. Many have argued that the novel's very messiness and indeterminacy were what appealed to these two great Russian innovators in the genre. Precisely this intractable failure of the great Russian novel to fit into a classical poetics led the twentieth century's greatest student of Dostoevsky, Mikhail Bakhtin, to posit the novel as a genre that is in principle *opposed* to both epic and drama. This dialogue between Bakhtin and Steiner, so suggestive and full of intricate complementarity, shall be pursued at the end of the essay. Let us turn first to the general lineaments of Steiner's juxtaposition of Tolstoy and Dostoevsky.

Chapter one sets the scene by marking similarities. Both novelists wrote immensely long books. But, Steiner notes, the length of these books was of a different order than the length, say, of *Clarissa* or *Ulysses*; for those latter authors, length was an invitation to elegant and precise mapping, to tying down, whereas for Dostoevsky and Tolstoy, "plenitude was an essential freedom" (14). Freedom and plenitude: out of these two ideas Steiner constructs his larger contribution to the history of the novel. Much ink has been spilt on comparisons between the "European" and "Russian" novel, Steiner remarks. But the more interesting and valid comparison is between the European novel, on the one hand, and on the other the Russian and the American novel—two generic strands fused, as it were, at the still half-savage periphery of Europe's sphere of influence. Steiner explains his typology. The European novel, he argues, arose as a private genre that was secular, rational, social. Its task was the successful portrayal of everyday life. But the genre was plagued from the start with a question of legitimacy: Could the prosaic and quotidian ever attain to the "high seriousness" expected of great art? The grand novels of the Romantic period were spared the full implications of that question, because Dickens, Hugo, Stendhal could abandon the familiar plots of classical antiquity and draw, for inspiration and grandeur, on the heroic (but still contemporary and local) events of the 1810s-40s, on the Napoleonic theme and its aftermath. The problem became more serious in the second half of the century, Steiner claims, when the mainstream European novel—tacking to and fro in search of a new word—confronted the pervasive and leveling "bourgeoisification" of everyday life. As a genre devoted to secular readings of ordinary experience, its predictable endpoint was Zola's dessicating naturalism and Flaubert's *catalogue manqué*.

According to Steiner, this "dilemma of realism" was felt less acutely at the periphery of the novel's reach. "The masters of the American and the Russian manner appear to gather something of their fierce intensity from the outer darkness," he writes, "from the decayed matter of folklore, melodrama, and religious life" (30). Melville and Hawthorne are the United States' Dostoevsky: writers on an untamed frontier, creating in isolation, plagued by crises of faith in their pre-Enlightenment societies, and radically insecure in the face of Europe's complacent cultural superiority. With such a set of problems, Russian and American novelists had no trouble filling their novels with "high seriousness." Having established the special compatibility of these two quasi-civilized European outposts, Steiner then returns to the classics —and shows the Russian novel to be the salvation of that profoundly civilized legacy.

The body of the book falls into two parts, each with its own thesis and demonstration: Tolstoy as Homeric bard, and Dostoevsky as tragic dramatist. For a critic such as Steiner, utterly uninterested in such hypotheses as the death of the author or the impossibility of authorial intention, the first thesis is perhaps the easier to document. For Tolstoy himself desired to be compared with Homer. Indeed, we sense intuitively that Tolstoy's novels have some kinship with epic: in their immensity, seriousness, spaciousness, in the serene confidence of their narrative voice. But certain other parallels have been neglected, Steiner claims. The most crucial of these are Tolstoy's specific structural imitations of Homeric epic, and the concordance between Tolstoy's epic manner and his anarchic Christianity (which Steiner will later bring unnervingly close to paganism, to an anthropomorphic "theology without God" [266]). Steiner's critical method here is leisurely and learned. He constantly weaves scenes from the *Odyssey* and *Iliad* into his own paraphrases of Tolstoyan plot and doctrine. One important byproduct of these subtle penetrations is Steiner's continual reassurance that Tolstoy's novels are not unworked "slices of life," not the fluid puddings or baggy monsters that Henry James christened them— for no one would deny a great epic poem the status of real art. If the great Russian novel had little influence on its European counterpart it was not because Russian novelists had no interest in craft; it was because the craft of these Russians was unreadable in the context of the Romantic or naturalistic Continental novel (49–58).

Classicists might balk at Steiner's bold, homogenizing definition of the "epic vision." But, as Steiner gradually sculpts this vision to fit his thesis about Russian writers, Tolstoy's novels take on an integrity— both artistic and theoretical—that their bulk and their sprawl of detail usually defy. Invoking as foil and counterexample the negated, manipulative world of *Madame Bovary*, Steiner points out the deeply epic reflexes of Tolstoyan novelistic prose: the sensuous, dynamic, personal energy that physical objects continually absorb from their human context ("The sword is always seen as part of the striking arm" [51]); the frequent elevation of tiny realistic detail to a matter of passionate significance; and the utter lack of sentimentality about death and individual tragedy ("War and mortality cry havoc in the Homeric and Tolstoyan worlds, but the centre holds. . . . 'Keep your eyes steadfastly to the light,' says Tolstoy, 'this is how things are'" [78, 77]).

Of great and disorienting importance in the Tolstoyan vision is the effective absence of God. Steiner devotes a portion of chapter four to this seeming paradox: a deeply religious thinker who constructs his Christian theology without the Church, and his Christ without a heavenly Father.[2] A partial answer might be found, again, in the Homeric model. Tolstoy is a pagan, Steiner insists, of the most sophisticated and ethically responsible sort. Within such a world view, neither confession as a sacrament nor faith in a miracle-working savior can remedy human error; error is righted only through something akin to stoic resolve, a willingness to change one's life as a result of pained contemplation or the act of an isolated conscience. We should not be misled by the superficial frivolity of the Greek gods and their irresponsible antics on and off Mount Olympus. The continuum of Homer's world—its ultraheroism for human beings and its semidivinity for gods— suggests precisely the sort of leveling of the secular and the divine that we would expect from the author of a treatise entitled *The Kingdom of God Is within You*.

Steiner is alert, of course, to those aspects of the epic that do not match up with Tolstoyan values. He notes, for example, that the ethic of Tolstoy is profoundly antiheroic (80) and that his pacifist self would never have approved (although it always deeply understood) the epic lust of the battlefield. However, the world views of Tolstoy and the epic do share one vital and quasi-religious dimension: "The humanity of the gods signifies that reality—the controlling pivot of man's experience—is immanent in the natural world" (267).

In these ways, then, Steiner aligns Tolstoy's novel with Homeric epic. Throughout his argument, the novel appears to be the tenor of the metaphor, cast in a sort of passive holding pattern, while the epic is the more active vehicle. But in one final comparison, Steiner makes an impressive contribution precisely to understanding the novel as a genre. This is his discussion, in chapter two, of the "double and triple plot structure" of epics and of Tolstoyan narratives. Steiner does not probe the formal implications of this structure for Tolstoy's larger ethical vision—for that one must repair to Gary Saul Morson's splendid monograph on *War and Peace*[3]—but he does make numerous acute observations that assist the reader in integrating this baffling novel.

Steiner acknowledges that multiple plot structure in the epic lends it a certain narrative grandeur and disinterestedness. He sees clearly that Tolstoy employs such multiplicity for very special purposes. (On the master list of talents that Tolstoy commands as novelist, disinterestedness must rank rather low.) "Double vision" and double plots can be polemical, of course, in the overtly didactic sense: they can reinforce and generalize a particular instance (thus making it more authoritative), or they can ironize and undercut an instance, trivializing the original statement, as well as later parodic replays of it. Although Tolstoy is surely no stranger to this kind of didacticism, Steiner suggests a third possibility: that multiple vision, in the form of many blunt-edged competing plot lines, can be deployed purely to thicken the texture of the work, "to suggest realness by making the design of a work dense, jagged, and complex" (98).

So far, no surprises. But Steiner then stresses that the purpose here is not to saturate the novel with realia for its own sake, or to despise—in the name of "realism"—the need to structure some sort of coherent story. He points out, correctly, that Tolstoy's plots incorporate every bit as much artifice and coincidence as the jerry-built, crisis-driven adventure plots of Dostoevsky. However, the mesh of narrative strands in Tolstoy is so dense, and the degree of "humanization" that even the most episodic characters receive is so high and precise, that coincidence and artifice do not shock us. With that much living material it seems only natural that a great deal of it will interact.

Steiner then speculates on the connection between this thickening of texture in Tolstoy's novels and the nature of Tolstoyan closure. The mass of meticulously tended plot lines and the open, often unresolved endings of the great novels prompt Steiner to regard length, complex plotting, and multiple vision as a "stringent test" for the "aliveness" of a character: "whether or not it can grow with time and preserve its coherent individuality in an altered setting" (104). In this insight—which will not be the last such curious overlay—we see the germ of the Steiner-Bakhtin debate. At base are their deeply incompatible notions of the potential of epic. For Bakhtin, the epic hero is defined as a closed and ready-made character who fits neatly into a prescribed plot with no slack or superfluity. Bakhtin's novelistic hero, by contrast, is a character in whom "there always remains an unrealized surplus of humanness, there always remains a need for the future and a place for this future must be found."[4] What Steiner does, then, is graft on to his epic model a novelistic sensibility that undoes some of Bakhtin's most famous dichotomies—and, in the current theoretical climate that has turned so many Bakhtinian terms into mental reflexes, this is a provocative revision. Through it, Steiner proves himself as strong a reader of Tolstoy as Bakhtin was a weak one.

As a bridge to his second major theme, Dostoevsky as tragic dramatist, Steiner discusses Tolstoy and the drama—and specifically the most scandal-ridden corner of that question, Tolstoy and Shakespeare. Tolstoy's vitriolic 1904 essay "On Shakespeare and on Drama," with its mockery of *King Lear* and (implicitly) of *Hamlet*, contemptuously dismisses Shakespearean language as tedious vulgarity and the Bard himself as an immoral fraud. The piece has long been relegated to that category of eccentricity permitted great writers. Steiner, however, takes Tolstoy's essay more seriously. For one thing, it contains a lengthy passage praising Homer (for seriousness and neutral narrative voice) at Shakespeare's expense; this broadside appeals to Steiner, for he sees in Tolstoy's gravitation toward the virtues of the epic and its faith in a "totality of objects" a lodestar of Tolstoyan aesthetics. Second, and more importantly, Steiner correctly stresses that Tolstoy's writings on drama are not the ravings of a man who rejected or misunderstood the stage. Tolstoy was an excellent and effective playwright. He rejects not drama itself, but only what he perceives as Shakespeare's inability to produce on stage the right sort of illusion.

Accordingly, Steiner deals with Tolstoy's rejection of Shakespeare in terms of "two different types of illusion." The first type is straightforwardly false (the seduction of Natasha at the opera in *War and Peace*); the second type Steiner refers to, unsatisfyingly, as "some undefined notion of 'true illusion'" (122). Steiner's argument here would have been stronger had he considered a key text on aesthetics that Tolstoy wrote six years before the essay on Shakespeare. For the Tolstoyan paradox of a "true illusion" is not at all "undefined," but lies, with important modifications, at the base of Tolstoy's treatise *What Is Art?*

In his attempt to answer that title question, Tolstoy avoids the simple binary opposition "true-false." With his passion for inventories and lists, he constructs a much more interesting evaluative model of (at least) two axes. Along the first axis, an artwork can be true or counterfeit. If counterfeit, the art simply won't "take," that is, it will be deficient in aesthetic effect. If true, we enter more dangerous territory—for the artwork can be good (moral) or bad (immoral). According to Tolstoy, true art (presumably both moral and immoral) must satisfy three criteria: it must be nonderivative, lucid, and sincere. These three traits bring on the "infection" of the reader or spectator by those very emotions that the author experienced during the act of creation. The resultant communication—in essence an act of solidarity between artist (infector) and audience (infectee)—constitutes the mission and justification of art. But artists can have genuinely bad feelings, and people can be genuinely infected by bad art. Here is where the problem of Shakespeare becomes acute. For Tolstoy insists that Shakespeare's plays are *both* counterfeit art (derivative, worse than their literary prototypes, poorly motivated, and—unlike Homeric epic—the work of an insincere author who "does not believe in what he is saying") and bad and immoral art (tempting spectators with corrupt or obscene plots, trivial ideas, deceptive language). But if Shakespearean drama is both counterfeit and bad, how did "infection" occur? How did the entire European nineteenth century collapse into idolatry before this false playwright?

Tolstoy's answer to this paradox takes up a large part of *What Is Art?*, but Steiner—fastidiously and perhaps wisely—does not call him on it.

For Tolstoy resolves the dilemma of false, immoral, and yet highly regarded art by an explanation as irrefutably crude and, as it were, somatic as the idea of infection itself, namely, "hypnosis," the baleful influence of fashionable critics and mere ugly vogue. Tolstoy's essay was not written to explicate Shakespeare, but to expose him. A glance at Tolstoy's letters and diaries of the time will easily document this preoccupation with the problem of "counterfeit reception." Tolstoy wrote to Vladimir Stasov in October 1903, for example, that the trouble with Shakespeare was not his aristocratism as much as "the perversion of aesthetic taste brought about by praise of unartistic works."[5] There is much that Steiner might have mined in this passion of Tolstoy's to unmask Shakespearean drama on behalf of the world's aesthetic health[6]—but here Steiner keeps his eyes perhaps too steadfastly to the light of his thesis about Tolstoy as epic bard. Three decades later, the author of *Real Presences* would have in Tolstoy a perfect candidate for his "republic of primary things," that hypothetical city from which all noncreating critics are banished. The nineteenth century's great Naysayer would keep that city from ever becoming a utopia.

If Tolstoy's understanding of the drama was hopelessly tied to a single voice with the authority of an epic narrator, then Dostoevsky represents for Steiner the opposite case: a novelist who looked to drama, and specifically to tragic drama, for both the structure and the spiritual focus of his novelistic world. Steiner begins chapter three with a most useful account of the nineteenth-century eclipse of tragic form. Music, darling of the Romantics, had accomplished less than had been hoped in the narrative arts, and the stage had been captured by popular melodrama and vaudeville. The "tragic vision" was thus picked up and perfected by Melville and Dostoevsky.

What does genuine drama require? In approaching this question, Steiner is both helped and hobbled by his reluctance to attend to specific requirements (or, for that matter, even simple definitions) of the novel as a genre. The essence of drama, for Steiner, is concentration, compression, "moments": all affects are piled into single mass confrontation, where it is imperative that "speech should move and motion speak" (163). In Steiner's view, however, this highly controlled and often stylized nature of drama does not in the least restrict its freedom of meaning, nor reduce it to cliché. This fact is of crucial importance for Steiner's next move, which is to attach to tragic drama, as a resolute genre attribute, what many (again, most famously Bakhtin) have considered the central achievement of the Dostoevskian polyphonic novel: the power to invest heroes and plots with genuinely free potential. As Steiner puts forward his thesis, "Dostoevsky, like all genuine dramatists, seemed to listen with an inward ear to the independent and unforeseeable dynamics of action. . . . [Thus] the characters seem admirably free from their creator's will and our own previsions" (173).

For Steiner, then, the "law of composition" in a Dostoevskian novel is dramatic in that it is "one of maximum energy, released over the smallest possible extent of space and time" (147). But this energy and compression are so volatile, so chemically unstable that the playwright cannot hope to do more than set up the scene, then stand back. Thus genuinely dramatic scenes always convey the sense that "things could be otherwise" (unlike, in Steiner's control case, the absolute determinedness of human action in the novels of Henry James). "The tightness, the high pitch of drama," Steiner writes, "are brought on by the interplay of ambiguous meanings, of partial ignorance with partial insight" (277). To be dramatic in Steiner's sense is not to be tied to specific unities, speech styles, or roles, but to be ever uncertain how the scene will end.

So much, then, for dramatic character in Dostoevsky, which is indeed saturated with polyphonic novelness. What about dramatic plot? At this point in chapter three, Steiner treats us to some European literary history (one of many such treats in the book) on a topic too often overlooked by Russianists. Steiner wishes to defend Dostoevsky's plots. These plots have taken a beating, both in their own and in our century—for their exaggerated pathos, their perversity, their apparent incompatibility with the sophisticated philosophy that Dostoevsky weaves around them in his novels. The extremism of these plots encourages critics (especially of the psychoanalytic persuasion) to seek in the personal psychology of their creator some abnormal or pathological core. But Steiner advises us to read Dostoevsky the creator against the background of *his* century, not our own. Our postmodern mentality now dismisses much of Dostoevskian thematics as low culture, as kitsch, or (in an alternative coping mechanism) we find it so repellent that we prefer to analyze it as a matter of "private obsession" (201). But violence against children, seduction of virgins, murder over mysterious inheritances, and related landscapes of eroticism, terror, and sadism were "the public material at hand"—that is, the set plots available to any European novelist, so familiar as to be almost invisible. This material was the indifferent, indeed the clichéd stock in trade of Gothic melodrama and the grotesque. The fact that Dostoevsky considered these conventions—which flooded the popular stage as well as the popular novel—to be acceptable material for high art provided him with a matchless opportunity. He could write best-sellers that compromised nothing in intellectual rigor; he could resurrect tragic drama on the basis of forms that were already part of the reading public's most basic literacy, namely, the Gothic romance.

Steiner argues this case with skill. What reservations one has about his thesis arise on different and prior ground, back at the point where the graft between drama and novel was originally joined. To take one example: in defense of his drama/novel analogy, Steiner notes at one point that "with each year, the list of dramatic adaptations of Dostoevskyan novels grows longer. During the winter of 1956–57 alone, nine 'Dostoevsky plays' were being performed in Moscow" (141). What Steiner does *not* note is that almost all the stage dramatizations of Dostoevskian novels have been spectacularly bad. This badness is not due to any lack of talent on the part of the playwrights; for example, Albert Camus's *Les Possédés*, a dramatization of Dostoevsky's massive novel-satire on revolutionary morality, *The Devils*, is clearly the work of an earnest and gifted writer.[7] It is simply that everything "Dostoevskian"—except for the melodramatic, Gothic skeleton of the plot—disappears.

In itself this is no bad thing, of course: adaptations need not imitate their parent texts, especially when cast in a new genre or medium. But the "derived" text must have its own vision and succeed on its own new terms. In this regard the adaptations and "dramatizations" of Dostoevsky—at least the ones with which I am familiar—fail more routinely and more miserably than do most such projects. This failure must at least partly be due to the temptation to extract that tragic-dramatic core that Steiner so clearly sees—to strip the novel of all that had obscured its originary scenic composition—and then to stop there. The sorry result is instructive, for the difference between the original and its stage adaptation is a measure of the crucial noncoincidence between the private, innerly realized world of the novel and the publicly performed world of drama. Dostoevsky may think through his plots as a dramatist, but he uses words as a novelist. As Bakhtin has argued this case, "drama is by its very nature alien to genuine polyphony: drama may be multi-leveled, but it cannot contain *multiple worlds*; it permits only one, and not several, systems of measurement."[8]

Near the end of chapter four, Steiner gives us one of those bold and lapidary juxtapositions that are his trademark. In what he engagingly calls a "myth of criticism, a fancy through which to re-direct our imaginings," he proposes "to read the Legend of the Grand Inquisitor as an allegory of the confrontation between Dostoevsky and Tolstoy" (328). There is much to recommend the exercise. The Inquisitor's indictment of Christ as carrier of "all that is exceptional, vague and enigmatic" is indeed Tolstoy's problem with the New Testament— and Tolstoy would like to replace its heady visions and parables with "thorough, unhesitating common sense" (337). Steiner does not take up the obvious counterargument, that the Inquisitor corrects Christ's work with the famous triad "miracle, mystery, authority" (hardly bastions of common sense), but never mind: in the tough old Cardinal there is not a drop of genuine humility or piety, and this is the point Steiner is resolved to make about that sophisticated pagan aristocrat, Leo Tolstoy. Dostoevsky, throughout his life passionately undecided about the nature of moral choice and deeply convinced that "no system of belief, however compelling, could confer immunity from guilt, doubt, or self-contempt,"[9] remained ever willing to take a chance on genuine mystery.

In the blunt contours of his Tolstoy-Dostoevsky comparison, Steiner is certainly correct. Many other students of the two novelists have elaborated this difference before and since, but one eloquent variant on the thesis can serve us as summary. In 1929, Prince D. S. Mirsky, the great Russian literary historian and critic then an émigré in England, observed that the problem of Tolstoy was indeed complicated—but, he added,

I do not imply that he was a particularly complex character. There was no very great variety of ingredients to his personality. He cannot in this sense be compared to Rousseau, to Goethe, to Pushkin, or to Gogol. He was one of the most simply composed of great men. . . . His mind was essentially dialectical, in the Hegelian sense. . . . But, unlike Hegel's system, Tolstoy's mind did not surmount the contradiction of "thesis" and "antithesis" by any synthesis. Instead of Hegel's "triads," Tolstoy was all arranged in a small number of irreducible and intensely hostile "dyads". . . . Dualism is the hall-mark of the

ethical man. The essence of ethics is a dualistic pattern, an irreducible opposition between right and wrong or good and evil. As soon as a third element is
introduced, as soon as anything *one* is allowed to stand above good and evil,
the ethical point of view is adulterated and ultimately lost.[10]

Perhaps here, through Mirsky's insight on Tolstoy, we can integrate
the various contradictory genre traits that Steiner sees in his two great
subjects. The Tolstoyan novel, for all its expansiveness and intricate
multiplicity, is "unitary" in the way the Manichean universe is unitary.
Thus its epic narrator, albeit often subtle in judgments of right and
wrong, tends to keep the audience distanced from the meanings of
events and does not invite new or uncontrolled synthesis. In contrast,
the Dostoevskian novel—for all its compression and ideologically precise juxtapositions—continually gives rise to genuinely new confu-
sions. In Steiner's terms, Dostoevsky's art is open-ended dramatic
conflict, with only the most minimal interference from authorial stage
directions.

How viable is Steiner's thesis today? And what is the "feel" of this
classic essay amid the comings and goings of current theory and criticism? What strikes us first about *Tolstoy or Dostoevsky* is how wonder-
fully it is written. For cadence and complex poetry of style, perhaps its
only competition in Russian studies is the highly personal prose of
Isaiah Berlin. It is a truism—and, like most truisms, largely true—that
in this age of ideological criticism the plain art of writing well has
become terribly debased. Ground down by the ugly and careless, however, it is easy to forget the power that a perfectly tuned sentence can
have. Some of Steiner's formulations stop you in your tracks. "Both
The Death of Ivan Ilych and *The Kreutzer Sonata* are masterpieces, but
masterpieces of a singular order," he writes. "Their terrible intensity
arises not out of a prevalence of imaginative vision but out of its narrowing; they possess, like the dwarf-like figures in the paintings of
Bosch, the violent energies of compression" (283). Or on the urban
landscape: "Dostoevsky moved with purposeful familiarity amid a
labyrinth of tenements, garrets, railway yards, and tentacular suburbs. . . . Tolstoy was most thoroughly at home in a city when it was
being burnt down" (198).[11] Steiner has a special way with the lower
animals. "Gania's house [in *The Idiot*] is one of those Dostoevskyan

towers of Babel from whose dank rooms an army of characters pours forth like dazzled bats" (159); and "D. H. Lawrence's dislike of the Dostoevskyan manner is notorious; he hated the strident, rat-like confinement of it" (208).

Closely related to this exquisite literacy is a trait that Steiner shares with Vladimir Nabokov in the latter's pedagogic mode: an unembarrassed willingness to retell large amounts of plot and cite huge chunks of primary text. It is the sort of thing we always warn our undergraduates against: "Assume," we say, "that the person grading your paper will already know the plot." Now Steiner assumes that his readers will know a great deal—the depth, spread, and light touch of his allusions make that clear—but he nevertheless walks you, episode by episode, through twenty pages each on *Anna Karenina*, *The Idiot*, and *The Possessed*, for what seems to be the sheer pleasure and love of it. "Just look at how good this is," he appears to say over and over—much in the spirit of Nabokov's lecture notes on Chekhov and Tolstoy, which often do little more than note and annotate the primary author's moves over a wide stretch of text (when Nabokov really dislikes an author, as he does Dostoevsky, we get scornful and rather abstract analysis).[12]

On one level this is doubtless a common-sense acknowledgment that readers can love a novel but still benefit from some rehearsal of the plot before being asked to follow an analysis of its more subtle moves. More importantly, however, plot summary seems to be Steiner's way of leaving his readers with a fuller taste of the primary text than of its secondary critical effluvia. When the critic himself is a gifted writer, this is not an easy task. Although Steiner, to be sure, is much more the mediator and literary tour guide than Nabokov, both seem to nurse a nostalgia for that "city of primary things" from which critics have been banished.

A final general observation might be made on Steiner's evaluation of his own contribution to scholarship. At the end of chapter one, Steiner apologizes to the professionals in Russian literature: "I shall be approaching the Tolstoyan and Dostoevskyan texts by way of translation. This means that the work can be of no real use to scholars of Russian and to historians of Slavic languages and literature" (44). This is nonsense. If Steiner were analyzing poetry, or doing textological work and close reading for dialect or style, then of course; but the bulk of Dostoevsky's and Tolstoy's genius is eminently translatable. Furthermore, this body of work has been subject to at least as many constricting or superficial readings by native speakers and readers of Russian as by gifted outsiders. To assume that humanistic thought must always work with the grain of "original national languages" in order to make an authentic contribution to scholarship is to underestimate the power of ideas, the power of translation, and the value of great minds from different cultures working on one another.

Only occasionally does one remark the relative thinness of Steiner's sense of the Russian context, and the effect of these alien moments is negligible.[13] By and large, the benefits that Steiner's broadly cast net can bring to Slavists far outweigh the occasional local misprision. Through their richly nuanced European context, many of Steiner's readings oblige Russian literature professionals to confront yet again a question that never seems to go away: How much in Russia's great writers is irreducibly Russian (as the writers themselves, caught in a massive identity crisis along with their nation, would like to claim), and how much overlaps and duplicates the experience of Western Europe? We recall Steiner's thesis in chapter one: the European novel knew itself, but the American and Russian novel was always—and often unhappily—in search of itself.

Two examples from Tolstoy. What in the field is called a Tolstoyeved (a specialist on Tolstoy or, in the Soviet academic context, a scholar who has spent his or her life ingesting literally every text and commentary in the ninety-volume Jubilee Edition) will have a thick cloud of references to back up the genesis of every one of the master's ideas. All contradictions have already been classified; the novelist has long been a product, and at times even a prisoner, of his own extensive self-documentation. So has the Tolstoyeved. Steiner brings a different sort of ballast to the task—and, as it were, loosens Tolstoy's text for a moment from the paper trail of its author's life.

Consider the First Epilogue to *War and Peace*. Steiner reads these final domestic scenes in a highly peculiar—because so unredeemably negative—way. " 'Brightness falls from the air' " (108), Steiner says. Natasha has become stout, stingy, untidy; Sonya is weary; the old Countess is senile. "The saddest metamorphosis is that of Pierre. With marriage to Natasha, he has suffered a sea-change into something neither rich nor strange" (109). "Tolstoy's iconoclasm is relentless," Steiner writes; "each character in turn is seen corroded" (109).

True, Steiner does see some small surviving light in the larger picture. The Epilogue can be read in two ways, he suggests: "In its corro-

sive account of the Rostov and Bezukhov marriages there is expressed
Tolstoy's nearly pathological realism" (that is clearly the bad side); but
there is also the good side, a formal loophole implicit in the very
openness of the ending, which "proclaims the Tolstoyan conviction
that a narrative form must endeavor to rival the infinity—literally, the
unfinishedness—of actual experience" (112). Both are sound and possible readings. Then Steiner hints, albeit without enthusiasm, at a potential third reading: that Tolstoy, although he records "with the hard
irony of a poet" all of Natasha's "parsimony, untidiness, and querulous
jealousy," nevertheless does enunciate through her person "essential
Tolstoyan doctrines" and thus probably intends us to applaud her "ferocious standards of monogamy and . . . utter absorption in the details
of childbearing" (110). What is missing, however, from this earnest
postscript in redemptive reading is any serious attempt on Steiner's
part to respect or, better, to understand from within, Tolstoy's own
world view.

Why does this matter? Because anyone familiar with the long, subtle
genesis of Tolstoy's views on families and on love will agree that the
Epilogue provides us not with a "pathological realism" but with scenes
of genuine prosaic bliss. In the late 1850s, in the final volume (*Youth*) of
his childhood trilogy, Tolstoy outlined a three-part typology of love
from which he henceforth never deviated. Types one and two—
respectively, the "beautiful-romantic" and the "self-sacrificing" modes
of loving—are mercilessly exposed as false and internally contradictory. Only type three, "active love," is genuinely worthy of the name,
and its purpose is not to encourage in one's mate more of the "rich and
strange," but rather to anticipate everyday necessities, to clarify, bind,
and infiltrate the other life, to *serve the quotidian need*. Both Natasha and
Marya accomplish that in their married states. Unmarried, Natasha
was irresistible, yes, but she was also unstable, too full of self and
uncertain where to invest it, a type one (so, for different reasons, was
her brother); Sonya was, and remains at the end of the novel, a sterile
type two. The rhythms of family—which Tolstoy deeply understands
but never idealizes or presumes to be without cost—can only succeed
with type-three lovers. In reading the Epilogue as negative and "corro-
sive," Steiner, the model pan-European, gives himself away. Courtly
Renaissance moorings and conventional Tristan-and-Isolde reflexes in
matters of love are precisely what Tolstoy has set out to refute with his
scenes of everyday, and thus imperfect and real, human commitment.

Let us consider one more example. In his discussion (129–31) of Tolstoy as dramatist, Steiner devotes some time to his final play, that "colossal fragment" *The Light That Shines in the Darkness*. Steiner correctly reads the play—essentially a chunk of Tolstoy's own diaries cast in dramatic form—as an exercise in autobiography. Comparing Tolstoy with Molière, who is alleged to have "satirized his own infirmities in *Le Malade imaginaire*," Steiner asserts that "Tolstoy did something crueller: in his last, unfinished tragedy he held up to public ridicule and indictment his own most hallowed beliefs" (129). As Steiner interprets the play, its hero—the patriarch and pacifist Saryntsev— comes out the loser in almost every dramatized encounter with his family or ideological opponents. "With pitiless veracity Tolstoy shows the man's blindness, his egotism, and the ruthlessness which can inspire a prophet who believes himself entrusted with revelation. . . . Nowhere was Tolstoy more naked," Steiner concludes. "He presented the anti-Tolstoyan case with uncanny persuasiveness" (129).

In the light of the other writings and proclamations of Tolstoy during his final decades, this reading of the play is quite astonishing. For, however much we might wish to reassure ourselves, there is little indication that Tolstoy meant us to see Saryntsev, the light that shone in the darkness, as blind or ruthless. On the contrary, Saryntsev was making morally correct choices. The outer world—the outer darkness —would inevitably judge these acts in terms of the suffering they brought others and thus call them blind or cruel. That cruelty, however, is the inescapable byproduct of ethically consistent behavior and must be borne.

The dilemma here thus resembles the one surrounding Prince Myshkin in *The Idiot*: by his Christ-like goodness, the prince ruins every life he touches. How does Dostoevsky resolve this disagreeable truth? Steiner is very good on Myshkin in this regard: "The 'idiot' is love incarnate," Steiner writes, "but in him love itself is not made flesh. . . . Myshkin's 'crime' is the excess of compassion over love" (171). Such humility, alas, is not Tolstoy's. Tolstoy was unable to finish his final play, I suggest, not because he was embarrassed or stricken by the "pitiless veracity" of its hero's failure—but because Tolstoy, as playwright, had not yet found a way to make his point of view more irresistibly persuasive. Tolstoy was no advocate of the overly clever "problem play." Rather, he believed in the theater as a crucible for the right sort of "infection," one whose first task was to move human feelings. Mere outrageousness or run-of-the-mill unhappiness hardly mattered to the rightness of a moral position (witness Tolstoy's relish at the scandal over "The Kreutzer Sonata," and his subsequent insistence that he stood personally behind its plea for marital celibacy). In short, the unfinishedness of *The Light That Shines in the Darkness* can sooner be attributed to Tolstoy's frustration over the proper portrayal of his "positive hero"—in this sense, the parallels with Dostoevsky's quest are sharp and intriguing—than to any special discomfort on the part of Tolstoy at his own "nakedness" in a perfectly crafted self-parody.

In both these readings, Steiner reads and reacts as a sophisticated, culturally flexible European, a genuine comparativist. Inevitably, some of his balanced good sense and breadth rub off on his subject. For Slavists who read Tolstoy and Dostoevsky within these novelists' own more savage, insecure worlds, this can be an excellent and often enlightening corrective. In this connection we might note an instructive equivalent to Steiner among world-class scholars working on Russian themes today: Joseph Frank. Frank learned Russian late, made a mid-career shift to Slavistics, and is currently completing this century's definitive biography of Dostoevsky.[14] In a territory dominated by mystic philosophy and messianic overstatement, the intricate, refined European underpinnings of the scholar are everywhere in evidence. "The Dostoevsky who emerges from Frank's pages is a man far less singular, impassioned, extreme than he is usually conceived to be," Donald Fanger has written in a review of the biography's third volume; scrupulous attention to evidence and sifting of legend brings the life story much more into the European mainstream, and what extremism there is finds its place "through a process of osmosis that lets Frank's own sovereign balance and reasonableness seep into the character he is recreating."[15] At crucial moments in his own essay, Steiner has much the same civilizing, almost "airbrushing" effect on the image of his two unruly Russian master novelists.

In conclusion let me return to the comparison, mentioned in the opening pages of this essay, between Steiner and Bakhtin. In Steiner's poetics, Tolstoy is at heart an epic writer, and Dostoevsky is a tragic dramatist. In Bakhtin's poetics, neither novelist by definition can be either of those things—because the essence of the novel lies, first, in transcending the stasis and impenetrable "absolute distance" of epic, and second, in surpassing the easy performability and mere "compositional dialogue" (almost always monologic) characteristic of drama. For Steiner, the "epic" aspects of Tolstoy are revealed in a lack of sentimentality, in a passion for the pitiless effect of circumstances and things on human beings, and in a pagan insistence that all moral dilemmas must be resolved in *this* world—without recourse to the miracles, mysteries, and authorities of God. Aspects of Tolstoyan aesthetics that do not fit the Homeric model (Tolstoy's rejection of heroism, for example) Steiner does not hide, but he also does not elaborate. Well he might not, because to a very large extent Tolstoy's militant antiheroicism is what makes the Tolstoyan novel what it is.

The case is more complex with the analogy between Dostoevsky and tragic drama. At the base of the problem is Steiner's rather uncomplicated notion of dialogue, which he sees as a continuum from its novelistic to its stage-drama poles. "It should be noted," Steiner remarks in his discussion of *The Idiot*, "that our difficulties in perceiving all the levels of action at a first reading [of this scene in the novel] are strictly comparable to the difficulties we experience when first hearing a complex piece of dramatic dialogue in the theater" (161). But they are not "strictly comparable" at all, if readers of the novel attend to the intricate layers and "voice zones" that permeate even the simplest narrative filler between slices of direct speech. Bakhtin's major concern—how words work in novels—is not Steiner's. That Steiner does not engage his texts at this level has little to do with the language barrier and much to do with the indwelling "unspeakability" of novelistic worlds (especially Dostoevsky's worlds), their potential to be several voices at once, and thus their resistance to even the most subtle intonation on stage—which would embody them too aggressively and thus flatten them out.

At several points, Steiner aligns Dostoevsky with the Aristotelian notions of dramatic catharsis (213) and a fusion of "'thought' with 'plot'" (228). Significantly, Bakhtin resists both these moves. "Tragic catharsis (in the Aristotelian sense) is not applicable to Dostoevsky," Bakhtin writes. "The catharsis that finalizes Dostoevsky's novels might be—of course inadequately and somewhat rationalistically— expressed this way: *nothing conclusive has yet taken place in the world, the ultimate word of the world and about the world has not yet been spoken, the world is open and free, everything is still in the future and will always be in the future.*"[16] Steiner intimates the radical freedom of Dostoevsky's characters, their freedom both from "their creator's will and our own previsions." He senses the polyphony that Bakhtin makes explicit, but then he attaches it to the dramatic, not to the novelistic. There are advantages to Steiner's thesis. Among them is that his "dramatization" of Dostoevsky's verbal art can serve as robust corrective to some of Bakhtin's blind spots. One such spot shows up with special naivete in the latter's discussion of *Notes from Underground*, which Bakhtin reads rather benevolently in terms of "words with a loophole," the permanent noncoincidence of a self with itself, and the right of selves to counter every word cast in their direction with a new, fresh, free word.[17] Equipped with his less permeable definition of the word, Steiner sees the matter more darkly. In his reading—not an uncommon pattern for postwar readings of Dostoevsky—the mission of the Underground is to "lay bare the hypocrisies of high rhetoric" (218), and the failure of the Underground Man is connected not with the abused glory but with the shame of being human (225–26).

Here a return to Joseph Frank is in order, for he also resists Bakhtin, and in ways that Steiner would find compelling. The major difference between these two pan-European comparativists on this masterwork of Russian literature can be found in Frank's insistence that Dostoevsky, in giving voice to the dilemma of the Underground, is not an existentialist—that is, in no way does he endorse its dead ends and rhetorical traps as necessary complements to human freedom. Frank reads *Notes from Underground* as ice-cold Swiftian satire, as a deadly serious parody of certain patterns (absorbed naïvely and uncritically from the West) in Russian intellectual thought.[18]

According to Frank, some of these utopian patterns—such as the "rational egoism" of Chernyshevsky—are seductive, even compelling, but a head-on, negating resistance to them (the task of the Underground) is neither dialogic nor liberating. The Underground Man desperately seeks a moral anchor. Steiner misses the parody. He, too, posits the tragic nature of the Underground, but sees Dostoevsky buying in to it, sympathetic to its merciless "critique of reason" (227) and thus also to a human being's no-exit entrapment by this critique. Wedded as he is to the monologic notion of Dostoevsky as dramatic tragedian, Steiner has trouble detecting the independent—and polemically untrustworthy—voices of Dostoevsky's narrators.

To conclude, then. In this refitting of Tolstoy and Dostoevsky back into epic and tragedy, that is, into the two genres most central to a classical poetics, we feel most palpably the "oldness" of Steiner's Old Criticism. This sense of the richness of the old, its ever-present relevance, is surely one of the most liberating aspects of Steiner's essay. For in contrast to so much in modern critical practice that reduces the past to a pale, and always inadequate, reflection of the values and politics of the present moment, Steiner starts with the assumption that all great literature is richer than any single subsequent time could possibly appreciate in full.

Again, Bakhtin might be an appropriate guide to Steiner's larger intent. In 1970, near the end of his life, Bakhtin was invited by the editorial board of Russia's leading literary journal to comment on the future of Soviet literary studies. In his open letter Bakhtin wrote: "Authors and their contemporaries see, recognize and evaluate primarily that which is close to their own day. The author is a captive of his epoch, of his own present. Subsequent times liberate him from this captivity, and literary scholarship is called upon to assist in this liberation."[19] Now "liberation" is a fighting word. But in his letter Bakhtin intends the word in a sense quite contrary to the radical intent so commonly invested in it by radical critics. For Bakhtin, "liberation" meant a *suspicion* of the impulse to measure all of past culture by the social or political standards of the present day. Precisely that narrowing of vision makes an author—and a reader—a "captive of his or her own epoch." Releasing us from that captivity is the most important service that other times, past and future, can render us; this is *what great novels are for*. Thus to "liberate authors from their epochs" is not to read them into contexts that are immediately politically relevant. In Bakhtin's world view, more likely the opposite obtains: to liberate authors is to make them as open as possible to as many times as possible.

This conviction lies at the base of Steiner's critical world view as well. In *Real Presences* he takes severely to task the hardcore pretensions of literary theory—starting with the "absolutely decisive failing" that occurs when theoretical approaches attempt more than linguistic description and classification, "when such approaches seek to formalize meaning."[20] In *Tolstoy and Dostoevsky*, the ancient past is revealed as a richly surprising source for present relevance. Or, as Bakhtin put this point, "Dostoevsky has not yet become Dostoevsky, he is still becoming him."[21] More than anything, such faith qualifies George Steiner as a resident in his own republic of primary things.

Notes

1. The book was first published in 1959. All citations for this essay are taken from George Steiner, *Tolstoy or Dostoevsky: An Essay in the Old Criticism* (New York: Dutton, 1971). Page numbers are included in parentheses in the text.

2. In his discussion of Tolstoy's religious beliefs, Steiner presciently notes what later scholars have amply documented, that despite Tolstoy's much-advertised "conversion" of 1881–82, continuity rather than break was the norm: "Actually, most of the ideas and beliefs expounded by the later Tolstoy appear in his earliest writings and the live substance of his morality was plainly discernible during the years of apprenticeship" (242). For a comprehensive exposition of this continuity thesis, see Richard F. Gustafson, *Leo Tolstoy: Resident and Stranger* (Princeton: Princeton University Press, 1986).

3. Gary Saul Morson, *Hidden in Plain View: Narrative and Creative Potentials in "War and Peace"* (Stanford: Stanford University Press, 1987).

4. Mikhail Bakhtin, "Epic and Novel," in *The Dialogic Imagination: Four Essays by M. M. Bakhtin*, ed. Michael Holquist (Austin: University of Texas Press, 1981), 37.

5. Leo Tolstoy to V. V. Stasov, 9 October 1903, *Tolstoy's Letters*, ed. and trans. R. F. Christian, 2 vols., vol. 2: *1880–1910* (New York: Scribner's Sons, 1978), 633.

6. The absurdity of Tolstoy's argument is clear in this crude form, but it is sobering—and not reassuring—to see how his idea (on the baleful influence of fashionable critics and vogue) has resurfaced in current politicized theory of literary value.

7. In his "Preface" to the play, Camus reinforces much of the Steiner thesis: "For almost twenty years . . . I have visualized its characters on the stage. Besides having the stature of dramatic characters, they have the appropriate behavior, the explosions, the swift and disconcerting gait. Moreover, Dostoevsky uses a theater technique in his novels: he works through dialogues with few indications as to place and action. . . . And yet I am well aware of all that separates the play from that amazing novel! I merely tried to follow the book's undercurrent and to proceed as it does from satiric comedy to drama and then to tragedy. Both the original and the dramatic adaptation start from a certain realism and end up in tragic stylization." For an English version, see Albert Camus, *The Possessed: A Play*, trans. Justin O'Brien (New York: Vintage Books, 1960).

8. Mikhail Bakhtin, *Problems of Dostoevsky's Poetics*, ed. and trans. Caryl Emerson (Minneapolis: University of Minnesota Press, 1984), 34. Later Bakhtin expands on the implications for stage performance: double-voiced language of the sort we get in dialogic novels "is difficult to speak aloud, for loud

and living intonation excessively monologizes discourse and cannot do justice to the other person's voice present in it" (198).

9. The phrase is Aileen Kelly's. See her excellent essay "Dostoevsky and the Divided Conscience," *Slavic Review* 47, no. 2 (Summer 1988): 239–60, esp. 239.

10. D. S. Mirsky, "Some Remarks on Tolstoy," *London Mercury* 20 (1929): 167–75, reprinted in *D. S. Mirsky: Uncollected Writings on Russian Literature*, ed. G. S. Smith (Berkeley: Berkeley Slavic Specialties, 1989), 304.

11. One compromising side effect of Steiner's relentless pursuit of elegance, however, is a certain rhetorical imprecision: "railway yards" and "tentacular suburbs" are not really characteristic of Dostoevsky's cities, but rather of novels by Dickens or Zola set in Paris and London—or by an American novelist such as Theodore Dreiser.

12. Compare, for example, Nabokov's admiring discussions of *Anna Karenina*, "The Death of Ivan Ilych," and "The Lady with the Little Dog"—all annotated plot summaries—with his vituperative putdown of Dostoevsky's banal plots and "neurotic" heroes. Vladimir Nabokov, *Lectures on Russian Literature* (New York: Harcourt Brace, 1981).

13. It shows in conventions of Russian naming and address: discussing *The Idiot*, Steiner properly refers to "Gania" and "Aglaya," but does not sense why one must call the heroine (a well-bred woman of experience) "Nastasya Filippovna," by name and patronymic as Dostoevsky always does, never just "Nastasya" as is Steiner's habit.

Only once does Steiner hazard an important thematic point based on an uncertain detail in translation. Nastasya Filippovna, having cast Rogozhin's one hundred thousand rubles into the flames and rejected Gania's suit, flees with Rogozhin. To Myshkin she shouts: "Farewell, Prince, for the first time I've seen a human being" [Prosh chai, kniaz, v pervyi raz ya cheloveka videla]. Working with an inadequate English version—"I have seen man for the first time in my life"—and unaware of Russian's lack of definite and indefinite articles, Steiner makes a questionable call. He wants to hear in Nastasya Filippovna's parting words to the Prince that she has seen "man" in all his "extremes of nobility and corruption" (168), but in Russian the addressee of her final cry is not "man" in general, but clearly the saintly person of Myshkin—to whom the heroine will compulsively return.

Imprecise labeling also somewhat miscasts discussion of *Notes from Underground* (216–28). Steiner refers to this work throughout as "Letters from the Underworld"—quite wrong. They are not letters but *zapiski*, "jottings" or "notes," an honorable nineteenth-century Russian genre with an important genealogy (Gogol, Turgenev, and Tolstoy all wrote works with that title). Not only is the Underground Man not composing an epistolary novel; part of his agony is precisely that he doubts he will have any addressees or readers at all. And—attending to the second half of the title—to render the Russian *podpol'e* ("underground" or "under the floorboards") as the "underworld" suggests Lucian ("Dialogues with the Dead") and other pagan satires. Steiner does indeed invoke this classical subtext (216), but it is arguably inappropriate to Dostoevsky's work, with its painful Christian genesis.

Likewise, in his treatment of the conflagration that closes *The Possessed*, Steiner begins at his own most "at-home" point, which is precise to the extent that it is Europe (i.e., Flaubert's reaction to the incendiarism of the Paris Commune) and increasingly blurred as we move closer to Russia itself. The fires that end the novel are indeed linked with "the traditional Russian theme of a fiery apocalypse" (183), but they were directly inspired by the real-life burning of Saint Petersburg in the spring of 1862. The nefarious campaign to pin blame for these events on the new generation of "nihilists" in the capital deeply agitated Dostoevsky.

14. Three volumes by Joseph Frank have so far appeared: *Dostoevsky: The Seeds of Revolt, 1821–1849* (1976); *Dostoevsky: The Years of Ordeal, 1850–1859* (1983); and *Dostoevsky: The Stir of Liberation, 1860–65* (1986), all by Princeton University Press.

15. Donald Fanger, "Turning Point" (a review of *Dostoevsky: The Stir of Liberation*), *New Republic* 196 (27 April 1987): 42.

16. Bakhtin, *Problems of Dostoevsky's Poetics*, 165–66. Emphasis in original.

17. Ibid., 50–54.

18. In an elaborate footnote near the end of chap. 21 in his *Dostoevsky: The Stir of Liberation* (346), very much in Steiner's capacious spirit, Joseph Frank comments on his own weaning from the Bakhtinian world view. There he resists two of Bakhtin's most colorful claims: first, that Dostoevsky was the founder of a "wholly new kind of polyphonic novel," and second, that Dostoevsky's novels are best understood as part of an ancient tradition of Menippean satire (the so-called carnivalesque) rather than the more accessible, and much more readily documented, tradition of eighteenth- and nineteenth-century European literature. In reading the *Notes from Underground* as satire, not as morbid philosophical truth, Frank cuts through a century of sentimentalism and existential despair. This satire has nothing to do with Menippean satire or carnival, with their rejuvenating guffaws, blasphemous mumbo jumbo, indestructible bodies, and easy exchange of masks; and it also is distant from the benign scenario in Bakhtin's Dostoevsky book, where even the tortured moves of the Underground Man come to represent a celebration of unrealized potential, the right to postpone forever the final word.

19. M. M. Bakhtin, "Reply to a Question from the *Novy Mir* Editorial Staff," in *Speech Genres and Other Late Essays*, trans. Vern W. McGee (Austin: University of Texas Press, 1986), 5.

20. George Steiner, *Real Presences* (Chicago: University of Chicago Press,

1989), 81. Steiner defines literature (and art and music as well) as "the maximalization of semantic incommensurability in respect of the formal means of expression" (83).

21. Mikhail Bakhtin, "Toward a Reworking of the Dostoevsky Book [1961]," in *Problems of Dostoevsky's Poetics*, 291.

George Steiner and the
Greekness of Tragedy

TRAGEDY IS THE BASIS of Steiner's work. His only book devoted to a single text—the only text, he says, to express the "constants of conflict"—is on Sophocles' *Antigone*. Throughout his work Steiner is concerned with the essence and possibility of tragic form: with tragedy's prime elements, their Greek roots, their life in current Western imagination. I shall address these questions and their relation to other aspects of Steiner's thought. My main starting point is *The Death of Tragedy*, and the work of redefinition evident in the 1984 *Reader*, in *Antigones*, *Real Presences*, and the 1990 "Note on Absolute Tragedy."

In Steiner, everything is connected with everything else. Writing about him entails some taking apart. I do this through a series of topics which may feel en route like unconnected fragments, but they should add up to wholeness at the end; and the fragmentation is itself important, for it bears upon how Steiner has come to see possibilities of the tragic in our time.

A Record of Encounter

All Steiner's work enacts encounter. Reading him requires us to relive the conflict, risk, and responsibility endemic to his own image of reading. The act of reading—an act of love, of surrendering your passport on a strange border—brings us "face to face with the presence of offered meaning." The reading self, engaging with the other, resees itself. The model for this engagement is tragic dialogue: "All dialogue is a proffer of mutual cognizance and a strategic re-definition of the self. The Angel names Jacob at the end of their long match, the Sphinx compels Oedipus to name himself, to know himself as *man*."[1] Naked encounter is the core of Steiner's dream of both reading and tragedy: "I take *Berenice* . . . to be the touchstone of absolute tragedy in modern western literature. A man and a woman saying *adieu*. For ever. In which termination all light is momentarily gathered and put out."[2] The way Western art represents encounter—human to human, human to divine—fore-stages our encounter with art itself:

Great poetry is animate with the rites of recognition. Odysseus proceeds from one recognition to the next in a voyage towards the self that is Ithaca. Dante recognizes the timbre of Brunetto Latini's voice out of the ghost-smoke. Titania is "ill-met by moonlight". . . . Religious thought and practice metaphorize, make narrative images of, the rendezvous of the human psyche with absolute otherness. . . . These intuitions and ceremonials of encounter, in social usage, in linguistic exchange, in philosophic and religious dialogue, are incisively pertinent to our reception of literature, of music and of the arts. . . . We are the "other ones" whom the living significations of the aesthetic seek out.[3]

Tragedy's life is the record and the ceremony of such encounter. Sophocles' *Antigone*, for instance—Steiner's Angel or Sphinx—is made of conflict, and *Antigones* is a record of Steiner's encounter with the play. It both presents the text as the sum of many encounters over the centuries—encounters by scholars, dramatists, translators, actors—and confronts the play as a record of encounters between old and young, male and female, the living and the dead.[4] Steiner's understanding of the confrontations of tragedy is not only inseparable from his account of reading; it formed that account, and goes on doing so. What he says about reading, therefore, always illumines his definitions of tragedy.

The Royal Enclosure

Steiner's ideal condition for encounter with a text is identical with his image of the human condition in tragedy: unhoused. But paradoxically, the ideal arena for representing such encounter is enclosed. The "thalamos" of a Racine court, the ambiguous space of a Greek tragedy set "before the door" of a palace: both offer a compact emblem for the sealed enclosure of art, of musical form.[5]

So, however, does the chessboard. From *The Death of Tragedy* to "A Death of Kings," Steiner sees chess, too, as an open record of encounter. "In a card game, the adversary's cards are hidden; in chess, his pieces are constantly open before us, inviting us to see things from their side."[6]

Agon is the word for the scene in a Greek tragedy in which two speeches tilt against each other, disclosing a fundamental moral and situational rift between the speakers. The word meant "contest" or "struggle," a core notion in ancient Greek, especially classical Athenian, culture. From this word came, quietly at first, the word *agonia*. This originally meant "struggle" or a visible, athletic "contest." It was not, at first, much used. Slowly, in the fourth century B.C., it began to be used of mental struggle. Not until Christian Greek—until, say, reportage of Gethsemane—does *agonia* gather semantic hold on internal struggle, on mental or spiritual pain: struggle within a conflicted self. The element of conflict is essential and internal to the history of "agony." Tragedy and chess both enact some conflict in the outer world which gives form to conflict and struggle within.

The mutual illumination of tragedy and chess. . . . In a so far unpublished lecture for an "Art and Chess" symposium at the Tate Gallery, 1991, Steiner spoke of the "hatred of the other" which drives "masters of arcane disciplines" such as philology and chess. Of the pawn who encapsulates "the mystery of human vulnerability," a vulnerability that can "turn to infinite power." Of the chess encounter as image of love and hate, power and weakness: an encounter of sustained violence where not a move can be taken back. All this is a hieroglyph of tragic conflict. Witness this Sophoclean encounter, in which different pieces—one pawn, the threat of another, the chorus, the queen—move in on the King of Thebes:

Messenger: I pulled out the pin that pierced your feet.
Oedipus: I carried that terrible shaming brand from infancy.

Messenger: From that misfortune you got the name you have.
Oedipus: For the gods' sake, tell me: was it my mother or my father,
  who did that?
Messenger: I don't know. The man who gave you to
  me may know more.
Oedipus: What? Did you get me from someone else?·
Messenger: Another shepherd—he gave me the baby.
Oedipus: Who was he? Do you know him? Can you describe him?
Messenger: They called him Laius' servant.
Oedipus: Laius?
  The King who once, long ago, ruled here?
Messenger: Yes. He was Laius' herdsman. . . .
Oedipus: Do any of you know the man he speaks of . . . ?
Chorus: I think he means the very man,
  [the one survivor of King Laius's death],
  you asked to see just now. But the Queen,
  Jocasta, could best tell you that.
Oedipus: Madam, you know the man we sent to fetch?
  Is he the very same this stranger means?
Jocasta: Whom do you mean? Don't fuss about it.
  Forget what has been said. It's not worth the bother.
Oedipus: No! With these clues I cannot fail
  to make clear my birth.
Jocasta: For the gods' sake,
  as you care for your life . . . please let this drop!
  Enough that I am suffering.[7]

Jocasta sees the true position first. But in tragedy, as in chess, no one can "forget," nor can a move or word be lost. Two unthought-of shepherds become agents of destruction to royalty. The movement is a record, in little space, of a death of kings.

The House of Minos

In the same lecture, Steiner spoke of the prehistory of chess, this image of encounter and courtesy in a closed world where lines of force, one mirroring the other like Creon and Antigone in the Theban palace, are drawn on squares of white and black. A geometry of good and evil shared between selves in conflict, adversaries on a ground privileged by its enclosedness: the image is as old as Western images of royalty. In the West, it goes back to the Bronze Age, above all to the palace of Minos at

Knossos, the palace that was also the labyrinth. In one corridor was found a checkered game board, made about 1600 B.C., inlaid with ivory, rock crystal, faïence, lapis lazuli, and gold foil. Steiner pointed also to a modern chess set—made by Michael Ayrton, the British artist possessed by Greek myth—in which the king was horned, reminding us of deep relations between the labyrinth and chess.

Dealing with tragedy, with Steiner on tragedy, with tragedy seen in terms of chess, one cannot very long escape Crete; any more than Bronze Age Greece could escape the reality of Minoan power, or classical Athenian imagination could escape the power of Cretan myth. Cretan ingredients are a vital part of Greek tragedy and its legacy.

> Tout a changé de face
> Depuis que sur ces bords des dieux ont envoyé
> La fille de Minos et de Pasiphaé.

So Racine's Hippolyte describes how Greece and Greek relations were transformed when Phèdre brought with her the whole monstrous Cretan package, Minos, Pasiphae, labyrinth, Minotaur. The last line here, says Steiner, "Opens the gates of reason to the night. Into the courtly setting . . . bursts something archaic, incomprehensible, and barbaric."[8]

Racine's vision is a burnished, seventeenth-century French evocation of barbaric intrusion on a royal court, but it accurately reflects a fifth-century Athenian sense that "Crete" means some part-bestial, part-royal irruption into the civilized. In Euripides, the boat that carried Phaedra from Crete "flew ill-omened to glorious Athens." Phaedra is open to Aphrodite's savagery through her family inheritance. In a fragment from Euripides' lost play *The Cretan Men*, Phaedra's mother, Pasiphae, asks ironically (presumably in an agon scene in which someone else vilified her for wanting sex with the bull):

> Why should I have fallen for the bull?
> For his lovely clothes
> and languishing flirtatious glances? No!
> This was the work of Minos's *daimon*!
> It filled me too with destruction.[9]

The whole family was "filled" with sexually destructive daemon.

Tony Harrison's *Phaedra Britannica* inverts the Cretan sexual inheritance and the civilization into which it breaks. Phaedra is a British Memsahib, a foreigner supposedly more "civilized" than the land and gods she comes to. But she comes of rotten stock. When she met Hippolytus, she was overwhelmed by local divinity: "The gods of India were there / Behind the throbbing heat and stifling air." At first, India seems like "Crete": alien, pulsing with half-beast divinities. But Phaedra is susceptible to this because she carries "Crete" within her. India's gods call up her own darkness:

> Mother, driven by the dark gods' spite
> beyond the frontiers of appetite.
> A *judge's* wife! Obscene! bestialities
> Hindoos might sculpture on a temple frieze! . . .
> Sister! Abandoned! . . . by him too . . . left behind . . .
> driven to drugs and drink. . . . Out of her mind![10]

Harrison's reworking of Racine puts elements of Greek fantasies about Crete, still radioactive in European imagination, into play against each other. Steiner paints Racine's own theater as "an enclosed place, fortified against disorder by the conventions of the neo-classic style." Into this enclosure Minos's daughter brings "an alien and barbaric world." When Phèdre learns that Hippolyte loves Aricie, "the last authority of reason is shattered. . . . The maddened queen brings into the seventeenth-century playhouse presences begotten of chaos and ancient night. She is a daughter of the sun; the whole of creation is peopled with her monstrous and majestic ancestry. Her father holds the scales of justice in hell." At the end of act 4, Phèdre, the outsider, the excluded, her language frenzied with "jalouse rage," knows herself outside the pale—"je respire à la fois l'inceste et l'imposture"—and craves revenge. For this end, she calls on the exemplars of male power surrounding her ancestry and marriage: Minos, Theseus, Zeus.

After revenge? "Le ciel, tout l'univers est plein de mes aieux." She cannot escape consciousness of her own damnation. Her father is waiting "dans la nuit infernale," judging the dead.[11] Damned in her erotic fury, damned in her ancestry, Phèdre is in a tragic bind. She cannot kill herself: her father would judge her. Her ancestors are everywhere: in hell (Steiner insists how literally Racine and his audience would take that) and in the sky. Pagan and biblical interact. The same alternative, sky or underworld, is despaired of in Psalm 139 (known, of course, to Racine):

> Whither shall I go from thy spirit? or whither shall
> I flee from thy Presence?

If I ascend up into heaven, thou art there; if I make
my bed in hell, behold, thou art there.

Racine "invokes the presence of Jehovah *and* the Minoan sun-god."[12]
In Greek tragedy the cry, "Where can I hide, can I fly to the sky or
plunge below the earth?" answers itself. Neither escape is possible. The
play's pain is visible even in its most far-flung "escape odes."[13]

On Phèdre's *aporia*, Steiner comments: "Not since the blood-
streaming heavens in Marlowe's *Faustus* has nature presided with more
animate fury over a scene of human damnation. If I were to stage the
play, I would have the background grow transparent to show us the
dance of the Zodiac and Taurus, the emblematic beast of the royal
house of Crete."[14]

In Racine, Euripides, Tony Harrison, and Steiner, the bestial and the
barbaric are alive in the human: in the background of the royal court, in
the zodiac that rules us from the sky. They meet us if we make our bed
in hell.

The Crete of Athenian tragedies presents in an acute form the paradox of Steiner's characteristic challenge, the barbarism at the heart of
civilization, the silence and betrayal at the center of courtly language.
The royal enclosure, space of wrought concentration on the arts—for
which Minos's palace is the supreme mythic example in the West—
may be the most deadly empowerer of barbarism. Crete is one source
of Steiner's vision of "absolute tragedy": a universe where there is no
hope because the place that distills what is best in what human beings
do is also the place of repression. The cabinet of rarities, the chamber of
courtesy, is also the chamber of horrors, torture, gas. The master artist
creates a home for the monstrous hybrid, the man-beast. Tragedy
makes us face the brutality within the human, the violence in the royal.

In my view, but not I think in Steiner's now, tragedy is also capable
of hinting the opposite. In the inner shell of tyranny, the heart of
Bluebeard's dungeon, the brutalities of the labyrinth, the hope of love
and courtesy may be at work. This insight has its overall place in
Steiner's thought—he explores aspects of it fictionally in the theological debate in the gas chambers—but he now excludes it from his definition of absolute tragedy.[15]

The Foreign in the Self

In *Antigones*, Steiner argues that Greek myths form the syntax of Western imaginations.[16] This is strongly true of his own imagination, shaped not only by Greek myths but also by the Athenian culture that codified these myths into tragedy. In his understanding of European tragedy, local intuitions of the fifth century B.C. which went into the making of Athenian tragedy—insights into passion, divinity, exile, and the foreign—are oddly vital. His response to the history of his own age is also deeply shaped by his closeness to Athenian tragedy, which entails very precise Athenian perceptions both of the self and of foreignness. Its talismanic demon is Erinys, the Fury in the heart. It is obsessed with foreigners and foreignness.[17] Its main currency is myth that precedes its own existence. Often this myth is from Crete (most tragedies set in Crete are lost, but we know of them through reports and fragments): a Crete that is both Greek and other, as fatally involved with Athens as Germany, traditionally, with France.

For me, the heart of Western tragedy is Racine's *Phèdre*. Reading this, we are possessed by two great tragedies at once, those of Euripides and Racine, while in the future loom versions of Lowell, Harrison, and Marina Tsvetayeva. Wherever it lands, tragedy has a feel of foreign origins, always presenting some image of the other in the self. Something feral that comes from another language, another culture, yet that is also, already, naturalized in its target audience. For British Jacobean and Elizabethan dramatists, it was Spain.

This picture of one culture playing with the drastic representations of another is characteristically Greek and European. From Athens onward, it belongs with tragedy's central representation of passion as the other in, the foreign presence in, the self.[18] All this is at work in Steiner's tragic understanding of Europe's barbaric *civilitas*.

The Weight of Darkness

Steiner uses images of blackness for tragedy. When Titus and Bérénice say farewell forever, "all light is momentarily gathered and put out. As in a pearl, flawlessly black." Transforming the legend of Phaedra and Hippolytus, Racine "imposed shapes of reason on the archaic blackness of his theme." The archetypal modernist painting, "black on black," has now become his image for the tragic absolute.[19]

This blackness has a precise field. As in archaic Greek poetry, and in Greek theories of vision, light stands very sharply for hope, life, and meaning. Blackness is their cancellation. Steiner's fascination with the impact of artificial lighting on European culture reminds us that darkness is our natural condition for at least half our life: "There are intricate, deep-felt contiguities between obscurity and silence on the one hand and loquacity and light on the other. . . . The history of artificial lighting . . . cannot be separated from that of consciousness itself. In what ways have the conventions . . . of linguistic exchange been modified by the voluntary prolongation of the lit portions of existence?"[20] This perception is informed by his awareness of the enormous role of light imagery in Greek thought:

The history of our vision of and feel for light has yet to be written. Even as there are doctrines of light in religious thought and mythology or in neo-Platonic philosophy, so there are, both implicitly and explicitly, in art. Our political awareness but also . . . our readings of the hours and the seasons, of wind and of water, are modified by the uses of light in the flat deeps of Piero della Francesca, by the light from Vermeer's casements. . . . Concomitantly, observe the mutations in the weight of darkness after Rembrandt's etchings, after Goya's "black paintings" or Ad Reinhardt's *Black on Black*.[21]

Two central, and intimately connected, aspects of light in the hermeneutical situation are reading and relationship. Reading is the ultimate act of communication in solitude. It is also in the deepest sense a political act, binding and thrilling people who cannot see or hear or physically touch each other. "The model of true reading is . . . a political model." Reading is an image of relationship which illumines. A book is "talisman" against death, whose classic Greek image is darkness.[22] Within the walls of civilization, reading needs illumination. So, for much of the hours we live, does personal encounter. We need light to read, to face each other. Lighting home or street changed the polis, changed the ways human beings understood each other and themselves.

In all this, language stands for light, the light by which self understands other. Silence is darkness. Words illumine the dark of our being in the world. We are dark to each other, unless we communicate. In Steiner's relentlessly alchemical and deeply Greek imagination, this light—of language, humanity's hope—is an image for divinity. Light is the classic Western metaphor for God, as well as for impulses or powers that come from outside and yet are in us: inspiration, reason, intellect. The "lamp" of consciousness. . . . Ancient Greek light metaphors expressed through Steiner's insights have long governed our ways of thinking about thought and understanding.[23]

The Lightning Flash

As preface to *Antigones*, Steiner quotes Walter Benjamin on the "lightning bolt," the illuminatory flash of insight, of urgent response, to a text. "The text is the thunder-peal rolling long behind." When we meet a person or a text, there comes a flash of recognition, *anagnorisis*. Then actual experience catches up. "The deepest shocks of recognition unfold patiently out of immediacy."[24] This notion of flash is crucial to Steiner's work. The "lightning bolt" of understanding, a violence that joins heaven and earth and that opens the self to the other, is a *sine qua non* of reading; and of the seminal encounters and *anagnorisis* of tragic dialogue.

It is increasingly, I think, important for Steiner that this flash comes from elsewhere, from outside. In our culture so far, we have behaved as if there were a flame of meaning that is external to the closed cell of self-and-other. A light to see by, to read the other by. Something that is not only us. A light that is challenged by deconstruction. In *Real Presences*, Steiner argues we have exhausted that light source. Divinity provided a source of meaning and otherness which until now, in most cultures, was seen as transcendent. Now, "what we say" takes divinity for granted as source of illumination; but we ourselves do not.[25] Cut off from the implications of our own language, we simultaneously use and deny its illumination.

This thought follows from the argument of *The Death of Tragedy*: "Tragedy is that form of art which requires the intolerable burden of God's presence. It is now dead because His shadow no longer falls upon us."[26] In tragedy, divinity is the source of meaning and otherness. It illumines otherness.

Human love can share this role. Titus and Bérénice lose the possibility of each other's presence, which illumined their lives and gave the world meaning. For Cleopatra, Antony's death means "there is nothing left remarkable / Beneath the visiting moon." For her and hers, "Our lamp is spent, it's out." As she orders the asps, she hears: "Finish, good lady; the bright day is done, / And we are for the dark."[27]

The dust jacket of *Real Presences*, lit only at the point where the gaze of two figures meets, is dark as Iras's words to Cleopatra, but its message could not be clearer. The source of light for human beings is between two faces. It glows through the hand of a child. Encounter, the meeting gaze: relationship is what illumines the darkness in which human figures stand. Love, connection, relationship between two people—or that other interdependent relationship, divinity and humanity—is central, vital. We are all for the dark, unless we face each other. Between face and gaze is the source of meaning. Divinity is active between people; or it is nowhere, and we are left darkling.

Real Presences tracks an argument—which its author claims he never wanted, but which was driving his work from the beginning—that human meaning depends on the presence of God. A presence manifest, until now, in art. Tragedy is his first paradigm. *Real Presences* argues that the God-shaped appearances are still "in" what we say. We go on needing them. If this is right, then, whatever the death chronicled and foretold in *The Death of Tragedy*, we must still be in touch with at least the shell of the tragic.

Tragedy has been divinity's precinct from the beginning. "Nothing to do with Dionysus" was an ancient Athenian phrase meaning "inapposite" (said to have started as a complaint against tragedies deemed unsuitable for the festival).[28] Intermittently a few scholars have argued that tragedy itself, despite being written for his festivals and performed on his ground, has indeed nothing to do with Dionysus. But the fuller, and I think juster, response has always been, and still is, that tragedy has very deeply "to do with" him. It may be that for fifth-century Athenian imaginations, the whole formal presentation of a tragedy had Dionysus *as* its meaning. That the whole contradictory persona of the god in whose precinct tragedy was performed—all aspects of him, both the bitter and the sweet, the mad and the nurturing, violent destruction and glowing *communitas*—*was* tragedy.[29]

Inheriting tragic form and preoccupations, Christian tragedy absorbed Dionysus as a *deus absconditus*, through whom elements of Greek religious intuitions were made manifest in scenic and lyric structure. Christianity gave tragedy a new basis for the connectedness of divinity and form. In Judeo-Christian thought, unlike Greek thinking, the creation of human beings is crucial. Steiner argues that we comprehend form and create because we have been given—been created—form ourselves. "There is formal construction because we have been made form."[30] Form—what we are and what we make—presupposes divinity.

This thought underlies the formal structures of Steiner's own works. The interwoven organization of *After Babel* "was itself meant to illustrate, to enact, the underlying theme of metamorphic transformation and semantic transfer."[31] The conflicts of *Antigones* enact the relationships of which they speak: a book about tragic conflict, about the antagonisms of philosophy and poetry or of Germany and France, expressing these antagonisms within its own movement and form. The form of Steiner's texts incarnates their messages: passion, as he says of Racine, within form. *The Death of Tragedy* is a tragic arc of loss, ending with a "threefold possibility": tragedy is dead, or it "carries on its essential tradition despite changes in technical form," or it might—just might—come back to life.[32]

"Changes in Technical Form"

In a conversation published in 1966, Steiner elicited from Lévi-Strauss an ideal formulation on the interrelation of form and meaning: "I think the Jungian approach is entirely mistaken because it is based wholly on the consideration of content and not at all of form . . . I believe that content never has a meaning in itself; that it is only the way in which the different elements are combined together which gives a meaning."[33] Steiner's own position is not so clear-cut, but has affinities with this; as his Racine, that ivory master of scene form, plot form, verse form, bears witness: "All that happens, happens inside language. . . . With nothing but words—and formal, ceremonious words—Racine fills the stage with the uttermost of action. As nothing of the content of *Phèdre* is exterior to the expressive form, to the language, the words come very near the condition of music . . . , where content and form are identical."[34] Form and content, identical? What, then, about changes in technical tragic form and their bearing on tragedy in our time?

Steiner has drastically redefined his position on this, first in his "Introduction" to the *Reader*, then in his "Note on Absolute Tragedy." It is worth following the change. *The Death of Tragedy* stresses the absence of dramatic form implied by Chaucer, in the first European account of tragedy: a "characteristic mediaeval definition," making explicit "the universal drama of the fall of man." Tragedy is a narrative:

"The life of some . . . personage who suffered a decline of fortune toward a disastrous end," "a descent from prosperity to suffering and chaos":

> Tragedie is to seyn a certeyn storie,
> As olden bookes maken us memorie,
> Of hym that stood in greet prosperitee,
> And is yfallen out of heigh degree
> Into myserie, and endeth wrecchedly.

In the 1560s, tragedy was magnetized away from narrative, toward dramatic, form. A tragedy became a play dealing with tragic things.[35]

Steiner charts the running conflict *about* tragedy. On the one hand, there are the "open" Elizabethan forms. Popular dramatic forms, rising from the medieval imaginative undergrowth, revitalized tragedy. Elizabethan playwrights, especially Shakespeare, "violated every precept of neo-classicism" (20). The demotic breathed new rough life into tragedy. Against this performed gusto stood the neoclassic ideal, yearning for written form: a Roman legacy, a tight prescriptive version of Greek tragic form. Neoclassicism is perfected in Racine, in which "controlling poise is maintained between the cool severity of the technique and the passionate drive of the material. Racine poured molten metal into his unbending forms. At every moment, one expects the structure to yield under stress, but it holds" (80). In *Esther* and *Athalie*, Racine uses the technical oddity of a chorus, "outcome of a theory of drama implicit in [all his] work" (77). For "always in Racine's mind was the ideal of a ritual or court theatre, of a theatre of solemn occasion, as there had been in Athens" (76).

Steiner argues that neoclassic theories were themselves built round a tension or paradox, that "true realism is the fruit of intense stylization" (36): a paradox that maybe no one but Racine understood. Racine alone saw that the conventions underlying neoclassic tragedy were "myths emptied of active belief" (37). In the English-speaking world, Milton upheld neoclassicism against Shakespeare's rough magic. *Samson Agonistes* expresses "the lost totality of Greek drama" (32) with its unreachable choric musicality.

Neoclassicism versus the wryneck spell of Shakespeare: tension between these competing versions of tragedy arose in "the great division of ideals" in the late sixteenth century and "shaped the history of the European theatre" (18) until Ibsen. Ibsen, freed by the great nineteenth-century change, when "the centre of expressive language had to shift from verse to prose," fulfilled "ideals of tragic form which derived neither from the antique nor the Shakespearian example" (33–34).

The paradox here, I take it, is that the "ideals of tragic form" which Ibsen fulfilled had lived as wild yeast in the air, as unhoused intuitions of symbolic and poetic possibilities derived from past forms. They were roving ideals of form which had, until then, no form.

Both *The Death of Tragedy* and "A Note on Absolute Tragedy" address this paradox; but the new "Note" gives it teeth. We inherit a sense of tragic form: a compound, presumably, of the neoclassical and the rough, an ideal driven by its own interior tension. Where did we get it from? Tragedies. Yet most of the tragedies that gave it to us do not fulfill it. In Steiner's "Note," the number of "true" tragedies is tiny, "a handful."

It is as if the sense of tragedy we have been given has mostly not been cashed. There is a myth of tragic form which (as Lévi-Strauss might put it) dreams us. Yet from the mass of actual plays written and produced, only a fraction live up to the dream. This takes a lot of looking at. *The Death of Tragedy* argues that tragedy, like a tragic hero, fell. Despite Ibsen and Chekhov, tragedy died—in, roughly, the first three decades of our century. The "ash was too thick in its mouth." Eliot, Cocteau, and Yeats were all haunted by an image of theater which "should never have been summoned back to the electric light." They called up Greek antiquity, then were bedeviled in their own work by a numbingly sterile version of Greekness. "No amount of theatrical ingenuity will make the Furies [in Eliot's *The Family Reunion*] look natural in the modern world" (329).

By an accident of Fortune (or was it accident? did their remoteness free them?), Ibsen and Chekhov, the heroes who might have saved things, wrote in little-known languages, remote from "the geographical centres of taste." Parisians, Dubliners, Londoners read them only "through a veil of translation." If they had not, "the course of modern drama might have been different." Unfortunately, Eliot and Cocteau saw Ibsen and Chekhov only as "skilful artisans of realism, not the great creators of myth and symbolic form which they in fact were. They observed the scaffolding of realistic conventions and drawing-room scenes, yet were blind to the poetic life within. The realism of Ibsen or Chekhov is a discipline of unfolding insight whose authority leads from the real of the letter to the more real of the spirit" (305). And so the early twentieth-century tragedies were Greek *revenants*, breathing only of the embalmer. This passage shows us the kind of tragic "form"—symbolic form, mythic form—to which Steiner is looking. This is what is carried on while technical forms work their change.

"Moments"

The Death of Tragedy was published in 1961. The work it represents gathered shape, I assume, in the mid-1950s. *Sweet Bird of Youth* was staged in 1959; *The Night of the Iguana*, in December 1961. It could not have been clear while *Death of Tragedy* was being written that Ibsen and Chekhov had some sort of living heir. I doubt Steiner would accept him. Tennessee Williams and Lorca, the names I would put after Ibsen and Chekhov as new masters of a "realism" with "poetic life within," of a tragic "discipline of unfolding insight," are absent from his 1984 retrospective "Introduction" to the *Reader*. Instead he considers criticism that he left Beckett, Ionesco, and Pinter out of the last chapter of *The Death of Tragedy*: "On this point, I remain unconvinced. If there has been any recent advance into authentic tragedy, it is, very probably, that of Edward Bond's dramatic parables. . . . The undoubted genius of Beckett, the talents of Pinter, still strike me as essentially formal. In their plays, we find an internalized epilogue to an eroded tragic vision. The brilliance and the grief lie in the language."[36] In *The Death of Tragedy* itself, Steiner looked for counters to the thesis that tragedy was dead and for the possibility that "perhaps tragedy has merely altered in style and convention," becoming a sequence of "moments," as in the "black fantasies" of Beckett: "There are moments in *Waiting for Godot* that proclaim with painful vividness the infirmity of our moral condition: the incapacity of speech or gesture to countenance the abyss and horror of the times."[37] Or moments on the stage. In Brecht, for example:

There comes a moment in *Mutter Courage* when the soldiers carry in the dead body. . . . They suspect he is the son of Courage but . . . she must be forced to identify him. I saw Helene Weigel act the scene. . . . As the body of her son was laid before her, she merely shook her head in mute denial. The soldiers compelled her to look again. Again she gave no sign of recognition, only a dead stare. As the body was carried off, Weigel looked the other way and tore her mouth wide open. . . . The sound that came out was raw and terrible beyond any description. . . . But, in fact, there was no sound. Nothing. The

sound was total silence. It was silence which screamed. . . . And that scream
inside the silence seemed to me to be the same as Cassandra's when she divines
the reek of blood in the house of Atreus. It was the same wild cry with which
the tragic imagination first marked our sense of life. The same wild and pure
lament over man's inhumanity and waste of man. The curve of tragedy is,
perhaps, unbroken.[38]

I want to hang onto this concept of "moments," of an encapsulated
cry against inhumanity, and turn to a new motif in the 1990 "Note on
Absolute Tragedy." Here, nearly thirty years and many books and
thoughts later, including a study of Beckett, and six years after the
Reader, Steiner does make place in the canon for Beckett: "On the
evidence we have . . . the list of absolute tragedies is short . . . *Oedipus
the King, Antigone*, a number of Euripides' plays . . . , the main plot of
Marlowe's *Faustus*, Shakespeare's *Timon of Athens*, Racine's *Bérénice*
. . . and Racine's *Phèdre*; Shelley's *The Cenci* (together with Artaud's
adaptation); Büchner's *Woyzeck*; the black holes in the *guignol* and
monologues of Beckett."[39]

It may be that our experience, both dramatic and cultural, over these
thirty years, has made us all more liable to see the symbolic form of
tragedy in a "pure," isolate "moment" rather than in structured scenic
form. Steiner seems to be choosing one particular possibility out of the
three at the end of *Death of Tragedy*: tragedy is changing in technical
form.

This new form, tragedy's form in our age, by which the culture's
sense of tragic symbolic form is fulfilled, is the fragment: "Where the
postulate of the absolutely tragic . . . is made articulate, the performative act . . . will be fragmentary. . . . It cannot be of any great length
because the vision it embodies is indeed unbearable. . . . Human
imagining and presentation endure only a spell of unabridged doom;
they can dramatize, fictionalize . . . that spell only by extreme compaction."[40]

Trilogy, Tetralogy, and Satyr Play

In the new formulation, Steiner appeals to the unknowability of the
earliest mature form of tragedy. His argument invokes two points
about Greek tragedy in its original, fifth-century performance. He
argues that the form in which the Greek tragedies reached their public
was a triptych. Because we mainly have only single plays, we cannot

judge Greek tragic form (and maybe, therefore, any tragic form) completely: "With one exception, we know no complete trilogy, only
complete sections. The *Oresteia* is . . . a *commedia*. It . . . ends in redemptive absolution and personal-political hope. We simply do not
know whether Aeschylus' triptych was an exceptional instance or the
norm." However, through the culturally traumatic years at Athens
between 468 and 404 B.C., tragedy's form in this respect changed radically. Even in the early fifth century, unconnected single plays were
possible. The trilogy form is particularly associated with Aeschylus,
but even he did not always use it. In 472 B.C., for instance, he grouped
The Persians with plays that had no subject link.[41] The *Oresteia*, 458
B.C., was revolutionary in many ways we cannot fathom: it may have
been the first tragedy to be performed in front of a backdrop; it may
also have been one of the last great trilogies. By midcentury, trilogies
were still coming out, but, apart from Aeschylus, very few trilogies are
recorded, and it was taken for granted that playwrights could put on
three separate tragedies.[42] The great plays we have from after 458—
Antigone, for example—are singletons.

It depends how you put it. You can say with Sir Richard Jebb, the
great Sophocles scholar, that "two forms of trilogy were in concurrent
use down to the end of the fifth century": one in which the three
tragedies were links in a single story (as in the *Oresteia*), another in
which there was no story link, in which the plays were unrelated.[43]
Steiner needs this way of putting it for his argument.

On the other hand you can say, as I prefer, that by the midcentury
most dramatists stopped using the trilogy form and concentrated their
formal precisions on the unit of a single play. Then you argue either
that the Athenians' sense of tragic form changed with their experience
of tragedy, or (a softer, Aristotelian argument) that the change enabled
tragedy to grow toward its pure and (maybe) natural form, the single
tragedy.

For me, the decisive point is that by midcentury the audience and
judges *judged a single play*, awarding the prize to a tragedy as a single
unit. The judges based their decision on audience response to single
plays. Sophocles' *Oedipus Rex* was defeated for first prize (according to
a tradition dating back to the second century B.C.) by a tragedy by the
poet Philocles. The norm was competition between single plays, discrete units, concentrated explorations of one mythic moment.

In this hothouse competitive environment, each maker of these discrete plays watched the others. They influenced each other. At least eight fifth-century dramatists wrote an *Oedipus*. As for Phaedra: Euripides' play *Hippolytus*, as we have it, was a rewrite, in 428 B.C., of his first *Hippolytus*. The earlier play was set in Athens and showed Phaedra deliberately seducing her stepson. When Hippolytus rejected her, she accused him to Theseus out of spite. The Athenian setting must have grated on Athenian sensibilities. Theseus, the great local hero-king, was duped in Athens, and Phaedra killed herself when her cover was blown: the audience hated it. The play flopped. But then (this is the chronology suggested by the most magisterial modern editor of *Hippolytus*) came Sophocles' play *Phaedra*, which removed Theseus entirely—he was thought to be dead—and created a sweet-minded and noble, not lecherous, Phaedra. She killed herself in remorse, not because she was exposed. Euripides' second *Hippolytus*, the play we have, must have been galvanized by Sophocles' play. It removed everyone from Athens to the coast of the Peloponnese, the setting Racine chose. Its Phaedra is virtuous. She struggles against love. The Athenians adored it. It won Euripides one of the only four prizes he ever got.

This and other examples suggest that increasingly at Athens what dramatists, audiences, and judges cared about was the structuring of a single moment of myth. Euripides learned from Sophocles' play and produced a new one of his own, whose coiled-steel form thrilled the local audience and, of course, posterity. What stirred Racine, it seems to me, was the purity of the tragic episode, the different pressures that go to make one explosive tragic act, within a single play.

Sometimes, it is true, in the second half of the fifth century a dramatist used the fact that he was presenting three tragedies to make an overarching point. We know the plays put on with *The Trojan Women*: they also were set at Troy and were full of the black pessimism of this particular year. Scholars have called them Euripides' "Trojan trilogy." But it was not really that. Each play had a separate theme, time, and cast list. They were not causally related, like Aeschylus's *Oresteia* or the problematic Prometheus trilogy.

Even within the fifth century, therefore, it would be fair to say that tragedy altered in form, responding to a changing society. The norm became the single play, not the trilogy. This is the more understandable because we see tragedy changing formally in other directions, too. As Sophocles and Euripides inherited it, tragedy depended on a counterpoise between the personal single voice, the single actor, and the communal voice of the chorus. Interplay among them exposed the play's concerns shiftingly. It voiced its themes at two levels: personal and individualizing on the one hand, public and universalizing on the other. Much of the impacted power of the Greek texts depends on this tension, which itself depended on the way the poet used the choral odes. Centrifugal, associative, and decoratively mythological though they were, these songs crucially mirrored the pain and preoccupations of the action. But toward the end of the century, there was a trend—reflected in late Euripides—toward choral odes that were simply decorative and unrelated to the play's cares. After Euripides, dramatists might write *embolima* ("things to be thrown in"): choral odes to keep in a drawer, for ad hoc use in any play.[44]

We know a bit about fourth-century tragedy: what Euripidean tragedy became.[45] Public and private split apart somehow. The stage was raised, separating actors from the singers in the orchestra, incarnating a thematic and formal separation of the choric from the individual, the plural from the singular. Tragedy's form, therefore, sensitive to shifting local preoccupations, did suffer important changes even in its first seventy Athenian years of life. Changes in the writing and staging of tragedy reflect an increasing stress on inwardness—the long Western slide toward individualism—apparent elsewhere in Greek culture at the beginning of the fourth century. Within the changing forms of tragedy rose the staging of the agony of inwardness, which is crucial for later manifestations of tragedy. It was articulated especially in the monologues of Euripides, master shaper of European soliloquy and the dramatist for whom Racine felt most affinity.[46]

It is not the case, then, that the form of the Greek tragedies is one unitary thing, unknowable to us. In the perceptions of the culture for whom it was per-formed (made apparent "through form"), the form changed through the century. We have some texts. What is formally unknowable is the emotional context, the festival resonance of which tragedy was one element.

Steiner's first point is vital, therefore, but I think, as far as pure form is concerned, it can be met. His second point concerns the satyr play. Tragedy's moment, when the audience faced the unendurability of the human condition, was short. Steiner argues that we cannot fully comprehend its structure because it finished with something we no longer have. Each tragedian rounded off his group of three tragedies with a satyr play, which both completed and undercut the effect of the tragedies.

In the early years a tragedian did not offer a trilogy but a tetralogy. Sometimes even the satyr play was thematically related to the tragedies. Aeschylus's Theban plays in 467 B.C. came as a tetralogy: *Laius, Oedipus, Seven against Thebes*, and the satyr play, *Sphinx*. Steiner argues that we cannot know what this genre was like and therefore cannot grasp the form of tragedy, to which the satyr play belonged.

In the festival as a whole, the satyr play was only the first of two ways in which tragedy's effect was undercut. The dramatist wrote it for performance after three tragedies, on the same day. We have two fragmentary satyr plays and the plot lines of many. Much scholarly care has gone into reassembling the elements and tone of the genre. Although much is speculation, it is clear that the satyr plays explored "human culture as through a fun-house mirror." Satyr drama continued tragedy's illusion and fictiveness. It did not parody tragedy. The laughter lay with the character of the satyrs, their out-of-placeness in the situation. They were packed little amalgams of selfishness and animal response—qualities bleached out of most tragic figures— stumbling into a mythic or epic scenario and responding to it in an endearingly boorish, ignoble way.[47]

It is true that all this is mostly lost. But I am not convinced that our understanding of tragic form is therefore lacking. The loss means lack in another direction. "Without satyric drama we cannot know enough about the way the Greek spirit survived catastrophe," writes Tony Harrison in his "Introduction" to his version of *Ichneutai*, Sophocles' satyr play. "With the loss of these plays we lack important clues to the wholeness of the Greek imagination, and its ability to absorb yet not be defeated by the tragic. In the satyr play that spirit of celebration, held in the dark solution of tragedy, is precipitated into release."[48]

What we have lost is something that undercut the effect of the tragedies—not necessarily the form of the tragedies themselves. I do not think we can argue that a satyr play completed this, any more than the two other tragedies, in the group presented by each tragedian, affected the audience's judgment of a single play.

Furthermore, comedy's subversion of tragic vision was in many ways more radical. It came as it were on the Thursday, after three days on which three tragedians each presented three tragedies and a satyr play. Comedies, written and put on by different dramatists, not the tragedians, mocked tragedy's stage illusion, addressed the audience directly, and parodied tragedy's language, stage business, intellectual preoccupations, and plots. They also were part of the festival, whose own huge structure must have expressed the wholeness of the Greek dramatic imagination. This is the structure we cannot get back.

Satyr drama and comedy, in their complex relations to tragedy, are irreplaceable pointers to fifth-century Athenian imagination. Once launched on the satyr play, you might well look back to the preceding three tragedies differently. By the end of Thursday, you would see them in retrospect differently again. But that would not take away your immediate grasp of the form of each tragic play. Your view of Monday's tragedies would be affected also by Tuesday's. But responding to separate forms was what you were there to do.

So I do not think that satyr drama, any more than comedy does, affects the form of tragedy. Rather, its presence affected the shifting value of separate tragedies retrospectively within the festival. The tragedies were moments in the festival, structurings seen by the Athenians as whole forms. They were short. They were accompanied in the festival by other forms that challenged the sealed blackness of the tragic vision. But each one could win a prize awarded specifically for that form. In this sense, the content and form of a single tragedy made their own unique impact on the audience. You could even argue that the following drama, the separate form of a satyr play, was needed because the impact of tragic form was indeed absolute.

Form in "Fragments"

In *The Death of Tragedy*, Steiner sees tragedy's history not as continuous tradition, but as tragedy expressing itself, miraculously, in specific cultures at specific moments: most vividly, fifth-century Athens, Elizabethan and Jacobean England, and seventeenth-century Spain and France:

If we consider the twenty-five hundred years which separate us from Greek tragedy, the history of tragic drama will strike us as having in it little of overt continuity or tradition. What impresses us is a sense of miraculous occasion. . . . In the long view . . . it is the existence of a living body of tragic drama, not the absence of it, that calls for particular note. The rise of the necessary talent to the possible occasion is extremely rare. . . . What we should expect, and actually find, are long spells of time during which no tragedies . . . [are] being produced.

He also deals with the times of failure. For Romantic poets—who dramatized experience and idealized the dramatic—tragedy was the supreme goal they never reached.[49]

Politics was partly responsible, especially after the end of the eighteenth century, when the glow of the French Revolution faded, and the middle classes, once a source of revolutionary energy, betrayed the dream that human nature was perfectible and fortified themselves in prosperous conservativism (126). But changing ideas of crime and guilt also helped. The Romantics were optimists about human nature. Responsibility for crime and evil lay outside, with the environment, society, or (the Freudian version—Freud being Romanticism's heir) the parents. But the Romantic thesis that "evil cannot be wholly native to the soul" will not do for tragedy, where it must be native to the soul *and* abroad in the world.

Political and moral ideas combined, therefore, to stop the Romantics (except for a while in Germany) from creating authentic tragic drama. True tragedy is anti-Romantic. In it, "the redeeming insight comes too late to mend the ruins or is purchased at the price of irremediable suffering." Human beings "run against the grain of inexplicable and destructive forces that lie 'outside' yet very close"; and "there is no answer. Why should there be? If there was, we would be dealing with just or unjust suffering, as do parables. . . . Not with tragedy." There is no "compensating Heaven" like that which Romanticism dreamed (128–29).

Houselessness

> It is clear that the city-state is a natural growth, and the human being is by nature a political animal. The man who is *apolis* by nature (not by fortune) is either something less or something more than a human being . . . and resembles an isolated piece of the board.
>
> (Aristotle *Politics* 1253a 10)

Let us go back to the act of reading as image of the tragic encounter. It dislocates the self by opening it to the other, to the "absolutely alien":

Serious painting, music, literature or sculpture make palpable to us . . . the unassuaged, unhoused instability and estrangement of our condition. We are, at key instants, strangers to ourselves, errant at the gates of our own psyche. . . . We can be, in ways almost unendurable to reason, strangers to those whom we would know best, by whom we would be best known and unmasked. . . . [Art and literature] tell of the obstinacies of the impenetrable, of the absolutely alien which we come up against in the labyrinth of intimacy. They tell of the Minotaur at the heart of love, of kinship, of uttermost confiding. . . . [Art makes us] if not at home, at least alertly, answerably peregrine in the unhousedness of our human circumstance.[50]

"Our" condition, as we see it illumined in art, and experience it in our encounter with art, is identical with the tragic condition as Steiner outlines it in his "Note on Absolute Tragedy": "An absolutely tragic model of the condition of men and women views these men and women as unwanted intruders on creation. . . . The absolutely tragic . . . [is] man unhoused in being." The compelling encounter takes place when human beings are, like Lear on the heath, "unhoused," where the human condition is ontological unwantedness.[51] A world in which human beings are atoms lost outside structure.

To be unhoused, fragmentary, unplaceable, stripped, outside: this is summed up in the Greek word *apolis*, "without-city," "uncitied." "Few words outside Scripture have drawn more intense commentary." The dialectic between the "housed" and the "unhoused" comes up at the beginning of *Antigones*. In Sophocles' play, with its clash between the domestic and the civic, the female and the male, a key question is, Which is the true *apolis*, Creon or Antigone?[52]

This notion of houselessness reminds us how precisely Steiner's insights are both tragic and Greek. The houselessness and fragmentariness that he ascribes to the tragic condition (and implicitly to our own), is the DNA of Greek nightmare. We hear it in Greek oaths and curses. It is what you wish on your enemies. As the gods swear by that which most horrifies them, the black death-river of Styx, so human beings swear by what most appalls them: exile, houselessness.

In the apocalyptic vision of Empedocles, this is what happens to fallen demigods, to a soul that defiled itself with bloodshed or swore a false oath:

> the air's force pursues him into the sea,
> the sea spits him out to the threshold of the land,
> the earth throws him to the rays of the burning sun
> and the sun into the whirlings of the air.

Of these souls, says Empedocles (whose philosophy assumes reincarnation), "I too am one: a fugitive from god and a wanderer, who trusted in mad strife." The Empedoclean soul pays for sinning in this world ("I wept and wailed when I saw the unfamiliar place"), by entering

> a joyless place, where Bloodshed and Anger,
> tribes of Fates, withering Plagues,
> Corruptions and Floods roam in the dark
> over a field of Ate.

Plutarch's *De Exilio* corrects Empedocles, but keeps his image of life and afterlife as a fugitive wandering: "Since the soul has come here from elsewhere, Empedocles euphemistically calls birth a 'stay abroad.' A comforting name. In truth the soul is a fugitive and a wanderer ever, driven by the decrees and laws of gods."[53] An apprehension of human life as a driven houseless wandering is both the tragic vision as Steiner formulates it in his "Note on Absolute Tragedy" and the condition in which we meet great art.

The Place of Joy

In Empedocles, the fugitive soul enters "a joyless place." In Steiner's "Note on Absolute Tragedy," the issue is precisely joylessness. Is there any place in tragedy now for joy?

Shakespeare's tragedies, he argues, are not absolute. Shakespeare's feel for the hybridity of life is too strong. Too much satyr play in the fabric. A note of redemption at the end of *Macbeth*, *Othello*, *Hamlet*, even *King Lear*, works with a pulse of humor or hope to deny these plays a claim to absolute tragedy. In absolute tragedy, the audience sees the human condition only as unflawed black. Only *Timon of Athens*, "that inexhaustibly perplexing, erratic bloc," is the real thing.

I think there is a case, however, for hearing even in *Timon of Athens* the same sad demi-healing as in *King Lear*, *Hamlet*, *Othello*: the end note that suggests "Cyprus will be governed efficiently by Cassio as it never could have been by Othello . . . [and] times in Denmark will be back in joint."[54] Athens will be more justly governed hereafter. Values live on by which Timon's nobility will be rescued and appreciated. "Bring me into your city," says Alcibiades. He will physic the city that cast Timon out: will "make each / Prescribe to other as each other's leech." But even so I am not persuaded that this means none of Shakespeare's tragedies is tragedy and that this sense of hope at the heart or end of darkness is alien to tragic form. Instead, I think the sense of hope belongs to tragic form, though it may be nomadic within it.

Steiner presents his austere category of absolute tragedy as a corrective or refinement to his earlier account. "I had not in *The Death of Tragedy* drawn the definition taut, or seen how limited is the class of the absolute." In his "Introduction" to the *Reader*, the first place I find the reformulation, he elaborates:

The notion of absolute tragedy, as we find it in classical Greece and seventeenth-century France, is alien to the . . . tragi-comic bias of Shakespeare. . . . The mature Shakespeare refuses to compact the universe into a "black hole." But it is precisely this compaction, this suspension of relativity and hope, that define the supreme formal expressions of human nothingness and despair in pure tragedy. . . . This distinction is implicit in *The Death of Tragedy*. But it is not hammered out and applied with sufficient clarity.[55]

In essence, however, the reformulation seems rather to undermine a claim that I take to be fundamental in *The Death of Tragedy*: that tragedy "fuses" grief and joy.

Things are as they are, unrelenting and absurd. . . . Yet in the very excess of his suffering lies man's claim to dignity. . . . Man is ennobled by the vengeful spite or injustice of the gods. It does not make him innocent, but it hallows him as if he had passed through flame. Hence there is in the final moments of great tragedy, whether Greek or Shakespearian or neo-classic, a fusion of grief and joy, of lament over the fall of man and rejoicing in the resurrection of his spirit.[56]

It seems to me that the new formulation, in which any tragedy not "immune to light" is not "absolute," goes back on this.

The new formulation needs the picture of a split in the Greek dramatic festival, an absolute division between the tragedies and, as it were, the afternoon of satyr drama, as well as (though the "Note on Absolute Tragedy" does not go into this) the Thursday of comedy. No joy in tragedy, not even, now, in sharing the suffering. Steiner makes the "moment" of strippedness, the black "flash" in which the waste of human lives is flung back as in an obsidian mirror at the audience, the only touchstone of tragic form.

This austerity expresses, I think, Steiner's understanding of two things at once. Of the ancient nightmare of houselessness, and also of current post-Communist, post-Freudian, postreligious sensibility, unhoused in any ideology, despairing of a fatigued humanism: a self-

vision that has precisely nowhere to go or be. From—I hazard—an
increasing intuition that the Empedoclean nightmare of a joyless place,
a place that is no place, fits the modern dilemma, he argues that "absolute" tragic texts stage this nightmare "unremittingly." In a sense this
argument, whether or not one buys it, is itself the most compact
possible expression of its own *Zeitgeist*.

Heracles' Nightmare

The nightmare of houselessness is articulated throughout Greek
tragedy. But no religious system can underwrite it completely: "I take
such a reading of the human case to be heretical. It presumes either an
unforgiving God whose pique breeds everlasting vengeance, or some
manichean dialectic in which . . . the negative principle prevails."[57] In
most tragedies, it is not worked through unremittingly, except perhaps,
as Steiner says, in the *Bacchae*. It is rather the defining moment of a play:
the counterpart experience presents to Erinys, the defining tragic demon.[58] Through this moment of insight—of the world as an alien place
whose only meaning, if it has one, is a random rejecting cruelty—the
characters and audience experience the destructiveness of both humanity and divinity. Of divinity at work in and through humanity.

Take, for example, a Greek hero whose goodness to humankind
parallels that of Shakespeare's Timon. His expression of houselessness
is his expression of despair at his own being.

The form of this play is *Hippolytus* inside-out. In *Hippolytus*, two
divinities stand at the beginning and end of the action like columns on
either side of a temple pediment. In the center human drama unfolds,
to their direction, but also in accord with human motivation. But
Euripides' *Hercules Furens* (*The Madness of Heracles*) opens and closes
with human efforts at evil and saving. Divinity rips through the center,
making Heracles mad, making him kill those whom he saved. At the
end, he is in some sort saved by the touch and negotiation of another
human being.

Heracles is self-defiled—he kills his own children—through the
agency of a self-confessedly amoral divinity. His moment of strippedness is a moment of truth, about himself in relation to divinity. But it is
not the only truth. Theseus, his friend, wants to find for him some way
of existing in the human world. Heracles, in the presence of his helpless
human father, flings his houselessness at Theseus:

Listen, that I may wrestle in words
against your advisings. I shall unfold to you
how unlivable, now and before, my life has always been.
First, I was begotten by a father
who killed my mother's ancient father
and then, a suppliant needing purification,
married her. Alcmena. She gave birth to me.
When the tribe's base-stone
is not laid right, the family must suffer.
And Zeus—whoever Zeus is—begot me
enemy to Hera.—No, old man, don't be angry—
I count you as my father. Not Zeus.

So begins the black exposition of the doubly and impossibly fathered
hero, as to why he should not live. Hera persecuted him when he was
an infant. His adult life—"why should I speak of the sufferings I
endured?"—has been a sequence of "labors" (the Greek word also
means "pains"). Now,

The last, this terrible murder.
Unhappy wretch, killing my children
I put the topstone of misery on my house.

Hera made him kill his sons. Polluted, he cannot stay in Thebes. No
one may speak to him. What altar or friend could he approach? He
cannot go to Argos: he is outlawed. He cannot go to a strange city: men
would stare and say, "There goes Zeus's son, who killed his wife and
children."

To the man who was called happy once,
reverses are bitter. The man
who always fared badly from birth—
he's not hurt when he meets misfortune.[59]

Heracles' position crystallizes the arrogance, as well as the agony, of
the unplaceable. No one comes near him in misery, and (in another
register) he can come near no one in friendship. All this is said to the
one man who will—in the Athenians' watching knowledge—"come
near" him in this misery. Theseus, too, will kill his child. He, too, will
suffer a reverse from "greet prosperitie" to supreme misery and alien-
ate gods through his dealings with his son. This is the man who offers
Heracles friendship and housing. For the Athenian audience, his very
person refutes Heracles' lonely claim.

Heracles embodies his apprehension of his self in a vision of pure
ontological unwantedness:

> I think I'll come at last to this last twist of fate,
>> when earth will make a sound
>> forbidding me to touch the land
> or cross the sea and well-springs.
> I'll be like Ixion,
>> wheel-driven in his chains.
> Best that no Greek sees me—
>> those Greeks among whom once
>> I was so prosperous, so blest.

The fantasy that earth forbids him to touch earth or sea—any possible
place where one may house oneself or travel—is echoed in an oath
reported in *Hippolytus*. Hippolytus swore he had not touched Phaedra:

> He called Zeus Horkios ["Zeus of Oaths"] to witness,
> and the plain of earth: "Grant that I perish
> without fame, without name,
> uncitied, houseless, a fugitive
> wandering the earth, and may neither sea
> nor land receive my flesh when I die,
> if I be this vile man!"[60]

Heracles assimilates his fantasy to Ixion, whirled on the wheel in
Hades because he tried to touch, erotically, the Queen of Heaven: the
crime of attempted rape, of which Hippolytus is accused. This is the
very queen who plunged Heracles into his pollution. Ixion is the Greek
Cain, the first to murder his own kind.[61] Purified of this by Zeus, he
tried to rape Hera. Both his crimes touch (that word again) on Heracles' crisis. We remember the unhoused untouchable "whirlings" of the
fallen in Empedocles.

Heracles sees his own houselessness in social and existential terms:

> best that none of the Greeks see me,
> among whom I prospered when I was happy.
> Why do I need to live? What gain
> in having a useless unholy life?

He is unjustly destroyed:

> Let her dance, that famous wife of Zeus,
> striking Olympus' holy floor with her shoe.

She's got what she wanted: she hurled down
the saviour of Greece, the foremost man.
Who shall pray now to such a goddess—who,
because of a woman, jealous that Zeus
had sex with her, destroyed the benefactor
of all Greece, guiltless though he was?[62]

Theseus's answer is to trust the human city. When relationships with divinity fail, human relationships must save. Alcibiades at the end of *Timon of Athens* picks up some pieces, providing a way by which better values may again take their place in the city that ousted Timon. Theseus plays this role here. The catastrophe was "Hera's work," but heroes must suffer, not die. Come and be purified at Athens, where he himself has "been given precincts" by those he saved from barbarism. Heracles, the other great Greek savior (a talismanic word for Heracles throughout the play), can have these lands, and be honored at Athens after death.[63] He is offered *place*.

Theseus's offer does not heal the vision of houselessness. It is a true vision, of a true thing. But Theseus, like Alcibiades, shows where a healing might start, and he offers a vision of a future in which past suffering can be celebrated, where the experience of houselessness is itself earthed in human land and memory. The formulation proposed by *The Death of Tragedy* fits Heracles exactly. He is "ennobled" by the gods' spite. "It hallows him as if he has passed through flame." There is the possibility that others may rejoice that his spirit endured the flame.

Most tragedies—not the tiny number Steiner designates as absolute—do offer this moment of alternative perspective, fusing it with the moments of blackness. The tragedies that have formed our notion of the tragic, by which we measure what a tragedy is, do compact, like a battery cell, a positive with a negative charge. They characteristically offer a moment that might start a healing, against the stronger moments in which the intuition of houselessness is absolute. Any dream of healing is imperfect and momentary. It does not redeem anything. It is not defining or compelling; not what we take away from the play. But in the presence of agony, the best that can be offered is this underthought: that the human must suffice when gods fail and hurt.

Many Greek tragedies had the shape Steiner calls "commedia," ending in some personal-political hope. The protagonist starts in stripped agony, like Aeschylus's Niobe in the lost play that bore her name, mourning her fourteen children killed by gods. Aeschylus's *Carians*

began with Europa, searching and then mourning for her glorious son
Sarpedon, killed because "Ares loves / to pluck the loveliest flowers of
the army." This shape may be particularly Asechylean. Aeschylus began several tragedies with a protagonist silent in despairing mourning,
such as Achilles mourning Patroclus at the beginning of *Myrmidons*.[64]
The unfolding tragedy brought the mourner back from silence into
language, as Heracles is brought back to the possibility of a city, of
living housed.

The grammar of these moments—the vision of waste and houselessness counterweighted by some possibility of makeshift healing—is
stamped in us "made in Greece," as deeply as the vision of houselessness itself. "Heroes must suffer, not die." Most Greek tragedies include
this possibility. Unless you are terminally ill, nightmare is finite. The
payoff comes in the sharing. Sharing nightmare, an audience touches
the possibility that we may know and come through it. Not compensation. Not "making it better." But it thrills us to share something in the
face of despair. "Since the expression 'To see the light' in Greek means
to live, the final sense [of a tragedy] is that of shared *life*," writes Tony
Harrison. "It is to that life that the masked upright figure of Hecuba
commits herself and us at the very end of the *Trojan Women*."[65]

This sense of tragedy came to us as Europa, mother of the Cretan
house, herself came to Greece: unhoused, from over the sea, brought
by divinity, bringing with her a precise syntax of suffering which
helped to define Europe. Fifth-century Greek vases sometimes painted
Tragoidia as a maenad in Dionysus's train.[66] From the beginning tragedy is a human form in a violent divinity's neighborhood, and it pits
the demonic cruelties Greece knew and feared well—violence, madness, absolute exile, mutilation, unjust persecution—against human
possibility.

Steiner's challenge is a paradox: that we learned tragic grammar
from the Greeks, yet most of their—and our—tragedies do not square
up to the sense we have of them. You might resolve the paradox by
appeal to the grammar's individual components, and say we derive this
sense of the tragic absolute from one element in tragedy's grammar of
houselessness. Heracles refusing Theseus's help, Juliet in her moment
of desolation: "Is there no pity sitting in the clouds / To see into the
bottom of my grief?" But this does not meet Steiner's call for the
absolute.

It may be that Steiner's is the demand of our age. The changes of technical form have ground exceeding small, until the only form that matches our sense of what we now perceive as tragic is the moment, the fragment. Steiner's vision of absolute tragedy expresses the unanswered absolutes of his own time. It stresses the moment; and inevitably in the Athenian festival stresses the division of the warm and comic from the tragic. In tragedy, blackness, grief, is all that there is.

What has Steiner done with the "joy" of his earlier formulation? Given the scale and theology of his associations to light he could answer, I suppose, that the illumination of uncompensated blackness, the flash of insight into it, is itself the joy. But I suspect this is different from the joy he meant thirty years ago. He is now questioning the place, in tragedy, of any note of hope for which "joy" may be a summary. The relation of joy to grief is now a nonrelation. The elements do not mix within the form of tragedy itself.

I do not share this vision. I like the old formulation. In my mythology, the spectacle of a "slow torture of a child" would come into the category, not of tragedy but a "fable of unjust suffering." But then, in terms of the "Note on Absolute Tragedy," I am a weak humanist. As *The Death of Tragedy* says, "in large measure, we are romantics still," and it is precisely the Romantics who failed to create tragedy.[67]

The exclusion of joy from tragic grief is expressed in Steiner's argument about trilogy and satyr drama. It is the drive behind his exclusion of Shakespeare from absolute tragedy.[68] It impels his insight into the barbaric at the heart of courtliness, "the Minotaur at the heart of love," and, above all, his exclusion from tragedy of the obverse intuition, that the courtly and the noble may be alive in the dungeon, the gas chamber. It may well be that the one who understands tragedy most truly in any age is one who both understands the innermost nerve of despair in his own times and can formulate it in terms of the oldest tragedies.

Ourselves as Fragments

Although absolute tragedy skipped most of the Romantics, it does live on, according to the "Note on Absolute Tragedy," in fragments, in "Alban Berg's *Lulu*, and the black holes in the . . . monologues of Beckett." Only here is "the postulate of the absolutely tragic thought through, 'staged' unremittingly." Only here do we "find fully expressed the conception of human life as lawless chastisement, as some hideous practical joke visited upon man, . . . the vision of reality as one best shown in the slow torture of a child or an animal." Tragedy lives today in black flashes, which display human lives meaninglessly torn. [69]

This position is explained by the argument of *Real Presences* that we create because we are created (or, the weaker version, because we perceive ourselves to be created). That we write tragedy in form because we are formed. The only form of tragedy possible now is momentary, a fragment or a flash, *because how we see ourselves has changed.* We see ourselves now as shards. Fragments without meaning, flakes of lost form.

Real Presences suggests that the form of the tragic insights we produce must responsibly mirror, for better or worse, the form in which we see ourselves. In our uniquely postreligious age, our God-shaped vacuum, it is basic to our sense of ourselves that the rubbish we see around us once made sense but does not now. Not to us. We have lost a way of seeing form in meaning, meaning in matter, and ourselves as formed.

The paradigmatic image of our condition is a night shot of a city. To the Greeks and even more to Augustine, the city emblematized divinely ordered, civilized meaning. "City" is what Alcibiades and Theseus offer at the end. It is now our image of self-created anarchy, where human beings are unanchored particles, exciting, destructive, vulnerable. Who knows what is at work, say our film-taught senses, in the city at night? The radical Steiner point, that the death camps forever changed our grasp of suffering, of human lives, of the meanings underlaying civilization, reminds us that we, in a way that was not possible before, see human beings as breakable fragments, without the light that always before stood for God, ordering, and hope. "Only the fragmentary, whose completeness is expressly that of mutilation . . . can be immune to light." [70]

Because of our experience of the scale of evil, and also of the loss of religion, we value—or we see sense in—the fragmentary, the momentary, in a way impossible to those who looked for meaning in the ordering of light. The possibilities of the tragic have changed, in keeping with our changing sense of our selves. Both now are immune to light. Aristotle's *Poetics* "is patterned on, it is not verified by, Sophocles' *Oedipus Tyrannus.* . . . Nothing in Aristotle's blueprint . . . could predict Büchner's *Wozzeck* and the deployment in tragic drama of inarticulate low life." [71] Inarticulate fragmentariness is where we now expect to see the tragic meaning available to us. Mutilation is the way we make sense.

Notes

1. George Steiner, *Extraterritorial: Papers on Literature and the Language Revolution* (Harmondsworth: Penguin Books, 1975), 72.

2. George Steiner, "A Note on Absolute Tragedy," *Journal of Literature and Theology* 4, no. 2 (July 1990): 150.

3. George Steiner, *Real Presences: Is There Anything in What We Say?* (London: Faber and Faber, 1989), 147. Hereafter cited as *RP*.

4. George Steiner, *Antigones: How the Antigone Legend Has Endured in Western Literature, Art, and Thought* (Oxford: Clarendon Press, 1984), 231. See Ruth Padel, "A Portrait of Teiresias: Steiner's *Antigones*," *Encounter* 64, no. 4 (November 1984): 44–49.

5. See George Steiner, *The Death of Tragedy* (London: Faber and Faber, 1961), 78–80 (hereafter cited as *DT*), on the "unbending forms" of Racine: "The space of action . . . is that part of Versailles in the immediate vision of the king." Cf. Roland Barthes, *Sur Racine* (Paris: Éditions du Seuil, 1963), 9–11, and Ruth Padel, "Making Space Speak," in *Nothing to Do with Dionysos? Athenian Drama in Its Social Context*, ed. John J. Winkler and Froma I. Zeitlin (Princeton: Princeton University Press, 1989), 355. Hereafter cited as Winkler and Zeitlin.

6. George Steiner, "A Death of Kings," in *Extraterritorial*, 63.

7. Sophocles *Oedipus Tyrannus* 1034–61.

8. Racine, *Phèdre* 1.1.34–36: "One of the most beautiful lines in the French language," says my Hachette edition. "All things are changed / Since the gods sent to these shores / The daughter of Minos and Pasiphae." *DT*, 87.

9. Euripides *Hippolytus* 759, and *Cretans* frag. 9.

10. Tony Harrison, *Phaedra Britannica*, 3d ed. (London: Collins, 1976), act 1. Minos, Phaedra's father, judge of the dead in the Greek underworld, becomes a British judge in rural India.

11. Racine, *Phèdre* 4.6.1255–80, and *DT*, 92–93.

12. *DT*, 81; emphasis mine.

13. See Ruth Padel, "Imagery of the Elsewhere: The Choral Odes of Euripides," *Classical Quarterly*, n.s., vol. 24, no. 2 (December 1974): 226–41.

14. *DT*, 92–93.

15. Cf. George Steiner, "Conversation Piece," in *Proofs and Three Parables* (New York: Granta Books/Penguin, 1993), 99–114.

16. Steiner, *Antigones*, 134–38.

17. See Edith Hall, *Inventing the Barbarian: Greek Self-Definition through Tragedy* (Oxford: Clarendon Press, 1989).

18. See Ruth Padel, *In and Out of the Mind: Greek Images of the Tragic Self* (Princeton: Princeton University Press, 1992).

19. Steiner, "A Note on Absolute Tragedy," 150; and *DT*, 85.

20. George Steiner, "The Distribution of Discourse," in *On Difficulty and Other Essays* (New York: Oxford University Press, 1978). Hereafter cited as *OD*.

21. *RP*, 188.

22. See George Steiner, "Text and Context," in *OD*, 15; and George Steiner, "After the Book?," in *OD*, 192; and cf. R. Lattimore, *Themes in Greek and Latin Epitaphs* (Urbana: University of Illinois Press, 1942).

23. See, e.g., Plato *Timaeus* 45B-46C, 67C-68D.

24. *RP*, 187.

25. *RP*, 211. *RP*'s subtitle is, *Is There Anything in What We Say?*

26. *DT*, 243.

27. Shakespeare, *Antony and Cleopatra* 4.13.67, 85; 5.2.192.

28. See A. W. Pickard-Cambridge, *Dithyramb, Tragedy and Comedy* (Oxford: Clarendon Press 1962), 124–26.

29. See Winkler and Zeitlin, 3–5, 98ff., 336; and Albert Henrichs, "Loss of Self, Suffering, Violence: The Modern View of Dionysus from Nietzsche to Girard," in *Harvard Studies in Classical Philology*, ed. D. R. Shackleton Bailey (Cambridge: Harvard University Press, 1984), 88:205–40.

30. *RP*, 201.

31. George Steiner, *George Steiner: A Reader* (Harmondsworth: Penguin Books, 1984), 16.

32. *DT*, 351.

33. Claude Lévi-Strauss, in George Steiner, "A Conversation with Claude Lévi-Strauss," *Encounter*, 26, no. 4 (April 1966): 35.

34. *DT*, 96.

35. Chaucer, "Prologue," in *The Monks Tale*; and *DT*, 11–13, 16.

36. *George Steiner: A Reader*, 10.

37. *DT*, 353, 349, 350.

38. *DT*, 353–54.

39. Steiner, "A Note on Absolute Tragedy," 148; cf. Steiner, "Of Nuance and Scruple," in *Extraterritorial*.

40. Steiner, "A Note on Absolute Tragedy," 147–48.

41. Pickard-Cambridge, *Dithyramb, Tragedy and Comedy*, 61.

42. Polyphradmon's *Lycurgeia*, Philocles' *Pandionis*, Meletus's *Oedipodeia*, Sophocles' *Telepheia* (see Pickard-Cambridge, *Dithyramb, Tragedy and Comedy*, 62nn. 1–4): when you remember that eighteen tragedies appeared every year between 475 and 400, this number is tiny.

43. Sophocles, *Antigone*, ed. Richard Jebb (1891), xlix.

44. See Padel, "Imagery of the Elsewhere," 240n.5.

45. See G. Xanthakis-Karamanos, *Studies in Fourth-Century Tragedy* (Athens: Akadēmia Athēnōn, 1980).

46. See R. Patterson, *Tennyson and Tradition* (Cambridge: Harvard University Press, 1979), 26–28, 156–57n.11; and *DT*, 81, 76, 106.

47. François Lissarrague, "Why Satyrs Are Good to Represent," in Winkler and Zeitlin, 228–37. See further V. Steffen, "De fabularum satyricarum generibus," *Eos* 65 (1977); R. Seaford, "Introduction" and "Commentary," in *Euripides' "Cyclops"* (Oxford: Clarendon Press, 1984); and David Konstan, "An Anthropology of Euripides' *Kyklōps*," in Winkler and Zeitlin, 207–27.

48. Tony Harrison, "Introduction," in *The Trackers of Oxyrrhynchus* (London: Faber and Faber, 1990).

49. *DT*, 106–7, 123, 127.

50. *RP*, 139–40.

51. Steiner, "A Note on Absolute Tragedy," 147.

52. See Steiner, *Antigones*, 11, 255.

53. Empedocles frag. 115, 118, 121DK; and Plutarch *De Exilio* 607D.

54. Steiner, "A Note on Absolute Tragedy," 149.

55. Ibid., 148; and *George Steiner: A Reader*, 9–10.

56. *DT*, 9–10.

57. Steiner, "A Note on Absolute Tragedy," 155.

58. See Padel, *In and Out of the Mind*, 170–72.

59. Euripides *Hercules Furens* 1255–93.

60. Ibid., 1294–300; and Euripides *Hippolytus* 1025–31.

61. Pindar *Pythian Odes* 2.31ff.

62. Euripides *Hercules Furens* 1300–1310.

63. Ibid., 1311–37.

64. See Oliver Taplin, "Aeschylean Silences and Silences in Aeschylus," in *Harvard Studies in Classical Philology*, ed. G. P. Gold (Cambridge: Harvard University Press, 1972), 76:57–97. On Europa, see Aeschylus, frag. 100N.

65. Harrison, "Introduction," x.

66. See W. Burkert, *Greek Religion*, trans. J. Raffan (Oxford: Blackwell, 1985), 185.

67. *DT*, 129, 135.

68. See Steiner, *Antigones*, 236.

69. Steiner, "A Note on Absolute Tragedy," 148.

70. Ibid.

71. *RP*, 75.

On Difficulty: Steiner, Heidegger, and Paul Celan

wie heißt es, dein Land
hinterm Berg, hinterm Jahr?
Ich weiß, wie es heißt.
Wie das Wintermärchen, so heißt es,
es heißt wie das Sommermärchen,
das Dreijahreland deiner Mutter, das war es,
das ists,
es wandert überallhin, wie die Sprache . . .
—Paul Celan, "Es ist alles anders"

W H A T   I S   I T for a text (or anything at all) to resist our efforts to make sense of it? On this question George Steiner's writings seem to point us in all the right directions. The question exposes us, for example, to the elemental experience of the translator, which one might summarize by saying that it is before everything else the experience of the nonidentical, or of the irreducible singularity of all that exists, but especially of human beings and their languages.[1] This experience is both ethical and open-ended. One tries to make the other plain and transparent within one's own language and cultural scheme, but the other cannot be objectified in this way precisely because it belongs to its own world and cannot be uprooted from it without great violence. Latin antiquity understood this when it associated translation with the conquest of cities, the taking of slaves and removal of treasures—in short, the making of empire; but this (or any) translative event has uncontrollable consequences. It exposes the translator to what cannot be contained within his or her self-identity, and this exposure must be understood in the strong sense of being turned inside-out, because in translation one appropriates the other within one's own self-intimacy, which henceforward can never be just the same.[2] Steiner puts it in another context, "the 'otherness' which enters into us makes us other."[3] One might put it that there can be no translation except under conditions of epistemological crisis, that is, conditions that require that one's self and one's world be reinterpreted or restructured so as to find a place in it for alien wisdom. Latin antiquity and the Renaissance constitute our large examples of this sort of crisis, and of course the history and philosophy of science continue to celebrate it.

Translation never just occurs on paper; it is always a movement toward conceptual revolution or, in nonscientific terms, toward ethical and cultural transformation. Think of how the lives of Augustine and Petrarch bring this point home. One cannot understand the alien text until one has first translated or converted oneself into one who can understand it, that is, someone who can experience the alien world from within as one who dwells there and who can read the alien text with the eyes of a believer in it.[4] This means taking leave of oneself and one's history in a radical way. The translator must always become an outsider before anything can be translated, and it remains an open question whether the translator ever becomes anything else. This also helps to explain why outcasts and wanderers make the best translators, not to say the best poets.

This is undoubtedly the moral of Steiner's story. "I have no recollection of a first language," he writes in *After Babel: Aspects of Language and Translation* (1975). "So far as I am aware, I possess equal currency in English, French, and German. What I can speak, write, or read of other languages has come later and retains a 'feel' of conscious acquisition. But I experience my first three tongues as perfectly equivalent centres of myself" (115). It is as if Steiner harbored within himself some principle of nonidentity with which three nonidentical (although of course not *radically* nonidentical) languages could feel themselves at home.[5] The question that puzzles Steiner is really what sort of person, or people, would have no experience of the nonidentity of alien languages. Obviously only someone nonidentical every which way could have such an experience, because it is not the languages in question which are interchangeable, but only the subject who speaks each of them equally well without belonging to any one of them. Only such a stranger could wander within himself across boundaries that hem the rest of us in. "It was," Steiner says, a habitual, unnoticed practice for my mother to start a sentence in one language and finish it in another. At home, conversations were interlinguistic not only inside the same sentence or speech segment, but as between speakers. Only a sudden wedge of interruption or roused consciousness would make me realize that I was replying in French to a question put in German or English or vice versa. Even these three "mother tongues" were only part of the linguistic spectrum in my early life. Strong particles of Czech and Austrian-Yiddish continued active in my father's idiom. And beyond these, like a familiar echo just out of hearing, lay Hebrew. (116)

This echo is a sort of hint of an answer to the question of nonidentity vis-à-vis multiple and conflicting mother tongues.

This polyglot matrix was far more than a hazard of private condition. It organized, it imprinted on my grasp of personal identity, the formidably complex, resourceful cast of Central European and Judaic humanism. Speech was, tangibly, an option, a choice between equally inherent yet alternate claims and pivots of self-consciousness. At the same time, the lack of a single native tongue entailed a certain apartness from other French schoolchildren, a certain extraterritoriality with regard to the surrounding social, historical community. (116)

Extraterritoriality, or apartness (*Abgeshiedenheit*), has great critical and even philosophical resonance. It is, first of all, foundational for Steiner's own theory of literary modernity, because modernity is understood as a crisis (which Steiner, following Mallarmé's "Crise de vers," is happy to locate somewhere in France in the early 1870s) consequent upon the language of poetry setting itself apart as something external to discourse or to what Habermas would characterize as the everyday world of communicative praxis monitored by cultural experts and above all by philosophy as the discipline dedicated to keeping everyday communication transparent or self-identical. Philosophy, says Habermas, whatever else it may have become since Plato's time, remains "the guardian of rationality."[6] So naturally one notices how the conceptual structure of this crisis duplicates the originary event of exclusion memorialized in book 10 of Plato's *Republic*. Or, again, it duplicates the inaugural moment in the history of aesthetics when the category of the beautiful was constructed as precisely that which remains external to the discourses of knowledge, truth, and practical decision. Or (one final time) it corresponds to that more elemental rupture that Michel Foucault tries to get at in *Les Mots et les choses* (1966) when, drawing on the eminent interpretation of Mallarmé developed by Paul Valéry and, later, by Maurice Blanchot, he speaks of the nineteenth-century origination of literature, where literature is no longer one discourse among many—no longer a discourse that is inter-translatable with those discourses in which we try to make sense of things—but instead

> encloses itself in a radical intransitivity; it becomes detached from all values that were able to keep it in general circulation during the Classical age . . . , and creates within its own space everything that will ensure a ludic denial of them (the scandalous, the ugly, the impossible); it breaks with the whole definition of *genres* as forms adapted to an order of representations, and becomes merely a manifestation of a language which has no other law than that of affirming—in opposition to all other forms of discourse—its own precipitous existence; and so there is nothing for it to do but to curve back in a perpetual return upon itself, as if its discourse could have no other content than the expression of its own form.[7]

Already in some of the essays collected in *Language and Silence: Essays on Language, Literature, and the Inhuman* (1967), Steiner was developing his version of this theory of rupture, which he characterizes in terms of the withdrawal of the poet from communication and representation. What Steiner calls "The Retreat from the Word" is a retreat from the postrhetorical (postclassical) or Enlightenment theory that language is a system for framing representations and that successful discourse or mutual understanding is a matter of coming to agreement concerning our concepts. Call this a theory of philosophical language. One wants to say that Steiner's own originary and eccentric experience of language as multiple, heterogeneous, unrestricted to self-identity, and irreducible to deep structure could never be comprehended by this theory. So it is no accident that his conception of modern writing emphasizes the resistance of poetry, and indeed of language itself, to a culture committed to making language transparent, open to view, conceptually coherent, and reducible to propositional form—an instrument, in short, of communicative efficacy. The long chapter "Word against Object" in *After Babel* is Steiner's most sustained and detailed meditation on this resistance, which, with donnish understatement, he summarizes with the word "difficulty." In modern poetry, he says, we encounter "an entirely new, ontologically motivated order of difficulty" (178).[8] Modern poetry is not so much a failure of discourse as a refusal of it; call it a self-reflexive movement in which poetry recognizes, after centuries of struggle to integrate itself into Western culture, that it is not one discourse among others, that it is external to discourse as such, and that its incommensurability in this event is not a defect to be overcome but a constitutive withdrawal or exclusion that preserves language (and therefore the world) from the attempt to bring it under the control of representational and communicative action. Language (and therefore the world) is not for us, and it is this deep truth that poetry registers in its refusal of our efforts to make sense of it.

What is this truth, exactly? Or, to put it another way: What moral are we to draw from the ontological difficulty of poetic speech? The idea, after all, is not that we need to break through this difficulty and so undo it, but rather that we should understand how this difficulty reflects on us—how it speaks (as nothing else can) to what the matter is with us. (We shall see that this is how the poetry of Paul Celan speaks.)

Nothing in our philosophical or conceptual experience prepares us for this line of thinking, which is why we still do not know how to pursue it. The insights of Steiner in this regard show his unique encounter with Heidegger, who has given us, in his essay "Der Ursprung des Kunstwerkes" (1935–36), the most coherent theoretical account of the "ontological difficulty" of art that we are likely ever to have; but it is an account whose coherence we are likely to miss, for Heidegger has given up the traditional language of aesthetics for a vocabulary appropriated from (among other places) the poetry of Hölderlin. "The Origin of the Work of Art" is an attempt to understand the work of art, not as an object of aesthetic judgment or subjective experience, but in terms of the truth of its work, that is, in terms of what happens in the event of its being.[9] For Heidegger the work of art is not (or not just) an entity within the world; it is an originary event that opens up the world and exposes us, as beings, to time and history. As Heidegger says, "the work holds open the Open of the world" (31/45). Nothing comes into presence or withdraws into absence except with respect to the open space opened up in this event.

However, the being of the work is not exhausted in this event. On the contrary, the paradox of the work of art (which the staunchest Heideggerians themselves tend to miss) is that its work of disclosure is also a work of resistance and refusal: call it "ontological difficulty." Heidegger explicates this difficulty in several ways, starting with the essay's whole first part ("The Thing and the Work"), which, under the pretext of asking about the thingliness of the work of art, concerns itself with the refusal of the thing to answer to our concepts of it. This is not because of the weakness of conceptual thinking (which, on the contrary, is characterized as being aggressive and violent with respect to things); rather, "this self-refusal [*Sichzurückhalten*] of the mere thing, this self-contained independence, belongs precisely to the nature of the thing," that is, it is part of the truth of things to be "strange and uncommunicative" (17/32–33). In the essay's second part ("The Work and Truth"), this self-refusal of things becomes the distinctive character of that which also belongs to the event of world disclosure, namely, the foregrounding or bringing forth of the earth. In contrast to the opening up of the world, the earth is that which remains closed, or, as Heidegger puts it:

The earth appears openly cleared as itself only when it is perceived and preserved as that which is by nature undisclosable [*Unerschliessbare*], that which shrinks from every disclosure and constantly keeps itself closed up. All things of earth, and the earth itself as a whole, flow together into a reciprocal accord. But this confluence is not a blurring of their outlines. Here there flows the stream, restful within itself, of the setting of bounds, which delimits everything present within its presence. Thus in each of the self-secluding things there is the same not-knowing-of-one-another [*Sich-nicht-Kennen*]. The earth is essentially self-secluding [*Sichverschliessende*]. To set forth the earth means to bring it into the Open as the self-secluding. (33/47)

For Heidegger, world and earth belong together in a fundamental opposition or strife (*Streit*). "The world," says Heidegger, "in resting upon the earth, strives to surmount it. As self-opening it cannot endure anything closed. The earth, however, as sheltering and concealing, tends always to draw the world into itself and keep it there" (35/49). This strife itself opens onto a deeper or more originary conflict (*Urstreit*), which, as if against all reason, Heidegger calls truth (*Wahrheit*). Truth here is no longer a philosophical concept, or rather (like the thing) it is something excessive to or excluded by the history of attempts to clarify the concept of truth. Truth is the event of opening or clearing (*Lichtung*) in which everything makes its appearance (and from which, as if in the same stroke, it disappears). As Heidegger says, "that which is can only be, as a being, if it stands within and stands out within what is lighted in this clearing" (40/53). Truth is this unconcealment (*Unverborgenheit*). At the same time, however, "a being can be concealed, too, only within the sphere of what is lighted. Each being we encounter and which encounters us keeps to this curious opposition of presence in that it always withholds itself at the same time in a concealedness. The clearing in which beings stand is in itself at the same time concealment [*Verbergung*]" (40/52). So truth is not the pure presencing of beings; the truth of beings also means their withdrawal, their reserve, their ungraspability; it means their ability to disguise and dissemble themselves according to the ancient concept of the *pseudos*.

Indeed, we will not feel the force of Heidegger's notion of truth unless we linger over his German—for example, *Verbergung* is "concealment." *Bergen* means "to shelter" or "keep safe." *Unverborgenheit*, "unconcealment," is thus not (or not just) a word for revelation, which is perhaps how most Heideggerians construe it; it also means exposure. Truth is the exposure of beings, whose entry into the Open also means a deprivation of shelter. Moreover, as beings, our own relation to the Open, that is, our being in it (our truth), does not mean that we are happily or even rationally and justly situated. "We believe we are at home in the immediate circle of beings," Heidegger says.

That which is, is familiar, reliable, ordinary. Nevertheless, the clearing is pervaded by a constant concealment [*Verbergen*] in the double form of refusal and dissembling [*des Versagens und des Verstellens*]. At bottom, the ordinary is not ordinary; it is extra-ordinary, uncanny [*un-geheuer*]. The nature of truth, that is, of unconcealedness, is dominated throughout by a denial [*Verweigerung*]. . . . *This denial, in the form of a double concealment, belongs to the nature of truth as unconcealedness.* Truth, in its nature, is untruth. (41/54)

All by itself this last statement is preposterous, of course, but Heidegger's point is to get us out from under the idea that truth is simply a logical concept. Ontologically it is an excessive and even violent event.

It follows that the truth of the work of art is not something that can be translated into a discourse of meaning and significance.[10] Heidegger is notorious for the way he seems to guard against such translation. In the essay's third part ("Truth and Art"), he speaks of truth as that which establishes (*richtet*) itself in the work "as the conflict between lighting and concealing in the opposition of world and earth" (50/62). The work is structured as a *rift* (*Riss*) of earth and world—although "structured" is not quite the right word, because the work is not to be thought of as a formal unity of opposites. Its gestalt, Heidegger says, is more event than form, and in saying this he lays special emphasis upon the way in which the work "sets forth" the earth. "In the creation of the work," he says, "the conflict, as rift, must be set back into the earth, and the earth itself must be set forth and used as the self-closing factor

[*Sichverschliessende*]. This use, however, does not use up or misuse the earth as matter, but rather sets it free to be nothing but itself" (52/64). In plain English this means that the work of art will always be too much for the world. The work of the work of art is disclosure, but the work itself remains self-closing in the manner of the earth. This is the ontological difficulty of the work of art. It is not for us. It is self-standing, not just autonomous in the Kantian sense, but forceful and active in its self-refusal, meaning that its work with respect to the world does not come to an end; rather, it is a persistent trouble to any world that merely settles into place and sees the Open only in terms of itself or through its own eyes. Heidegger characterizes the relation of the work to the Open of the world as a *Stoss* and *Anstoss*, a thrust and an affront. "The more essentially this thrust comes into the Open," Heidegger says, "the stranger and more solitary [*befremdlicher und einsamer*] the work becomes" (53/66).[11] The consequence is that the Open always remains open in the sense of being a place of exposure. "The more solitary the work . . . stands on its own and the more cleanly it seems to cut all ties to human beings," Heidegger says, "the more essentially is the uncanny [*Ungeheure*] thrust to the surface and the long-familiar thrust down" (54/66). As if to emphasize this theme of the uncanny, Heidegger entails the nature of art under the name of poetry, where *Dichtung* is to be understood not as the art of writing verses, but ontologically as an event in which "everything is other than usual . . . [and] everything ordinary and hitherto existing becomes an unbeing" (59/72).

It is important not to draw back from the radical character—the deep ontological difficulty—of Heidegger's aesthetics. In a section of *L'espace littéraire* that is a close paraphrase of "'The Origin of the Work of Art," Maurice Blanchot, who in many respects is the best reader Heidegger ever had, puts it as plainly and darkly as one can: "Through the work there takes place in time another time, and in the world of beings that exist and of things which subsist there comes, as presence, not another world, but the other of all worlds, that which is always other than the world [*ce qui est toujours autre que le monde*]."[12] It is precisely for this reason that the work of art, whatever sense we might try to make of it, always remains ontologically external to the world. The work, Blanchot says, belongs to history, yet "it escapes history. In the world where it emerges to proclaim that now there is a work—in the usual time, that is, of current truths—it emerges as the unaccustomed, the unwonted [*l'insolite*]. Never is it affirmed on the basis of familiar, present reality. It takes away what is most familiar to us. And always it is in excess: it is the superabundance of refusal" (304/228). A superabundance of refusal.

Blanchot's reading is valuable because he knows that this refusal is not simply a refusal of meaning; difficulty is ontological before it is philological. "The work of art is linked to a risk," Blanchot says; "it is the affirmation of an extreme experience" (316/236). Heidegger had developed this idea in "Wozu Dichter" (1946), where Being is said to draw beings into being by drawing them toward itself, but, because Being withdraws in this same movement, it creates something like a draft or void in which beings are "flung loose," radically ungrounded as if suddenly free of gravity.[13] Thus if Being is the ground of beings, it is so only in this antifoundational sense of being a risk or venture (*Wagnis*) into which beings are thrown or drawn. Accordingly, we should think of the Open not as a place of enlightenment and plenitude, but as a condition of being caught in the wake or void of Being. Historically human reason seems always to have tried to overcome this condition by securing itself against Being, fixing itself in place, bringing everything that surrounds it under the control of this fixity. This is the task of metaphysics and, by extension or application, of technology, and in the modern world we have renewed this task with an unprecedented and willful fury. Blanchot, however, reminds us that we long since abandoned our efforts to enlist the collaboration of art and poetry in this task. "Art is for us a thing of the past," said Hegel in a famous line. This means, Blanchot says, that there is no place for art in "the world [where] subordination reigns: subordination to ends, to measured proportion, to seriousness and order. On one front science, technology, the state; on another, significance, stable values, the ideal of the Good and the True. Art is 'the world turned upside down': insubordination, disproportion, frivolity, ignorance, evil, non-sense" (287/216). As we know from Emmanuel Levinas, turning the world upside down in this way—Levinas calls it "the breakup of essence," "the breakup of identity"—is the beginning of the ethical, where the ethical has to do with our relation or exposure to the other rather than with securing (fixing in place) our concepts, values, and beliefs.[14]

The task of poetry is to hold open the Open precisely by turning the world upside down. Its mediation, says Blanchot, is "insubordination, disproportion, frivolity, evil, non-sense." The consequences of this task are not just formal and linguistic: namelessness, wandering, madness, and suicide are as constitutive of poetry as fragmentation and intransparency. "When Saint-John Perse named one of his poems *Exile*," Blanchot says, "he named the poetic condition as well. . . . The poem is exile and the poet who belongs to it belongs to the dissatisfaction of exile. He is always lost to himself, outside, far from home; he belongs to the foreign, to the outside which knows no intimacy or limit, and to the separation which Hölderlin names when in his madness he sees rhythm's infinite space" (318/237). Or, again:

> Error is the risk which awaits the poet. . . . Error means wandering, the inability to abide and stay. For where the wanderer is, the conditions of a definitive here and now are lacking. . . . The wanderer's country is not truth, but exile; he lives outside, on the other side which is by no means a beyond, rather the contrary. He remains separated, where the deep of dissimulation, that elemental obscurity through which no way can be made and which because of that makes its awful way through him. (319/238)

This does not rule out a poetry that is eminently civilized and that gives the world a concept of itself that can be recognized and celebrated, as in Valéry's case, for example, in which the construction of the poem is a work of analytical reason and control. Instead, it means that, as Philipe Lacoue-Labarthe suggests in *La poésie comme expérience*, a poetry such as Celan's discloses an originary uprootedness, an *Abgeschiedenheit*, which deprives Celan's suicide of its contingency.[15] The risk of poetry is not simply that we will be unable to understand and interpret it.

Steiner is not wrong to conceive *Abgeschiedenheit* as privacy, which is the concept that guides his Celan interpretation in *After Babel* and again in the essay "On Difficulty."[16] But perhaps it is better to distinguish the private from the secret, that is, the secreted, where what is set apart is not merely something to which we are not privy, like another's thoughts that a word might betray, but rather something that is constituted as such in its being out of reach, a pure elsewhere. What is characteristic of Celan's poetry is not that it is unintelligible, only that it causes a hemorrhage in our discursive space, whence a once-familiar language drains away from us. Imagine not the poem but ourselves (or the world) left, not speechless entirely perhaps, but—

Die nachzustotternde Welt
bei der ich zu Gast

gewesen sein werde, ein Name, herabgeschwitzt von der Mauer,
an der eine Wunde hochleckt.   (*GW*, 2:349)[17]

(What world is this? No longer ours; no longer answerable to our
concepts and intentions: call it, after Heidegger, a world expatriated.)

> Mit den Sackgassen sprechen
> vom Gegenüber,
> von seiner
> expatriierten
> Bedeutung—:
>
> dieses
> Brot kauen, mit
> Schreibzähnen.
>   (*GW*, 2:358)[18]

Unlike a Joycean text, which (as Derrida says) speaks many languages at once, and so seems to have, Pantagruel-like, internalized the
world, Celan's is constituted as a conversation in which no one can take
part and from which Celan seems at times to have been excluded—a
conversation in a language not made for us, "a language not for you and
not for me" (*GW*, 3:170), which not even the poet can make his own.[19]
It is true that Derrida reads Celan's text as if it were Joycean, that is,
made of multiple languages (the poem "In Eins" is his example), but
his point is that *Schibboleth* is the watchword of Celan's text, the coun-
tersign that refuses not our understanding, but our belonging.[20] This
pushes the question of difficulty beyond the merely linguistic onto
truly ontological grounds, where the density or refusal of the text is no
longer the text's problem—that is, no longer a defect in the text which
critical methods can hope to repair. Rather, it is now a counterstatement (*Gegenwort*) that arraigns our whole form of life (including, one
might as well say, the poet's) and opens us onto another that, alas, (as if
for anthropological reasons) can make no sense to us, which is why we
are left with the experience of worldlessness or exile:

> Weggebeizt vom
> Strahlenwind deiner Sprache
> das bunte Gerede des An-
> erlebten—das hundert-
> züngige Mein-
> gedicht, das Genicht.

Aus-
gewirbelt,
frei
der Weg durch den menschen
gestaltigen Schnee,
den Büßerschnee, zu
den gastlichen
Gletscherstuben und -tischen.

Tief
in der Zeitenschrunde,
beim
Wabeneis
wartet, ein Atemkristall,
dein unumstößliches
Zeugnis.   (*GW*, 2:31)[21]

What is recognizable here is the world left behind; but to what are we
being exposed?[22] It is purely a world elsewhere, nonidentical, as if it
could have no other meaning or definition except in its difference from
what we inhabit; it is just the exile's world. (So Celan: "The poem
intends another, needs this other, needs an opposite. It goes toward it,
bespeaks it. For the poem, everything and everybody is a figure of this
other toward which it is heading.")[23] The other is not a homeland; it is
a place of exposure, an open in which we are bereft of our conceptual or
cultural resources. (*La poésie ne s'impose plus, elle s'expose* [*GW*, 3:181].)
And this bereavement, says Levinas, opens us to the ethical.

Every effort at reading Celan, including (most famously) Peter
Szondi's memorable essay (among the first really sustained efforts of
Celan interpretation), has had to confront its own critical helplessness
before the intrepid darkness of Celan's text.[24] Szondi said that Celan's
poems are not representations of reality, but "reality itself" (but not
one we can recognize as ours). No one has read or could read Celan
more rigorously or resolutely than Szondi, but it has taken Steiner's
counsel to convince us that the task is not so much to decipher and
explain Celan's poems as to contextualize them historically, and that
means above all to understand ourselves in the light of Celan's history
and experience—not, to be sure, (just) his own subjective experience,
but the history that above all leads up to and away from the Holocaust.
In this event our task is not decipherment but acknowledgment ("Lies
nicht mehr—schau!" [*GW*, 1:197]).[25] This is the hardest reading of all,

namely self-exegesis, standing exposed *before* the text of Celan, occupying *its* present, transported by it, no longer trying to appropriate it as usual within our historically and morally indifferent analytical space.

In *Real Presences* Steiner speaks of the way texts happen to us, that is, intercept us and situate us in their company, taking us forever out of our way. How this comes about no one can say; there is no method for it—it is entirely outside the competence of literary criticism, that is, outside of our instrumental control. It is as if poetry could only speak to our weaknesses, our receptivity or exposure, rather than respond to our mastery and strength. "The text, the musical structure, the picture or form, fulfill, in what may be, almost literally, a spatial sense, awaitings, needs we knew not of. We had been expecting that which we may well not have known to be, and to be complementary to us. The shock of correspondence—it can be muted and nearly indiscernibly gradual—is one of being possessed by that which one comes to possess" (179). Steiner's example of being thus possessed by a text (read by it)—which is, historically, the most fundamental of hermeneutical experiences—is, not surprisingly, his encounter with the text of Celan: "It was between trains, in a Frankfurt station bookstall, that I picked up and leafed through, scarcely attentive, a very thin book of poems, the rather odd name of whose author had caught the corner of my eye. Almost the first line I skimmed across or towards spoke of a language to be composed 'north of the future.' I do not now recall whether I caught the intended train, but Paul Celan never left me" (180).

und zuweilen, wenn
nur das Nichts zwischen uns stand, fanden
wir ganz zueinander.   (*GW*, 1:217)[26]

Notes

I am grateful to John Matthias for his many suggestions for this essay, as well as to Krzysztof Ziarek for allowing me to read his unpublished manuscript "The Ethical Direction in Celan's Poetry."

Epigraph: *Gesammelte Werke*, 5 vols. (Frankfurt am Main: Suhrkamp, 1983), 1:285. References to Celan's writings will be to this edition, cited as *GW*. For an English translation, see *Poems of Paul Celan*, trans. Michael Hamburger (New York: Persea Books, 1988), 219:

what is it called, your country
behind the mountain, behind the year?

I know what it's called.
Like the winter's tale, it is called,
it's called like the summer's tale,
your mother's threeyearland, that's what it was,
what it is,
it wanders off everywhere, like language.

1. See George Steiner, *After Babel: Aspects of Language and Translation* (New York: Oxford University Press, 1975), 48: "The fact that tens of thousands of different, mutually incomprehensible languages have been or are being spoken on our small planet is a graphic expression of the deeper-lying enigma of human individuality, of the bio-genetic and bio-social evidence that no two human beings are totally identical. The affair at Babel confirmed and externalized the never-ending task of the translator—it did not initiate it."

2. John Henderson, writing on Terence, remarks that "an educated Roman's Latin was in an important sense 'a good translation'" of Greek, meaning that the stylistic norms of classical Latin are determined by what counts as a good Latin translation from the Greek. See "Entertaining Arguments: Terence *Adelphoe*," in *Post-structuralist Classics*, ed. Andrew Benjamin (London: Routledge, 1988), 195.

3. George Steiner, *Real Presences* (Chicago: University of Chicago Press, 1989), 188.

4. Hence the basic principle of romantic hermeneutics: "To understand the text at first as well as and then even better than its author." See Friedrich Schleiermacher, *Hermeneutics: The Handwritten Manuscripts*, ed. Heinz Kimmerle and trans. James Duke and Jack Frostman (Missoula, Mont.: Scholars' Press, 1977), 112. This hermeneutical task requires that the interpreter resituate him or herself in the time and place of the text's composition; but it requires more—namely that "the interpreter transform himself . . . into the author" of the text (150).

5. *Radically* nonidentical languages would be those that had never come into contact with one another—the sort of alien condition stipulated in W. V. O. Quine's theory of radical translation in *Word and Object* (Cambridge: MIT Press, 1960). French, German, and English share a common history, not so much because they are each Indo-European as because they are the principal vernaculars in which cultural modernity established itself.

6. Jurgen Habermas, "Philosophy as Stand-In and Interpreter," in *Moral Consciousness and Communicative Action*, trans. Christian Lenhardt and Shierry Weber Nicholsen (Cambridge: MIT Press, 1990), 17.

7. Michel Foucault, *The Order of Things* (New York: Random House, 1970), 300.

8. See George Steiner, "On Difficulty," in *On Difficulty and Other Essays*

(New York: Oxford University Press, 1978), 40–47. In *Real Presences* Steiner characterizes this condition in terms of a "broken contract" between language and the world, where contract is to be understood less in social and conventional terms than in the biblical sense of covenant, that is, a foundational bond that, once broken, brings the order of the intelligibility as such crashing down (92–93). Cf. Gerald L. Bruns, *Modern Poetry and the Idea of Language: A Critical and Historical Study* (New Haven: Yale University Press, 1974).

9. Martin Heidegger, "Des Ursprung des Kunstwerkes" (1935–36), in *Holzwege* (1977), vol. 5 of *Gesamtausgabe*, 63 vols. (Frankfurt am Main: Vittorio Klostermann, 1976–91), 1–74; and Martin Heidegger, *Poetry, Language, Thought*, trans. Albert Hofstadter (New York: Harper and Row, 1971), 15–87.

10. John McCumber speaks of the relation of earth and world as a relation of "presignificance," as opposed to a "context of significance" opened up by the work of art. See *Poetic Interaction: Language, Freedom, Reason* (Chicago: University of Chicago Press, 1989), 128–42.

11. The English text at this point misprints "stronger" for "stranger."

12. Maurice Blanchot, *L'espace littéraire* (Paris: Gallimard, 1955), 303; trans. Ann Smock as *The Space of Literature* (Lincoln: University of Nebraska Press, 1982), 228.

13. Heidegger, *Holzwege*, 279; and Heidegger, *Poetry, Language, Thought*, 101.

14. See Emmanuel Levinas, *Autrement qu'être ou au delà de l'essence* (Le Hague: Martinus Nijhoff, 1974).

15. Philipe Lacoue-Labarthe, *La poésie comme expérience* (Paris: Christian Bourgois, 1986). Cf. "Hölderlin et les grecs," *Poetique* 40 (1979): 465–74.

16. See Steiner, *After Babel*, 182–84; and Steiner, *On Difficulty*, 44–45. See Celan, "Der Meridian," in *GW*, 3:197.

17. Michael Hamburger translates as follows:

World to be stuttered by heart
in which
I shall have been a guest, a name
sweated down from the wall
a wound licks up.
      (*Poems of Paul Celan*, 325)

18. For an English translation, see *Paul Celan: Last Poems*, trans. Katharine Washburn and Margret Guillemin (San Francisco: North Point Press, 1986), 119:

To speak with blind alleys
about the face-to-face,

about its
expatriate
meaning—:

to chew
this bread, with
writing teeth.

19. Jacques Derrida, *Ulysse gramophone: Deux mots pour Joyce* (Paris: Éditions Galilée, 1987), 28. See also Hans-Georg Gadamer, *Wer bin Ich und wer bist Du? ein Kommentar zu Paul Celans Gedichtfolge "Atemkristall"* (Frankfurt am Main: Suhrkamp, 1986), 10.

20. See Jacques Derrida, *Schibboleth* (Paris: Galilée, 1986).

21. Michael Hamburger translates as follows:

Etched away from
the ray-shot of your language
the garish talk of rubbed-
off experience—the hundred-
tongued pseudo-
poem, the noem.

Whirled
clear,
free
your way through the human-
shaped snow,
the penitents' snow, to
the hospitable
glacier rooms and tables.

Deep
in Time's crevasse
by
the alveolate ice
waits, a crystal of breath,
your irreversible witness.
    (*Poems of Paul Celan*, 231)

22. See Gerhard Buhr, "Über Paul Celans Gedicht 'Weggebeizt,'" in *Celan-Jahrbuch* (Heidelberg: Carl Winter, 1987), 9–56.

23. Celan, "Der Meridian," in *GW*, 3:197; and Paul Celan, *Collected Prose*, trans. Rosemarie Waldrop (Manchester: Carcanet Press, 1986), 49.

24. See Peter Szondi, "Lecture de 'Strette,' essai sur la poésie de Paul Celan," *Critique* 27 (May 1971): 378–92; an English version is available as "Read-

ing 'Engführung': An Essay on the Poetry of Paul Celan," trans. D. Caldwell and S. Esh, *boundary 2*, 11, no. 3 (Spring 1983): 231–64.

25. Stanley Cavell calls such reading "being read," because the intelligibility of the text derives from our exposure to it. See "The Politics of Interpretation (Politics as Opposed to What?)," in *Themes out of School: Effects and Causes* (San Francisco: North Point Press, 1984), 51–53.

26. Michael Hamburger translates:

and at times when
only the void stood between us we got
all the way to each other.
　　　　　　(*Poems of Paul Celan*, 159)

The Mind of a Critical Moralist:
Steiner as Jew

J E W I S H   T H I N K E R S think about the Holocaust. They think about it all the time. When thought shifts its venue so thinking centers on other issues, it still remains a thinking of the Holocaust in the manner of not thinking it. Those who refuse to privilege the Holocaust because it might threaten the positive value of traditional learning still ponder how they might have transmitted Torah in secret in the camps and ghettos of Eastern Europe. Epistemological reference point and moral obsession, Holocaust thinking is concerned neither with matters of fact nor with the relations of ideas, but is instead a kind of perpetual moral wakefulness, a cogitating of new scales for calibrating quanta of evil. George Steiner's work is in this vein: a Holocaust hermeneutics of language and culture.

Does the ubiquity of the Holocaust in Jewish thinking not vitiate all hermeneutical projects? Is a hermeneutics of culture possible after the Holocaust? If culture has been emptied of all meaning and value, the Eleatic principle, whatever is not can neither be thought nor spoken about, would seem to hold. An event of ultimate negation leaves nothing worth remembering or interpreting, not even the event of negation itself. But, if a hermeneutics of culture is possible, then thought is the master of the Holocaust, and its existence as sheer nihilation is sublated.

For those who choose the first alternative and interpret the Holocaust as sheer nullity, as ontological abyss, reason must be demolished, and either total silence or antisystem must replace systematic philosophy. Thus Theodor Adorno argues that if thinking "is to be true today . . . it must also be a thinking against itself. If thought is not measured by the extremity that eludes the concept, it is from the outset in the nature of the musical accompaniment with which the SS liked to drown out the screams of its victims."[1] Steiner's analyses of language and culture are efforts to avoid the extreme of nihilism on the one hand and the subjection of the Holocaust to the norms of categorical thinking which the Holocaust has itself made suspect on the other.

Two questions inform Steiner's hermeneutics: What must thinking be if it is to remain heedful of itself as inseparable from the Holocaust? What is the result of such heedful thinking when it is attentive to the artifacts of culture? For Steiner, to think is to interpret, and to interpret is to translate, not only from one language to another but from one temporal framework to another. "The French word *interprète* concentrates all the relevant values. . . . *Interprète/interpreter* are commonly used to mean *translator*."[2] One who explicates the meaning of a poem, a musical composition, a painting, is no less embarked on translation than one who renders a text from Finnish to French, for both are engaged in semiotic transposition. *"Inside or between languages, human communication equals translation"* (AB, 47).

As for the event of the Holocaust—Steiner prefers *Whirlwind* because *Holocaust* means ceremonial sacrifice (R, 14)—what linguistic matrix could provide *le mot juste* that would express sheer annihilation? Steiner argues that Christian imagery, with its graphic depiction of hell, is the language of reference, the source language that, with the loss of transcendence, is translated in wildly parodic form, into the receptor language of actual existence: "Needing hell we have learned how to build and run it on earth" (BC, 55). I believe Steiner's formulation can itself be translated into the older literary-critical language of T. S. Eliot: the Holocaust is the "objective correlative" of a lost transcendence.

Steiner is interested not only in the theological antecedents of the Holocaust but also in how it regiments the reading of the Western cultural past. If, as Steiner believes, the psychological stage for the

Holocaust is set by "the brain-hammering strangeness . . . of the monotheistic idea" (37), then this idea must be brought to light in all its protean manifestations, including the amorphous literary genres of modernity and postmodernity. Steiner is not proposing a naïve didacticism, a moral decoding of literature, nor is he attributing biblical theological constructs to the Hellenic literature that developed independently of them. Instead, a discursive space is opened in which the relation of literature to ethics in what he calls a postculture may be considered. Thus, far from envisioning a simplistic renewal of ancient values, Steiner is attentive to thinkers who exhibit the epistemic conditions for the breakdown of earlier idealities, as well as to the literary and philosophical texts in which these idealities are first articulated. Steiner scans the history of culture by remaining attentive to the tracks of transcendence and the efforts to eradicate them which, often enough, erupt in violent acts of semiotic transposition. His style is one of cascading metaphor and rhapsodic intensity, and the lineage of texts is as meticulously enumerated in his work as the chains of begettings in the book of Genesis.

In *Real Presences* there is a marked radicalization of his affirmation of transcendence. Meaning as articulated in cognitive language or artistic expression is validated by the assumption of the presence of God or by the felt presence of his absence even when translated into the *cri de coeur* of a contemporary postculture. Steiner reads texts through the nearly illegible spoors of transcendence that are their accompanying or countertexts and does so because the Holocaust, like no previous historical event, attests the pressure of a divine self-withholding. I shall argue that this semantic transposition, this reading of text with and through its countertext in both his early and later work, constitutes a Jewish hermeneutics of Western culture.

Although Steiner does not discuss the matter, the contrast between a conceptual language that is quintessentially Jewish, "the Jewish word," and the languages of the world is a recurrent theme in nineteenth-century Jewish literature from the pale of settlement. The Judaization of the outsider's language entails its ethical and religious transformation through an *ascesis* that involves acquaintance with Torah and Jewish suffering. For example, a Yiddish language poem, "The Alien Word," describes the pilgrimage of the personified figure of a strange language who "come[s] from the broad / field that sits on the world," and "from the crooked stone / [whose] water is like the clean heaven,"[3] to enlist the transformative powers of the founder of Hasidism, the Baal Shem Tov, Master of the Holy Name:

Before the thought of the Baal Shem Tov
Transfixed, oft stood
A word, alien,
And humbly small. . . .

"Hush, won't you? What do you want?"
He was asked by the Besht . . . .

"I want to become
An Israelite word"[4]

The alien word must learn the "alphabet" and "cantillation." It must also acquire the power of Torah interpretation and reexperience the woes of Israel until at last

. . . . the Besht sees
an Israelite crease

On the narrow brow
of the alien word.
Well-pleased
he stroked his beard

And he did bless him.[5]

Steiner's thought often Judaizes in something like the sense ascribed to the term in the verses cited, not because it exhibits great familiarity and commerce with traditional rabbinic sources, but because for him the Judaizition of culture is culture's passing through the prism of moral self-questioning. It can be so construed by virtue of two criteria proposed by the late Steven S. Schwarzschild: first, "the primacy of Practical Reason," the idea that human beings are moral agents before they are cognitive subjects and that logic, epistemology, and metaphysics are therefore the instruments of ethics; and second, the transcendence of the rational, the hypothesis that the ideal cannot be realized in the world of phenomena and "that everything in the world is fallible and subject to critique."[6] Thus for Steiner tragedy is concerned with the blind working of fate alien to the Judaic sense of the world. By contrast, "the Judaic spirit [exemplified in Job] is vehement in its conviction that the order of the universe and of man's estate is accessible to reason" (*DT*, 4).

In what follows, I first describe Steiner's perception of Judaism by examining the autobiographical statements in his writings, as well as his critical stance toward several modes of contemporary Jewish existence, religious orthodoxy, and Zionism. Next, I focus on the way in which the Holocaust affects his approach to literary texts. In so doing, I consider the problem of translation as a dialogical relation between what is to be interpreted (literary text, music, and the like) and the language of present-day reception of the text. Crucial to my argument is the contention that there is an accompanying countertext that shapes the discourse of the critic, the presence/absence of transcendence in the age of the Holocaust. In this connection, I discuss the role of silence in contemporary hermeneutics, "the failure of the word in the face of the inhuman" (*LS*, 51). Finally, I develop the idea of what I call a biblical hermeneutical mytheme that I define as a biblical story—building the tower of Babel, Jacob wrestling with the angel, stories of Moses and Aaron, and the like—that is not the *subject* of interpretation, but its instrument. I give to the term *mytheme* something of the meaning it has in Claude Lévi-Strauss, a malleable "element halfway between a percept and a concept."[7] In my usage, however, mythemes are not atomic simples, but complex narratives, which Steiner uses to bring to the fore the workings of cultural processes and the meanings of texts. I argue, too, that this use of biblical stories is an expression of Steiner's Jewishness, which enters the fabric of his work.

The Jew of Central Europe

If the Holocaust is to inscribe itself into interpretation, the interpreter must become a passageway for its annihilating power in the sense intended by Eckhardt when he speaks of self-emptying to create a space for the Holy Spirit, or in the sense of Heidegger when he thinks of the poet as the passageway for language. Yet, for Heidegger, not everyone can become the instrument of language. The poet is especially receptive to the meaningfulness and musicality of language and, in the present age, to the absence of the gods. Just as the poet is steeped in language, the critic who is to translate/interpret Western culture must be immersed in it; speak its principal tongues, French, English, and German; understand the interrelationships of its multiple literatures —their roots in Hellenism and Hebraism, the Roman world, and Latin Christendom—and, when possible, grasp the symbolism and local lore of Europe's regional subcultures. Through the accident of birth and rigorous self-shaping, Steiner has acquired these requisites.

This understanding is not the result of an inborn gift, but of the formative influences, the polishing effect of *Bildung*, an untranslatable term for the process of civilizing natural man through educating him in matters of manners and morals, as well as shaping his cultural literacy as it was defined in late nineteenth- and early twentieth-century Germany. Although Steiner is not of German Jewish descent—his father was born in Prague, and his mother's ancestry was probably Galician—central European Jewry was bound through language and culture to this ideal. The *Bildungsroman* of a somewhat earlier period combines the goals of Greek *paideia* and of the *Wanderjahre* as appropriated by German Romanticism into a single narrative of youth and was standard fare in the homes of German-speaking Jews. (Women were *erzogen*, "bred"; they may have been *gebildet*, "learned," but, if so, they were likely to have been thought bluestockings.) Wilhelm von Humboldt thought of *Bildung* as harmonizing intellect and morality. Greek thought and language were seen to refine sensibilities so that practical reason, in harmony with classical norms, could transcend national differences and overcome man's sensual nature.[8] Wary of *Bildung* because of its failure in shaping the morality of German national consciousness, Steiner is nevertheless its beneficiary.

Steiner himself was born in Paris and raised in both Paris and New York and thus is a generation removed from the *Bildung* ideal, which is still likely to have informed the ethos of his parental home. He recalls, somewhat nostalgically, a polyglot childhood in which he spoke English, French, and German concurrently and with equal facility. All, he writes, are "perfectly equivalent centres of myself" (*AB*, 115). If the idea of *Bildung* permeates German and central European Jewish life, the line of access to literary culture is skewed differently for central European Jews: "Strong particles of Czech and Austrian-Yiddish continued active in my father's idiom. And beyond these," Steiner avers, "like a familiar echo of a voice just out of hearing, lay Hebrew" (116). This "polyglot matrix" stamped his personal identity, "the formidably complex, resourceful cast of feeling of Central European and Judaic humanism" (116). It is Judaic humanism in a post-Holocaust version that guides Steiner's critical vision.

Steiner is thoroughly familiar with Heidegger's critique of humanism in the latter's *Letter on Humanism*. There Heidegger claims that, with its stress upon rationality as the essence of the human, humanism is parasitic upon a metaphysical conception of man and, as such, precludes a receptiveness to Being. In his book on Heidegger, Steiner shows that for Heidegger "the issue is . . . the *Seinsfrage*, . . . the gradual coming nearer to man of 'Being' and questioning" (*MH*, 54). Unlike Heidegger, for Steiner humanism is bound up with the study of the canonical literary texts of the West insofar as they deal with the image of humanity and with human conduct. But humanistic learning has not become humane culture, has not served as a buffer against the reality of the concentration camps. "Before we can go on teaching we must surely ask ourselves: are the humanities humane and, if so, why did they fail before the night?" (*LS*, 66).

One reason Steiner offers for the failure of the tradition is the gap between university culture and historical actuality, the abstractness of the written text and the concreteness of real events. With the focus of consciousness upon texts, a psychological investment in the imaginary may diminish rather than enhance moral acuity in the real world of affairs. To the extent that we are absorbed by the fictive creations of imagination, "the death in the novel may move us more potently than the death in the next room" (61).

A second reason is the all too ready acceptance of what Steiner calls the myth of "the garden of imagined literary culture," an idealized depiction of Western civilization that developed between the 1820s and 1915 (*BC*, 5). Steiner's description of it reads like a bill of lading enumerating English and German Enlightenment values: a high level of literacy, a society ruled by law, a reaping of the benefits of science. But this myth of present comfort and future promise concealed a substructure of poverty, class distinction, and the exploitation of underdeveloped countries (7). Steiner does not apply this analysis to the internal structure of the Jewish communities of Europe. Gershom Scholem, however, writes bitterly of German Jewry's acceptance of a comparable image of progress. Jews bought the myth of advancement and integration into middle-class society, Scholem contends, without recognizing its exclusionary character. Because of their intellectual heritage, post-Enlightenment German Jews saw themselves as fitting snugly into German intellectual life, but the short-lived "love affair of the Jews and the Germans remained one-sided and unreciprocated." For Scholem (although, as I shall show, not for Steiner) only a Jewish homeland could put an end to these false hopes.[9]

Reconquering the Future

If humanism fails as Steiner's perspicuous criticisms would seem to indicate, should the dead past not bury its dead? Is it not pointless to collect the ashes of a defunct civilization? Or are there within that civilization embers that may still be fanned? Steiner responds that the sciences, and the languages of mathematics and logic, constitute "the 'forward dreams' which define us" (128). This may appear to be something of a tour de force in light of the woes that have come to be associated with the principal outcomes of scientific research: the development of ever more lethal weaponry and the destruction of the environment, points that Steiner concedes are by now commonplaces (135). But there are reasons for this hope quite apart from Steiner's admiration for what intelligence can produce.

To be sure, Steiner as polymath and *enfant terrible* embraces the sciences, as well as mathematics, out of sheer love for the "deep elegance, . . . quickness and merriment of the spirit" (*BC*, 129) that they exhibit. But, I would urge, there is something deeper in Steiner's enthusiasm for science and mathematics than an eros for the feats of intellect. A clue is to be found in several dilatory remarks in his writings on chess linking it to mathematics and music. It could be argued that Steiner's love for the game is a kind of fetishism reflecting a central European's passion for the game. But, for Steiner, even if mathematics, music, and chess are value-free in the sense of offering no moral prescriptions, they are freighted with moral meaning. To be sure, they do not in natural language or visual imagery body forth a view of the human, yet each in its unique fashion opens up a vision of infinitude. Thus, Steiner exults, there are more possible moves in a game of chess than, it is calculated, "the generally assumed sum of atoms in the universe" (*FF*, 54). This is compounded when the grand master plays numerous boards simultaneously (*E*, 56).[10] Mathematics, music, and chess at the highest reaches may be practically useless and morally neutral, but each, by virtue of its endless possible combinations of sounds or symbolic relations, marks off a potentially unending stream of time. Although Steiner does not carry the argument in this direction, Emmanuel Levinas asserts (with Descartes) that the infinite always exceeds any idea we can have of it and that, by going beyond the bounds of consciousness, the infinite's sheer excessiveness and uncontainability opens up the dimension of transcendence.[11] In the case of science the infinite is expressed as what lies ahead: for scientists, "their

evenings point self-evidently to tomorrow" (*BC*, 135). The importance of this shred of hope is obvious when one reflects that these
activities restore a sense of the future and that "genocide is the ultimate
crime because it pre-empts on the future" (*LS*, 164).

Is science then to replace the humanist tradition? If so, why does
Steiner continue to write unceasingly of Homer and the tragic spirit, of
Virgil and Dante, Shakespeare and Ben Jonson, Racine and Corneille,
Ibsen and Beckett? Does he support a version of Derrida's argument
that the old metaphors of philosophy and literary culture are like worn-
out coins, but that these metaphors are the only currency we have?[12]
Steiner's continuing attachment to Western culture is restrained by the
crucial caveat that our mode of reading be altered so as to ethicize,
to morally impassion, the process of interpretation. Kafka's injunction
is definitive for him. Steiner cites Kafka thus: "If the book we are reading does not wake us, as with a fist hammering on our skull, why
then do we read it . . . what we must have are those books which come
upon us like ill-fortune, and distress us deeply, like the death of one
we love better than ourselves, like suicide. A book must be an ice-axe
to break the sea frozen inside us" (67). "A neutral humanism," Steiner
contends, "is either a pedantic artifice or a prologue to the inhuman"
(66).

Thus far, I have argued that the Holocaust functions as a perpetual
placing in question of Western culture as a source of meaning and
value, but, despite this moral obligatto that accompanies the artifacts of
literary and visual culture, Steiner does not reject the aesthetic produc-
tions that the West has created. Instead, developing a double response,
he turns to what C. P. Snow calls the "other" culture, that of science
and mathematics (as well as to music and chess) as a reserve of value
because of their purchase upon the future. At the same time, he calls for
a new hermeneutics of culture that would break open our moral sensibilities, for Nietzsche's hammer and Kafka's ice-axe as interpretive
tools. I shall soon turn to what I think such a hermeneutic entails for
Steiner. At present it suffices to notice that—and in this he sees himself
in league with Israelite prophecy—Steiner exposes the growing gap
between the text and the existential claims it places upon the reader.

Zionism, Orthodoxy, and the "Jew of Culture"

To understand Steiner as Jew, it is important to examine his reasons
for rejecting two by now standard Jewish responses to the events of the

twentieth century, responses for which he is not without sympathy despite his harsh criticism of them: Zionism and Jewish orthodox practice in their post-Holocaust forms. In what is perhaps the most autobiographically revealing text concerned with these matters, "A Kind of Survivor," he argues that, crucial to his view of himself as Jew, is the "burden of ancient loathing" and "savagery" that he bequeaths to his children. Steiner argues that the orthodox believer looks at his children "not as hostages that bear the doom of his love, but in pride and rejoicing. . . . They are alive not because of a clerical oversight in a Gestapo office, but because they no less than the dead are part of God's truth" (141). What is more, Steiner sees himself as excluded from a communion based upon observance of the Law.

His summary account of orthodox piety ignores a fissuring of consciousness even in the most rigorously fundamentalist communities that both affirm transcendence and, no less than he, quake for their children. At the same time, Steiner misses the diversity and inflectedness of many of the theological responses of modern orthodoxy to the Holocaust. Although their abundance precludes anything more than summary mention of some principal positions, these allusions may suggest their range. [13] Emil Fackenheim, in what is by now a staple of inner Jewish dialectic, argues that traditional Judaism must be maintained in order not to grant Hitler a posthumous victory through a post-Holocaust surrender of Jewish faith. Michael Wyschogrod responds that, in the absence of living faith, the Holocaust constitutes no reason to continue Jewish life and practice. If Judaism is to remain alive, it must affirm its positive content despite the Holocaust. Irving Greenberg sees the covenant as having been traduced by the Holocaust, so the loss of religious observance is understandable, but he finds solace in the numerous defiant expressions of faith. Eugene Borowitz (a traditionally minded Reform theologian) argues that, if there is no transcendent criterion of holiness, then there is no standard by virtue of which Auschwitz can be judged evil. A central figure in shaping religious Zionism, Rabbi Abraham ha-Cohen Kook, sees in the eclectic spirit of both secular and religious Jewish thought a kernel of sanctity, an outgrowth of Kook's mystical doctrine that the souls of all Jews, despite their diversity, are holy. While Kook's Jewish ecumenicity is an exception in Jewish right-wing circles, his position allows for a positive attitude toward Steiner. Although Steiner's view of Jewish orthodoxy is sympathetic, if wistful and nostalgic, it nevertheless slides into dismissiveness without addressing orthodoxy's recent theological literature.

Steiner's rejection of Zionism as an option for himself is bound up with his general suspicion of nationalisms. Acknowledging the necessity of nationhood and self-defense, Steiner nevertheless maintains that "the nation-state bristling with arms is a bitter relic, an absurdity in the century of crowded men. And it is alien to some of the most radical, most humane elements in the Jewish spirit" (154). The essay in which this comment appears was written in 1965 and so antedates the crystallization of the issues that sparked the Peace Now movement in Israel, but his familiarity with Buber's work makes it more than likely that he was then aware of the Yihud group that supported a binational Jewish-Arab state founded by Judah Magnes and endorsed by Martin Buber and Ernst Simon. Unlike either of these groups, Steiner argues from the standpoint of a Diaspora Jew opposed to all nationalisms while endorsing the survival of a Jewish national state. There is no thought on his part of dissolving the state on the one hand, nor is it clear to him how a state is to survive without the accouterments of power and sovereignty on the other.

The mood of uneasiness with Zionism in the early work gives way to denunciation in the essay "Our Homeland, the Text," written twenty years later (1985). There Steiner does not criticize specific Israeli policies or actions, but thinks in terms of historical laws from which he derives, in quasi-deductive fashion, imagined historical outcomes of Jewish nationhood. First, for him all nationalisms—Zionism no less than others—must degenerate into violence, which can end in genocide. Thus he writes that "there is no singular vice in the practices of the State of Israel. These follow ineluctably on the simple institution of the modern nation-state, on the political-military necessities by which it exists with and against its nationalist competitors" (*HT*, 22). Second, along with violence, the displacement of peoples is simply a byproduct of nationalism from which Zionism is not exempt. Third, paradoxically Steiner shares with Zionism its ideal of post-Holocaust Jewish self-preservation. Employing what could be called an endangered-species argument, he contends that after the Holocaust the lives of Jews must not be concentrated in any one place because such close ingathering makes them vulnerable to extermination. What is more, in the long run it is a law of history that "nation[s] are laid waste" (21) and the best way to avoid this is to scatter. His final and for him most existentially compelling point is that, even if nations disappear, texts and their transmitters endure. The relation to texts is not a mere concession to survival, but the expression of Jewish greatness. The text is home; "each text rightly established and expounded . . . a homecoming of Judaism to itself and to its keeping of the books" (19).

It can be argued that Steiner's position is itself a species of Romanticism bound up with nineteenth-century notions of national greatness. To be sure, instead of economic and military strength, intellectual excellence and the willingness to produce and care for the treasures of culture now qualify a people for its place in the sun. Yet the ideal of national greatness persists. What is more, it is hard to see how the mission of rescuing culture squares with Steiner's critique of its previous failure to prevent the Holocaust. Nor is it easy to understand how there can be safety in dispersion when the Holocaust occurred in the widely scattered Jewish communities of Europe. Steiner's ultimate agendum is, I suspect, bound up with his understanding of what he believes to be the moral task of Jews: to remind humankind that the treasures of its collective memory must be judged in light of its excesses of bestiality and that so dangerous a job can only fall to its victim-priests, men and women who have been shaped by culture and who have also suffered its depredations.

In short, Steiner chooses to become what Phillip Rieff has called "a Jew of Culture," one who is the reverent caretaker of culture in a period of far-reaching social change.[14] His or her function is to fend off the barbarians at the gate by sustaining at least the memory of the authoritative interdicts that once governed Western societies. On this reading, the university, like the Talmudic academies at Sura and Pumbeditha, transmits the lessons of antiquity in a setting of relative isolation. In Steiner's terms, the Jew "is a cleric. . . . No other tradition or culture has ascribed a comparable aura to the conservation and transcription of texts" (17).[15] Like Luther's Christian, the lover of texts both rules and serves: as critic, such a one is master and judge of the text; as reader, she or he is placed at the text's disposal (R, 95).

Steiner, like Rieff, believes that Jews have a special talent for what has been called a hermeneutics of suspicion. "The long confinement of the Ghetto, the sharpening of wit and nervous insight against the whetstone of persecution, had accumulated large reserves of consciousness" (LS, 145) that enabled Jews to transfigure the content of Western thought. Steiner goes on to say: "That which has been destroyed . . . embodied a particular genius, a quality of intelligence and feeling which none of the major Jewish communities now surviving has preserved or recaptured. Because I feel that specific inheritance urgent in my own reflexes, in the work I try to do, I am a kind of survivor" (145).

This position is argued with varying nuances and different degrees of intensity by other Jewish critics of art and literature, including Lionel Trilling, Clement Greenberg, and, more recently, Harold Bloom, who writes that "many of us shape an inchoate and still heretical new Torah out of the writings of Freud, Kafka and Gershom Scholem."[16] The persistence of the Jew of culture in eastern Europe—Adam Michnik in Poland and George Conrad in Hungary—is astonishing in light of the minuscule numbers of Jews in those countries. Although he does not touch on Steiner's 1965 essay specifically, Gershom Scholem criticizes alienation as an existentially viable Jewish stance. The idea that Jews as alienated exemplify the human condition does not assure an appreciation of the Jewish contribution to culture on the part of a hostile world, Scholem asserts. Far from reflecting on the human lot generally, the state of homelessness remains for those who are truly rooted a term of opprobrium and serves only to sever the outsider's connection with his or her own traditions.[17] Scholem's argument successfully disposes of the view that, because estrangement contributes to the creation of culture and Jews are estranged, gratitude for their contributions will ameliorate their life circumstances. But Scholem slides over the issue of whether the culture to which the Jew contributes is worth saving. What is more, as I argued earlier, the *Bildung* that shapes Jewish scholarship (including Scholem's own) results in an indissoluble amalgam with non-Jewish elements that is often disingenuously described as purely Jewish thinking.

Ambiguity and a Holocaust Hermeneutic

Steiner's stationing himself alternately within each extreme of a pair of oppositions—central European and Jewish, for example—moving from horn to horn of some existential dilemma, and his refusal to resolve it by fixing upon an Artistotelean mean or midpoint, suggests that something like a hermeneutical tactic is at work. I hope to show that this tactic is one of carefully thought out, deliberate ambiguity. I shall argue that Heidegger's phenomenological description of ambiguity is the backdrop against which Steiner's appropriation of ambiguity must be grasped, and I shall discuss key instances of its use in the context of Steiner's Jewish concerns. Finally, I hope to suggest some lines of comparison between Steiner's view of culture and that of Jacques Derrida, an Algerian Jew, in which ambiguity plays a key role. Despite Steiner's fierce criticism of deconstruction in *Real Presences* on the grounds that deconstruction dissolves meaning into sheer textuality, his invoking of the Holocaust to call into question the artifacts of culture suggests closer affinities with Derrida than this later appraisal allows.

In *Being and Time*, Heidegger analyzes ambiguity—the German original, *Zweideutigkeit*, connotes not only undecidability but also doubleness and duplicity—in the context of the phenomenon of fallenness or the way in which *Dasein*, human Being, loses itself through absorption in social existence and the world of things. Fallenness is a state of bewitchment, a fascination that plunges *Dasein* into inauthentic existence, into anonymity, into the sphere of faceless others, into the they-self. The term is not to be understood as indicating a capitulation to sin or a descent from primordial purity, but as descriptive of *Dasein*'s situation as a being thrown into the world. Ambiguity is a manifestation of fallenness, which for Heidegger is "the impossibility to decide what is disclosed in genuine understanding and what is not."[18] In ambiguity nothing is concealed from the understanding. Ambiguity is simply the "uprooted" condition of *Dasein* in its everydayness, a *Dasein* that is "everywhere and nowhere."

Although Steiner does not discuss ambiguity specifically in his book about Heidegger, he takes up the issue of fallenness. Taking his cue from Heidegger's assertion that fallenness is something positive and not merely privative of some prior ontological fullness, Steiner asserts that "the 'positivity of fallenness' in Heidegger's analysis is an exact counterpart to the celebrated *felix culpa* paradox, to the doctrine which sees in Adam's 'happy fall' the necessary precondition for Christ's ministry and man's ultimate resurrection. Through the inauthenticity of its being-in-the world, *Dasein* is compelled to search out the authentic" (*MH*, 99). Like the fallenness of which it is an expression, ambiguity or *Zweideutigkeit* exposes the doubleness of human existence, a loss and return to self, which Steiner will transform into a tactic of textual interpretation.

Steiner interprets fallenness less as loss than as an opportunity for self-transcendence. The fallenness that belongs to everydayness (what Virginia Woolf called the dailyness of life) can be grasped authentically through care and solicitude, so that *Dasein* is brought face to face with itself. But, for Steiner, the doubleness of ambiguity, the back-and-forth movement of binary oppositions, occurs because interpretation cannot avoid dwelling upon the question that accompanies these oppositions. A Holocaust hermeneutics requires that texts justify themselves in the light of their actual or potential failure to create a conscience that would preclude, or at least protest, the extermination of peoples. Interpretation for Steiner is a kind of inquisition that bears down on texts with the force of Kafka's ice-axe. Thus Steiner writes that "a theory of culture, an analysis of our present circumstances, which do not have at their pivot a consideration of the modes of terror that brought on the death, through war, starvation, and deliberate massacre, of some seventy million human beings in Europe and Russia, between the start of the first World War and the end of the second, seem to me irresponsible" (*BC*, 30).

A hermeneutics of ambiguity, when maintained in its purity, can produce a result that runs directly counter to its intent. By stationing oneself within a moral extreme so repugnant as to appear to lack a point of opposition, the moral import of the analysis may be lost. Thus, one could ask, what would count as the lexical opposite of Nazi anti-Semitism? Philo-Semitism? Liberal democracy? I shall consider this problem in greater detail in connection with Hitler's speech in Steiner's novel *The Portage to San Cristóbal of A.H.* At present it suffices to notice that texts not only present philological, historical, and aesthetic problems but also disclose themselves to interpretation in their moral ambiguity.

The binary oppositions, the either/or that cultural artifacts present, are a major focus of Steiner's critical writings. Consider the tension of the terms *particularity* and *universality* as they are used in the context of the social and political philosophy of Steiner. For him they are not logical or epistemological categories, but freighted with moral meaning. For example, Marx, Trotsky, and Jewish Marxist intellectuals such as Georg Lukács and Ernst Bloch are thinkers who appeal to universal categories and utopian ideals that offset the destructive character of eastern European regional loyalties, whose divisiveness Steiner perceived long before the emergence of ethnic conflict in post-*perestroika* Europe. By contrast, as I suggested in connection with his remarks on Jewish nationhood, Steiner sees "nationalism [as] the venom of our age. . . . It drives the new states of Asia and Africa like crazed lemmings" (*LS*, 152). On the other hand, Steiner concedes, genocides are often directed against particular peoples when utopian ideals founder. Thus Stalin's terror was aimed against not only ideological enemies but also kulaks, Jews, and other ethnic groups.

There is little doubt that Steiner leans strongly toward a definition of humankind that would blur national distinctions. Yet his penchant for universalism does not preclude his conceding that particularism functions as a moral counterpoise to the excesses of universalist utopias. The tension of these opposites—what propels Steiner in one direction or another in a rebounding dialectic—is the potential of each for sparking the destruction of peoples. No hermeneutical perspective is exempt from the Holocaust question that makes ambiguous every interpretive stance and implicates the interpreter, at least potentially, in its conceptual opposite.

Steiner identifies Judaism as the intellectual root of the West's most profound moral expressions of universalism. Jews, he argues, invented monotheism, individual conscience, and messianism. With Freud, he posits a causal relationship between all three and the rise of modern anti-Semitism. "By killing the Jews, Western culture would eradicate those who had 'invented' God" and suppressed instinctual life (*BC*, 41). The demands of the Hebrew prophets for justice are incised into individual consciousness, where they suppress instinctual expression, as well as self-love. What is more, the message of atheistic socialism is an outgrowth of prophetic eschatological promise. Nothing is more akin to the prophetic quest for justice than the Socialist vision of the destruction of the bourgeoisie, he argues. In an impassioned passage, Steiner declares that "monotheism at Sinai, primitive Christianity, messianic socialism: these are the three supreme moments in which Western culture is presented with . . . 'the claims of the ideal.' These are the three stages, profoundly interrelated, through which Western consciousness is forced to experience the blackmail of transcendence" (44).

Yet it is Israel, a particular people, that is the recipient of punishment for having inflicted bad conscience upon the West. It is here that ambiguity is born: Steiner's Jew is Israel in its *Leibhaftigkeit*, its flesh and blood particularity, and at the same time an archetype of humankind as such. As Steiner describes him, the Jew is a taxonomical anomaly (in

Mary Douglas's language):[19] particular and universal, and as such bearer of a negative sacrality that has resulted in near extinction. Similar considerations govern Steiner's relation to literary texts. He extols the multilingual, transnational character of the writings of Borges, Beckett, and Nabokov, as well as modernist abstraction in literature and painting, as expressing a desirable universalism. Thus Nabokov is seen as "a great writer driven from language to language by social upheaval and war, . . . an apt symbol for the age of the refugee" (*E*, 11).[20] Yet Steiner acknowledges the impoverishment that results when myths that are time-bound and site-specific are lost or supplanted. To be sure, for him such specificity is generally tied to Greek or Latin sources that are shaped by the traditions of epic and pastoral poetry, but they are, for all that, the mythical "antecedents" that enable members of a society to achieve identity (*BC*, 3). Even Kafka—who is, for Steiner, the premier polyglot writer of our time— is enriched by the particularities of place, including "the Zlatá ulička, the Golden Lane of the Emperor's alchemists, and . . . the castle on Hradčany Hill," which Steiner associates with that of Kafka's *The Castle* (*LS*, 120). Steiner's preference for polyglot writers and his cavalier dismissal of what he calls "neoprimitive" non–Western cultural, literary, and artistic creations, should not obscure the role mythic sources play in his interpretive framework.[21] Without them, the classical world of Homer, Hesiod, Pindar, and Greek tragedy would disappear.

It can be argued against Steiner that in the realm of action the hermeneutics of ambiguity paralyzes choice. "The reader is one who (day and night) is absent from action" (*HT*, 5), he writes. It is astonishing that Steiner, who is so acutely aware of the failure of European intellectuals to take decisive steps against nazism and of the American intellectual's failure to speak out when the facts about the existence of concentration camps began to trickle in, does not address the problem raised by Sartre in *Les Mains Sales*, withdrawal from action because speculation by its very nature opens numerous seemingly equivalent moral options. Unable to select from among them, the intellectual seeks by fatuous argument to evade the world's work, just the outcome that Steiner seeks to avoid.

Another difficulty inherent in a hermeneutics of ambiguity is the possibility that one of the poles in a pair of oppositions is so repugnant that stationing oneself within it risks a certain rubbing off of its taint on the interpreter. Steiner incurs this danger when he analyzes Nazi racial theory and focuses on one of its assumptions, that the idea of a master race is parasitic on the biblical doctrine of election. Thus he writes that "the concept of a chosen people, of a nation exalted above others by particular destiny, was born in Israel. In the vocabulary of Nazism there were elements of a vengeful parody on the Judaic claim" (*LS*, 153). Steiner recycles this assertion in fictional form in *The Portage to San Cristóbal of A.H.*, but, as one reviewer suggests, in the mouth of Adolph Hitler, a central figure in the novel and rather favorably depicted, the contention, controversial even in the analytic writings, begins to acquire an eerie plausibility.[22] When Hitler pronounces oracularly, "To slaughter a city because of an idea, because of a vexation over words. Oh that was . . . a device to alter the human soul. Your invention. One Israel, one *Volk*, one leader" (*P*, 163), the parodic character of the words is obscured by their rhetorical force.

The risk Steiner takes in showcasing the Hitler speech is especially puzzling in the light of his own fierce criticism, in his essay on Louis Ferdinand Céline, of racist fiction that echoes the racist prose writings of an author (*E*, 39). Those who because of failed insight or deliberate bad faith want to rehabilitate the literary reputation of Céline overlook the moral spillover of his extreme bigotry, which, as Steiner contends, damages the aesthetic surface of his work. In this context Steiner reiterates one of his most compelling insights: the creation of beauty can be conjoined in a single sensibility with a sadistic politics. It is the task of the critic to bring this out and to return literature to its vocation. The innovative literary techniques of Céline do not exonerate the anti-Semitism of his fiction.[23]

If these arguments hold, why does Steiner highlight the perverse politics of Hitler? When Steiner is asked about the provocative character of the Hitler speech in an interview with D. J. R. Bruckner,[24] he responds that equal time has been granted to the "litany of suffering" spoken by the Nazi hunter Lieber. It is of course possible to interpret Lieber's words as a rebuttal of Hitler's arguments, but to do so is to grant these arguments a certain legitimacy, to presuppose conditions of debate in which all participants fall within the framework of recognizably moral discourse. Perhaps Steiner saw this when he added that Milton's Satan and Dostoevsky's Grand Inquisitor proffer no "real answers" because evil is imponderable. *Teku*, the name of one of the novel's characters and the Hebrew word for a query whose answer lies beyond human wisdom, suggests the imponderability of evil that haunts moral inquiry.

Like Richard Rorty, Steiner recognizes that there is no profit to be had in juxtaposing incommensurable discourses, in this case those of Hitler and the Nazi hunter Lieber. But, unlike Rorty, once it is conceded that the discourses have no common measure, Steiner would find it bizarre to conclude as Rorty does that Nazis are "folks just like us" who simply base their actions on a social consensus different from that of liberal democracies and that "lightening up" might help us to demystify the difference.[25] For Rorty, "human beings are centerless networks of beliefs and desires and their vocabularies and opinions are determined by historical circumstance,"[26] whereas Steiner holds that radical evil is incomprehensible. Still, Steiner appears to believe that we can, however obliquely, experience something of its imponderability when we give the position, however odious, its discursive space.

I proposed earlier that Steiner's work be examined in the context of other Jewish critics of culture. On the face of it, Steiner's predilection for the classical tradition suggests affinities with conservative Jewish figures such as Leo Strauss and Allan Bloom or the non-Jewish Eric Voegelin. Yet for none of these is a Holocaust-driven hermeneutics of ambiguity, in the sense in which I have described it, a feature of his work. Despite Steiner's harsh criticisms of deconstruction in *Real Presences*, the bulk of his critical writings, those informed by the problem of the Holocaust, exhibit affinities with Derrida's effort to expose the false consciousness of language and text. In fact, Steiner concedes, given its premises, "deconstruction does seem to me irrefutable" (*RP*, 132).

For Derrida ambiguity is inescapable and follows at least in part from his contention that texts conceal the law of their composition. Texts are duplicitous in the etymological sense, exhibiting a doubleness that goes all the way down. Thus they have no "true" meaning that can be brought into full presence. What cannot be made present (their mode of temporalization, the fact and manner of their dissimulation, in short the way in which they are fissured or differ from their supposed essences) is covered over by concepts such as unity, identity, and presence. Derrida does not wish simply to reverse the order of opposed philosophical concepts. For example, in considering the opposed terms *speech* and *writing*, philosophers since Plato have interpreted writing as ancillary to speech. But Derrida does not simply want to rehabilitate writing, but rather to show that language is always already writing-like (graphematic) even when spoken.[27] Although Derrida is generally interested in the esoteric properties of language, in tracking the spoors of its metaphysical presuppositions, in his "Otobiographies" he considers a word's potential for debasement, an ambiguity that is bound up with the future unfolding of the word's semiotic potential.[28] In a passage that could have been written by Steiner, Derrida comments on a text of Nietzsche that discusses the necessity for a guide or *Führer* to supplant democratic education: "Doubtless it would be naive and crude simply to extract the word 'Führer' . . . and let it resonate all by itself in its Hitlerian consonance, with the echo it received from the Nazi orchestration of the Nietzschean reference, as if the word had no other context. But it would be just as peremptory to deny that something . . . passes from the Nietzschean Führer, who is not merely a schoolmaster and master of doctrine, to the Hitlerian Führer."[29] Derrida goes on to say that philosophical language is unstable, so interpretation is inherently undecidable. For example, there are left and right Hegelians, Heideggerians, and Nietzscheans such that "the one can always be the other, the double of the other."[30]

In *Real Presences*, Steiner asserts that the understanding of language and the experience of meaning are "underwritten by the assumption of God's presence" (*RP*, 3). Thus, the perpetual question posed by the Holocaust is resolved by positing a divine center with which meaning and value are in accord. Nothing, it would seem, could be further removed from Derridean usage. Yet, even in his most manifestly theological work, Steiner is driven to posit a counterlogos to explain language's clouded doubleness, the speech that articulates the death camps, actualizes and "deconstructs the humane," and is not merely privative but a demonic positivity. Does not the counterlogos play the role of the Egyptian god Thoth in his guise as poisoner of language in Derrida's essay "Plato's Pharmacy"? Steiner's remark that deconstruction "ironizes into eloquence, the underlying nihilistic findings of literacy . . . as these *must* be stated and faced in the time of epilogue" (132) could well be applied to aspects of his own work.

Jewish Hermeneutical Mythemes

If Derrida's view of language focuses on writing, on the physical topos of the page, then the white spaces of writing must constitute a key feature of language. For Steiner, language is primarily utterance, and the *Urnatur* of language is silence: first, the silence that antedates speech, what there was before there was utterance; second, the circumambient silence of transcendence that surrounds and limits all language; and, finally, the silence of night, the Holocaustal silence of an absent Presence. Of the first silence, Steiner writes, "the human person has broken free from the great silence of matter" (*LS*, 36).

The second and third modes of silence are perceived and made sensuously present through the works of three central European Jewish figures: Franz Kafka, Hermann Broch, and Arnold Schoenberg. Not only do references to them abound, but the analyses of their works are conducted with unusual intensity, as if physically to ingest the core of their aesthetic and moral visions. Steiner writes:

Kafka used every word, in a language which he experienced as alien, as if he had purloined it from a secret, dwindling store and had to return it before morning intact. Hermann Broch . . . recognizes in the act of poetry, in a commitment to language, a blasphemy against life and the needs of man. One would also want to include the new uses of silence in the music of Schoenberg . . . and in particular the "failure of the word" which is the dramatic substance and climax of Schoenberg's *Moses and Aaron*. (*E*, 72)

Steiner sees the three as virtuosi of silence, and his effort to give an account of their work (and that of others who wrestle with silence) is mediated by biblical "hermeneutical mythemes" as I defined this term earlier: complex stories that are not the subject of interpretation, but interpretive instruments. Because they recur frequently in Steiner's work, I shall focus particularly on the tales of Babel, Jacob's wrestling with the angel, and the struggle between Moses and Aaron.

For Steiner the story of Babel is the controlling figure for hermeneutical activity itself. The salient features of the story from the standpoint of its interpretive function are the existence of a single language spoken by the whole earth, the effort of the people to build a city and a tower that would reach to the heavens in order to make a name for themselves, God's anger at their overweening ambition, their dispersion, and the multiplication of the earth's languages. The move from the Edenic transparency of a single language to manifold languages constitutes a primal act of humanization.[31] To be human is to translate, to reach for a semiotic equivalence across the phonic and lexical differences of numerous languages. The true genius of our age, on Steiner's account, is the genius of Babel, the polyglot writer who needs no visa to pass across the frontiers of several languages. Steiner is often quoted as saying that trees have roots and men have legs (*LS*, 152), implying that mobility in space and language, rather than static rootedness, is quintessentially human.

I noted earlier that there is, for Steiner, a prelapsarian silence and the deathly quiet of a postapocalyptic world, the world after Babel. This double silence is found in opposing predictions of the Kabbalah: that there would come a time when the pellucid language of divine speech would return, but also when words would cease to have any meaning, would "'become only themselves, and as dead stones in our mouths'" (*AB*, 474). Steiner reads Broch's *The Death of Virgil* as an envisagement of this final silence. The work centers on Virgil's decision to destroy the manuscript of the *Aeneid* because language can never be adequate to "human suffering and the advance of barbarism" (*LS*, 103). Thus the work is itself a chronicle about the failure of language in the face of humankind's anguish and pain. For Steiner, Kafka also lives at the edge of this silence, for even if "Kafka names all things anew," these acts of nomination take place "in a second Garden full of ash and doubt" (50). The stillness that succeeds the tumult of Babel is a fall deeper than the fall into multiple tongues from a single divine language.

Jacob's wrestling with the angel is the hermeneutical mytheme through which Steiner explicates the emergence of psychic individuation and artistic creation. To understand Steiner's view, it is important to notice that, in order to account for artistic creation, he does not introduce the myth of Prometheus, who breaches the chasm between heaven and earth with his theft of fire from the gods. Instead, Steiner turns to Jacob, who wrestles with an angel ("man" in the newer translations) throughout the course of a night, forces the angel to bless him, and receives the name Israel. Prometheus is hideously punished for his theft, but Jacob's striving with God and mortals goes unpunished. Steiner uses the Jacob story almost allegorically: to force the divine blessing from God is the equivalent of commandeering the poetic word. Thus Steiner can say of Kafka: "Overarching the whole Kafka enigma is the conflict between Judaic iconoclasm—the injunction that there can be only one true revealed body of writing—and the impulse to fiction, to rivalry with the Torah."[32] Grappling with the creator, seizing the transcendent word and exploiting it, is literary creation. Steiner's focus on the Moses story is bound up with Schoenberg's opera *Moses and Aaron*, so much so that Steiner's use of it is incomprehensible without attending to Schoenberg's reconfiguring of the biblical narrative. For Schoenberg, the same story is explicans and explicandum, both the opera's subject and the hermeneutical mytheme through which Steiner explicates his theory of fiction. I want to suggest, following Robert Alter, that the significance of the original biblical version of the story may be discovered in a *Leitwort*, a theme or motif revealed by a key word (or a synonym for it) that expresses and develops the meaning of the story.[33] It could be argued plausibly that the key word of the original biblical story is "obedience." But in Schoenberg's free rendering of the Moses tales, the key lexical items are the terms *image* and *idea*, which, for Steiner, will undergo a significant shift to become *speech* and *silence*.

Schoenberg's work, composed in the period 1930–32 and never completed, is a complex of interwoven musical, verbal, and theatrical elements that transcends the genre of opera. Act one distinguishes the role of Moses, the prophet in direct contact with God, from that of Aaron, the channel to the people of the divine word delivered by Moses. (Moses often speaks his lines, whereas Aaron sings his.) In the absence of empirical proof, the people reject the new God until Aaron performs concrete miracles and promises a land of milk and honey. Act two explicates the crisis of meaning instigated by Aaron's fashioning of the golden calf. An orgiastic display of sex and human sacrifice is the result of sacralizing a material thing. Horrified, Moses castigates Aaron for making an image out of an idea, but Aaron disdains the tablets of the Law as themselves images. This act ends with Moses' outcry: "O Wort, du Wort, das mir fehlt."[34]

One need not posit explicit borrowing in order to see that Schoenberg's interpretation exhibits the neo-Kantian mind set condensed in Hermann Cohen's oft-cited remark about the impossibility of loving anything but an idea. What Cohen meant is that the concept of monotheism is the highest expression of ideality and therefore the most worthy object of human love. For Cohen, if God were to become actual, he would acquire the properties of phenomenal existence, and thus, in the nature of the case, he can have no actuality.[35] This is the position that Schoenberg's Moses pits against the idolatry of the concrete.

Steiner can no longer adopt a straightforwardly neo-Kantian reading of the Moses cycle in light of the linguistic turn taken by contemporary philosophy. It is now increasingly difficult to speak of words as mirroring an antecedent reality. If words cannot refer straightforwardly to things, if a theory of truth that posits a positive relation of meaning and reference is suspect, then the crisis of meaning appears to be unsurpassable. For Steiner, the Moses cycle reveals the possibility that language is incapable of capturing signification and that therefore all language lies, or, more precisely, fabulates. "Golden-tongued" Aaron tolerates the lie of the golden calf, but for Moses, the stutterer, "no words are available with which to articulate the essential, the election to suffering that is history, and the real presence of God as it was signified to him in the tautology out of the Burning Bush. . . . Human saying lies" (*RP*, 112).

Far from lamenting the lie of language, Steiner finds in it the human opportunity to wrest, from the aporia between transcendence and words, the possibility of literary fiction. In everyday usage, to lie is to say that which is not. But, if we had only the capacity to express what is, all human existence would be an endless and mindless chain of positive iteration. Only by imagining what is not can we register dissent, protest against the world, and imagine counterworlds. Thus both ethics and literature depend upon our ability to express counterfactuality (*AB*, 217–18).[36] The lie that the Moses and Aaron story reveals differs from the "noble lie" told by the rulers of Plato's *Republic* in the interest of a higher truth in that the former is intrinsic to language itself. Nor is the lie that is subject to dialectical sublation the lie that Steiner discovers. Steiner's lie is the event that comes to pass when human artistry exercises a godlike prerogative by imagining worlds that are not. The field for counterfactual speculation is infinite, so writing and interpretation are infinite tasks in the Kantian sense.

Steiner's rejection of some standard expressions of Judaism (Zionism and religious orthodoxy) does not preclude his developing a Jewish hermeneutics of culture and texts. Jewish "rootless cosmopolitanism" is construed positively as the condition for a post-Holocaust Jewish central European humanism. Yet even positions that are endorsed may in the end be made ambiguous by the power of the Holocaust. What is more, Steiner invents a biblical hermeneutic in which narratives are hermeneutical instruments: Babel, a vehicle for grasping interpretation as translation; Jacob and the angel, a means for understanding individuation and artistic creation; Moses and Aaron, a way of seeing the relation of fiction to lying, counterfactuality, and negation.

Notes

1. Theodor Adorno, *Negative Dialectics*, trans. E. B. Ashton (New York: Continuum Publishing, 1973), 365.

2. George Steiner, *After Babel: Aspects of Language and Translation* (London: Oxford University Press, 1975), 27–28. Hereafter cited in the text as *AB*. Works by Steiner are abbreviated and cited in the text as follows: *The Death of Tragedy* (New York: Knopf, 1961). Cited as *DT*. *Language and Silence: Essays on Language, Literature, and the Inhuman* (New York: Atheneum, 1967). Cited as *LS*. *Extraterritorial: Papers on Literature and the Language Revolution* (New York: Atheneum, 1971). Cited as *E*. *In Bluebeard's Castle: Some Notes towards the Redefinition of Culture* (New Haven: Yale University Press, 1971). Cited as *BC*. *Fields of Force: Fischer and Spassky in Reykjavik* (New York: Viking Press, 1973). Cited as *FF*. *On Difficulty and Other Essays* (New York: Oxford University Press, 1978). *Martin Heidegger* (New York: Viking Press, 1978). Cited as *MH*. *The Portage to San Cristóbal of A.H.* (New York: Simon and Schuster, 1981). Cited as *P*. *George Steiner: A Reader* (New York: Oxford University Press, 1984). Cited as *R*. "Our Homeland, the Text," *Salmagundi* 66 (Winter-Spring 1985): 4–25. Cited as *HT*. *Real Presences* (Chicago: University of Chicago Press, 1989). Cited as *RP*.

3. This poem is found in Yiddish in J. I. Siegel, *Letzte Lieder* (Montreal: J. I. Siegel Foundation, 1955), 327. I am indebted to my student Mr. Harold Berman for calling my attention to it. The translation is mine.

4. Ibid.

5. Ibid.

6. Schwarzschild's position is explicated in Kenneth Seeskin, *Jewish Philosophy in a Secular Age* (New York: State University of New York Press, 1990), 4–5.

7. Claude Lévi-Strauss, *The Savage Mind* (Chicago: University of Chicago Press, 1966), 18.

8. See George Mosse, "Scholem as a German Jew," *Modern Judaism* 10, no. 2 (May 1990): 123. Mosse shows that the thought of Gerschom Scholem, whose works on Kabbalah and Hasidism are frequently cited by Steiner, was permeated by the concept despite Scholem's late repudiation of German national culture on the ground that Jews, contrary to their self-delusions, were excluded from it.

9. Gershom Scholem, "Jews and Germans," in *On Jews and Judaism in*

Crisis: Selected Essays (New York: Schocken Books, 1976), 86. The essay was first written as a lecture, "Juden and Deutsche," and delivered at the World Jewish Congress, Brussels, 2 August 1966. It was translated by Werner J. Dannhauser.

10. During the 1950s and 60s, Paul Wyschogrod, my father-in-law, a chess grand master and a student of the late nineteenth- and early twentieth-century Hungarian grand master Geza Maroczy, played as many as thirty boards blindfolded, often at the Rossolimo Chess Club frequented by Steiner (*E*, 56). But he frequently spoke of multiple board playing as mere flummery that impressed the crowd, insisting that the real challenge in chess was the encounter of two master players.

11. See Emmanuel Levinas, "Philosophy and the Idea of Infinity," in his *Collected Philosophical Papers*, trans. Alphonso Lingis (The Hague: Martinus Nijhoff, 1987), 47–60.

12. Jacques Derrida, "White Mythology: Metaphor in the Text of Philosophy," in *Margins of Philosophy*, trans. Alan Bass (Chicago: University of Chicago Press, 1982), 207–72.

13. Accounts of the theological positions I summarize can be found in Eugene Borowitz, *Choices in Modern Jewish Thought* (New York: Behrman House, 1983), 187–217; and Kenneth Seeskin, *Jewish Philosophy in a Secular Age* (Albany: State University of New York Press, 1990), 169–225. For a variety of positions on the Holocaust in Jewish theology in the 1970s, including those of Emil Fackenheim and Irving Greenberg, see *Auschwitz: Beginning of a New Era? Reflections on the Holocaust*, ed. Eva Fleischner (New York: K'tav Publishing, 1977). An assessment of Jewish theology in the last decade, including the role of the Holocaust, is in Kenneth Seeskin's "Jewish Philosophy in the 1980's," *Modern Judaism* 11, no. 1 (February 1991): 157–72.

14. See Philip Rieff, "'Fellow Teachers,'" *Salmagundi* 20 (Summer-Fall 1972): 5–85. There were numerous German Jewish "Jews of Culture" in New York City from the 1940s to the early 70s. Some, like Hannah Arendt, Ernst Cassirer, and Hans Jonas, entered mainstream American intellectual life. Others, who produced works of considerable sophistication, remain virtually unknown. Sigmund Krakauer, a Frankfurt School film critic, has only recently received serious attention in film circles. Hermann Broch, a novelist neglected in the English-speaking world, has begun to come into prominence, largely through Steiner's own efforts. Erich Gutkind, author of an important theological work, *The Body of God: First Steps towards an Anti-Theology* (New York: Horizon Press, 1969), tends to be remembered as a footnote in Scholem's *On Jews and Judaism in Crisis*. Interactions between this circle and American Jewish intellectuals were sporadic. When Rieff speaks of "Jews of Culture" he appears to have in mind American Jews such as Lionel Trilling, Irving Howe, and himself, whereas Steiner thinks of the cultivated refugee

novelists, poets, and scholars who lived and died in obscurity.

15. In "A Challenge to Jewish Secularism," *Jewish Spectator* 55 (Summer 1990), Jonathan Sacks, Chief Rabbi of Britain, reproaches Steiner for extending the notion of Torah to include texts in general. Against Steiner, Sacks writes that if Jews found a homeland in the text, "it was not *a* but *the* text, the Torah, the written record of the Divine covenant. . . . The texts of the Greeks were to be studied. At worst they led to heresy. At best they were *bittul Torah*, a distraction from Torah-learning" (28). Sacks's criticism is suggested *in nuce* in his *Traditional Alternatives: Orthodoxy and the Future of the Jewish People* (London: Jews' College Publications, 1989), 238, 242, passim. One could infer from this that, in creating a reverence for texts, Judaism has succeeded too well. But Sacks overstates his case when he argues that Steiner's pantextuality divinizes all great texts. Although art is a wrestling with transcendence, this does not entail for Steiner a literal canonization of literary texts. To the contrary, Steiner questions their failure to prevent historical catastrophes. Eugene Borowitz's remarks in "A Soft Word to Writers," in his *How Can a Jew Speak of Faith Today?* (Philadelphia: Westminster Press, 1969), predate Sacks' criticism but remain suggestive: "If Jews want the intellectual in the community they must cherish him for what he is and let him be that. He must always be allowed his distance, judging, criticising, using his intelligence in a never-ending search for greater honesty and understanding" (155). I am most grateful to Nathan Scott, an editor of the present volume, for calling my attention to Sacks' article.

16. Harold Bloom, "The Pragmatics of Contemporary Jewish Culture," in *Post-Analytic Philosophy*, ed. John Rajchman and Cornel West (New York: Columbia University Press, 1985), 126. Something of this sacralization occurs in Thomas J. J. Altizer's interpretation of Western literary history as a sequence of episodes in a progressively expanding Christian and post-Christian canon. Thus in *Genesis and Apocalypse: A Theological Voyage towards Authentic Christianity* (Louisville, Ky.: Westminster/John Knox Press, 1990), he writes: "Apocalyptic faith . . . has been renewed . . . in each of the great revolutionary transformations of Christian or Western history, as reflected not only in the epic poetry of Dante and Milton, but also . . . in the vision of Blake" (9).

17. Scholem, "Jews and Germans," 82.

18. Martin Heidegger, *Being and Time*, trans. John Macquarrie and Edward Robinson (New York: Harper and Row, 1962), 217.

19. Mary Douglas, in *Purity and Danger: An Analysis of Concepts of Pollution and Taboo* (Harmondsworth: Penguin Books, 1970), discusses the fear of liminal or borderline forms of life in nonliterate societies.

20. In a review of Brian Boyd's biography of Nabokov in the *New Yorker*, 10 December 1990, Steiner surfaces some reservations: "There is compassion in Nabokov, but it is far outweighed by lofty or morose disdain" (157).

21. Despite the range of his erudition with regard to Western texts, it is possible that Steiner's knowledge of non-Western cultures, especially South Asian, pre-Colombian, and African ones, is limited. It is otherwise difficult to account for such remarks as "it is a truism or ought to be that the world of Plato is not that of the shamans . . . that the inventions of Mozart reach beyond drumtaps and Javanese bells" (*LS*, 120).

22. See Morris Dickstein's account of *The Portage to San Cristóbal of A.H.* in the *New York Times Book Review*, 2 May 1982, 13, 21. Robert M. Adams, in his review of the same work in the *New York Review of Books* 29 (12 August 1982): 11, argues that romanticizing such arguments is wrong and, in this case, an attention-getting device. Bernard Bergonzi, writing in the *Times Literary Supplement*, 12 June 1981, states that, although it risks antagonizing certain Jewish readers, he finds it "a fiction of . . . power and thoughtfulness" (680). Robert Boyers, "Steiner's Holocaust: Politics and Theology," *Salmagundi* 66 (Winter-Spring 1985): 26–49, defends Steiner's Hitler portrait, arguing that negative criticism results from forgetting its fictional character, whereas Hyam Macoby, "George Steiner's 'Hitler,'" *Encounter* 58, no. 5 (May 1982): 27–34, sees it as unjustifiable propaganda.

23. In my *Saints and Postmodernism* (Chicago: University of Chicago Press, 1990), 249–51, I argue that Julia Kristeva's writings on Céline exhibit a doubleness, an expression of abhorrence, but also a willingness to speak the transgressive words through the mouth of another, which Steiner excoriates in other recent efforts to rehabilitate Céline.

24. D. J. R. Bruckner, "Talk with George Steiner," *New York Times Book Review*, 2 May 1982, 13, 20.

25. The gist of Rorty's remarks and the phrases cited were contained in his talk at Queens College of the City University of New York, April 1991, and my recollection of them is confirmed by several colleagues who were present.

26. Richard Rorty, *Objectivity, Relativism, and Truth*, Philosophical Papers, vol. 1 (Cambridge: Cambridge University Press, 1991), 191.

27. For an analysis of the secondary status of writing, see Jacques Derrida, "Plato's Pharmacy," in *Dissemination*, trans. Barbara Johnson (Chicago: University of Chicago Press, 1981), 63–171.

28. See Jacques Derrida, *The Ear of the Other: Octobiography, Transference, Translation*, trans. Peggy Kamuf (Lincoln: University of Nebraska Press, 1988), 1–40. "Otobiographies" is translated by Avital Ronell.

29. Ibid., 28.

30. Ibid., 32.

31. See Walter Benjamin, "The Task of the Translator," in *Illuminations*, trans. Harry Zohn (New York: Schocken Books, 1969). Benjamin, whose view of translation strongly influences Steiner, argues that "where a text is identical with truth or dogma," it is "unconditionally translatable." In that

sense "the interlinear version of the Scriptures is the prototype or ideal of all translation" (82).

32. George Steiner, in his review of a biography of Kafka by Pietro Citati: "Man of Letter," *New Yorker,* 28 May 1990, 109.

33. Robert Alter, *The Art of Biblical Narrative* (New York: Basic Books, 1981), 180. Geoffrey H. Hartman, in considering the story of Jacob and the angel, makes a similar point about a leitmotif that for him extends through the story's chain of interpretations. In his "The Struggle for the Text," in *Midrash and Literature,* ed. Geoffrey H. Hartman and Sanford Budick (New Haven: Yale University Press, 1986), he argues that although "we cannot define Scripture . . . we have redefined fiction in the light of Scripture" (12).

34. Steiner notes how rarely the opera has been produced (*LS*, 130). The extraordinary Hans Neugebauer production at the New York City Opera on 6 October 1990 was its long-awaited New York stage debut.

35. See my "The Moral Self: Emmanuel Levinas and Hermann Cohen," in *Daat: A Journal of Jewish Philosophy and Kabbalah* (Winter 1990): 41.

36. For an account of possibility and counterfactuality as the space of fiction and ethics, see my *Saints and Postmodernism,* 52–58.

Heidegger in Steiner

"THE PERTINENT CATEGORIES of inference and felt intelligibility are theological and metaphysical. But they inhere in language."[1] So Steiner writes, in a recent book, affirming and celebrating a logocentrism, a commitment to the onto-theological mystery of language, which has characterized his work from its inception. He continues, significantly for this essay: "My case can only be made if I can render plausible a view of language and of meaning, of the limits of language in regard to certain orders of meaning, which differs from the views now most generally held and practised" (ibid). Heidegger's influence (and to some extent Walter Benjamin's) bears mostly upon Steiner's pressing desire to "render plausible a view of language and of meaning." Gradually, as his reading of Heidegger has deepened, Steiner's hermeneutical position has changed and, as a consequence, clearer articulations of his engagement with the meaningful, of the sacrament of reading, have emerged.

This essay shall explore Heidegger's influence on Steiner's hermeneutics. It shall do so by examining what I discern to be four distinctive "periods" of Steiner's *ouevre*—his pre-Heideggerian hermeneutic, his early encounter with Heidegger's work, his interpretation of

Heidegger, and, finally, what he would call his "ingestion" of Heidegger in recent years, which has led to even more ambitious orchestrations of themes that have long dominated his work.[2]

Steiner's Pre-Heideggerian Hermeneutic

In the beginning Steiner expended much intellectual energy defining his hermeneutical position. The opening section of his first book, *Tolstoy or Dostoevsky: An Essay in the Old Criticism*, is devoted to methodology. In its wake, in a wave of articles in the early 1960s, Steiner distinguished the best of Marxist critics (Lukács, Adorno, Benjamin) from the Leninist *Tendenzpoesie*, and he embraced the Romanticism of individual genius, the importance of education, and the centrality of the classical tradition as promoted by such critics as F. R. Leavis in England and R. P. Blackmur in the States. Steiner's explicit apologia for the "old criticism" involved the uneasy welding of two modes of thought—the liberal (and philological) with the "para-Marxist" (and dialectical). We need to examine this uneasy welding more closely, for its presence is felt throughout Steiner's work, and it accounts not only for the distinctiveness of his cultural criticism but also for his penchant for paradox.

The liberal dream—of humanism, rationalism, literacy, and the political commitment to what Leibniz termed "un instinct général de societé"—has always been dizzy with nostalgia, because it balanced on the shoulders of tradition. It looked back, in its appeal to *auctoritas*, and affirmed as necessary the interrelationship of social élitism, philosophical universalism, and the cultured (*gebildet*) consciousness. Historically, its final *mise en scène* was the Weimar Republic, with Ernst Cassirer as its philosophical impresario. Its anthropological optimism was founded upon a faith in education and human perfectability. But its optimism began to wane, "sometime around 1890," according to Fritz K. Ringer.[3] It became increasingly tempered by a sense of declining values, a sense of a certain entropy. Finally, there was *Krisis*, in the wake of World War I, and the emergence of a critique of liberalism (that was still governed by the values implicit in liberal thinking). The work of Adorno, Horkheimer, and Benjamin gave unforgettable form to the sense of writing in a time of epilogue. Steiner sums up what these critics share:

The belief that literature is centrally conditioned by historical, social and economic forces; the conviction that ideological content and the articulate world-view of a writer are crucially engaged in the act of literary judgement; a suspicion of any aesthetic doctrine which places major stress on the irrational elements in poetic creation and on the demands of "pure form." Finally, they share a bias towards dialectical proceedings in argument.[4]

We can see from Steiner's summary how, in his campaign against the New Criticism, Steiner might find an arsenal in the work of the Frankfurt School. But his plea for the "old criticism" could also be undermined by "dialectical proceedings," aiming, as Adorno suggested, at a "consciousness which does not succumb in advance to the fetishization of the intellectual sphere. Dialectics means intransigence towards all reification."[5] As one scholar has succinctly put this, Adorno's goal was critical enlightenment through "the dialectical negation of idealism."[6] The Frankfurt School's understanding of dialectics couples liberal nostalgia with a reactionary, demythologizing fervor. Humane literacy and negative dialectics sit uneasily together, and the syntax of their coexistence is paradox. The Frankfurt School method of critique foregrounded the either/or.

Steiner, who said himself that his writings were "a kind of epilogue" to the Frankfurt School of "philosophic criticism, sociology and aesthetics,"[7] emerges in the late 1950s and early 60s dreaming the liberal dream, but hearing the call to awaken; writing about a "humane literacy" while hearing a "sub-human jargon." The tensions in his work become understandable. For Steiner adopts the "process of dialectical analysis" (LS, 342) he admires so much in the work of "para-Marxist" critics. This is a process that analyses a text in its dialectical relationship to its sociohistorical context, a process in which the text is examined in terms of how it reflects, creates, and acts as a critique upon that context. It is a process that, as Adorno wrote, "cannot, therefore, permit any insistence on logical neatness."[8] But Steiner also proceeds to trace logical development and to argue toward an idealistic synthesis[9] or a messianic revolution.[10] Thus in his writing there emerges a complex weave of trenchant social critique and Romantic idealism. But unlike the writers of the Frankfurt School, Steiner's employment of "dialectical analysis" is not concomitant with a political and philosophical program. He employs the technique in order to breathe a new life into "old criticism" and its belief in civilizing values; but these are values that "para-Marxist" dialectics are calling into question.

We can appreciate the tensions in Steiner's thought by looking briefly at his first two books: *Tolstoy or Dostoevsky* and *The Death of Tragedy*. In the first book, two contradictory and towering geniuses are analyzed in terms of a dazzling series of encounters between their work and the times in which they lived. Social, biographical, historical, geographical, theological, psychological, and literary contexts are employed to define Tolstoy's and Dostoevsky's stature and the difference between their individual achievements. Then, in the final section, the two men confront each other[11] and the argument between them proceeds dialectically, with the confrontation culminating in a penultimate paragraph, one sentence long, outlining the contraries their work represents, the contraries from which Steiner's cultural preoccupations emerge. The two men and their *oeuvres* are then clasped in a concluding sentence by Montaigne: *"C'est un grand ouvrier de miracles que l'ésprit humain. . . . "* The structure of the work, the confrontational dialectic, is end-stopped by a taut synthesis. It is the vaguely universal but undefined *ésprit humain* that embraces both a Tolstoy and a Dostoevsky.

In *The Death of Tragedy*,[12] instead of a movement toward synthesis, an ever-increasing dissolution is traced. The dissolution is identified through a chronological narrative of contrasting texts and historical contexts, all of which are related back to the Sophocles of Aristotle's *Poetics*. We move inexorably toward "the metaphysics of Christianity and Marxism [that] are anti-tragic. That, in essence, is the dilemma of modern tragedy" (*DT*, 324). The decline in a classical form indicates for Steiner, *a fortiori*, a decline in sensibility. But the decline, having been traced, then abruptly plunges into another key. A terrifying personal note is sounded that is at odds with the seeming finality of tragedy's death. The book concludes with a narrative in which the ashes of Auschwitz are momentarily tasted, the animal realm feeds upon the human, and God retreats into a sad corner of the synagogue. There is a "wild and pure lament over man's inhumanity" (354), and the obsequies for tragedy's death are overtaken by despair (with a hint that from such despair tragedy may have once arisen). But the reader is uncertain whether this despair (or even the historical situation narrated) is a product of the decline of tragedy or whether it constitutes the interruption of such a decline. This ambivalence, it seems to me, results from Steiner's uneasy exploration of liberal values through the critical strategies of the "para-Marxists"—critical strategies that have been divorced from a philosophy of history and a social theory that is suspicious of culture.

In both books, the hermeneutics of suspicion and critique is at odds with an idealism and a desire for rhetorical wholeness. Tonal ambivalences are generated because Steiner is unclear about the ontological and epistemological framework within which he is working. The resolutions are terse or ruptured or paradoxical. *The Death of Tragedy* concludes with a cry in which "there was no sound. . . . It was silence which screamed" (354). Heidegger has much to say about "the peal of stillness."

Steiner's Early Encounter with Heidegger

The move toward the paralysis of paradox (often coupled with a recognition of the ambivalence of silence in Steiner's early work) is nowhere more evident than in the 1963 essay "Humane Literacy." "Barbarism prevailed on the very ground of Christian humanism, of Renaissance culture and classic rationalism" (*LS*, 23). The liberal humanist hermeneutic, countered by a twentieth-century inhumanity, demanded that "the art of reading, of true literacy . . . be reconstituted" (29). The search for grounds enabling such a reconstitution is the crux of the task Steiner increasingly realizes is before him: a definition of culture following the incommensurability of the Shoah.[13]

Heidegger is first mentioned in an article that appeared the following year, "A Note on Günter Grass." His debut is not promising. Steiner notes, with evident approval, Grass's "deadly pastiche of the metaphysical jargon of Heidegger" (139). The "arrogant obscurities of German philosophic speech" only encouraged the slide of the German language into Nazi doublespeak. At this point, in Steiner's attempt to turn Adorno's statement—"To write poetry after Auschwitz is barbaric"—into a question, Heidegger is not on the side of the angels. Steiner's subsequent appreciation of the work of Heidegger never underestimates the moral dubiety of his *Blut, Boden,* and *Volk* vocabulary. But something changes in the tone of Steiner's work in the mid-1960s, and Heidegger is most certainly linked with it. Steiner becomes preoccupied with the relationship of eloquence to silence. Parallel to articles that explore his own response to the death camps ("A Kind of Survivor" and "Postscript") there emerges a new metaphysic, even a negative theology, which focuses upon language's relation to silence. We find it in his interpretation of Schoenberg's Moses and "the tragic paradox of the drama, the metaphysical scandal which springs from the fact that the categories of God are not . . . commensurate to those of man" (159). We find it in Steiner's appreciation of Broch, Wittgenstein, and Rilke, who "make the reader aware of other dimensions which cannot be circumscribed in words" and who "commend us to silence" (112). But it is in the 1966 essay "Silence and the Poet" in which Heidegger makes an explicit appearance, that Steiner's deeper awareness of the "paradox of silence" (69) achieves an unforgettable articulation. New notes are sounded, and they seem to me echoes of a change of heart about Heidegger's "metaphysical jargon."

The essay opens with a new question—concerning not the corrosion of language, but the whence of the word, the Word's relation to words. The first two sections, on language in relation to light and music, considerably develop Steiner's logocentric, and therefore ontotheological, thinking. Inspired by Dante's language as it arches back toward the Adamic paradise (inspired, too, by Benjamin's messianic philosophy of the Name), Steiner speaks of language as bordering on "a transcendent presence" of "divine meaning surpassing and enfolding ours. What lies beyond man's word is eloquent of God" (58–59). An explicit ontological idiom is employed, and words are an "affirmative outrage, a manifest proof of being, of that which surpasses all human speech" (60). Such eloquence is then juxtaposed with the silence of current linguistic "devaluation and dehumanisation" (69) and the "death of language" (71). This devaluation and death are most particularly evident, for Steiner, in the German language during and following nazism. The result of this juxtaposition is, once again, paradox: the silence of the Sirens, which is both a "fatal weapon" (Steiner is quoting Kafka) and "ready for the wonder of the word" (74).

The antinomy of eloquence and silence, representation and presence, is informed in this essay by a new onto-theological appreciation of language. The question of language, Heidegger's *Das Fragen nach Sprache und Sein*, both its nature and its origin, is foregrounded here in a way that foreshadows Steiner's later work *After Babel: Aspects of Language and Translation*.

There are significant differences between Heidegger's and Steiner's handling of the question of language's relation to Being. These differences are partly veiled by Steiner taking up from Heidegger's work that which most clearly corresponds to his own. But it is already evident that there is a profound methodological difference between Heidegger's and Steiner's exploration of the nature of language. We need to examine this more closely in order to understand how Heidegger is influencing Steiner at this early stage.

The hermeneutical phenomenology that issued from and informed Heidegger's analysis of *Dasein*, the method characteristic of *Sein und Zeit* (1929), was, to use Heidegger's famous phrase, "stepped back from" in his later work. In his *Gesprach von der Sprache*, Heidegger summarizes his new position. When asked by a Japanese professor: "How would you present the hermeneutical circle today?," Heidegger replies: "I would avoid a presentation as resolutely as I would avoid speaking *about* language."[14] In a sense, we return to section 33 of *Sein und Zeit* and the claim that assertive discourse presupposes an interpretation. But now we step back into that more primary "interpretation" —the human being as Hermes, listening to, and bearing, a saying that comes to him. We have shifted from speaking *about* language (sections 34–35 of *Sein und Zeit*) toward Heidegger's thinking-that-waits: "The in-dwelling in releasement to that-which-regions would then be the real nature of the spontaneity of thinking."[15] The method informing and issuing from Heidegger's new hermeneutic is one of following the path that thinking opens up as it listens to the appeal being made to it. It is a thinking that is being approached by a moment of appropriation (*Ereignis*), a moment that thinking is simultaneously approaching. We engage in the operation of this circular hermeneutic in Heidegger's meditations upon the work of Stefan George and Hölderlin in *Das Wesen der Sprache*, on the poetry of Georg Trakl in *Der Sprache im Gedicht*, and on Rilke in *Wozu Dichter?* But, as Paul de Man points out in his essay "Heidegger's Exegeses of Hölderlin," "one cannot speak here of 'method' in the formal sense of the term, but rather Heidegger's very thought in relation to the poetic."[16] A distinctive dialogue is opened between Heidegger, the poet, and Being, in which each position is believed to feed into, affirm, and promote the unfolding of the others. But the result is exegetical violence—"Heidegger goes against the established canons of literary scholarship."[17] Heidegger's interest lies in the intercession of language and an anthropology defined by human beings as *zoon logon echon*. He listens intently to what of the concealed and the ineffable is called forth by the in-dwellingness of things—that for which " 'Being' remains only the provisional (*Vorläufige*) word."[18] His "method" is inseparable from his understanding of the nature (*Wesen*) of language.

At this early stage in Steiner's work, Heidegger influences not so much his "method" as his sense of "the necessity of re-establishing the science of language on foundations which are ontologically more original."[19] Once more, Steiner is detaching an interpretative strategy (with its corollary of exegetical violence) from its philosophical basis. Only this time, it is not the strategy that is retained, but Steiner's reading of its ontological foundations. What we have to examine now is how this philosophical framework (which is Steiner's interpretation of Heidegger's thought) relates to what we have already traced as a conflict between the philology and classicism of "the great tradition" and the sociohistorical critique of such a tradition by the Frankfurt School.

It was at this point in Steiner's career, 1971, that *In Bluebeard's Castle* was published. The book is thematically related to Horkheimer and Adorno's *Dialectic of Enlightenment*, which Steiner refers to in the closing pages.[20] Both books are an examination of anti-Semitism, modern technology, the culture industry, and the present crisis of humanism. Both are politically ambivalent toward the elitism of "mandarin rights" and the "democratization of high culture" (85). Both books swing paradoxically between the positive and the negative aspects of a contemporary culture that privileges science and mathematical meta-languages. At the same time, in *In Bluebeard's Castle* Steiner is conscious of his own profound nostalgia for "the garden of liberal culture" (14) and the "safety of the *faubourg*" (15). It is within this context that Steiner begins to make an appeal to "the grammar of being" (13), the "ontological and hermeneutic aspects of the modulations between a language-culture and death" (88). The struggle to relate these three perspectives within this searingly honest course of lectures becomes overwhelming. The intention to compose *Some Notes towards the Re-definition of Culture* (the book's subtitle) collapses three-quarters of the way through: "It is not, therefore, 'some notes towards a re-definition of culture' that I feel able or competent to put forward" (74). The pessimism of "A Season in Hell" and its consequent "Post-Culture" cannot easily be redeemed. The "centrality of the word . . . [may be] informed by . . . the trope of transcendence" (87), but it is equally true that "language is close-woven with lies" (94). Steiner closes by attempting to locate hope between "stoic acquiescence . . . [and] Nietzschean gaiety in the face of the inhuman" and an admission that "even the term *Notes* is too ambitious for an essay on culture written at this moment" (106–7).

Steiner introduces Heidegger's ontological idiom into his *In Blue-*

beard's Castle because he recognizes that culture needs to be "rooted in a gamble on transcendence" (71). Therefore, an onto-theological interpretation of Heidegger's exploration into the call of Being within language becomes attractive. But Steiner's stretching of various interpretative strategies over Heidegger's ontological frame makes certain tensions become more pronounced. Heidegger symbolizes the paradox Steiner cannot resolve: "One of the principal works that we have in the philosophy of language . . . was composed almost within earshot of a death camp" (63). Heidegger seems, on the one hand, to promise a new redemption for language, yet, on the other, provides Steiner with a poignant example of moral betrayal at the heart of the aesthetic, which, as Steiner knows, can easily become an anesthetic.[21]

It is the paradox of language as both rhetoric and real presence that informs the breadth of the argument in *After Babel*. To understand exactly in what way, and why, Heidegger becomes important for Steiner in this book we need to examine the paradox of language as Heidegger understands it.

Central to Heidegger's analysis of *Dasein*, and his phenomenological method, is the idea that an act of understanding *is* an act of interpretation. Central to Heidegger's later thought on language is the idea that language does not correspond to what is there, word to object, but creates what is there. There is no world independent of language and interpretation. This is not to say that there is no outside—*Nichts*, from which presence issues and to which it returns, has substance in German. There is an event of appropriation (*Ereignis*) which determines the manifestation and the withdrawal, the revelation and the concealment of Being, but "appropriation is *not* to be thought,"[22] the "awakening to appropriation is to be experienced" (53). The experience of presence is a gift of *Ereignis*, but in being recognized as such it withdraws. Because of this, language, which enables us to recognize the withdrawal of presence, walks a thin, indeterminate line between having no external reference and giving expression to the primal origins of Being. Language is *poiesis*, but its creativity responds to, leaves a trace of, and conceals Being. It is both a said (*Gerede*, or common speech) and a saying of (double genitive) the event of appropriation: "Language is not only ontic, but from the outset ontic-ontological" (51). This ontic/ontological difference, the immanent/transcendent split, is at the heart of the paradox of language for Heidegger. Steiner, in *After Babel*, explores this two-sided character of language in terms of the accidental differences between each tongue (differences that constitute the world view of each language) within the essential unity of the logos, "the universal principle of relational meaning" (*AB*, 310).

For Heidegger, language's paradox informs his later method—the way he explores his own thinking process as it tries to understand the ontic/ontological difference. For the "thinker's thinking would thus be the relatedness to the Being of beings."[23] In *After Babel* Steiner includes a shift from Frankfurt School dialectics to a hermeneutical phenomenology. The attempt to integrate these two methods governs the structure of *After Babel*. It is by means of this structure that Steiner eventually embraces Heidegger's thinking while not allowing the ahistorical aspects of phenomenological method to predominate.

The first four chapters of *After Babel* analyze the nature of language—and "a theory of translation is a theory of language" (279) —in terms of dialectical opposites: the physical and the mental, the past and the future, the private and the public, truth and falsity. But chapter five, "The Hermeneutic Motion," is an account of the practice of translating, and it is here that Steiner draws upon "phenomenological ontologies [that] look very much like meditations on the 'transportability' of meanings" (278). Prior to this chapter, the reader has been balancing a series of arguments and theories, but now Steiner turns his attention to the experience of translating. We are shifted from philosophies of language that can support the phenomenon of translatability against philosophies of language that deny the possibility of translation, to a phenomenological account that *demonstrates* that translation is a fundamental operation of all understanding. This hinged structure— the move from discursive argument to the phenomenological description of a process—can be found again in " 'Critic'/'Reader' " and *Real Presences*. "The logic comes after the fact" (295), Steiner writes, and a description of the fact (of translating, of reading) is given. The phenomenological account describes how all translating (or reading) only makes sense as an elicited response to the transcendent. It does not argue the case; rather, the mimetic presentation of the case *is* the argument itself.[24]

By means of this methodological shift, Steiner can bring together the emphases on the rational, the moral, and the religious in liberal culture, the sociohistorical critique of the Frankfurt School, and the ontological idiom of Heideggerian phenomenology. It seems to me that Steiner, who is a deeply Hegelian thinker, aspires toward a synthesis of these three approaches to culture. If such a synthesis is possible, it may then also be possible to complete those notes toward a redefinition of culture that crumbled before the unthinkable in Bluebeard's castle.

Heidegger's Bavarian *Holzwege* begins to make substantial inroads into Steiner's work. But there is a need for caution when assessing the extent of Heidegger's influence on Steiner, and perhaps here is the best place to demonstrate the point. For *After Babel* also reveals the considerable influence of Benjamin on Steiner's hermeneutics. Benjamin's essay "The Task of Translators" stands firmly behind Steiner's theory of translation, just as Benjamin's essay "On Language as Such and on the Language of Man" and the "Allegory and Trauerspiel" section of *The Origin of German Tragic Drama* help to shape Steiner's theory of language. The theme of *After Babel* can be viewed as an expansion of Benjamin's statement that "it is necessary to found the concept of translation at the deepest level of linguistic theory."[25] Of course, as Hannah Arendt has pointed out, Benjamin's views on language have much in common with Heidegger's.[26] They were both (as is Steiner) conscious heirs of the legacy of *Sprachphilosophie* left by Hamann, Herder, and Humboldt. But it was Benjamin, following in the footsteps of Rosenzweig, who fused Romantic vitalist conceptions of language with "para-Marxism" and Kabbalistic mysticism. It is *he*, then, to whom Steiner is listening as he composes that Kaddish-like conclusion to *After Babel*. Here words can either be redeemed by reentering "the translucent immediacy of that primal speech shared by God and Adam" or become "only themselves, and as dead stones in our mouths" (474). *After Babel* is end-stopped with a paradox: language as either pure semantics or pure semiotics. This is, *in nuce*, the paradox of Benjamin's own position.[27] Benjamin's work, like Steiner's, reveals the tension of a hermeneutic trying to marry a metaphysical ground for poetry (the ontology of naming) with an emphasis upon the historicity and social psychology of creativity. The dialectical poles that emerge in Benjamin are often Manichean. By dwelling upon Heidegger's work, Steiner is preserved from a similar position.

We can assess Heidegger's distinctive influence on Steiner by comparing the conclusion to *After Babel* with its recapitulation at the end of *Real Presences*. For it is between these two books that Steiner engages in a thorough study of Heidegger's work. A messianic eschatology remains, but the redemption is one of attaining "the Utopia of Sunday" (*RP*, 232). The metaphors are distinctly Christian, and the logocentrism is Christocentric. The dialectic remains: we are now caught between Good Friday and Easter Sunday, suffering and liberation. But "ours is the long day's journeying of the Saturday"—the dialectic does not paralyze into paradox. It perpetuates the journeying that produces the poetry and the music that mediate between the pain and the hope. The dialectical tension issues from and articulates "an immensity of waiting which is that of man." The conclusion is not silence, but the infinite ingression into a definite future. The profundity of Heidegger's influence lies in the difference between this ending and *After Babel*'s, and it gathers about that very Heideggerian word "waiting." Heidegger writes that "waiting means: to release oneself into the openness of that-which-regions," that "in waiting we are released from our transcendental relation to the horizon."[28] From the passivity of waiting issues the call (Heidegger's *des Singens der Abgeschiedenheit*) to creatively respond.

Steiner's Interpretation of Heidegger

There is one further difference between the conclusion to *After Babel* and the conclusion to *Real Presences*. There is a difference in tone. A note of optimism which sounds even at the portcullis of Bluebeard's castle gathers volume in *Extraterritorial: Papers on Literature and the Language Revolution* (1971) and *After Babel* (1975). The language revolution sets Steiner sailing toward new intellectual horizons, and the dark clouds of negativity (generated by liberalism in decline, illustrated by the Frankfurt School, and evidenced in the sheer intractability of Auschwitz) part for a moment. The act of interpretation does seem to point, if not exactly to Chomsky's *grammatica universalis*, then to topologies of culture, to "a single curve of meaning" (*AB*, 436), and to "a genetic code of transmitted consciousness" (463). A certain Hegelianism is implicit in the threefold structure of translation: the moving out in trust; the experience of difference in the very foreignness of the other language; and the appropriation of that experience into the mother tongue. The experience of difference becomes the precondition for the reexperience of identity through the hermeneutical appropriation and "the transcendence of difference" (379). The Other is made familiar by an appropriation that travels through the hermeneutical circle. That this is Hegelian is evident. That Steiner also believes this to be Heideggerian is implicit in the use of terms such as "expropriation" and "appropriation" and phrases such as "the organic autonomy of the saying and the said" (380). Heidegger's hermeneutical phenomenology is interpreted along Hegelian lines: "Hegel and Heidegger posit that being must engage other being in order to achieve self-definition" (301). This interpretation of Heidegger is highly important for understanding how Steiner tries to locate a theory of contemporary culture in an ontological frame. The tone of the conclusion to *Real Presences* is more muted, uncertain, and equivocal. This change is related to a disassociation of Heidegger's work from Hegel's.

It is in "'Critic'/'Reader'" and *Heidegger* that it clearly emerges how Steiner has interpreted Heidegger's work throughout the 1970s and early 80s. In "'Critic'/'Reader'" Heidegger provides a philosophical infrastructure for a phenomenology of reading (we meet this again in *Real Presences*). The critic/reader relationship is investigated in terms of a "fiction of contrastive absolutes"[29] forming a constellation of theses/antitheses (epistemology/ontology, realism/idealism, immanence/transcendence, syllabus/canon, the past/the future). The change in vocabulary is quite marked. The ontology of reading is described in distinctly Catholic (Heidegger's theological background) terms: "transubstantial," "real presence," "sacramental," "incarnation," "icon," and "revelation." Steiner is conscious of the rhetoric involved—tropes are not necessarily truth and, like Heidegger, Steiner reiterates that "there is nothing occult or mystical about this entrance" into the text (91). Nevertheless, Steiner wishes to claim that this experience of transcendence is ultimately underwritten by theology. For only theology, "if this word is allowed its widest compass," guarantees "the validity of metaphor and analogy" (96). Much is unresolved here, as it is unresolved in Heidegger. But it does not remain unresolved for the same reasons in both writers. In both Steiner and Heidegger we are unsure to what extent the ontological model propounded corresponds to or deconstructs the theological metaphors that enable its presentation.[30] But in Heidegger there is a recognition that this ambiguity constitutes the heart of the openness, the heart of the incommensurate *Differenz* between the ontic and the ontological. In Steiner it is unresolved because he is attempting to interlace a sociology and an ontology of literature. He wants a synthesis of the ontic and the ontological, and it is all too easy to create the synthesis by being "eloquent of God." What remains unresolved here is the central issue for any definition of culture after Auschwitz: Where does the rhetoric end and the real presence begin?

The dislocation of meaning and metaphor—Heidegger's avowed and repeated conviction that Being is not another word for God, inscribed in an idiom redolent with incense—is the secret struggle at the heart of Steiner's monograph *Heidegger*. If again the resolution is unconvincing, it is because it is achieved only with hermeneutical violence and is fraught with tonal tensions. For Steiner underlines Heidegger's emphasis on finitude and the fact that "we are at the antipodes to Plato."[31] He points out (without really unpacking) Heidegger's notion that *"Das Nichten des Nichts 'ist' das Sein"* (146). Yet still he wishes to end his work by drawing Heidegger into the orbit of Coleridge and a "kind of mystery of immanence" (148). Epithets such as "a kind of"; subclauses such as "adopts almost at every point" and "to this reader at least"; nebulous allusions to "post-theologies" and "metatheologies," to Nietzsche's death and Buber's eclipse of God—all testify to the cloudiness of Steiner's conclusion. But by giving little or no weight to Heidegger's insistence on *die Spur des Unter-Schiedes, Ereignis, der Schritt zurück*, and the post-Hegelian thinking articulated both in "The Onto-theological Constitution of Metaphysics" and "Time and Being," Steiner is able to maintain his picture of Heidegger as the liberal Romantic.

Steiner has been helped and encouraged in his tracing of this picture by Emmanuel Levinas (whose readings of Heidegger have often been questioned)[32] and two earlier appropriations of Heidegger's work for aesthetics—Gadamer's *Wahrheit und Methode* (1965) and Ricoeur's *De l'interprétation* (1965). This picture of Heidegger offers philosophical support for Steiner's classical aesthetic values. Why this support is required is a question touching upon the nature of Steiner's vocation to *Kulturkritik*: to construct, in the all too personal face of Auschwitz, an aesthetic theory, a definition of culture. The aesthetic theory he constructs closely corresponds to the Romantic doctrine of the sublime. He interprets Heidegger, therefore, as "the great master of astonishment" (*H*, 150). He accentuates the ethics of *Entsprechung* (which restores the humanity to *humanitas*) and the transcendence of *Erstaunen*. What are emphasized in Heidegger's work are language as the house of Being, and poetic language as the site of "epiphanies," "revelations," "miracles," and "presence." Heidegger provides Steiner with philosophical descriptions of the immediacy of poetic experience and an authenticity through poetry. Steiner does not read Heidegger as articulating the *question* of

Being and *Ereignis* as the experience not of Being but *"die Differenz als Differenz."*[33] He does not read Heidegger as qualifying any talk of immediacy, or of the return, via the hermeneutic circle, to what Ricoeur would call "second naïveté." He does not read the Heidegger who in his "Dialogue on Language (Between a Japanese and an Inquirer)" wrote: "I: But this necessary acceptance of the hermeneutic circle does not mean that the notion of the accepted circle gives us an originary experience of the hermeneutic relation (*der hermeneutische Bezug ursprünglich erfahren ist*). J: In short, you would abandon your earlier view (*Auffassung*)? I: Quite . . . that talk of a circle always remains superficial (*vordergrün-dig*)."[34] The understanding of the hermeneutic circle in *Being and Time* is "stepped back from" as Heidegger struggles with *Ereignis*—the experience not of logocentric presence and underlying unity, but of logo-centric absence. For Heidegger, the difference between the ontic and the ontological can provide only a "hint" of the saying in the said. In other words, there are points in the later Heidegger where language is not the *tertium quid* between beings and Being that Steiner requires; where language articulates *"die Stille des Unter-Schiedes"*[35] and that we are always only "on the way."

Steiner's analysis pitches Heidegger on a note of high moral and aesthetic grandeur:[36] "The unity of thought and of poetry, of thought, of poetry and of that highest act of mortal pride and celebration which is to give thanks" (*H*, 150). Hegelian synthesis is wrapped in Eucharistic vestments. It jars, because the most "authentic" piece of writing in the book is made up of the eleven pages devoted to Heidegger's 1933–34 pronouncements. Here Steiner finds that the "idiom of the purely ontological blends with that of the inhuman" and that Heidegger's complete silence "on Hilterism and the holocaust" after 1945 "is very nearly intolerable" (118). What remains, as Steiner quite rightly points out, "is the question of how this silence . . . is to be accorded with the lyric humanity of Heidegger's later writings" (121). It is a question that seems to be forgotten in the final pages. No aesthetic theory or defini-tion of culture in the later twentieth century can return to Heidegger as if the Holocaust had not occurred. Unless, that is, it is merely "lyric humanity," a rhetorical gesture. Steiner knows this. If Heidegger, then, is to remain the philosophical framework within which to erect such a definition, he must be read again. In Steiner's next major work he returns to the theme in his writing most closely related to the cultural dilemma posed by the Holocaust: tragedy.

Steiner's "Ingestion" of Heidegger

Antigones: How the Antigone Legend Has Endured in Western Literature, *Art, and Thought* (1984) is born of Steiner's prolonged wrestling with the Heideggerian angel, and the book's deepening sense of the unavoidability of the tragic will dictate the ambivalent mood that pervades *Real Presences*. The book's historical genesis lies in lectures delivered in 1979, but its metaphysical genesis lies in Heidegger's undeveloped and covert sense of the tragic. We can sense the tragic potential of Heidegger's *Dasein* in statements such as: "In the ex-istent freedom of *Da-sein* there is accomplished a dissimulation of what-is in totality, and therein lies the concealment (*Vorborgenheit*)."[37] Human nature cannot but deceive itself. It cannot grasp "what-is in totality." In order to be there (da-sein), to be a distinct identity, it must select and interpret and dissimulate. Insofar as *Dasein* then "clings to the certainties of self-hood" (196/345), it must forget and deny the revelation of what is in totality. *Dasein* must necessarily forget its own mystery and so "humanity builds up its 'world' out of whatever intentions and needs happen to be the most immediate" (196/344). As Heidegger observes, "error is part of the inner structure of *Da-sein*" (195/343). Humanity's tragic potential is grounded in this ontological and anthropological paradox. Furthermore, Heidegger's most explicit exploration of this tragic potential comes from his own analysis of Sophocles' *Antigone* (in his *Introduction to Metaphysics*).

Steiner's *Antigones* develops his thinking on "the hermeneutic motion," thinking that Heidegger and Benjamin have governed. It is a book about the interpretative contexts within which seminal texts are translated, transmuted, and transmitted. Even the core question— Why is it that a handful of Greek myths map out the contours of the Western imagination?—is about the inception of the hermeneutic circle and why the human condition interprets itself through these metaphors. Steiner postulates that the whence of myth is the structure of language itself, and we are back with Heidegger's reevaluation of the emergence of *Dasein* as the emergence of language.

Heidegger's shadow is long and distinct, but ostensibly it remains a Hegelian Heidegger. This produces a tension between the metaphysics of a unifying "presence" and Steiner's recognition "that it is not the Hegelian hope of an evolutionary synthesis . . . which best expresses the Sophoclean sense of the play."[38] Tragedy, which "confronts the possibility of nothingness . . . which western religiosity, metaphysical idealism and the common pulse of the imagination would deny" (281), stands in a necessary and insoluable conflict with "presence." Tragedy points to a "generic human infirmity" (298), and the meaning for which it expresses a yearning may be either "messianic or antimessianic" (303). "Presence" takes on more sinister connotations, especially in the final section of the book. What is earlier described as Heidegger's "Arcadian ontology"—the *déjà vu* "which makes our experience of great art and poetry a homecoming" (127)—gives way to descriptions of "undecidable finalities of conflict" (254). The appraisal of "language in its original state of truthful nomination and concealment" (131) becomes a meditation on "an irreconcilable dialectic" (258). The "up beat, pendulum swing towards hope" (280), traced in Steiner's work from *In Bluebeard's Castle* to "'Critic'/'Reader,'" returns again to the deep freeze of paradox: the "dialogue of noncommunication" (251) and "anarchic lawfulness" (252).

The meaning and the tone of "presence" shift throughout. There is "significant presence" or "felt meaning" if a text accords with our own intuition of the human condition. There is "vestigial presentness," which is the approach or the bequest of the holy (a holiness that is sometimes a Johannine incarnation and sometimes a Pascalian otherness). There is "presence" as the encounter with the chthonic night, where "the living wait in blackness for their end" (288). We are looking over the edge here into the pluralized and polyvalent "presences" of Steiner's next book: presentness as an anthropological, theological, and rhetorical creation.

In terms of Heidegger, Steiner has fulfilled his own prescription: "I want to work forward from Heidegger's argument without, necessarily, adopting its Arcadian ontology and suppressed religiosity" (133). The ontology, as we have seen, is severely qualified, but what remain are, first, the method of a hermeneutical phenomenology, and, second, the distinction between authentic and inauthentic speaking (Heidegger's *Rede/Gerede*). This "working forward from Heidegger" brings Steiner closer to readings of Heidegger's work by postmodern critics.[39] The postmodern Heidegger cannot be used metaphysically to ground the liberal cultural dream; he stands with his back to Hegelian dialectical synthesis. Tragedy brings Steiner, once more, to the inescapability of antinomies and the hermeneutic of paradox developed by Benjamin, Adorno, and Horkheimer. Phenomenology's investigation of the encounter with otherness has uncovered "presence" as either plenitude or void. We arrive at the "wager" of *Real Presences* and the proposal made by serious art, that the "density of God's absence, the edge of presence in that absence, is no empty dialectical twist" (*RP*, 229). It is a "wager," as Steiner realizes, that might be "wholly erroneous" (4).

Real Presences plays out, first dialectically, then phenomenologically, the polyvalence of "presence." Part one, "A Secondary City," extols hermeneutics as *poiesis*. Interpretation is presented as an encounter with the meaningful and authentic. The presentation is an explication of late Heideggerian method, where the form of the encounter between the philosopher and his text emerges from a response to the call of the text's "presence." Both Steiner and Heidegger would agree: a critical response is a performance and a participation. Such a response is only found in a Primary City, but such a city, devoted to true aesthetic immediacy, rests upon a Romantic *Nebelmeer*. Steiner recognizes this, and so he attacks with the severity and verve of negative dialectics our cult of the secondary, our reification of culture. Part one concludes with a paradox all too evident to Heidegger: "By the logic of dialectical inversion . . . the very methodologies and techniques which would restore to us the presence of the source, of the primary, surround, suffocate that presence with their own autonomous mass" (47). The eclipse of the humanities, as well as the humane, becomes inevitable, and the cry for reexperiencing the "life of meaning in the text" (50) is forced to become prophetic. The logical tensions here are evident, and they prepare the way for Steiner's repetition of "wager."

In attempting to ground an argument for the theological and metaphysical as "they inhere in language" (50), part two of *Real Presences*, "The Broken Contract," develops a Heideggerian logocentrism. It is a logocentrism supplemented by Steiner's insight into grammar as "the formal articulation of the conceptual and imaginative phenomenality of the unbounded" (55). But it is a Heidegger no longer annexed to Hegel—Heidegger's exploration of *Nichtigkeit* is foregrounded, the "midnight of absence" of which "deconstruction is the spectral trace" (133). The resonance of "trace" (a word favored by Heidegger, Levinas, and Derrida) is telling. The irony and doubling that resound throughout this part strike a distinct chord here. Steiner recognizes the paradox at the heart of the hermeneutical enterprise. For interpretation *assumes*, first, that it passes from Heidegger's *"das Gedachte"* into *"das Ungedachte,"* and, second, that what is unthought is what is ultimately meaningful. But the hermeneutic circle might be chasing the wind. For what is unthought has to be thought, and what is voiceless presence has to be voiced in order to be heard. So that plenitude opens itself to be interpreted merely as the endlessness of self-perpetuating signification. "The hermeneutic circle . . . is the very arena for the deconstructive game" (130). That is the paradox of the oxymoronic broken contracts: "The two principles of indeterminacy and of complementarity . . . are at the very heart of all interpretative and all critical proceedings and acts of speech in literature and the arts" (76). The ironies, antinomies, and dialectical twists that counterpoint this part are the result of Steiner teasing out the complexities (and profundities) of this paradox. There is no *tertium quid*, no Hegelian *Aufhebung* teleologically integrating negativity into a higher unity in the Absolute. The tone of Steiner's polemic against "postmodernism and deconstruction" is shot through with ambivalences, because deconstruction issues from the very preoccupation with language which inscribes the philological and logocentric. Deconstruction articulates a "real absence" *in* the "real presence"—and, as Steiner points out, "there is here an absorbing paradox" (128). Ultimately, the argument of Steiner, his "grounds for rebuttal" (128) of this negative semiotics, cannot become an argument: "On *its own terms and planes of argument* the challenge of deconstruction does seem to me irrefutable" (132). Hermeneutics enters a maze of mirrors in which what is being refracted is Heidegger's dictum "die Sprache spricht."

Even so, it is a commitment to "a hermeneutic and reflex of valuation" (134) and whether this can "be made intelligible . . . to the existential facts, if they do not imply . . . a postulate of transcendence" (134), that allows Steiner to proceed. Heidegger, then, problematizes any final grasp of what is meaningful while opening, through hermeneutic phenomenology, a track leading to a *Lichtung*. If this is the junction of modernism and postmodernism, the preoccupation with the Absolute folding back upon the preoccupation with *le degré zéro*, is also the site of both Heidegger's and Steiner's later work. It locates them both in the cleft heart of a culture born of barbarism and violence.

They seem to answer to each other's call in part three, "Presences"— a phenomenological account of the hermeneutical encounter that Heidegger would call a thinking about thinking (*"das sich selbst denkende*

Denken") and that Steiner would call a reading of reading. For both it is the pursuit of the saying within the said, for they are both haunted by the possibility of dialogue. If there is only one explicit reference to Heidegger in this last part, it is because the resonating stillness they both hear is recognizably the same. We register the echoes of what has been "ingested." Other voices are present also—the explicit theologizing of Heidegger's thought owes much to Von Balthasar's *Mysterium Paschale* and to the Jewish metaphysics of Benjamin, Buber, and Levinas. An earlier Hegelianism is overshadowed by a new appropriation of Kant (whose metaphysics has often attracted Jewish theologians). But it is Heidegger whose method and idiom orchestrate much of the discussion. *Unheimlichkeit* becomes "uncanniness," *das Haus des Seins* echoes throughout, often transposed into metaphors of homecoming and welcoming. "Trace," "waiting," "gathering," and "recession" take on Heideggerian weight. There is the centrality of being-toward-death constituting "thereness," the frequent appeal to the Leibniz question that provoked Heidegger's *Introduction to Metaphysics* ("Why are there essents rather than nothing?"), and the phenomenology of "the coming into being of being" (204). Heideggerian rhetoric becomes part of the very fabric of Steiner's argument: "There is no mysticism in this monition" (224), and "The distancing is . . . charged with the pressures of a nearness out of reach" (230).

More importantly, this later, almost symbiotic dialogue between Steiner and Heidegger qualifies the character of "presence." Phrases speaking of "immediacy" and "epiphany" are mostly toned down, in the light of an increasing awareness of mediation, the possibilities of hermeneutical violence, and the ambiguities of imitation. Now a philology is called for "with self-ironizing alertness to the verbal" (172). Steiner now fully accepts the possibility that his account of the arts on the threshold of the transcendent "may be pure fantastication" (182). Now an immutable "secondarity" adheres to the very nature of mimesis, so all "presence" is re-presented, and, therefore, "the experience of meaningful form" is "a presumption of presence" (214). *Poiesis* can be *either* "a rhetorical flourish" or "a piece of theology" (216). It is because of this that there is something ironic about attempting to argue for a wager. For there is neither winning nor losing in a situation that can never be defined.

It is this wager as a theological analogue of faith which finally distinguishes Steiner from Heidegger. For both, there is an encounter with otherness, the "gathering [of] form and pure consciousness of form out of a 'great emptiness'" (223). Heidegger writes that "it is precisely the presently present and the unconcealment that rules in it that pervades the essence of what is absent."[40] Steiner writes that "the density of God's absence, the edge of presence in that absence, is no empty dialectical twist" (229). For Steiner, what is presenced is an absence that is either a "negative theism" or the "zero theology" of the "always absent" (229)—either plenitude or void. Yet the imagery he uses to describe both experiences is theological. In other words, when faced, the void is masked by religious rhetoric. It is as if the wager is never really taken, because the situation has already been read through theological metaphors. Heidegger keeps his thinking open—*Nichtigkeit* is aptly ambivalent, it is neither theological nor nihilistic. Steiner maintains a belief in the implicit theology of hermeneutics. In fact, he sees this belief as an inescapable aspect of hermeneutics, despite talk of his thesis as possibly "erroneous." It is this belief in hermeneutics that enables Steiner to complete his notes toward a redefinition of our present culture. This commitment allows him to define today's cultural circumstances as "transitional" (231), and it is the movement implicit in this epithet (Heidegger's *die Bewegung, der Weg,* and *wagen* lie behind it) that leads to the reaffirmation of the "wager." The commitment defeats the paralysis of paradox while postponing idealism's golden synthesis. Our culture is read into the narrative and metaphorics of Good Friday, Holy Saturday, and Easter Sunday. Ours is "the long day's journey of the Saturday" (232)—ours the experience of the in-between, the space not reported on (231). The openness to the future and the debt to the past that galvanize hermeneutical phenomenology allow Steiner to speak of emptiness, rupture, tragedy, and waste "in the name of hope" (232), if not hopefully.

Something yet remains of that call for "self-ironizing alertness to the verbal" (171)—something that almost dissolves in a superficial reading of the lyricism of Steiner's concluding paragraphs (paragraphs, like those at the end of *The Death of Tragedy* and *After Babel,* that call for, yet do not articulate, a philosophy of history). There is irony in a Jewish writer locating the redemption of culture in a Christian narrative. The question *Is there anything in what we say?* remains a question. For are we really experiencing a cultural Holy Saturday or are we being seduced by a rhetorical gesture? The irony surfaces because Steiner faces his most self-searching question. It is a question that profoundly relates him to Heidegger—the question of the ethics of one's own eloquence.

◊ ◊ ◊

"Influence" in this essay wishes to evoke its Latin origin (*influere*), because Heidegger's influence upon Steiner's work cannot be wrapped up like a box of ideas. That inflow has met, changed, and deepened contributory influences. This essay has attempted to trace the course of a conversation that shall no doubt persist—because "persistence" (Heidegger's *der Austrag*) is the very heart of that "immensity of waiting" (232) which leaves the way "open for what we are waiting for."[41]

Notes

Where it is possible, references to Heidegger's German texts are to the definitive *Gesamtausgabe*, 63 vols. (Frankfurt am Main: Vittorio Klostermann, 1976–91).

1. George Steiner, *Real Presences: Is There Anything in What We Say?* (London: Faber and Faber, 1989), 50. Hereafter cited as *RP*.
2. Independent of Steiner's work, there has been a change in the way Heidegger has been interpreted over these years. The change is best represented by a comment made by Jean Beaufret in 1962 that is quoted in *On Time and Being*, trans. Joan Stambaugh (New York: Harper and Row, 1972), 49: "In France the impression was widely predominant that Heidegger's thinking was a recapitulation . . . of Hegel's." By 1979 a book edited by William V. Spanos, *Heidegger and the Question of Literature: Toward a Postmodern Literary Hermeneutics* (Bloomington: Indiana University Press), could speak of the old phenomenological and the new poststructuralist Heidegger (x). More recently, Heidegger's "alterity" has been examined in the works of Mark C. Taylor, John Sallis, Robert Bernasconi, and Philip Lacoue-Labarthe.
3. Fritz K. Ringer, *The Decline of the German Mandarins* (Cambridge: Harvard University Press, 1969), 253.
4. George Steiner, in *Language and Silence: Essays, 1958–1966* (1967; reprint, London: Faber and Faber, 1984), 340.
5. Theodor Adorno, *Prisms* (Cambridge: MIT Press, 1967), 31.
6. Susan Buck-Morss, *The Origin of Negative Dialectics* (Sussex: Harvester Press, 1977), 36.
7. "Preface" to 1984 ed. of *LS*, 16.
8. Adorno, *Prisms*, 33.
9. Cf. George Steiner, *Tolstoy or Dostoevsky: An Essay in Contrast* (London: Faber and Faber, 1959).

10. Cf. George Steiner, *After Babel: Aspects of Language and Translation* (New York: Oxford University Press, 1975). Hereafter cited as *AB*; and *RP*.

11. This same technique was favored by Adorno, who liked to pit Valéry against Proust, or Schoenberg against Stravinsky, or Kant against de Sade.

12. Steiner's *The Death of Tragedy* (London: Faber and Faber, 1961) (hereafter cited as *DT*) is itself is a counterstatement to Nietzsche's *The Birth of Tragedy* and owes much to Benjamin's *The Origin of German Tragic Drama*, which was also designed as a counterstatement to Nietzsche's emphasis upon "the tragic myth as a purely aesthetic [rather than historical-philosophical] creation." See Walter Benjamin, *The Origin of German Tragic Drama*, trans. John Osborne ("Introduction" by George Steiner) (London: New Left Books, 1977), 102.

13. The paradox is still very much alive in Steiner's 1989 Armistice Day sermon in King's College Chapel. Here, speaking of the death camps, an appalling aporia opens, for "men and women, apparently sane, could flog and incinerate guiltless victims during their working day and recite Rilke and play Schubert . . . in the evening." *Cambridge Review* 111 (March 1990): 37. The paradox echoes thesis 7 of Benjamin's "Theses on the Philosophy of History."

14. Martin Heidegger, *Unterwegs zur Sprache* (1985), 12:81–146; and Martin Heidegger, *On the Way to Language*, trans. Peter Hertz (New York: Harper and Row, 1971), 1–54. References to German ed., 142–43; English ed., 51.

15. Martin Heidegger, *Gelassenheit*, in *Aus der Erfahrung des Denkens* (1983), 13:65; and Martin Heidegger, *Discourse on Thinking*, trans. John M. Anderson and E. Hans Freund (New York: Harper and Row, 1966), 82.

16. Paul de Man, *Blindness and Insight* (London: Methuen, 1983), 246–66. Reference to 247.

17. Ibid, 249.

18. Martin Heidegger, *Vortrage and Aufsatze* (Pfullingen: Verlag Gunther Neske, 1954), 25; and Martin Heidegger, *Early Greek Thinking*, trans. David Farrell Krell and Frank A. Capuzzi (New York: Harper and Row, 1975), 78.

19. Martin Heidegger, *Sein und Zeit* (1977), 2:220; and Martin Heidegger, *Being and Time*, trans. John Macquarrie and Edward Robinson (Oxford: Blackwell, 1962), 209.

20. George Steiner, *In Bluebeard's Castle: Some Notes towards the Redefinition of Culture* (London: Faber and Faber, 1971), 104–5.

21. Cf. *RP*, 143–45. Heidegger is also a symbol of the ambivalent relation Steiner perceives between true literacy and totalitarianism.

22. Heidegger, *On Time and Being*, 42.

23. Martin Heidegger, *What Is Called Thinking?*, trans. J. Glenn Gray (New York: Harper and Row, 1968), 86.

24. Both dialectical and phenomenological hermeneutics involve the reader in the exploration and are, therefore, mimetic enterprises. When reading

Walter Benjamin's essay "Some Motifs in Baudelaire" or Adorno's essay "Perennial Fashion—Jazz," one re-creates and experiences the dialectical movement of ideas. The reader moves back and forth as the argument leaps from, say, Proust to Freud, from the crowds on Parisian pavements to fascism, prising, through paradox, ideological appearance from sociological reality. The argument is maintained by the rhythm of thought which constructs the rhetoric of persuasion. Phenomenological accounts of language, of poetry, of painting, of translating are not attempts to argue for, but to discover the nature of, something and investigate the activity whereby that thing appears and is received. They are a form of praxis as performance in which the rhetoric of persuasion constructs the nature of the argument. Both dialectical methods and phenomenology arise from encountering the Other, encountering negation. Both instigate a teleological process. But dialectical method abstracts as it necessarily reifies. It works with and upon concepts, with and upon ideologies. It constructs interpretative contexts for the text. Phenomenological method works with and upon existential data—anxiety, trust, violence, strangeness, appropriation. It operates at the level of intentionality—texts are not analyzed, but experienced. With Heidegger, the analysis of the intentionality of the subject (the hermeneutics of *Dasein*) is pushed toward an analysis of the intentionality of being sub-ject (human nature as the response to the call of Being). It constructs interpretive pre-texts for the texts. But as Heidegger (and Steiner) is aware, dialectic becomes dialogical, and analysis becomes conversation and translation. There is always an element of each in the other. Heidegger: "Ob der Dialog notwendig eine Dialektik ist und wann, dies lassen wir offen." *What Is Philosophy?*, bilingual ed. (Plymouth: Vision, 1963), 66.

25. Walter Benjamin, *Illuminations*, trans. Harry Zohn (London: Fontana, 1973), 117.

26. See Hannah Arendt, "Introduction" in *Illuminations*. My remarks here on Benjamin's influence upon Steiner are cursory and require another essay for their full exposition.

27. Walter Benjamin, *One Way Street*, trans. E. Jephcott and K. Shorter (London: Verso, 1979), 119.

28. Heidegger, *Gelassenheit*, 54–55 / Heidegger, *Discourse on Thinking*, 72–73.

29. George Steiner, "'Critic'/'Reader,'" *New Literary History* 10 (Spring 1979): 423–52. Reprinted in *George Steiner: A Reader* (New York: Oxford University Press, 1984), 96.

30. It is a problem evident also in Benjamin's angels and demons. More significantly, it is the problem of citing adequate *Grundzüge* when the understanding of language as communication of ideas—the transparent means for conveying information and propositions—is overwhelmed by the conscious-

ness that "all language communicates itself" (Benjamin). Hence we dance on the burning sands where all truth may be rhetoric and all meaning mimetic. The mime-mimesis-mimicry axis locates the very ambiguity itself. Logocentrism and *écriture* are two paradoxically distinct and yet inseparable ways of interpreting the same phenomena.

31. George Steiner, *Heidegger* (London: Fontana, 1978), 103. Hereafter cited as *H*.

32. We can trace this questioning of Levinas's interpretation from Derrida's essay in 1963, "Violence and Metaphysics," in *Writing and Difference*, trans. Alan Bass (London: Routledge and Kegan Paul, 1978), to David Boothroyd's essay in 1988, "Responding to Levinas," in *The Provocation of Levinas*, ed. R. Bernasconi and D. Wood (London: Routledge and Kegan Paul, 1988).

33. Martin Heidegger, *Identity and Difference*, bilingual ed., trans. Joan Stambaugh (New York: Harper and Row, 1960), 117.

34. Heidegger, *Unterwegs zur Sprache*, 142 / Heidegger, *On the Way to Language*, 51.

35. Heidegger, *Unterwegs zur Sprache*, 32.

36. This emphasis upon the ethics of Heidegger's thinking runs contrary to Levinas's insistence that Heidegger's ontology is neutral, not ethical. It is Levinas who develops the ethics of the one for the other. This points, perhaps, to the fact that Steiner reads Heidegger through his appreciation of Levinas, Benjamin—whose ontological thinking was ethical—Franz Rosenzweig, and a Jewish understanding of "epiphany."

37. Martin Heidegger, *Wegmarken* (1976), 9:193; and "On the Essence of Truth," trans. R. F. C. Hull and Alan Crick, in *Existence and Being* (London: Vision Press, 1949), 340.

38. George Steiner, *Antigones: How the Antigone Legend Has Endured in Western Literature, Art, and Thought* (New York: Oxford University Press, 1984).

39. See note 1 above.

40. Martin Heidegger, *Holzwege* (1977), 5:347; and Heidegger, "The Anaximander Fragment," in *Early Greek Thinking*, 35.

41. Heidegger, *Gelassenheit*, 49 / Heidegger, *Discourse on Thinking*, 68.

Steiner's Fiction and the
Hermeneutics of Transcendence

AMONG THE MANY extraordinary moments in George Steiner's novel, *The Portage to San Cristóbal of A.H.*, surely it is Hitler's final speech that has generated the most controversy. As though the subject were not risky enough in itself, Steiner concludes the novel by including in Hitler's self-defense many of the ideas—and not a few of the phrases—that Steiner had himself used in his own essays. *In Bluebeard's Castle: Some Notes towards the Redefinition of Culture*, for example, had described three stages of "the blackmail of transcendence" by which Jews had pressed on Western civilization "a summons to perfection": the invention of "monotheism at Sinai, primitive Christianity, [and] messianic socialism."[1] The demands of this idealism proved so great that the civilization built up "murderous resentments" against the Jews, branding them "the 'bad conscience' of Western history" (*BC*, 45), and later trying to exterminate them and the threatening idealism they had come to represent. In his speech at the end of *The Portage*, Hitler uses Steiner's very phrase ("Three times the Jew has pressed on us the blackmail of transcendence"), then goes on to an explanation of the three stages, which in many respects resembles Steiner's.[2] Although some critics have drawn the astonishing and surely mistaken conclusion that Steiner must therefore have been sanctioning Hitler's position,[3] clearly Steiner's gesture of self-quotation is significant, and it bears directly on any consideration of the relationship between his fiction and essays.

Nobody is more aware than Steiner of this past decade's reconsideration of the relationships among genres, of its withering critique of essentialistic conceptions of generic purity, and of its insistence that a precise distinction between "creative" and "critical" writing cannot be sustained. Steiner does, finally, want to preserve the latter distinction, but not without a deep sense of both the difficulty of drawing boundaries and the rich potential for serious play across those boundaries.

There are many ways in which the defining features of Steiner's work are tied up with precisely this violation of boundaries. His critics say that his criticism is preposterously overwritten and that his fiction is too concerned with ideas. A more charitable way to put the point might be to say that in his critical and theoretical work he often writes like a novelist and that in his fiction his concern with ideas makes him seem theoretical. For Steiner to foreground ideas in his fiction and his own style in his criticism is to invite a certain misunderstanding. But clearly he does so with full awareness, and one wonders if his critics on this point are not relying on unexamined formalistic assumptions that all too simplistically distinguish the aesthetic from the intellectual, or the imaginative from the theoretical, ignoring the crucial crossovers.

Nor is this the only regard in which critics have been mystified by Steiner. To ask—as apparently his colleagues at Cambridge did rather uncharitably a decade ago—"What exactly is his field?" was not simply to ask whether he was a Renaissance specialist or a Modernist, but rather whether he was in "English" at all. Who is this man writing about Tolstoy and Lévi-Strauss and Benjamin, to say nothing of chess, music, mountain climbing, topology, the Holocaust, and linguistics? Even in our current academic/literary configurations, where the old model of historical "fields" has been increasingly eroded, Steiner continues to stand betwixt and between. In some ways he writes for that mythical figure, the "general reader"; in some ways he writes for the most esoteric specialist. He is often accused of being arrogant in his writing, but, as we shall see, he is as nakedly modest as any critic alive. Although there may be a grain of truth in caricatures of him as pompously delivering papal declarations, there is no critic whose work is so deeply grounded in the serious posing of original but unanswered questions.

"Consciously or not," says Steiner in the "Introduction" to *George Steiner: A Reader*, "I thought of myself as some kind of courier carrying urgent letters and signals to those few who might respond with interest and, in their turn, pass on the challenging news."[4] The image of Hermes shuttling across borders, crossing frontiers, ranging from field to field seems perfectly apt not only to Steiner's passionate antagonism to nationalism and his commitment to the values of the cosmopolitan Diaspora but also to his central work as a literary and cultural critic and a writer of fiction. For it is the ideal of translation, in this radical, fundamental sense that Steiner develops in *After Babel: Aspects of Language and Translation*—as a carrying across from one field or locus or realm into another—that is Steiner's model for all hermeneutic acts, as well as his most pervasive trope for comprehending experience, in both his fiction and his essays. To see him whole we need to understand just how deeply this notion of translation informs his vision and his sense of his work as an agent of movement or exchange across borders—from one language to another, from field to field, across cultures and historical periods and genres, across the permeable but important boundary between the creative and the critical, and, most significantly in his recent work, from the secular world of immanence to what he often calls the *"mysterium tremendum"* of transcendence.

To illuminate the connections between Steiner's fiction and criticism, I want to focus on his most ambitious work of fiction, *The Portage*; on its connection with his most ambitious theoretical work, *After Babel*; and on his recent critical book, *Real Presences*. Although the debates about Paul de Man remind us of the dangers of glibly speculating about relations between hermeneutics and actual historical horrors, with Steiner there is no escaping the intimate connection between his understanding of the Holocaust and his theory of interpretation and thus translation.

According to Steiner, the Holocaust—or, as he now prefers to call it, the "Shoah"—enacted "the travesty of all meaningfulness."[5] "A thousand years you men have argued, ravelled, spun words," says a woman on her way into the Nazis' gas chambers in Steiner's fable "A Conversation Piece": "You have read yourselves blind, crooked your backs, poring over the single letter or the missing vowel . . . as if truth could be caught in your fingers. You have burrowed for meaning like starved mice and pounded the words so fine they have fallen to dust. . . . To what end? Have you found those syllables which make up the secret name of God? . . . Was it all for *this*?"[6] To have posed this skeptical declaration, this chilling interrogation on the way to the gas chambers is to suggest that the question of meaning and interpretation —the whole hermeneutic dilemma—must be taken up in the urgent historical context of the Holocaust, an event that for Steiner forever transformed not only our sense of the possibilities of human conduct but also our very sense of language—of its import, its power to deceive and corrupt and destroy.

In *The Portage*, molding and transforming the conventions of the thriller, the historical novel, and the *roman philosophique*, Steiner explores the disquieting implications for interpretation of the whole phenomenon of Hitler. To put the matter in this way is to suggest a crass readiness to move too quickly from brutal historical fact to speculation and theory—a tendency that this novel does not, emphatically, demonstrate. But for Steiner, Hitler inevitably poses the most fundamental problems of meaning: How can we make sense of him and what he did, particularly because he was, in Steiner's view, a master manipulator of language and meaning himself?

The fundamental structural premise of *The Portage* is that Hitler is a text to be interpreted. Discovered alive in a remote South American jungle by an Israeli search party at the beginning of the novel, Hitler is carried through the heart of darkness on a wildly symbolic mission of retrieval, which becomes a brilliant parable and enactment of translation as a carrying over from one place to another: a transportation, a "portage." The task of making sense of Hitler and his capture, of comprehending this infinitely reverberating bundle of signification, is both monumental and terrifying. The very structure of the novel can be seen as a network of variously congruent or discordant translations of Hitler into meaningful constructs that the various interpreters unknowingly revert to in order to comprehend what finally remains elusive.

For the younger generation, for example, Hitler is "a figure out of the dim past, somewhere between the neolithic and the almost equally remote day-before-yesterday . . . all part of a school syllabus and television past. Totally unreal. Categorized for examination purposes or entertainment" (*P*, 142–43). For the Americans he becomes not a historical text, but a psychological one, a mere pattern of pathology. "The psychologists will have their day" if the Americans get hold of him, says the French under-secretary of state: " 'The Rehabilitation of Adolf

Hitler; the elucidation of his childhood traumas.' The triumph of the therapeutic" (142). In the Röthling chapter, Hitler becomes a legal text, somebody who has generated a file of "convolutions, proliferating codices, minority reports and thousand-page addendum . . . the prodigality of conjectured happening, the ramifications of invoked precedent and counterexample docketed in his file were such as no other legal body could hope to equal" (121–22).

The rush to make sense of Hitler breeds a chaos of interpretations, of desperate attempts to move in on the prey and capture him. "So many signals were poring in, so many indices of feverish advance somewhere just beyond the horizon" (147). The battered radio transmitter that the search party uses to keep in touch with the outside world becomes an emblem of the frailty of our instruments of communication and comprehension. Barely functional because eaten through by jungle rot, at one point it is "picking up a signal though it could no longer amplify or sort it out" (55).

Beyond the jungle the Soviets are scrambling to translate the discovery of Hitler into their own official version of reality, a version that one Nikolai Gruzdev had his fingernails ripped out for earlier contradicting. When he is asked now whether he thinks Hitler could possibly be alive, he responds in a way that points again to the shaken foundations of meaning in every sense: "I will say whatever you wish me to say. Possible, gentlemen? Everything is possible. *Everything*" (38). It is a point Steiner himself had made in his 1966 essay "Postscript": that after the Holocaust we are "now instructed as never quite before—and it is here that history *is* different—of the fact that 'everything is possible.'"[7]

The French, in their turn, see only the prospect of an embarrassing reopening of the question of their wartime complicity with the Nazis. In the United States the secretary of state reverts to bureaucratic jargon about "the current eventuality," and "the accused's mental condition and degree of responsibility" (154), while a journalist seeks his assurance "that due process will be followed and, most especially, that the accused will be given every legal aid for his defense" (155).

That otherwise important matters such as due process and the right to legal defense seem utterly beside the point here is simply to say that, like the other "translations" of Hitler, this one trivializes the appallingly complex reality of its text. Steiner drives home this point in the ultimate vulgarizations of the American Marvin Crownbacker, who appears one day in the squalid hut of an intelligence operative,

Rodriguez Kulken, very close to the scene of the search party. "This was the biggest story of the century," he tells Kulken:

Bigger than Lindberg. . . . Bigger than Jonestown . . . this was the hottest news break since Jesus got off his slab. This was like being at tombside . . . they'll have to come to us, Mr. Kulken, 'cause we'll have the contracts, the sole and exclusive right to deal with and negotiate for the sale of subsidiary and other rights within all territories covered by said agreement, i.e. newspaper and magazine serialization, anthology digest quotation and abridgement, dramatic, film, radio and television, microphotographic reproduction and picturization, reproduction by phonograph records and other mechanical means whether by sight, sound or a combination thereof. (107)

Last on the outrageous list, as though all the other items had not already been instances of translation: "translation into any foreign language and that, sir, includes Bantu, Toltec, Easter Island and/or Yiddish" (107).

"To *trans/late*," says Steiner in the "Introduction" to his *Penguin Book of Modern Verse Translation*, is "to carry over from what has been silent to what is vocal, from the distant to the near. But also to carry back."[8] "When he can't walk," says Benasseraf about Hitler, "we'll *carry* him. . . . We'll take turns *carrying* him. Like the ark" (23; emphasis mine).

After Babel, which grew directly out of Steiner's speculations in his early anthology of verse translation, is an extended meditation on both the "burden" and the "splendour" of Babel,[9] a meditation that takes its bearings from the claim that translation between and within languages is the model of all understanding and interpretation. Understanding, that is to say, is correct or effective translation. Culture is understood by Steiner to be a tissue of translations, an enormously complex web constituted by the continual reordering and reshaping of previous meanings and configurations of meanings. "It is no overstatement," he claims, "to say that we possess civilization because we have learnt to translate out of time" (*AB*, 30–31).[10]

The stakes of translation could not, then, be higher, a point on which Steiner cites the authority of Goethe writing to Carlyle: "Say what you will of its inadequacy, translation remains one of the most important, worthwhile concerns in the totality of world affairs" (*MVT*, 25). Goethe's emphasis matches Steiner's precisely, giving equal weight to both the inadequacy of translation and its necessity. In this respect *The Portage* is at one level a fable about the perplexities and possibilities, the limitations and urgencies, of translation. However inadequate, "the attempt to translate must be made," says Steiner, "the risks taken, if that tower in Babel is to be more than ruin" (29). Once the search party in *The Portage* captures its man, it confronts the soul-rending task of what to make of him. Interpretation and evaluation, comprehension and judgment can no more tidily be separated with regard to Hitler than with a work of literature, so here the issue of accurate judgment shades quickly into the question of justice.[11] "For Thou art judge," Elie Barach prays early in the book. "Thine is the vengeance and Thine the pardon. . . . Guard us from certitude. . . . Do not ask of us, O Lord, that we do vengeance or show mercy. The task is greater than we are. It passes understanding" (*P*, 22). We shall see, when we turn later to *Real Presences*, that this sense of humility when confronted with judging another human being has its analogue in acts of literary interpretation and evaluation, which, Steiner will argue, must finally be underwritten by the transcendent. But however perilous the act of translation may be, however fraught with difficulty and uncertainty and the possibility of radical misunderstanding, it must be undertaken. One does what one can, as the search party does at the end of the novel when it does indeed put Hitler on trial. "Where there is a temple," Elie tells Asher just before the trial,

let the rabbi speak. Where there is only a rabbi let the unlearned hold their peace. Where there are ten simple men left, let them join in counsel. Where there is but one man left, let him be steadfast as the temple was, let him seek out the meaning of the Law as the rabbi did, let him take counsel with himself as if a score of just men inhabited his heart. We have only ash in hand to kindle a great fire. (157)

One begins a translation, then, in trust, which constitutes the first of the four stages or motions that Steiner outlines for the act of translation in *After Babel*. The parallels with *The Portage* are striking. Translation begins with the assumption, not so obvious as it might at first appear, that "there is 'something there' to be understood . . . an investment of belief . . . epistemologically exposed and psychologically hazardous" (*AB*, 296). The very premise of the search party, that Hitler is alive in the jungle, seems the maddest gamble, exposing them to every conceivable form of doubt about the meaning of their venture. In one sense, then, their situation represents a dramatic enactment of precisely that radical exposure and hazard of which Steiner speaks in *After Babel*, though in the novel it is both intensified and symbolized by the enormity of physical danger that they confront throughout their mission. "No man," a local priest had explained to them, "could live in the unmapped quicksand and green bogs beyond the falls," nobody could survive the black rains that "lashed the clothing off their back," or the infernal swarms of insects as the members of the search party literally crawled the last thirty miles "inchwise. On their knees and with loosening bowels" (*P*, 17–18). But these men are in the obsessive grip of a vision, directed by their leader via radio from Tel Aviv: Emmanuel Lieber, a survivor who had "crawled out from under the burnt flesh in the death pits of Bialka" with "a perception so outside the focus of man's customary vision" that he could pursue his "one incessant dream" with a will utterly "inviolate to any other claim of life" (16–17).

"The second move," says Steiner, "is incursive and extractive. . . . . Comprehension, as its etymology shows, 'comprehends' not only cognitively but by encirclement and ingestion. . . . We 'break' a code; decipherment is dissective, leaving the shell smashed and the vital layers stripped" (*AB*, 297–98). Desperately, those on the periphery try to break the search party's code. Kulken, for example, lies awake listening "through the static and the oily wash of music" from the regional radio stations to "a code out of Revelation, an alphabet reversed and permuted out of Chronicles and Malachi" (*P*, 79). In Steiner's dramatization, the effort of decipherment is not only aggressive and dissective but also bone-shatteringly arduous work. "There were nights when his fingers had swollen to pale grubs just transcribing the stuff, trying to separate the syllables as they crackled or whispered out of the jungle. There had been thorns in his ears; he had felt them bleed" (80). That Steiner can sustain this symbolic rendering of the spiritual dynamics of translation/interpretation without compromising either the sheer literary suspense or the urgent historicity of the central plot is not least among the triumphs of this inspired fable; what is even more remarkable is that the subtext about translation achieves a power and resonance of its own that is virtually mythic in its portrayal of interpretation as a primal hunt for meaning.

Nor do the obstacles to be overcome cease with the seizure of the object. If the first step outlined in *After Babel* is trust and the second is aggression, the third is incorporation. "The import, of meaning and of form, the embodiment, is not made in or into a vacuum. The native semantic field is crowded" (*AB*, 98), as witness the array of semantic fields waiting hungrily on the jungle's periphery: Kulken and Crownbacker with their P.R., Röthling with his legal precedents, the French, Soviet, and American officials ready with their own structures of understanding to absorb and domesticate even this wild new piece of reality. But they are all anxious because "the act of importation can potentially dislocate or relocate the whole of the native structure. . . . No language, no traditional symbolic set or cultural ensemble imports without risk of being transformed" (299). It is here, I think, that we can begin to understand *The Portage* itself as a radical act of translation: a meditation on Hitler and the crisis of meaning, which aims to reshape our understanding of both the Holocaust and the nature of meaning itself.

The fourth and final stage of translation is "the enactment of reciprocity in order to restore balance" (300). The initial movement of trust and the fact that "we come home laden" cause "disequilibrium throughout the system by taking away from 'the other' and by adding . . . to our own. . . . The hermeneutic act must compensate . . . it must mediate into exchange. . . . The over-determination of the interpretive act is inherently inflationary . . . [and] enlarges the stature of the original . . . the latter is left more prestigious" (300–301). It is in this context that we can best understand those attacks on *The Portage* that claim the novel lends Hitler something of Steiner's own authority. For Steiner certainly does, at one level, enlarge the stature of Hitler, though it is important to emphasize that to do so is not to sanction or endorse Hitler—which has been a preposterous charge against Steiner and a complete misreading of *The Portage*—but rather to give Hitler his full due as an object of understanding. It is not that Steiner is impishly flirting with controversy or yielding to sensationalism, but rather that his view of language and understanding itself compels him to examine what might seem to be outrageous ambiguities, ironies, and resonances.

In a telling phrase in *After Babel* Steiner describes the third, the penultimate, stage of translation as "the *portage* home of the foreign 'sense' and its domestication in the new linguistic-cultural matrix. . . . It instances . . . the issue of 'alternity'" (333; emphasis mine), an issue central not only to this novel and his theory of translation but to all of his work. *After Babel* begins with an apparently innocent question:

Why are there so many languages? It is a question that Steiner, in a fashion characteristic of his best work, wants to dissociate from the deadening context of the obvious. As with so many of his searching questions, this one is meant to awaken our astonishment at what might before have seemed familiar. For Steiner it is a source of constant amazement to reflect that there are literally thousands of natural languages. "Why," he asks, "should human beings speak thousands of different, mutually incomprehensible tongues?" (49). His answer is that the main function of language is not to communicate information. "The outwardly communicative, extrovert thrust of language is secondary," he says. "The primary drive is inward and domestic" (231–32). The main function of language, then, is to create alternities, by which he means "the 'other than the case,' the counter-factual propositions, images, shapes of will and evasion with which we charge our mental being and by means of which we build the changing, largely fictive milieu of our somatic and social existence" (222). Language, he says, "is the main instrument of man's refusal to accept the world as it is" (217–18), which means that concealment, protection of one's identity and interior life are perhaps even more central functions of language than the outward movement of communication. "Distinct groups intent on keeping from one another the inherited, singular springs of their identity, and engaged in creating their own semantic worlds" speak different languages precisely in order to shape and preserve those identities and semantic worlds (232).

   If the essential genius of language is thus "creative [and] 'counter-factual'" (235), then the relation between lies and creativity becomes crucial. Steiner draws our attention to that relation in his numerous references to Hitler as a monstrous master of language. Gideon, for example, says of Hitler that "there is nothing he could not do with words. They danced for him" (P, 97). Steiner further emphasizes the relation in his controversial partial identification with Hitler through two types of allusion: having Hitler use some of the ideas and language from Steiner's own essays, and, even more shockingly, giving Hitler a withered arm, which Steiner himself has. In a manner that in curious ways recalls the coy self-allusions of Byron, both gestures violate the boundaries of historical and fictional actuality with the same kind of devilish abandon with which they leap across genres. The messiness of language is not, for Steiner, its defect but its vital energy; ambiguity, polysemy, the capacity to lie are "not pathologies of language but the roots of its genius" (*AB*, 235).

Falsity, then, becomes "an active, creative agent. The human capacity to utter falsehood, to lie, to negate what is the case, stands at the heart of speech" (214), which is one reason that Steiner's fascination with Hitler and the problem of meaning should not be passed off as indulgence or as insensitivity to historical suffering in the name of theory. "Central to everything I am and believe and have written," Steiner tells an interviewer for the *New York Times Book Review*, "is my astonishment, naive as it seems to people, that you can use human speech both to bless, to love, to build, to forgive and also to torture, to hate, to destroy and to annihilate."[12] "You must not let him speak," Lieber tells his men after they have caught Hitler:

Gag him if necessary. . . . If he is allowed speech he will trick you and escape. . . . His tongue is like no other. . . . All that is God's, hallowed be His name, must have its counterpart, its backside of evil and negation. So it is with the Word. . . . When He made the Word, God made possible also its contrary. . . . He created on the night side of language a speech for hell. . . . Let him speak to you and you will think of him as a man. . . . Words are warmer than fresh bread; share them with him and your hate will grow to a burden. (*P*, 44–46)

Robert Boyers, in his rebuttal to critics who have read Hitler's monologue as a vindication by Steiner, points out that one cannot interpret that speech outside the context established earlier by Lieber's monologue, from which I just quoted. "Hitler's speech," Boyers says, "is not a formal presentation of ideas; it is an elaborate self-defense mounted by a *character*. . . . The final speech demonstrates that a Hitler can appropriate a Steiner for his purposes by willfully ignoring, and thus violating, the *spirit and intent of Steiner's original utterances* and turning them to totally alien purposes."[13] Although Boyers does not make this point, his phrasing provides an almost perfect indication of what I take to be central here: that by violating the spirit and intent of Steiner's original, Hitler has, as it were, rendered a bad *translation* of Steiner. To put the matter in this way is obviously to suggest that Steiner is scrambling conventional divisions of chronology, to say nothing of the relations between fictional and historical realms. But it seems clear to me that, in a novel everywhere concerned with the problem of translation, we ought to read Hitler's self-defense as still another attempt—not unlike Röthling's and Crownbacker's and all the others'—to make sense out of the whole phenomenon of Hitler. In light of Lieber's earlier warning that Hitler will twist the truth, it seems much more plausible to take Hitler's use of the ideas and language of Steiner not as Steiner's attempt to vindicate Hitler, but rather as a wildly inaccurate translation of Steiner himself. There may be grains of truth in what Hitler says—and Steiner does clearly intend his speech to be provocative in this sense of challenging complaisant views—but the final result is an appallingly self-serving distortion on Hitler's part, a distortion that any careful reader of Steiner will recognize. Nonetheless, this extraordinary, Borgesian gesture of literary self-consciousness is consistent with Steiner's characteristic crossing of boundaries, with his continual trans-lation.

This movement from one world to another is a familiar theme in *The Portage* in other ways as well. In the throes of a raging malarial fever in the darkest depths of the jungle, Gideon, who had suffered terribly in the Holocaust, begins imagining another world. "Listen *zadik*," he tells Elie, "we'll go to the seaside you and I. Sit on a bench all day till the wind blows us clean. And say marvelous words like 'What time is it' or 'Stop picking your nose' or 'Do you want chocolate ice or vanilla?' Words human beings use" (*P*, 99). The world beyond the jungle feels like the merest dream, as though reality as it had been understood before the Holocaust were itself a kind of marvelous alternity or, as Steiner might put it, a kind of dreaming backward. "A man whose child has been burnt alive, whose wife has led another of his children into the gas, should use the future tense sparingly" (69).

Earlier in the novel Gideon confronts this sharp sense of disjunction when he looks at a post card containing scenes from his Parisian life before the war. The world that floods back into his memory is one of sidewalk cafés, of "Boursin with its shade of garlic and a pear . . . , bread . . . new as morning . . . her hair smoke-brown as September grass" (67). How, Steiner, wants to know, can that world be reconciled with the one Gideon now inhabits, or with the world of the Holocaust? The post card "arrested in a waking dream the otherness of the world, the illusion of total possibility without which the soul falls to a dusty heap" (68). This is the same language that Steiner uses to describe alternity, that urge to the extraterritorial that is both the glory and the bane of human imagining. Steiner sees it as a principle of radical free-

dom, dangerous because unpredictable, leading—painful as it may be
to contemplate—to the creations of both a Sophocles and a Hitler. "If
the Word can create, can it not," Steiner asks, "unmake and annihilate?" (*R*, 17). From the vantage point of the Holocaust, the familiar
world seems a dream, but the world Hitler created must also be understood as a dream—a cruel and perverse imagining, but an alternity
nonetheless. "It was he," says Lieber of Hitler, "who turned the dream
into day" (*P*, 51)—a point that could as easily be made of a great artist.

Steiner underlines the association between alternity and the mad
creations of Hitler by surrounding the fictional Hitler with a brooding
radiance, which arises as much out of silence as anything else, an
intensity of being that is shockingly Heideggerian, with something of
the awful immensity of Blake's tiger or Yeats's "rough beast." The
jungle itself embodies the fierce contraries of life and death, creation
and destruction, which leap to life when a bat is killed: "The ground
sprang alive. In a moment the white maggots were at its belly and a
dung beetle had its scissors in the dead wing" (90). Even the lair where
Hitler is snared has the aura of the extraterritorial: "Pure hell I'd imagine. . . . No one really knows. . . . So far as we can tell there's never
been a party beyond the falls. . . . And they're a thousand miles from
nowhere" (12). Hitler resides in a moral or imaginative territory that is
literally off the charts, a place where "the maps went mute" (17). It is
because of that fact, because the terrible enormity of his being and his
creations cannot be readily comprehended in the usual languages of
human understanding, that to understand him requires an act of translation, which, like any great translation, alters the contours and structure of the language into which it is translated.

"One of the things I cannot grasp," says Steiner in his early essay
"Postscript," "is the time relation." He is "trying to get . . . into some
kind of bearable perspective" the horrors visited upon two men during
the Holocaust:

At a previous point in rational time, Professor Mehring was sitting in his
study, speaking to his children. . . . And flayed alive . . . Langner was, in
some sense, the same human being who had, a year earlier, . . . walked the
daylight street, done business, looked forward to a good meal, read an intellectual monthly. But in what sense? Precisely at the same hour in which Mehring
or Langner was being done to death, the overwhelming plurality of human
beings . . . were sleeping or eating or going to a film or making love or
worrying about the dentist. This is where my imagination balks. The two

orders of simultaneous experience are so different, so irreconcilable to any
common norm of human values, their co-existence is so hideous a paradox
. . . that I puzzle over time. (*PS*, 156)

Time and again in *The Portage* we confront these contrasts between
two worlds that seem utterly irreconcilable. It is precisely that sense of
hysterically outrageous juxtaposition, welding Nazi brutalities hideously together with images of domestic tranquility and noble aspiration, that makes Lieber's epic catalogue of horrors so powerful. It is this
same principle of contrast that makes the opening movement of the
novel so jarringly effective, moving seamlessly as it does from the
discovery of Hitler in the hellish jungle to the polished sheen of oiled
book bindings and fine-grained furniture in the inner sanctum of an
élite British university.

Perhaps the most recurrent theme in Steiner's writing about the
Holocaust is the inadequacy of what he calls "pragmatist-positivist
levels of argument" (*LLM*, 61). "Understandably," he says in *In Bluebeard's Castle*, "in an effort to make the insane material susceptible and
bearable to reason, sociologists, economists, political scientists have
striven to locate the topic in a rational, secular grid." But none of these
approaches can explain the "active indifference . . . of the vast majority
of the European population," or the Nazi decision to liquidate the Jews
instead of exploiting them "towards obvious financial and practical
ends," or the "persistence of violent anti-Semitism where no Jews or
only a handful survive. . . . The mystery, *in the proper theological sense*,
is one of hatred without present object" (*BC*, 34–36; emphasis mine).
Steiner is not denying the need for "pragmatical systematic studies"
of the Holocaust; he is simply underlining their limitations and their
failure to illuminate "the deeper-lying roots of the inhuman" (*LLM*,
57–58).

This is not the place to examine the details of Steiner's complex and
controversial attempts to provide more illuminating explanations. For
our purposes the important point is that for Steiner the origins of the
Holocaust are as complex as its meaning, and any hypothesis about
them that is worth pursuing "cannot be 'proved'; the evidence for it is
not of an empirical or quantifiable kind. . . . Only a theological-
metaphysical scale of values . . . can hope to throw some light—I do
not lay claim to more—on the aetiology, on the causal dynamics of
Jew-hatred and of the Auschwitz experience" (59). The only language,

that is to say, into which the Holocaust can be intelligibly translated, is the theological. [14]

Anyone who has followed Steiner's recent forays into hermeneutics should be struck by this claim that the only way to understand the Holocaust is to approach it from the perspective of the theological. For Steiner has been making roughly the same argument with regard to interpretation itself, which in recent years has had its own crisis confronting the question of meaning. "Today," Steiner says in the 1984 "Introduction" to *George Steiner: A Reader*, "more and more of my work is an attempt . . . to discover whether and in what rational framework it is possible to have a theory and practise of understanding (hermeneutics) and a theory and practise of value-judgements (aesthetics) without a theological reinsurance or underwriting" (*R*, 8). Any serious theory of interpretation, Steiner insists, requires the underwriting of "a theology or, at the least, of a transcendent metaphysics. . . . I cannot arrive at any rigorous conception of a possible determination of either sense or stature," he says in his 1985 Leslie Stephen Memorial Lecture at Cambridge, "which does not wager on a transcendence, on a real presence, in the act and product of serious art." [15]

After all the concessions to ambiguity in *After Babel*, after all the disclaimers that communication is the central function of language, after all the encyclopedic cataloguing of the difficulties and limits of translation, Steiner still concludes that "translation is desirable and possible" (*AB*, 253). However multifaceted and elusive the great work of art may be, however difficult it may be to comprehend the Holocaust, the attempt must be made, as Steiner's nearly obsessive rethinking and reworking of the Shoah over the years and in a variety of forms suggest. Despite, or perhaps because of, the crisis of meaning created by the Holocaust and deconstruction, a leap of faith is required in any act of interpretation, something like that first stage of trust in the four steps of translation that Steiner outlines. "Without some axiomatic leap towards a postulate of *meaning-fulness*," he says in the Leslie Stephen Memorial Lecture, "there can be no striving toward intelligibility or value-judgement however provisional." Consequently, "we must read *as if*. We must read as if the text before us had meaning" (*LSML*, 17–18). If the text is a serious one, this meaning will be neither single nor ahistorical, and it will never be exhausted by commentary or interpretation. But without this "as if," without this "axiomatic conditionality," "literacy becomes transient Narcissism" (18–19).

Steiner's recent critical book *Real Presences* works explicitly from this premise, developing a fascinating and, as always, controversial argument about the necessary relationship of art and the transcendent. Although space prevents me from examining that argument more fully in this essay, I want to emphasize that the question of how one bridges those two realms is closely connected with the question of translation.[16] What we are confronting here is the central paradox, for Steiner, of translation: its difficulties are virtually limitless, but it remains a vital and essential task and must be undertaken with all the skill and knowledge and sensitivity and wisdom that one can muster.

But "the ideal [of translation], never accomplished," Steiner has said, "is one of total counterpart or re-petition—an *asking again*—which is not, however, a tautology" (*AB*, 302; emphasis mine). Precisely because of translation's insistent paradox—its ideal can never be accomplished but must always be pursued—it is the question, the "asking," that becomes the signature of Steiner's distinctive style of translation. Without exploring the central influence of Heidegger in this regard, it is worth noting the connection, for Steiner's explication of the role of questions in Heidegger has more than a little relevance for his own work. "Questions . . . are only worth asking," Steiner says, "of that which is worth questioning, of that 'which is questionable in a sense implying not the guarantee of an answer, but at least that of an informing response.'"[17]

That an answer may not be forthcoming is not a problem for Steiner. Time and again in his work it is his brilliant and provocative formulation of questions that matters most and cuts most deeply. I referred earlier to his attempt to recover from the deadening context of the obvious the question of why there are so many languages in the world. Steiner is constantly urging us to see issues freshly, to recognize, as he says of Heidegger, that "the font of genuine thought is astonishment" and that "questioning" is "the translation of astonishment into action" (*H*, 57). "Again," Steiner says about a question he has just posed in *Antigones*, "I ask: Why should this be so? . . . I am not certain that we have registered an appropriate sense of astonishment" (*A*, 122–23).

In the last section of *In Bluebeard's Castle*, as he turns to the final set of issues that he wants to examine, Steiner poses a question, then says something quite remarkable: "This is the last question I want to touch on. And by far the most difficult. I can state it and feel its extreme pressure. But I have not been able to think it through in any clear or consequent manner" (*BC*, 135). We need to pause over this frank admission of the limits of one's understanding and notice how rare it is— rare at any time, but particularly so in our present critical climate. Given the extent to which skeptical presuppositions now inform critical thinking and practice, it is rather ironic that one does not encounter more humility. One reason, of course, is that it has become conventional to assume an equality of author and critic, text and commentary, a situation that obviously elevates the status of the critic. It is thus doubly ironic that in such a universe of critical discourse someone such as Steiner, who has vigorously opposed the erosion of this distinction and the consequent elevation of the critic, should be considered arrogant.

From his earliest essays and books to his most recent, Steiner has, more than any other critic I know, continually emphasized both the provisionality of his claims and the limits of his understanding. What has misled his more uncharitable readers is that this consistent skepticism and stringent sense of limits have not led Steiner to renounce the quest for understanding, much less to deny its possibility. On the contrary, it has led him to seek it with such relentless passion and singleness of purpose that he sometimes adopts a prophetic voice, which is often misinterpreted as an indication of self-righteousness. What that voice does indicate is an extraordinary intensity and earnestness, both of which can threaten people, to say nothing of the vastness of Steiner's learning. What business does this man have working constantly outside his "field"? Time and again Steiner is taken to task by specialists in this or that academic field for some alleged inaccuracy, and indeed there are instances when the charges are warranted. But it seems to me that in the vast majority of cases the real grievance is unstated: Where does Steiner derive the authority to make pronouncements about my territory? Where does this man get off violating every conceivable established boundary?

It would be difficult to exaggerate the frequency with which Steiner thematizes questioning, both in his fiction and his essays, and it would be equally difficult to exaggerate the centrality that questions— carefully formulated but often unanswered ones—occupy in his work as a whole. He does, of course, often try to answer the questions that he poses, but the sense of provisionality is so insistent, the assertions are so obviously being kept at risk, that Steiner's humility is easily mistaken for disingenuousness, particularly in light of his vast learning, his impatience with cant, and his occasional—and they *are* only occasional—lapses into papal pronouncement.

This unfamiliar combination of ambition and modesty, of lofty purpose and humility, is not only a function of the paradox of translation; it is also related to the issue of transcendence. "At most," Steiner says in the final paragraph of *In Bluebeard's Castle*, "one can try to get certain perplexities into focus. Hope may lie in that small exercise" (141). The posture puts one readily in mind of a kind of theological humility, a stance toward understanding transcendent meaning and mystery, which has its clear analogue in Steiner's hermeneutics. Repeatedly, reading Steiner, one is grateful for the questions he poses, for the way he brings complex issues into focus, teases out strands of an argument, tries out hypotheses, speculates boldly but always provisionally. In one sense there is an important parallel, in terms of humility, with Socrates, who knew enough, he said, to know how much he did not know. But in another sense Steiner's humility is un-Socratic in much the same way that he says Heidegger's is:

To question truly is to enter into harmonic concordance with that which is being questioned. Far from being initiator and sole master of the encounter, as Socrates, Descartes and the modern scientist-technologist so invariably are, the Heideggerian asker lays himself open to that which is being questioned and becomes the vulnerable locus, the permeable space of its disclosure. (Again, the parallel with religious models, . . . with the risk of nakedness implicit in the dialectic of prayer, is unmistakable.) (*H*, 56)

The questioner lays himself open, that is to say, to the "real presence" of that which is being questioned, which discloses itself in the act of translation. The questioner's humility arises both from the inherent difficulty of his task and from his respect for the "real presence" that he now approaches. Interpretation thus becomes for Steiner a kind of secular petition, a "re-petition," as he calls it, an "asking again," in which one trains one's most concentrated, virtually prayerful attention not on God but on the text, which becomes the divine analogue. Of course "text" encompasses here not only literary texts but also cultural and historical ones, in the full modern sense derived from semiotics. Steiner's assiduous concern with the Holocaust, for example, should be understood in this context as just such a "re-petition," and it arises from that same radical sense of astonishment. Anxious lest the Holocaust come to be perceived as "a rational fact of life, a platitude," not unlike our jaded sense that of course there are many languages, Steiner argues that "we must keep in sharp focus its hideous novelty. . . . We must keep vital in ourselves a sense of scandal so overwhelming that it affects every significant aspect of our position in history and society. . . . I cannot stress this enough" (*BC*, 48).

The danger of hectoring is clear, not only because the Holocaust is so inherently painful to contemplate but also because a certain re-petition is required if that sense of scandal is to be kept vital. The line between vitalizing re-petition and dulling repetition is a fine one. Moreover, Steiner presses his quest for understanding into precisely those aspects of the subject that have been forbidden because they are so controversial. There is indeed a certain feistiness about Steiner, a love of "mental fight," which occasionally slips over into an indulgent flir-tation with controversy for its own sake. Frequently, Steiner speaks in a prophetic voice that, like all prophetic voices, is easily parodied. Edward Said refers to Steiner's "absurdly theatrical generalizations"; Ihab Hassan suggests that "he can seem too vehement, hortatory, over-bearing" and that "he raises his voice in public"; Terrence Des Pres says that Steiner "wears his learning on his breastplate"; and Morris Dick-stein claims that his "most ambiguous trait" is "the moral anguish he wears on his sleeve."[18]

Together with his occasional impishness and what Steiner himself might call his dark, Dostoevskyan (as opposed to Tolstoyan) streak, his feistiness has touched more than a few raw nerves among his critics. But one has to wonder if the more extreme reactions to Steiner's incessant probing of the Holocaust might not be related to a phenome-non that he has so often explored in his fiction and essays: the fear of the Jew as the "bad conscience" of the human race.[19] For the questions he raises are not only unpleasant; they are repeated, recast, reasked with the kind of urgency that we would do well to see not as hectoring and sensationalism, but rather as re-petition in the theological sense to which I referred.

One is reminded in this connection of a memorable character in Elie Wiesel's *Night*: Moché the Beadle, who was the young Elie's religious teacher before he was taken away with all the other "foreign Jews" by the Hungarian police. When Moché miraculously escaped and re-turned to Elie's town with horrifying stories of babies being used as machine-gun targets, nobody believed him. But what sticks with Elie about Moché is his teacher's notion "that every question possessed a power that did not lie in the answer. 'Man raises himself toward God by the questions he asks Him,' he was fond of repeating."[20]

"We have the obligation," says Steiner in a symposium on the responsibility of intellectuals,

> of pressing the unpleasant questions, the questions which are in bad taste, the embarrassing questions, the taboo questions. Being so privileged as we are it is almost our imperative job not to ask the nice questions, not to ask the comfortable questions. At the moment, of course, looking about us even in the most liberal of societies, there is an astonishing list of taboo questions, the raising of which ruins one's professional hopes, or one's friendships, or whatever. Well, if that is what matters most then the intellectual is in the wrong business.[21]

The fury unleashed upon the publication of *The Portage* and the production of its theatrical version on the London stage testifies to Steiner's point.[22] Hitler's monologue does indeed constitute an upping of the ante, but the gamble is in the service of pressing precisely these kinds of unpleasant, embarrassing, even taboo questions. It is not exactly true that Steiner translated his essayistic concern with both translation and the Holocaust to fiction fairly late in his career, for there are important respects in which the three stories that constitute *Anno Domini*, originally published in 1964, also deal with these issues. But in *The Portage* Steiner seems to have found a way of making questioning, in this theological sense of re-petitioning, a fundamental structural principle that is tied up with the central tropes of translation and alternity. Teku's one-word response to Hitler's speech, "proved" (P, 170), comports both an appropriate ambiguity and a final interrogative posture that is consistent with the Talmudic meaning, as Steiner explains it in an interview, of Teku's name: "that there are issues here beyond our wisdom to answer or decide" (*NYTBR*, 20).

Steiner has been cautious about moving more fully into the writing of fiction, but I think we see with *The Portage* an increasing attraction, as he puts it, to "the kind of patience of apprehension and open-endedness of asking which fiction can enact."[23] Fiction becomes a more appropriate genre to create and explore alternities, to explore those theological dimensions of the Holocaust and of the drama of meaning that Steiner now considers impervious to empirical study and rational analysis. The disjunction between those realms, which is the deepest source of the astonishment that issues in questioning, is explored in his recent story, "A Conversation Piece." In the tradition of midrash, Steiner reexamines the story of Abraham and Isaac from a multiplicity of viewpoints, including Sarah's, and in the process he weaves a dense and suggestive fable about the status of meaning in a world that, he is again astonished to acknowledge, could actually have included the Holocaust. The story begins *in medias res*, with a character citing an early seventeenth-century commentary on the biblical narrative, so we have the sense of entering the middle of an endless conversation whose object is interpreting the sacrifice of Isaac. The characters try to untangle the perplexities of freedom, faith, and obedience; they meditate and quote commentaries on the nature of silence, nationhood, and temptation; they cite authorities on the similarity of God and Satan; they speculate about Christ and sacrifice and the exclusion of women, trying all the while to understand, to comprehend, to wrestle some sense out of things. What we find ourselves in the midst of, then, is an apparently seamless web of glosses, interpretations, translations, re-visions, re-petitions. We enter immediately into this dense thicket of textuality, so we quickly find ourselves moving in the same environment of interpretation, the same insistent context of translation, that Steiner images in the jungles of *The Portage.*

When, at the end of the story, it becomes devastatingly clear that the setting for this narrative is Hitler's gas chambers, which are at precisely that moment being turned on, the question is raised whether all this burrowing for meaning is not utterly in vain, and an outrageous luxury to boot. Steiner is pressing here the full weight of the argument for viewing interpretation and the problem of meaning in an exclusively historical, secular context. But the final speech of the story, which directly follows and responds to this powerfully persuasive and moving cry of skeptical anguish, gives voice to an equally compelling counterpoint: "Thought is the dance of the mind. The spirit dances when it seeks out meaning, and the meaning of that meaning. . . . The dance-steps of the soul are words. . . . The lords of the dance are we. Are we not dancing now?" (*CP*, 177). Are we not, this character asks, performing a kind of spiritual dance even now as we debate the nature of meaning? Interpretation from this perspective is an emphatically and inevitably spiritual activity, one that unavoidably involves the transcendent, and thus stands in a relation of dynamic tension with the secular and exclusively historical view. This tension also parallels something of the paradox of translation, which is for Steiner both fraught with difficulty and absolutely crucial, both an impossibility and, when it truly happens, a kind of miracle.

In another of his recent fictions, the brief piece "Desert Island Discs," Steiner seems to be coming even more fully into his own by examining what happens when he brings into juxtaposition an extraordinary range of events, images, ideas, tones, and planes of reality. From a surrealistic sound archive, the main character makes six selections, listening to recordings of such disparate sounds as Fortinbras's belch after a banquet following Hamlet's death, the scratching of Clausius's pen nib as he writes the fundamental equation of entropy, and the laugh of a woman in a dark London alley as her lover "drank of her."[24] The metaphor of music is critical here, for—and this is a recurrent theme both in the fiction and in the essays—Steiner considers music "the most 'iconic,' the most 'really present' essent known to man," and thus "that which most absolutely resists paraphrase or translation" (C/R, 443).[25]

"The evident reason for the irreducibility of the iconic," says Steiner, "is that that which declares and conceals itself in the text . . . is of the order of being rather than of meaning, or, more accurately, that it has force incarnate in but also in excess of sense" (442–43). Although the iconic is found in its purest form in music, "infolding and resistance of this kind characterize all living texts," says Steiner (443). The best interpretation will attempt to translate meaning, but it will also, when it fully succeeds, translate the original text's "being," and, though this is translation's greatest challenge, it is also its greatest triumph: to translate what is, paradoxically, untranslatable. By working with richly suggestive imagistic and conceptual juxtapositions and trying to render something very much like their unique and multifarious "melodies," Steiner in this story seems to be exploring, more daringly than ever before, the notion of "real presences" and their habitation within the odd and assorted nooks and crannies of both everyday and high intellectual/artistic life. As his concern with the transcendent moves into the foreground of his work, Steiner more and more turns to music as the *mysterium tremendum* of our relations to meaning, and thus increasingly he seems drawn to that "patience of apprehension and open-endedness of asking" that fiction, more than the essay, provides.

Notes

1. George Steiner, *In Bluebeard's Castle: Some Notes towards the Redefinition of Culture* (New Haven: Yale University Press, 1971), 44–45. Hereafter cited in the text as *BC*.

2. George Steiner, *The Portage to San Cristóbal of A.H.* (New York: Simon and Schuster, 1981), 166. Hereafter cited in the text as *P*. The novel originally appeared as a separate issue of *Kenyon Review*, n.s., vol. 1, no. 2 (Spring 1979). It won a PEN-Faulkner Stipend in 1983 and has been translated or pirated into nearly a dozen languages, though there is a prohibition on either a German or a Hebrew version of the novel and the play based upon it. In addition to *The Portage*, "A Conversation Piece," and "Desert Island Discs," all of which I discuss in this essay, Steiner's fiction includes *Anno Domini: Three Stories* (New York: Atheneum, 1964), reissued by Overlook (New York, 1986) and Faber and Faber (London, 1985); "The Deeps of the Sea," *Botteghe Oscure* 18 (1956): 303–21, which in 1958 was awarded an O. Henry Prize; and two more recent fables, "Noël" and "Proofs," which, together with "A Conversation Piece" and "Desert Island Discs," have just appeared in a new collection, *Proofs and Three Parables* (New York: Granta Books/Penguin, 1993).

3. See, e.g., Morris Dickstein, "Alive and Ninety in the Jungles of Brazil," a review of *The Portage to San Cristóbal of A.H.*, by George Steiner, *New York Times Book Review*, 2 May 1982, 13, 21; and Alvin H. Rosenfeld, *Imagining Hitler* (Bloomington: Indiana University Press, 1985), 83–102.

4. George Steiner, "Introduction," in *George Steiner: A Reader* (New York: Oxford University Press, 1984), 21. Hereafter cited in the text as *R*.

5. George Steiner, "The Long Life of Metaphor: An Approach to 'the Shoah,'" *Encounter* 68, no. 2 (February 1987): 56; hereafter cited in the text as *LLM*.

6. George Steiner, "A Conversation Piece," *Granta*, no. 15 (1985): 177; hereafter cited in the text as *CP*.

7. George Steiner, "Postscript," in *Language and Silence: Essays on Language, Literature, and the Inhuman* (1967; reprint, New York: Atheneum, 1974), 157. Hereafter cited in the text as *PS*.

8. George Steiner, "Introduction," in *The Penguin Book of Modern Verse Translation* (Harmondsworth: Penguin Books, 1966), 35. Hereafter cited in the text as *MVT*.

9. George Steiner, *After Babel: Aspects of Language and Translation* (1975; reprint, New York: Oxford University Press, 1976), 474. Hereafter cited in the text as *AB*. The second edition of this book was published after this essay was completed.

10. Steiner's most exhaustive application of *After Babel*'s claim that interpretation is translation is in *Antigones: How the Antigone Legend Has Endured in*

Western Literature, Art, and Thought (1984; reprint, New York: Oxford University Press, 1986), esp. 214–25. Hereafter cited in the text as *A*.

11. Steiner explores the mutual dependence of the interpretation and evaluation of literary works in "'Critic'/'Reader,'" *New Literary History* 10 (Spring 1979): 423–52. Hereafter cited in the text as *C/R*.

12. D. J. R. Bruckner, "Talk with George Steiner," *New York Times Book Review*, 2 May 1982, 20. Hereafter cited in the text as *NYTBR*.

13. Robert Boyers, *Atrocity and Amnesia: The Political Novel since 1945* (New York: Oxford University Press, 1985), 169–70; emphasis mine.

14. It is in this context that we ought to consider Steiner's controversial claims that the Nazi extermination camp "embodies, often down to minutiae, the images and chronicles of Hell in European art and thought"; that all the death camps of the twentieth century are *"Hell made immanent,"* transferred from "below the earth to its surface"; and that, with the waning of religious belief, "needing Hell, we have learned to build it and run it on earth" (*BC*, 53–56).

15. George Steiner, *Real Presences: The Leslie Stephen Memorial Lecture* (Cambridge: Cambridge University Press, 1986), 23. Hereafter cited in the text as *LSML*. The much-expanded, book-length version of this lecture/pamphlet is *Real Presences* (Chicago: University of Chicago Press, 1989). Hereafter cited in the text as *RP*.

16. I take up these issues in greater detail in "Creation and the Courtesy of Reading," my review of *Real Presences* in *Kenyon Review*, n.s. 13 (Winter 1991): 187–92; and in my essay "Interrogation at the Borders: George Steiner and the Trope of Translation," *New Literary History* 21 (Autumn 1989): 133–62.

17. George Steiner, *Heidegger* (London: Fontana, 1978), 29. Hereafter cited in the text as *H*.

18. Edward Said, "Himself Observed," review of *George Steiner: A Reader*, *Nation* 240 (2 March 1985): 244; Ihab Hassan, "The Whole Mystery of Babel: On George Steiner," *Salmagundi*, nos. 70–71 (Spring-Summer 1986): 332; Terrence Des Pres, "Kulturkritiker," review of *Antigones* by George Steiner, *Nation* 240 (2 March 1985): 241; and Dickstein, "Alive and Ninety in the Jungles of Brazil," 21. Although Dickstein is negative throughout his review, Hassan is extremely enthusiastic, as is Des Pres in his assessment of *Antigones*: "There is no doubt about his brilliance" (241). Said's view is more mixed. Steiner, he says, "is without peer in rendering and reflecting on patterns and motifs in modern, mainly German, culture" (244). "There is much to be learned from what he says" (246). According to Said, *After Babel* "demonstrates a learning and insight that are remarkably exhilarating" (245). But Said's condescension is often flagrant, as in his claim that "Steiner is . . . a kind of humanistic relic" (246).

19. See esp. Steiner, "The Long Life of Metaphor"; *The Portage to San*

Cristóbal of A.H.; and "A Season in Hell," in *In Bluebeard's Castle*, 29–56.

20. Elie Wiesel, *Night*, trans. Stella Rodway (1960; reprint, New York: Bantam, 1982), 2–3. For important parallels, see George Steiner, "A Kind of Survivor," in *Language and Silence*, 140–54.

21. George Steiner, "The Responsibility of Intellectuals: A Discussion," *Salmagundi*, nos. 70–71 (Spring-Summer 1986): 194.

22. Christopher Hampton's production of *The Portage*, with Alec Mc-Cowen playing Hitler, was first produced in London during the winter of 1982. It has subsequently been produced throughout the United States as well.

23. Letter from George Steiner, 18 January 1988. Compare Steiner's answer to an interviewer's question about why he would want to "use a novel to raise the moral issues canvassed in 'The Portage to San Cristóbal of A.H.'": "I believe that a work of art, like metaphors in language, can ask the most serious, difficult questions in a way which really makes the readers answer for themselves; that the work of art far more than an essay or a tract involves the reader, challenges him directly and brings him into the argument" (Bruckner, "Talk with George Steiner," 13).

24. George Steiner, "Desert Island Discs," *Granta*, no. 18 (1985): 26.

25. In *The Portage* Gervinus Röthling says that music is "irreducible to language" (113), an observation that is played off against the vulgar lyrics of a pop song that both Kulken and the search party hear on the radio. Hitler is almost desperate to hear music. "Let me hear the music," he says. "I haven't heard music" (72). Compare *In Bluebeard's Castle*: "In the absence or recession of religious belief, close-linked as it was to the classic primacy of language, music seems to gather, to harvest us to ourselves" (122); "A Reading against Shakespeare": "Outside language lie the imperative spheres of the transcendental, of aesthetic, ethical and, perhaps, metaphysical awareness. Outside language, also, lies music, whose expressive, inferential access to these spheres is, precisely, that denied to verbal discourse" (14); *Real Presences: The Leslie Stephen Memorial Lecture*: "It is more than likely that the performance and personal reception of music are now moving to that cultural pivot once occupied by the cultivation of discourse and letters. . . . At decisive points, ours is today a civilization 'after the word'" (6); and the "Introduction," in *George Steiner: A Reader*: "Music . . . grows indispensable [to me], as if it had become the elect companion of identity, the homecoming to that inside oneself which time has in its keeping" (18).

John Cowper Powys and
George Steiner: A Relationship

A S T U D Y of the relations of Conrad with the state of the art in modern fiction observes that the characters in his later novels are "uncomfortably conscious of their own fictionality."[1] That is a point not only
just and subtle in its context but also with far-reaching implications. It
might well be said that most characters in recent fiction are, on the
contrary, *comfortably* conscious of their own fictionality. What is clearly
a matter of some uneasiness for Conrad, as an artist and a romantic, has
become the normal and accepted artistic premise for the modern, or
what we have come to call the postmodern, novel.

Long before the current critical orthodoxies—now looking as much
like museum pieces as every other theory of art that has had its day—
George Steiner demonstrated his remarkable powers of analyzing and
synthesizing the modes in which the language of art changed, re-
formed, and returned to itself in unexpected forms. He has seen our
fictionality not as a discovery that in becoming self-conscious has
changed its whole nature, but as a real presence: a benign premise of
language working as art, forming and reforming, moving as endless
circularity. He not only refrained from casting his findings in new
tablets of Mount Sinai, but also tacitly negated the overweening con-

ceit of modern criticism, based on Derrida, that illumination from without had finally arrived. How could it? How could the modes and inventions of language, to which consciousness is subject, not continue to present us perpetually with new and wholly different pictures of themselves?

Pictures of ourselves as well. We are gratified today to think of ourselves as fictional beings, acting out our own fictions, creating others inside fictionality itself. But we may in time return to the same sense of uneasiness and deprivation which Conrad obscurely felt in his own creation between the *truth* he wanted *"to make you see"* and the fictional beings required by a story, beings "uncomfortably conscious of their own fictionality." Today "truth" has become as comfortably superfluous as the fictionality of which it is "known" to be a part.

Steiner has surely been right to ignore these portentous but essentially flimsy and ephemeral constructs and deconstructions and to concentrate on the real and scholarly substances of language and literature, the perpetuity they ceaselessly engender inside themselves. A marvelous masterwork such as *After Babel: Aspects of Language and Translation* is a celebration of the powers of language and its symbiotic relationships, its office as Heidegger's "mistress of man." Steiner suggests that Shakespeare is used by language to the point where he seems at times "to 'hear' inside a word or phrase the history of its future echoes."[2] The idea of passivity as seeming like inspired and active vision offers a profound insight into the way in which Shakespeare's language works, and the way it affects us. And not Shakespeare's only. Whereas most modern poets or novelists give the impression—a discouraging one—of being conscious masters of their own fictional constructs, others can strike us as being voices or media in which the whole of language is speaking, so—to paraphrase Wordsworth's line—we feel that they are greater than they know. Steiner has always been fascinated by this phenomenon, and it lies at the root of his unique sense of the workings of language in art. In *After Babel* he has pursued it into out-of-the-way corners, to which I shall presently return, but my chief exploration in this essay shall be into and by way of Steiner's enthusiasm for a writer who has remained on the margins of academic literary appreciation, despite his obvious stature, as well as the high regard in which he is held by many readers in all walks of life.

John Cowper Powys and the great novels he wrote—great in all senses; most are extremely long—affords in many ways a sort of creative parallel to Steiner's wide-ranging interests and absorptions as a critic. They meet in the field of language: in Steiner's immensely erudite and comparative interest in the nature and nuances of utterance, and in Powys's remarkable and indeed wonderful insouciance in the utterance he spreads so prodigally before us. There is no question of Powys's characters being "uncomfortably conscious of their own fictionality"; no question of Powys being concerned with fictionality in any way. The language of his novels is not that of a modern writer of fiction. It is this absence of self-preservation and of instinctive boundaries in his writing—one cannot in this context use the word *style*—which makes him, it seems to me, of special interest to Steiner, and to his view of the self-transmuting metamorphoses of language.

There is a further point in this connection. As a trilingual critic and thinker, in French, German, English, Steiner frequently has the air in his writings of having been visited with the gift of tongues. His own utterance often strikes the reader as not being self-created, but arriving out of the veins and deposits and resources of language available to him. He does not hunt for words; they proffer themselves to him every which way, as if they were animating a frontierless country, or swelling to capacity a chosen vessel. Today critics, no less than novelists, are careful to stick to their own jargon and trademarks, the signs and habits by which they can be recognized and through which they make their message known. In Steiner there is a striking absence of these self-appointed signs. He sometimes seems—to venture a little further into metaphor—like an immensely learned Petrouchka, a puppet animated by language as the supreme showman, and whose life and soul are created in him by its own excitements, its own unbounded appetencies. No disrespect is intended in this metaphor: on the contrary, the strengths of Steiner as a critic come from the generosity with which he seems to allow all these catholic and cosmopolitan animations to flow through him and to transform him in the act and gesture of exposition.

In describing this I might also have been describing the created imagination and tongues that, in biblical terms, fill all the house of Powys's fiction. The chief reason why Powys has remained so persistently unadmitted to the modern academic canon is not the difficulty of "criticizing" his novels—significant though that kind of unspoken difficulty can be—but the bountiful instability of their linguistic and vocal resources. Melville is, as it were, a Salinger or a Carver compared to Powys; Powys's "discourse" (a good word, which like "gay" has become flattened and abused by mechanical treatment into a narrow compass) simply cannot be evaluated in terms of any orthodox academic standards of good and bad. It exemplifies in one sense the extreme, almost the *ad absurdum*, point of what is academically most embarrassing in any example of the novel form itself. Some like it, some do not: some see the vision, others cannot.

The significant distinction, indeed, between Powys and other novelists, especially where criticism is concerned, is that there is not even any common ground from which to start. A Graham Greene enthusiast, say, who is writing about what he likes in Greene, would have no problem in securing the general agreement and sympathy of other Greene fans, however much they might differ in minor ways. But the "evaluation" of Powys has to be undertaken in spaces so wide that the critic is usually impelled to make his own little world in his own corner of the Powys one, preferring not to notice the other worlds. He becomes a legitimate expert on Welsh myth or on some aspect of Powysian theology, and his view of the writer inevitably falls into one of those mildly daft categories respected among Powysians and, indeed, amply licensed by the writings of the master himself. No critic who wishes to depreciate Powys, and to suggest that his work cannot either in whole or in part be taken seriously, has the smallest difficulty in finding cogent grounds for such opposition. Conversely, it is all but impossible to make a balanced defense of his writings as a whole in such a way as to convince a skeptic of their greatness.

It is in this context that the nature of Steiner's awareness of and enthusiasm for Powys shows a particular significance. The appreciation of Steiner is essentially a product of his own feeling for the transmutations of language, and for a writer who can make himself a conduit for its powers of metamorphosis. He sees the world of Powys as one that has not been cornered or taken over linguistically by the outlook and skills of an author—an author who wants to make his mark by his own manipulation of language. Powys is the opposite of a writer like Henry James on the one hand, as he is of one like Graham Greene on the other. The greatness of James is of course in his language, and in its powers of holding thought, idea, and consciousness in solution. Yet James as a writer is unremittingly fastidious; he cannot bear to use a word that is not worthy of him and of the personal felicities and standards his own powers as a writer have established. James is inseparable, as he freely claimed, from the subtle and powerful engine that he had created and that served him so faithfully. Language is not, in Heidegger's sense, his mistress: he is very much its master; and the mysteries of language seem perfectly indulgent—if one can continue the metaphor—in according him this mastery.

The case of a writer such as Greene is much more crude, and its implications are more obvious: style and technique in discourse are addressed to sealing off the area in which the writer is getting his special effects, which are essentially reassuring to the reader by reason of their predictability. Greene used to win the parody competitions in the *New Statesman* for parodies of his own style; it would be impossible to imagine Powys doing anything of that sort. The lack of a determining style, with all its marks of achieved status as an established writer, is a characteristic usually found in bad writing of all kinds, the amorphous stuff produced by someone who is either not very good at it or has not yet found his "voice." Critics who have objected to the "badness" of the writing in Powys's novels do so on the basis of this rule of thumb.

The achievement of a determining style by the novelist goes of course with the achievement of his own special sort of fictionality. Indeed, the novel form has developed logically toward the position in which the novelist secures his place and his public by presenting to them his own world, in terms of the language, the characters, the story. Having done this, he has achieved his own kind of reputation, as well as his own public, be it large or small. This is what happened in the 1930s to John Cowper Powys's brother T. F. (Theodore), who had at the time, and for some years afterward, a much higher reputation than John Cowper among critics and connoisseurs of the novel. This was because the peculiar kind of formalized word style that T. F. had created, most notably in *Mr. Weston's Good Wine*, with its effectively catchy title (silently borrowed from a casual sentence in Jane Austen's *Emma*) struck a chord with Cambridge intellectuals such as F. R. Leavis, who found it a highly original reimagining of a tradition in English narrative that went back to *The Pilgrim's Progress*. The point was that T. F. Powys, like most other novelists, had his style and his world, a world that could easily be taken up and taken over by a critic such as Leavis, a world in which the reader felt at home, as he did so in other separate worlds of fiction which had pleased, impressed, or stimulated him.

Unlike his brother, T. F. Powys possessed the efficient novelist's power of taking his reader captive for a while, holding him like the

Ancient Mariner, and forcing upon him a Coleridgean "suspension of disbelief." The reader's absorption implies his acceptance, for a while, of the *Weltanschauung*, or, as we should now say, the "textuality," of the tale. Afterward he can see all around it, see the way it works, and patronize it with depreciation or commendation. None of this process takes place where his brother is concerned. It is significant that modern methods of criticism are apt studiously to ignore John Cowper Powys; they would hardly be able to fit him into any of their procedural modes. That is where Steiner's humanity and catholicity of approach come into their own and can act as a genuine critical inspiration. Steiner's sense of the essential oneness of life, literature, and language finds its correlative in Powys's nonparticular genius; and especially in the way his language—unlike that of a novelist—works like Shakespeare's in an area of total receptivity, where acceptance or belief are irrelevant. We do not experience the sense of a "text" with Powys.

We have instead what Powys himself called "Life Illusion," a total sense of ourselves and our consciousness to which his own has been added on; the expansion provides a free and unbounded dimension of experience. The word *illusion* as used in this context by Powys is misleading in that it has nothing to do with illusions about oneself or others in the sense they are traded on in, say, Conrad's, or even in Austen's, world. Powys, like Shakespeare, never makes any distinction between illusion and reality. Life Illusion is for him the envelope of multifold consciousness in which we live, and through which appear and disappear varying kinds of idea and concept about our states of acting and being—an internal state of which the language of his books suggests a continuous and spacious externalization. Books are in one sense the key, for Powys often admitted to being "dominated by books," but his and our Life Illusions are emphatically not like texts in the sense that other novels are. Schemes of perception jostle each other in Powys without reaching either dominance or aporia, or even the ability to centralize and establish the world of a text.

Bakhtin's conception of the way in which Dostoevsky's novels work—their polyphonic and dialogical patterning—provides some degree of insight into Powys's novels. But it also can be misleading in this context; for Powys's mode of writing is self-evidently not a tactic or strategy, and his own presence as a consciousness, a sort of disembodied personal and literary benevolence, is with the reader all the time. Going with this sense of the personal is an equal and delightful sense of privacy, as if we were alone in our own world with Powys. It is a *polyindividual* rather than a *polyphonic* world, in which no one reader is privileged, or cognizant of a mystery that in any case is immanent, innocent of revelation. Life Illusion is in a sense the apotheosis of the amateur seeker, whose purpose is not to find, but to add the freedom of what D. H. Lawrence scornfully called "taste in the head" to the reflective possibilities of language in nature. In *A Glastonbury Romance* Evans is fascinated by the word *Esplumeoir*, which Powys had found in Jessie Weston's commentary on the Perceval legend, but he does not wish to understand it (the only assignable meaning is that of a cage or mew for a molting falcon), just as he does not really want the thing he most longs for—a vision of the Grail. In much the same way Wolf Solent, the central figure in the novel of that name, sees an alder root slipping "adroitly" into the dark water of a stream—a vision of the pleasure and the goal of his own pondering.

In many ways the richest and most satisfying of all Powys's novels, *Wolf Solent* exemplifies with a special fullness Steiner's own sense of life's oneness with language, and at the same time its powers of free individuation. Wolf himself is not part of any action the author sees him as involved in: author and character are like two separate readers, absorbed in their own unconcluding awareness of themselves and their world. Reflection in Powys—both in himself and in his characters—takes over from any determinacy of being: no character is fixed by the view of either the author or a fellow character. Neither is anyone fixed, of course, by the reader himself. Steiner's sense of the comparative, his astonishingly eclectic ability to subsume authorship and different languages as fellows rather than strangers, may well have suggested to him the strong though hidden similarity between a great Continental master such as Robert Musil, author of *Der Mann Ohne Eigenschaften* (*The Man without Qualities*), and the far more disheveled amateur world of Powys and his people. Musil, too, was convinced (though more systematically and meticulously, as one would expect of a German *Dichter*) that "qualities" or characteristics did not exist in the world of consciousness or, as Powys would say, of Life Illusion. In that world anyone may be anything, may think and be conscious of anything—the "eidola," as Powys would call them, passing through his mind like fish in the shallow waters of an estuary or in the depths of the sea. In one of Musil's stories abut women, "Tonka," the girl bears a marked resemblance to several of Powys's female characters (e.g., Wizzie in

Maiden Castle). She is unpredictable, and any characteristics she possesses appear to be given her by the men in her life, by herself, or by the author: as a being she seems to swim free from all these agencies, including that of her own personality.

Steiner's relish for and enjoyment of language as an equally comparative or fishlike phenomenon makes him able to appreciate both the subtle, densely worked style of Musil and the loose abundance of Powys. In his "Foreword" to a collection of essays on Powys, Jerome McGann remarks on the way that the weird beauties of Powys's prose can actually "work to contaminate and ruin the illusion of its own grandeur."[3] As the people, that is, so the prose. Neither one desires to maintain itself in a suitable, or even a "true," posture. Precision is as foreign to them as it is natural and inevitable in the sentence structure of Musil; yet in both dissimilar cases language operates to free what it describes from its own structures. McGann quotes the superb—deliberately superb—paragraph that opens the final chapter of *The Glastonbury Romance*. The paragraph is emphatically not a parody of old and epic grandeur, but displaces that grandeur into elevation and enthusiasm of another sort, removing rigidity and dignity in the process, and substituting the relaxed spaces of Powys's own personality. I doubt whether Steiner would agree with McGann that this is "the style discovered by Powys for maintaining the real presence of the gods in the abysmal residues of a late-empire world" (9). For Powys, gods are the playthings of Life Illusion, and their continued presence is a matter for language itself rather than for convictions of "real presence." Yet McGann is surely right about the way in which Powys's language fuses frivolity with magnificence to produce a new compound of consciousness—a compound of pleasure rather than power. Writing *about* Powys is necessarily a more portentous affair than reading him, and the discrepancy is of course increased by the phenomenon I have already noticed: the tendency for Powys studies to operate in separate compartments—the philosophical, the mythological—without mutual reference or acquaintance.

The friendly freedom of the Powys syntax, and the way it summons up at the same time all possible suggestions from historic use, is well illustrated by McGann's quotation of a phrase in that final Glastonbury paragraph, "For many a long year." It is, in every sense, a *worn* phrase, yet the unmisgiving eloquence of the Powys style still seems to bequeath to us the original absence of self-consciousness in the epic voice, the voice of oral poetry, dirge, and chant. History lives in this pseudo-antique phrase, blown upon and reburnished by Powys's use of it without any recourse to metaphoric quotation marks. Such insouciance seems to liberate us from the text itself, in the way that we are liberated as we read from the narrative, from its meaning or its philosophy. It is worth emphasizing that the phrase "For many a long year" has a wholly different status in the text from the one it would have in *Ulysses*, or in Joyce's story "The Dead." Joyce would examine it with deliberate deadpan humor, set it in a context of specific speech patterning, and probably refer it to a character whose use of it would determine his or her role and being in the narrative.

When I used the word *unmisgiving* of the Powysian eloquence, I did so with intent; for the way in which Powys uses such things summons up a special kind of spirit or ghost from the linguistic past: that of Keats writing at his best, in the odes or in "The Eve of St. Agnes," and using language already shop-soiled with gentility or archaism with the same unselfconscious ardor with which he saturates his text with his own personal kinds of linguistic enchantment. That eclectic and demotic power was brilliantly defined as "unmisgiving" by Leigh Hunt, who went on to suggest that Keats was wrong (as he himself no doubt knew) in his attempt to forge a consciously and carefully grand manner in "Hyperion." Powys's manner is never grand, but its implications are; for Powys allows himself to be in the grip of language in the way of Keats at his best: a trusting repose—"might half slumbering on its own right arm," as Keats phrases it—that never let either artist down. Of course there is a big difference between them, for Keats's view of poetry and himself depends on a devotional seriousness of which Powys had no need. The Keats who touchingly decided to ask Hazlitt what to read for a serious study of philosophy is rather different from the great amateur showman who used philosophy as a part of the props in his novels, synthesizing it—as indeed Keats himself might in time have come to do—with our daily experience of the erotic and the quotidian dreams of our Life Illusion. In *Weymouth Sands* the philosophically minded Richard Gaul imagines what would happen "if some student at Jena or Heidelberg were to ask the famous expounder of the philosophy of Representation what object or group of objects might most vividly 'represent' the sea-coast of his native land, he might very well reply: 'A couple of pairs of girls' stockings, carefully kept in their place by pebble-stones, and sprinkled with drifting sand.'"

Synthesis extends here even to the blithe confusion of syntax, which confounds Hegel and Kant with the speaker ("of his native land") and draws into a warmly comic area of generalization Powys's own preoccupation with girls' legs and stockings and other conventional items of masculine fantasy. (This emerges in *Maiden Castle*, where Wizzie and the hero's relations in bed are treated with a touchingly shrewd practicality and a bisexual understanding, beside which *Lady Chatterley's Lover* looks both sentimental and silly.) Sex is too splendid to be taken seriously, and so is philosophy; yet Powys is ironically close here to Heidegger and Derrida, philosophers who have stressed not the epistemological significance of Being, but its actuality, and that of irreducible experience. Powys's shifting and humorous suggestiveness parallels in its own fashion Derrida's use of erotic actualities to displace philosophic meaning, a tactic inspired by Nietzsche's rejection of philosophy as abstract and ascetic thought.

Powys and his characters reach physicality by introspection, instead of proceeding from the physical to the speculative. This again can produce a hiatus—itself almost a part of the general comedy—between his novels and their critics and expounders, who have to extrapolate from the physical back again into the mental. Steiner himself is one of the very few critics who are aware of the comedy of this process, as well as aware of the peculiarly English and amateur nature of the genius who gives rise to it. Steiner is fascinated by the styles of copious writing in three cultures—English, German, and French—which in their own ways use the novel not for the creation of a new sort of "fictionality," but for the continuous and unbroken exploration of what Powys would call Life Illusion.

Musil in Germany is in his own way a Powys blood brother, and Steiner would certainly claim the same relation for Proust (Powys's own favorite novelist) and even for Lucien Rebatet's massive novel *Les Deux Étendards*, a vast "secret" work of philosophico-erotic fiction, which has something of the same equivocal position in the battle order of the French novel that Powys holds in the English one. The three languages produce their own different—wholly different—kinds of personal world; yet the kind of unifying sensibility which Steiner himself might be said to represent—as critic and as creator—animates them all.

Steiner has a special interest in the strange conflict that art can exhibit between its own beauty and illumination, and the evil of those who appreciate and create it. A favorite example is the fact that the organizers and executives of the German genocidal atrocities should have been lovers of Mozart, as well as devoted fathers. What astonished Steiner about Lucien Rebatet is that so despicable a parasite of the German secret police in occupied France should have written a novel filled with an astonishing tenderness and understanding of human instincts and ideals—the religious ideal of abnegation and sacrifice on the one hand, and the wonders and complexities of the sensual life on the other.

Musil would have no trouble in understanding this, and Powys would have regarded it as the most natural thing in the world. Or would he? Steiner's sense of the matter—itself a vivid and stimulating sense—and his feeling that language and its spectrum of functions are closely involved are also foreshadowed in Powys's imagination. "Evil into the mind of God and man / May come and go" is a Miltonic sentiment with which the Powysian imagination is wholly at home; and it is equally at home with the possible consequences. Musil's Tonka is not deliberately stupid or wicked, but she is capable of anything, like Powys's down-to-earth and dreamy heroines, and both writers show forth in their discourse why this is and perhaps must be so. They are deeply unperturbed by the knowledge of evil, perceiving it as an aspect of the freedom of the consciousness, somewhat in the way that Coleridge saw moral evil as itself a product of the mind's associative powers.

Of course there is a difference between what is in the mind, even in its darkest and most obsessional matter, and the activity of the will in action. No doubt the will can starve consciousness to the point where both language and fantasy are paralyzed in the sheer obstinacy of wickedness, although that hardly explains how Rebatet could have been writing his novel in hotel rooms and railway carriages while acting as lackey to the Gestapo agents who were hunting down Jews and French dissidents. Yet Powys or Musil, as well as Dickens, could have understood that—even to the point of taking it for granted. In *Great Expectations* Dickens shows us the lawyer's clerk Wemmick dividing his being and time between the nightmare office of Jaggers the lawyer and the domesticities of home and friendship. "All reality," as Steiner put it in *After Babel*, "is encoded in a distinctive idiom" (125), and Dickens demonstrates this by ventriloquial means ("He do the police in different voices"), whereas a Musil or a Powys works through a comprehensive idiom that demonstrates an equal sympathy for every manifestation of mental awareness.

Steiner's chapter heading in *After Babel* "Understanding as Translation" reveals the part played by decipherment in our reading of behavior and motive in language. We translate in our own way whatever we read. Moreover, most intellectuals are barely conscious of the extent to which unconscious habit causes them to decipher the people they meet in the light of their own fictional worlds, the worlds of texts they inhabit. But Powys brings this ironically home to them in the way he takes for granted Wolf Solent's dependence on the same habit. It is thrown into relief by a variation on the picaresque idiom, as well as by the operation of a style in which "goodness" and "badness" both revive and refer us to old literary forms, even stale or outworn ones, while encoding them in a wholly new and absorbing way.

Steiner himself considers a seriocomic case of this in a close reading he supplies in the chapter "Understanding as Translation." One of Dante Gabriel Rossetti's "Sonnets for Pictures," which appeared in the periodical *Germ* in 1850, takes as its subject Ingres' painting *Angelica Rescued from the Sea-monster*, itself based on Ariosto's account in *Orlando Furioso*. As Steiner effectively demonstrates, the sonnet fails entirely at the work of *translation*: it neither produces a new version of the episode nor manages to revive by implicit comment the iconography of the previous ones. Unlike that of Powys, Rossetti's own idiom is appropriately dull, vacuously turgid, because it has no insight into what it is supposed to be encoding. Nor does the writer seem to feel any devotional relish, as Keats or Powys would have, in the demotic vocabulary—half archaic and half Victorian-emotional—that attempts to come to the sonnet's rescue. Ariosto presents the incident in a manner that is both excitingly picturesque and subtly deflationary. Ruggiero is much more interested in the maiden than in the monster, which he does not succeed in properly killing; and Angelica, after she has been liberated, is interested only in getting back to her own affairs and amours, even as Ruggiero, inflamed by her naked beauty, is feverishly trying to unfasten his armor so that he may enjoy it. Ingres both romanticizes the spectacle and retains its Renaissance panache: his knight errant looks suitably youthful and eager, and the maiden is swooningly helpless. But Rossetti, unable to avail himself of either mode of reality, yet determined to write his sonnet on it, languishes in a linguistic limbo, which is null and void.

Although Steiner does not mention the significance of these details, with which he is not specifically concerned, he is emphatic on the necessity for prolonged, even if instinctive, *interpretation*, which accompanies our reading of any text out of the past. And there is a sense in which all texts—such is the nature of literary language—are out of the past. A writer, and especially a writer such as Powys, may evolve an idiom so densely yet so straightforwardly "old-fashioned" that it bursts upon us as something new and not fictional at all, just as his characters carry no suggestion of fictionality, let alone any consciousness of it. Wolf Solent's traditional past in the *Bildungsroman*, and his author's separate awareness of this, have fused together into a real presence (to reuse the phrase in one of Steiner's titles), which seems wholly to desummon and dispel literariness. As a character Wolf Solent appears to decline the historic fictional office adumbrated almost involuntarily by his creator's linguistic consciousness: he appears to live for himself and not for the novel, just as Powys's own language gives the impression of doing. Powys would no doubt have appreciated Steiner's comments on the Rossetti sonnet. He would have seen the point about the self-defeating bombast in it; for his own language is always at work in the way Rossetti's *should* have been, reconstituting and remaking verbal history in the light of his consciousness of new worlds and new people, and of his own Life Illusion.

Powys is continually aware of the way in which Life Illusion verges on obsession: indeed, he presents obsession as the state in which most of his characters live—as in a larger sense does the whole human race. But the writer must himself avoid giving the appearance of obsession, just as he must avoid (as Rossetti in his sonnet conspicuously fails to do) appearing enmeshed in a self-nullifying code of fancy language. Powys always manages to achieve a sense of freedom and space in his books, as if the absorptions and fixations of his characters were seen in the wide panoramas of a landscape. The toils of their own psychology make them resemble the little black figures of primitive men on a down-land hilltop or Iron Age fort. There is a sense in which all Powys novels depend on the well-known axiom of landscape theory, as formulated by late eighteenth-century Romanticism, that a picture can look grander, emptier, more sublime, if it contains the small figures of human actors, than it would if only "Nature" were present.

The Russian Jewish philosopher Lev Shestov, whose books Steiner greatly admires, wrote long critiques of Tolstoy and of Dostoevsky in which he advanced a general theory that also shed light on Powys's novels and on the impression they give the reader. In an important respect Shestov anticipated Bakhtin, and the latter's exploration of the dialogic and polyphonic structure of Dostoevsky's fiction, because he also emphasized the ways in which a great genius of the novel form escapes from his own convictions and obsessions, allotting them their place in the imaginative work under construction, but himself remaining free and outside them. Shestov, a humanist and humorist with a sharp eye and sharp nose for authorial deceit, accused Tolstoy of pretending one thing and writing another: for example, making the seeker Pierre the hero and fine conscience (as Henry James would say) of *War and Peace*, while secretly placing himself and the reader on the side of Nikolai Rostov, the self-contented *honnête homme* and landowner. I have discussed the implications of Shestov's view in a study of Tolstoy;[4] and, although Steiner does not himself refer to Shestov in his own book *Tolstoy or Dostoevsky: An Essay in the Old Criticism*, all his writings express an awareness of the question involved, and of the kind of importance it has for a great work of fiction. All major novelists are, almost by definition, obsessed and self-obsessed, so how do they nonetheless contrive to render us and themselves free from obsession, while remaining—in some cases at least—recognizably and entirely their own men, their own personalities as speakers and authors?

In some cases at least: for Dostoevsky is not among them—as both Shestov and Bakhtin suggest, Dostoevsky himself remains, as it were, under the floor of his novels. Tolstoy and Powys are of course in the foreground of theirs. Yet each achieves his own sort of freedom, while remaining his own naturally obsessive self. In the case of Tolstoy this is what chiefly intrigued Shestov, who regarded human beings as divided between a natural solipsism and the kind of revelation that resulted from taking a leap into the void. He remarked dryly that the young Tolstoy secretly realized the truth of solipsism, but could not bear to confront it. Growing old compelled him to do so.

Solipsism is the negative form of obsession, and probably the deepest and most difficult achievement of both Tolstoy and Powys in their novels is the demonstration through their art of the relation between the solipsistic and the free spirit. Wolf Solent is conscious of having a life to lead and a career to make, and this itself obsesses him, apart from his complex entanglements with the two women, Christie and Gerda. But he also liberates himself and the reader by remaining outside his own enclosed and obsessional world: the novel enables him to do so. He sees the face of a man on the Waterloo Steps, a face that life has wholly defeated and destroyed, an image that remains with him almost by virtue of his exclusion of it. The moment is oddly comparable with a much more relaxed and unemphatic one in *War and Peace*, when Prince Andrei, during the retreat of the Russian army before Napoleon's invading forces, sees two little girls stealing plums in the garden of an abandoned country house. His own preoccupations disappear as he watches them, and he becomes fully persuaded for the first time of the reality of *other people*, as well as the absolute validity conveyed by their own kind of intentness.

It is a moment that Coleridge would have understood and appreciated; and it is the sort of moment, too, which Steiner's diversity of perceptions would pick up and allocate its place in the pattern. For he is himself, most definitively, an apostle and critic of freedom in an age of critical determinism, an age in which pseudo-technology and "the state of the art" has sought to box in the whole world of creative language. Steiner emphasizes the metamorphoses of language in art, and its powers of forming and reforming new discoveries of meaning. This goes with its power to establish a sense of real presence, as in the case of the face on Waterloo Steps, or the detail in *War and Peace* of the little girls stealing plums. Both the words we use and the obsessions that dominate us are not, in terms of art, the end of the matter; and Steiner's multiple talents—his passion for linguistic and ideological enquiry— help to show us why.

They also help to show us how great is the gap between Steiner and the mass trend of contemporary criticism, founded as it is upon a widespread acceptance of the Saussurean premise at least as slavish—in linguistic terms—as the Marxist-liberal premise once was in the political sphere. However controversial Steiner's own position, it is absolutely firm on the distinction it makes between what we can think or feel, and what we can say. This distinction is the animating principle of an attitude to language and art which Steiner shares with two spirits equally congenial to him—Powys and Coleridge. Steiner's emphasis on certain implications of his general position—for example, the inability of language to deal with certain kinds of contemporary horror ("What is there to *say* about Belsen?")—seems exaggerated and perhaps misleading. But the real strength of his position is the way it runs parallel to the freedom I have tried to indicate in my examples from

Powys and Tolstoy. Our language can equal our solipsism, even our obsession, in the sense that we cannot break out from it. Modern critics have laid a misleading emphasis on this fact. But in the same way that Powys or Tolstoy demonstrates the power of art both to reveal solipsism and to transcend it, so Steiner remains insistent that we can think or feel more than we can say; and that our sense of things—its transformations and, as Coleridge would say, its esemplastic powers—is the vital ingredient in those astonishing transformations that language in art can undergo. Thought and feeling in art remain the masters of language.

In the chapter "Word against Object" in *After Babel* Steiner suggests something of this kind. He also shows how he has managed to retain in equilibrium the concept of language forming the artist—Shakespeare lying in it as if in Abraham's bosom; Steiner himself, in my own metaphor, a marvelously erudite Petrouchka in a trilingual grip—with the other and equally powerful concept of the artist's freedom, from his language and even from himself. Steiner must have been struck by the tendency in modern fiction to surrender to the bonds in which modern semiotics has confined the artist. Not only are its characters aware of their own fictionality, but it can only treat facts—*things* themselves—as passive counters in its own discourse.

Things, objects—once such potent bringers of plot and fate (Othello's handkerchief, the heel and armor of Achilles, the sword and red coat of Sergeant Troy)—have now become devitalized baubles, signs and counters to be played with at the novelist's whim. The change in *Weltanschauung* is obvious and far from reassuring. In championing object and thing against word, Steiner has done his best to redress the balance. Like the young Elizabethan nobleman in Hofmannsthal's "Letter of Lord Chandos," he himself has experienced "a tongue of which not a single word is known to me, a tongue in which mute objects speak to me" (cited in *After Babel*, 184). It is the liberation and the excitement of that experience which Steiner has so triumphantly brought home to us, as did his predecessors and comrades in thought and language—Coleridge and John Cowper Powys.

The three are in a special sense rhetoricians, to whom the act of speech can itself determine the validity of utterance and the particular reality of the speaker. In his letters Powys often mentions with a nostalgic gusto the days when he did the rounds of the American lecture circuits, acquiring a fabled reputation as magician and performer. The reputation was nothing to him, for he was the most deeply and casually modest of men, but it was the speech and the performance that counted with him and gave him what in his novels he always spoke of as Life Illusion. By epanorthosis or reverse effect, the term conveys the actuality and vivacity of mental being, the truth that the acute Coleridgean sense of self and the other establishes inside the head. One of the profoundest and most casual insights of Powys occurs toward the end of *Maiden Castle*, when a fleeting comparison is made between a child's and an adult's kinds of certainty *"that what you were pretending"* is "the only real reality in your life."

Some geniuses live not by means of an "As If," like so many nineteenth-century thinkers from Matthew Arnold to Hans Vaihinger,[5] but also by the extraordinary vividness and authority by which they reveal to us the truth of what we are pretending. They are able to convince us of the absolute claims of our own mental and verbal freedom, the truth of what we require to feel in order to be. Such an escape from our own fictionality inspires us uniquely; and not least because the rapt absorption that produces it—and that travels to us from the producer—makes no claims upon us. No guidance or exhortation or law-giving is involved. We are not even called upon to honor the few critics and creators who have the gift and inspire us with it, but only to enjoy with them, and to be confirmed by them in the truth of our own pretenses. In our mental world they have then become the most real of presences.

Notes

1. Daphna Erdinast-Vulcan, *Joseph Conrad and the Modern Temper* (Oxford: Clarendon Press, 1991), 97.

2. George Steiner, *After Babel: Aspects of Language and Translation* (London: Oxford University Press, 1975), 4.

3. Jerome McGann, "Foreword," in *In the Spirit of Powys: New Essays*, ed. Denis Lane (Lewisburg: Bucknell University Press, 1990), 5.

4. John Bayley, *Tolstoy and the Novel* (London: Chatto and Windus, 1966), 250–80.

5. Hans Vaihinger, *The Philosophy of "As If": A System of the Theoretical, Practical and Religious Fictions of Mankind*, trans. C. K. Ogden (London: Routledge and Kegan Paul, 1924).

GERHARD NEUMANN

Translated into English by Elizabeth Naylor Endres

The "Masters of Emptiness" and the Myth of Creativity: George Steiner's *Real Presences*

To ask "what is music?" may well be one way of asking "what is man?"[1]

THE HERMENEUTIC SCIENCES have maneuvered themselves into an impasse. The parasitic loquacity of the moderns has, by its sheer abundance, stifled the authenticity of the great acts of creation. It has led to an inflation of signs. The human ego has become lost amid the uproar of discourses. George Steiner's book *Real Presences* sounds a fanfare of protest against this state of affairs and presents a politicocultural utopia that might succeed it. The book wagers on the validity of meaning, the power of creativity, the autonomy of self; it also wagers on the presence of God as the guarantor of these things. This conservative gesture, which gains its force of conviction from the author's wealth of cultural knowledge, accounts for the far-reaching effect the book has had, provoking as it has so much response—in rejection as well as acceptance.

Steiner's book is one of a long series of formulations of the hermeneutic problem that have appeared since World War II. It arrived at a time of crisis. How can one assess its contribution to the increasing self-assurance of the hermeneutic discipline? In 1946 Erich Auerbach's great work *Mimesis* raised the issue of literary mimesis—midway between imitation and representation—as it applied to the history of European literature. [2] Written during World War II, this book discusses the endless question of literary realism, placing it within the context of the European tradition that draws both on Greco-Roman antiquity and on the Jewish practice of discussing the nature of reality (a practice that has been adopted by Christianity). Auerbach attempts in this way to trace the dynamics of new thought in a changing sociohistorical situation. Emil Staiger's *Basic Concepts of Poetics*, which was published in the same year as Auerbach's book, endeavors to interpret human creativity (set apart from any historical considerations) from three constants of anthropological behavior, with reference to Heidegger's *Being and Time*. [3] In Staiger's view, human creativity has a phylogenetic source, defining the nature of humankind by its temporality, whence comes the uniqueness of human creations.

Ernst Robert Curtius's *European Literature and the Latin Middle Ages* (written in 1948) retraces the literary tradition as a system of argumentation that develops very slowly, with patterns of discourse that last for centuries and are sustained by a rhetorical and topical reservoir. [4] Curtius's book represents a rejection of creativity, a gesture that by this time went almost unnoticed by his contemporaries. This rejection of creativity is reflected in his refrain: "nothing-more-than" (*Nichtsweiter-als*). In Curtius's view every argument is only a topos from the age-old repertoire of an inexhaustible tradition, stored in the archives of rhetoric. Hugo Friedrich's significant work *The Structure of Modern Poetry* (1956) seeks a formula that could be specific to our own era to describe that which, with the formalism of the new aesthetics and its renunciation of "meaning" in poetry, its abjuration of stringent semantic rules, has contributed to a revolution in the lyrical use of language. [5]

The important work of the Frankfurt School and its circle led to a rearticulation of the problem twenty years later: sociological, Marxist, and psychoanalytical approaches were locked into a running dispute of methods appropriate for Gadamer's hermeneutic theory; each side of the argument insisted on contradictory postulates. In the final analysis every one of them was based on Adorno and Horkheimer's *Dialectic of Enlightenment* (written in 1947), [6] which develops a model, critical in terms of ideology, of a displacement of the store of ideas, signs, and images from the Enlightenment as they become part of mythology, the displacement of a way of thinking that once was liberating as it turns into something that now enslaves and subjugates.

In France, the reception of Heidegger and Nietzsche, no less than that of Saussure's linguistic theories and those of the Moscow, Tartu, and Prague linguistic schools, laid the foundations for the poststructuralist formulations of writers such as Roland Barthes and Michel Foucault.[7] Foucault's writings constitute perhaps the most successful attempt to reformulate the old question about tradition and spontaneous creation, about subject, work, and text within the current of European culture. Barthes juxtaposes the traditional, discordant image of the "mythical" with the new notion of "ideology," an idea that owes much to Foucault's theories.[8] Barthes' concept of the "Mythen des Alltags" is connected with Foucault's perception of discourses as patterns of speech that compete with and overlap with one another.[9] Foucault's model is concerned with the nature of anonymous power, and it goes so far as to suggest the dissolution of all the conceptual elements of creativity and of the subject proper, which of course is the center of such creativity, and attempts to describe certain dispositives as links within the chain of functioning of discourse systems—as generators of cultural change, as it were. This thought was then taken up by Julia Kristeva.[10]

Finally, Derrida and Paul de Man articulate the concept of a metamorphosis of literary acts into systems of readings that overlap one another and take the form of "allegories of reading."[11] They envision acts of reading that both underlie and overlie one another. These were all attempts to address a conception of art that grew out of the question as to the creative power of humankind, our capacity to make new beginnings and to produce the signs of civilization from the core of creativity within the body. (This was of course an old question that had been reformulated at the end of the eighteenth century.)

The answers to this question are as diverse as could be conceived. Staiger's idealistic model of civilization contrasts with Auerbach's realistic approach. Between the two, there is Hugo Friedrich's form-concept (*Formkonzept*) of a repertoire of function and structure that characterizes the era and goes beyond all considerations of reception or intertextuality, of the aesthetics of creation, or of research into influence. From Friedrich's concept can be developed the model of a European structural formulation of modernity. Curtius introduced the idea of the "formulae constraints" (*Formelkorsett*) of a centuries-old tradition of topics and rhetoric which allows very little room for repetition or variation. Curtius's notion is oriented toward tradition and rhetoric. In contrast to this there is Adorno's approach, a critique of ideology which sees an interplay between Enlightenment and barbarity, between establishment and reevaluation, between progress and regression—with all the sociological implications as well as the psychological ones. Discourse analysis, which for the first time calls into serious question the concepts of author, work, and text (concepts that have stabilized the system since time immemorial, perhaps since the time of Saint Jerome), is challenged in turn by deconstruction, which in its development from Derrida to Paul de Man has until very recently been the subject of vehement attacks (especially given the background of de Man's political role). The theory of deconstruction does away with the principle of the establishment of meaning, the constitution of unambiguousness or equivocality in literary texts.[12]

Steiner's book attempts, in the loose format of an essay, to find a new beginning, a resolution of these acrobatics that keep tying themselves into inextricable knots; it tries to sever the Gordian knot of the methodological dilemma. His approach is to make a *salto mortale* into the "real presence" of transcendence. Steiner is only interested in one issue: that of creative man and his language. He develops a theory of creativity; his interest is semantic—he investigates what is in the message of a work of art. *Is There Anything in What We Say?* is the book's intriguing subtitle in the British edition.[13]

In this emphatic form, the theme of creativity is perhaps not such an old question as Steiner's book would have us believe. The question as to the spontaneity of human creativity did not erupt in full force until the second half of the eighteenth century, with its interest in creative people and their "genius," as well as with the theme of the artist as someone excluded from the bourgeois world of normality, with which he or she was at odds—as an outsider, as an extraterritorial being. This theme was expressed in the attempts of, say, Diderot (*Rameau's Nephew*), Herder, or E. T. A. Hoffmann (*Ritter Gluck*), to make sense of the connection among creativity, truth, and semiotics, among pictorial, literary, or musical signs and their correspondence to body-language signs.

Steiner's essay, too, with all the author's broad erudition and mastery of quotation, and despite his general anthropological interest, concentrates on the last two centuries and attempts to address the issue of the artistic creation of meaning in three stages. The first section of his book offers a finding and demonstrates the predominance in our age of secondary discourse, those texts about texts that take the place of texts about the world. The second section attempts an *explanation* of this rift, the disconnection of cosmos and logos, of world and language—Steiner calls it the "break of the covenant between word and world." The third section seeks to assure us of *the nature of art itself* as immediacy, as experience of the unforeseeable, as "encounter" and epiphany.

An understanding of the authentic statements that are contained within works of art cannot, in Steiner's view, be provided by the proliferation of critical jargon, such as that developed by structuralists, poststructuralists, and deconstructionists; nor by mountains of secondary literature (thirty thousand doctoral theses per year; twenty-five thousand publications on *Hamlet* since the end of the eighteenth century) (25); and certainly not by copying logical or scientific models of verification or falsification according to Karl Popper's model of statistical probability and prognosis (71). The understanding of artistic works—a painting, a poem, a sonata—is much more likely to occur through the presentation of such works by the actor, the giver of a reading, the dancer, the musical interpreter (8–9). Creative assimilation of this kind also occurs when a theme in music is "criticized" by a set of variations on itself; or when, in literature, a myth is retold; or when different versions or variants of a work interpret its meaning. These, in Steiner's opinion, are not theories, metalanguages, or practices of method, but "narratives of formal experience" (86), as when Racine reworks Euripides, when Brecht reconstrues Marlowe's *Edward II*, when Boito writes a libretto for Verdi's opera from Shakespeare's *Othello*.

Steiner believes that even great traditional works of a fundamentally theoretical or critical nature can be understood as "narratives of formal experience," such as Longinus's *Peri Hupsous*, Ruskin's *Modern Painters*, and Proust's *Contre Sainte-Beuve*. For example, Proust explores, in a singular manner, the possibilities of literary storytelling (as a preliminary to *Remembrance of Things Past*), and he registers a certain disagreement in literary theory with the great literary critic Sainte-Beuve, also undertaking the hermeneutic investigation of great works of literature (e.g., the texts of Stendhal, Balzac, Baudelaire, and Nerval). And, with the lucidity of his creative spirit, Steiner ties all these themes together.

The second section of Steiner's book discusses the origins of this reformulation of the question as to the truth of the message of art and its form of expression. According to Steiner, the nineteenth century revealed a shift of paradigm in the relationship between word and world, which he calls the "break of the covenant." One of the only revolutions in the history of civilization that has been worthy of that name took place between 1870 and 1940: "It is this break of the covenant between word and world which constitutes one of the very few genuine revolutions of spirit in Western history and which defines modernity itself" (93). Among the protagonists of this revolution in the use of language are Mallarmé, with his thesis on the liberation of language from its referentiality; and Rimbaud, with his deconstruction of the first person singular.

It is the moment in the history of art when the status of "meaning" becomes dubious. At the same time, all those concepts that are becoming increasingly important for the science of art appreciation—the concepts of evaluation, interpretation, textuality, and responsibility for the text's meaning—once again come into play, but are immediately called into question: modern hermeneutic science is born. From this time on, signs begin to "circulate"; language no longer knows any conceptual bounds. In terms of aesthetic perception, there is no longer an Archimedean point visible outside discourse. To paraphrase Steiner, *before* this paradigm shift, cosmos and logos were oriented toward each other; *after* it, they split apart. The binary code takes the place of logos (90). It is the change of what Steiner calls "real presence," in the truly metaphysical sense, into "real absence," the change of logocentrism— "the intelligible face of the sign remains turned to the word and the face of God," Steiner quotes Derrida (119)—into the era that comes "after the Word" (93). The shibboleth of this situation turns out to be "the death of God" (93): "The deconstruction of the 'I' and of authorship separates the aesthetic from the ethical" (101).

Four major movements emerge in the wake of this revolutionary event (101ff.): Wittgenstein's demonstration of the loss of innocence in discourse, and the necessity of silence in the face of the unutterable; psychoanalysis as developed by Freud and his followers, notably Lacan, with his insight into the conflict between authority and spontaneity, between regulations and the creative impulse; post-Saussurean linguistics, which posits a semantics of internal relations, rather than a referential semantics; and the movement of language-criticism (*Sprachkritik*) founded by Fritz Mauthner, which, in the work of its most impressive exponent, Karl Kraus, denounces the social use of language in its fatal wavering between clichés and lies.

Steiner interprets Derrida and Paul de Man's deconstructionist "satyr-play" (118) as the end result of this fourfold division. He enumerates their characteristics: their metatheoretic quality; the fact that they give equal value to criticism and to creative activity; their refusal to make value judgments; their continuous transformation—that recognizes no limits—of texts into texts (a ubiquitous intertextuality); and their elimination of the categories of remembrance, individuality, and artistic integrity, which are so essential for the experience of "real presence." According to Steiner, Barthes staged the death of the author (and with it the "birth of the reader") through his concept of "desire for the text,"[14] and Derrida subverted the categories of meaning, truth, and the authority of the work with his concept of "language play."

The final section of Steiner's book is devoted to a phenomenology of the experience of art, which is clearly influenced by Heideggerian conceptions: fear and apprehension accompany the moment of bliss in the encounter with "the other," which is what art is; the work of art creates truth, rootedness, orientation, but at the same time—and this is its most powerful, transcendent quality—it becomes, through its form and content, a challenge to death. Rilke's exemplary gesture "change your life" (142) attests to a ritual of recognition and revelation; the "source of being" (151) is shown to be a form of freedom. For Steiner, the creative spirit reaches its utmost perfection in music: to him, music is time "made organic" (196); it is, quite simply, "the supreme mystery of man" (197).

The final—and most important—question raised by the book concerns the why of art: Why should art exist, why is there not nothing? (to modify a Kantian question). "There is aesthetic creation because there is *creation*," Steiner says (201); transcendence is the reason for its legitimacy. Creation (becoming) is the nature of the world; the *Homo significans* of this Eden is its first imitator and countercreator. He is creator *sicut deus*. Art thus becomes a "counter-creation" (203), "desire for the beginning of being"; God appears as the envied "other craftsman," as Picasso said (204).

This mystery of creation is expressed, finally, in the difference between the sexes. While the man, because of his natural inferiority as a creator of life, tends instead to the "creation of fictive forms," the woman, with her capacity "for engendering formed life" (207), feels no compulsion to wrestle with a jealous god. A man's being is characterized by his creativity, his striving for authorship, his rivalry with the creator god. But a woman, as bearer of children, is a stranger to this compulsion. By "wagering on transcendence," Steiner unhesitatingly dismisses the old either/or question that has emerged in the latest cultural disputes about gender difference: that is, either sex role or fiction, either sexuality or poetry. Steiner refers the question back to the creator of man and woman.

> An aesthetic theory is always an attempt to bring to
> bear on the joyous, libertarian scandal of resurrection
> the concept of historical and rational form. (210)

Steiner's brilliant exposition of a theory of creation on an anthropological basis is itself a mythical construct. When he calls the deconstructionists the "masters of emptiness," he proves himself a master of the "correct citation," as reteller of the key stories of humankind, which for him become foundation myths of civilization. Central to his outline are two creation myths. The first is the primal scene in Eden (90), in which God speaks to man and starts the game of molding and creating, prohibition and freedom. Adam is a man set free by a prohibition, who gives things their names thanks to the ability given to him by God the creator.

The second myth shows man seeking language in the sight of God. This myth is represented by Moses and Aaron: Moses, who speaks only in halting phrases, or not at all; Aaron, who converses fluently. Silence and language are the two forms in which man "answers" transcendence (Steiner's *Language and Silence: Essays on Language, Literature, and the Inhuman* is devoted to this dual theme).

The crisis that is latent within these two primal scenes finally erupts in what has been termed the "second Fall," in the confusion of tongues at the building of the Tower of Babel. (Steiner's chief work bears the title *After Babel*.) There is a force within God's tautological pronouncement of certainty ("I am who I am" [99]) that is also found in the merging process within the friendship between Montaigne and La Boëtie ("Because he was he, because I was I" [186]), in which it still provides evidence of communication, still leads to "real presence." Yet in Mallarmé's pronouncement that the word "rose" means "l'absence de toute rose," and in Rimbaud's legendary words "Je est un autre" (99), this same force becomes a breach of contract between language and world, between language and ego. As Steiner retells the story of the Fall in Eden, the story of Aaron and Moses, the burning bush, the friendship between Montaigne and La Boëtie, Mallarmé's rose and Rimbaud's alien self, he is practicing translation, the understanding of creation as re-creation; he tells of the way people behave between "language and silence," "after Babel," in the face of the transcendence that bears witness to "real presence."

Steiner's outline of a new aesthetics (which is actually the "old" aesthetics of forgotten human creativity) quite rightly emphasizes two concepts: semantics (of meaning, of the truth of the sign) and the ego (the creative subject)—and it uses these concepts as if there were a God, a lord of the signs and a master of the garden, who guarantees meaning and utters the prohibition in Eden. If there is such a God, then the parasitic nature of discourse appears as something that is merely external and that can be overcome by admission to the experience of transcendence, of the sight of God; it is something that has merely been foisted upon the communicative act of godless people. The lack of creativity and the anonymity of the modern ego are in that case revealed as alien to the nature of free-willed people, something merely superimposed on their individual personalities, and something that could be shaken off, just as one frees oneself from the bounds of convention, or from a father's judgment.

Steiner's outline overlooks the fact that the nature of a communication does not consist of a free exchange of signs between sender and receiver, that the medium itself is parasitic, that it is both background noise ("bruit parasite") and the enabler of communication at the same time, and that in this impure state it constitutes the one condition of the possibility of language (as Michel Serres' *The Parasite* has shown).[15] Furthermore, the outline overlooks the fact that confidence in the creative power of the ego and confidence in the power of the norms and laws of the modern world to exert a detrimental influence on the creative ego are two sides of the same coin. They represent both the blossoming of authenticity and the dissolution of individual difference; this goes for the relationship between father and son as much as it does for that between civilization as a whole and the individual (as Alice Miller has persuasively demonstrated in *Prisoners of Childhood*).[16] Finally, the outline overlooks the fact that the creation myths he tells have been the victims of infection by the parasitic from the very start: from the Fall, the serpent, and the Father's prohibition. The Fall, in the sense of being driven from the nearness of God, of the loss of "real presence," had already happened in Eden, not just in the nineteenth century.

Steiner's idea of the power of memory to create the arts, in which remembering of masterpieces is considered to be the epiphany of the spark of divine inspiration, presupposes the emphatic imagining of a primal scene, a beginning of creation. Here Derrida is Steiner's most direct antipode: for Derrida there is no beginning, no history that one could relate, and no myth that one could present as an epiphany. There is only present time, which in continuous *différance* shows past and future as indices of continued "deferment of the now."[17]

For Steiner, the possibility of an authentic language, of the truth of the language of poetry, depends on the acceptance of the presence of God (1–2). He opposes this to the deconstructionist "counter-theology of absence" (122). Steiner believes that the canon, or unchallenged series of eternal masterworks, is created through the "quickening of being which is ours when we experience" the work of art (64). With this fundamental Heideggerian insight, the issue of authentic remembering—of memory as the power of validation made manifest —has also surfaced. Steiner's theory of art privileges the *semantics* of the work of art, the *message* it brings, in a way that is possibly unique in recent aesthetics: "I would define literature (art, music) as *the maximalization of semantic incommensurability in respect of the formal means of expression . . . .* Each formal unit in the poem, the phoneme, the word, the grammatical bonds or elisions, the metrical arrangement, the stylistic conventions which attach it to other poems in the historical set or family, is charged with a semantic potential of innovation and inexhaustibility" (83).

A semantics of the ethical is postulated here: Steiner's reproach is directed against the deconstruction of the "I" and of authorship that separates the aesthetic from the ethical (101), and it deals a deathblow to semantics. Thus, art becomes the mouthpiece of meaning, that which makes humankind feel at home in the world. Encounter as a moment of bliss, apprehension with its dual meaning of fear and perception (139), and creation of meaning as a means of orientation in the world are the marks of such interaction with texts, paintings, and music. Recognition as an outstanding poetical form of memory is thus an expression of creative translation (146–47). Therefore it becomes important to read the *world*, rather than its *texts*, which are being produced in such abundance (195). Through the idea of the reception of art, literature, and music *by means of* art, literature, and music, art itself, with its interplay of forms and possibilities, sets the standard for real remembering. Thus Steiner's interpretation is opposed to the concept of the intertextualization of the world, which has emerged in recent decades. In his conception, acts of intertextuality are directed by authority, by God as the sign of all signs, who creates the world order and watches over the chain of canonical works. It is not civilization and its ensemble of signs seen as an intertextual system that Steiner construes as a dialogue (as conceived in the theory developed by Bakhtin),[18] but the thought that God is "dialogical" and that the arts are responding to him.

The most perfect of the arts can only, from this perspective, be music (this is a thoroughly Romantic theme): music as time "made organic" (196), as "the supreme mystery of man" (197). In music, the shape of perception reveals itself in its innermost being: art appears as "transcendental expression" (in the meaning intended by Kant). The discourse of music, the most perfect form of authenticity, representing the temporality of the world, belongs to God, who is the guarantor of all discourse and of all textual formations that produce authenticity.

Steiner's conception contradicts two theories that are significant for our cultural understanding of the present. The first theory is the perception that concepts of cultural remembering develop through an interplay of both personal and nonpersonal facts, a theme that has been thoroughly documented by research on memory in recent times; for example, in the work of Haverkamp and Lachmann, Assmann and Harth, and Greenblatt.[19] The second theory is the conception that the essence of a literary work is its developmental character, its mode of becoming, and that this is precisely what literary criticism must make clear.[20]

Steiner counters that the philological criticism of texts has basically become obsolete and that "the texts in the canon of Western poetry, drama and fiction . . . have been adequately and more than adequately edited" (34). Steiner ignores all the research into edition philology that, with its painstaking argumentation, has called into question the concepts of authorship, work, and text that were developed from the nineteenth century. In the case of those same authors chosen by Steiner to portray "real presence," such research has led to substantial new

insights into the connection between, on the one hand, text presentation, and, on the other, the status of authorship, work, and text production that is documented by the text presentation (e.g., in Kleist,
Hölderlin, and Kafka). Notable in works published by Beiner, Sattler,
and also by Reu, Killy, and the Paris "critique génétique," are experiences with texts that relativize the concept of the singular work by the
autonomous author-creator, as well as that of the body of texts, concepts that were handed down from the nineteenth century. These experiences have taught us to see the entire process of civilization as the
interplay of interlocking discourses. This approach no longer relates
the concept of the canonical to the mythical creation of a single monumental work, but instead recognizes the canonical in the interconnec-
tions and complicated reworkings of different textual formations,
reading these as a treatment of cultural aporias.

Perhaps Georg Büchner's texts bear witness most forcefully to this
other concept of text. His works grew out of a mêlée of psychiatric,
legal, pedagogical, military, philanthropical, and political discourses,
and they brought forward a new type of literary writing, first in their
fragmentary nature, then in the history of the effect they produced,
from naturalism to the documentary theater of the present day. These
texts no longer have anything to do with author, work, and text homo-
geneity, which are the traditional canonical tenets. But for this very
reason, they are an exemplary representation of the type of modern
literature and writing.

Can there be a secular poetics in the strict sense? (223)

Steiner's forceful argument for the concept of the authentic "I"—the
conception of the act of creation as the essential characteristic of human
existence, the notion of the message of truth conveyed by the work of
art—is an impressive declaration of loyalty to the venerable philosophical tradition of cultural identity and the postulate of the freedom and
inviolability of the individual, which supposes the latter to have passed
unscathed through history's changing patterns of language. It is the "I"
that recognizes itself in the postulate of its being something completely
"other," as the ideal: "It is, I believe, poetry, art and music which relate
us most directly to that in being which is not ours" (226).

This idealistic concept of Steiner's can be countered by another construct derived from the history of those same authors who themselves would choose his concept as their guarantor: from Montaigne and Pascal to Georg Büchner, from Heinrich von Kleist to Joyce, and from Kafka to Thomas Bernhard. (Female authors, whose voices could perhaps bear witness to this process still more clearly, are not mentioned by Steiner—quite in keeping with Christa Wolf's *Cassandra* and its message of the historical ineffectuality of the female voice.) This construct is of a world in which one's confidence in the creative power of the individual bears the undercurrent of the opposing forces of fear, violence, and the influence of laws, norms, and institutions. Nineteenth- and twentieth-century art deals not only with the desire for the magic and bliss of the creative beginning but also with its contemporaneous destruction by the faceless, anonymous forces of an industrial society dominated by parasitic media. It is this opposition of productive and destructive forces that literary texts demonstrate, and in which they are involved. This applies most of all, perhaps, to the texts of Kafka, because he, like no other, reenacts the "drama of the gifted child" over and over, the drama of the magic of the beginning, and the tragedy of the anonymous destructive forces that run counter to this, in a dramatic presentation of the cruel game of creation and destruction. This is the *Bildungsroman* of the new era that, in Bernhard's novel *Auslöschung*, sees the classical canon of literature as nothing more than a reading list with anarchy as its goal.

The predominant "parasitic" element that Steiner would like to banish from the discourse of modern culture reveals its value here. We see the fundamental principle of the parasitic nature of every message, and of the damage done to creativity and individuality, as can be seen in exemplary form in the case of Kafka (in *The Castle*, as well as in *The Judgment*, the *Kaiserlichen Botschaf*, and *Sorge des Hausvaters*). The texts of the artists demonstrate this principle, and it must be taken into account by the interpreters of these texts. To describe such structures is to understand them; the parasitic is the price of communication. It arrived in Eden with the serpent. We would have to eat from the tree of knowledge a second time for rediscovery to take place. Steiner's book pretends we have already done so.

Notes

1. George Steiner, *Real Presences* (Chicago: University of Chicago Press, 1989), 6. Hereafter all citations from *Real Presences* are in parentheses in the text.
2. Erich Auerbach, *Mimesis*, trans. Willard R. Trask (Princeton: Princeton University Press, 1953).
3. Emil Staiger, *Basic Concepts of Poetics*, trans. Janette C. Hudson and Luanne T. Frank (1953; reprint, University Park: Pennsylvania State University Press, 1990).
4. Ernst Robert Curtius, *European Literature and the Latin Middle Ages*, trans. Willard R. Trask (New York: Pantheon, 1953).
5. Hugo Friedrich, *The Structure of Modern Poetry: From the Mid-Nineteenth to the Mid-Twentieth Century*, trans. Joachim Neugroschel (Evanston: Northwestern University Press, 1974).
6. Theodor W. Adorno and Max Horkheimer, *Dialectic of Enlightenment*, trans. John Cumming (New York: Herder and Herder, 1972).
7. Roland Barthes, *The Pleasure of the Text*, trans. Richard Miller (New York: Hill and Wang, 1975). Cf. my essay "Barthes (*1915)," in *Klassiker der Literaturtheorie: Von Boileau bis Barthes*, ed. Horst Turk (Munich: C. H. Beck, 1979), 298–310; and Michel Foucault, "What Is an Author?," in *Textual Strategies*, ed. Josue Harari (Ithaca: Cornell University Press, 1979), 141–60.
8. Roland Barthes, *Mythologies*, trans. Annette Lavers (New York: Hill and Wang, 1972).
9. Michel Foucault's main works range from *The Birth of the Clinic: An Archaeology of Medical Perception*, trans. A. M. Sheridan Smith (New York: Pantheon Books, 1973), to *History of Sexuality*, trans. Robert Hurley, 3 vols. (New York: Pantheon Books, 1978–90), and to his inaugural address "L'ordre du discours," in *The Order of Things: An Archaeology of the Human Sciences* (New York: Pantheon Books, 1971).
10. Julia Kristeva, *Revolution in Poetic Language*, trans. Margaret Waller (New York: Columbia University Press, 1984).
11. Paul de Man, *Allegories of Reading: Figural Language in Rousseau, Nietzsche, Rilke and Proust* (New Haven: Yale University Press, 1979).
12. Cf. Jacques Derrida, "Titel (noch zu bestimmen)"/"Titre (à préciser)," in *Austreibung des Geistes aus den Geisteswissenschaften: Programme des Poststrukturalismus*, ed. Friedrich A. Kittler (Paderborn: Schöningh, 1980), 15–36; and Jacques Derrida, *Memoires: For Paul de Man*, trans. Cecile Lindsay, Jonathan Culler, and Eduardo Cadava (New York: Columbia University Press, 1986).
13. George Steiner, *Real Presences: Is There Anything in What We Say?* (London: Faber, 1989).
14. Barthes, *The Pleasure of the Text*.

15. Michel Serres, *The Parasite*, trans. Lawrence R. Schehr (Baltimore: Johns Hopkins University Press, 1982).

16. Alice Miller, *Prisoners of Childhood*, trans. Ruth Ward (New York: Basic Books, 1981).

17. Dirk Baecker, "Überlegungen zur Form des Gedächtnisses," in *Gedächtnis: Probleme und Perspektiven der interdisziplinären Gedächtnisforschung*, ed. Siegfried J. Schmidt (Frankfurt am Main: Suhrkamp Verlag, 1990), 337–59.

18. This connection between memory and intertextuality is developed in an exemplary manner by Renate Lachmann in *Gedächtnis und Literatur: Intertextualität in der russischen Moderne* (Frankfurt am Main: Suhrkamp Verlag, 1990).

19. Anselm Haverkamp and Renate Lachmann, eds., *Gedächtniskunst: Raum, Bild, Schrift: Studien zur Mnemotechnik* (Frankfurt am Main: Suhrkamp Verlag, 1990); Aleida Assmann and Dietrich Harth, eds., *Mnemosyne: Formen und Funktionen der kulturellen Erinnerung* (Frankfurt am Main: Fischer Taschenbuchverlag, 1991); and Stephen Greenblatt, *Shakespearean Negotiations: The Circulation of Social Energy in Renaissance England* (Oxford: Clarendon Press, 1988).

20. Cf. Wolf Kittler and Gerhard Neumann, "Kafkas Drucke zu Lebzeiten—Editorische Technik und hermeneutische Entscheidung," in *Franz Kafka: Schriftverkehr*, ed. Wolf Kittler and Gerhard Neumann (Freiburg: Rombach Verlag, 1990), 30–74; Gerhard Neumann, "Der verschleppte Prozeß. Literarisches Schaffen zwischen Schreibstrom und Werkidol," *Poetica* 14, nos. 1–2 (1982): 92–112; Gerhard Neumann, "Schrift und Druck: Erwägungen zur Edition von Kafkas *Landarzt*-Band," *Zeitschrift für deutsche Philologie* 101 (1982): 115–39; Gerhard Neumann, *Le manuscrit inacheve: Ecriture, création, communication*, ed. Louis Hay (Paris: Editions du centre national de la recherche scientifique, 1986); and Wolf Kittler, "Literatur, Edition und Reprographie," *Deutsche Vierteljahresschrift für Literaturwissenschaft und Geistesgeschichte* 65 (June 1991): 205–35.

ROBERT P. CARROLL

Toward a Grammar of Creation: On Steiner the Theologian

Siehe, ich lege in Zion einen Grundstein, einen bewährten
Steiner, einen köstlichen Eckstein, der wohl gegründet ist.
Wer glaubt, der sieht nicht.
          —Jesaja 28.16 (Martin Luther's *Die Bibel*: adapted, with
                    apologies to Isaiah and Martin Luther)

The prologues are over. It is a question, now,
Of final belief. So, say that final belief
Must be in a fiction. *It is time to choose.*
                    —Wallace Stevens, "Asides on the Oboe"
                              (emphasis mine)

◇ ◇ ◇

THE CRITICAL READINGS of George Steiner have always had
a metaphysical dimension, and, however his metaphysics may be described, the term *theology* will be at least proximately adequate. From
his *Tolstoy or Dostoevsky: An Essay in the Old Criticism* (1959) to his latest
essay or impassioned book review, the presence of *theos* (necessarily
undefined and distanced by metonym and allusion) has cast its shadow
across his entire work. Yet Steiner is in no conventional sense a theologian dedicated to the service of any ecclesia; he is instead a metaphysi-
cian of art, literature, and culture in the service of a larger bailiwick
than ecclesiastical interests, and some may therefore regard him as a
theologian *manqué*. His metaphysics, however, is never paraded for
inspection, and thus it is difficult to delineate the contours and content
of any theology he may embrace. Nevertheless, the theological is always there, and his *oeuvre* cries out for elucidation at this level. But,
rather than attempting so ambitious a project, this essay, by focusing
on his 1990 Gifford Lectures, will endeavor to assemble some of the
elements in his work which point toward the theological dimension of
the Steinerian universe.

The lectures—presented in Glasgow under the general title "Grammars of Creation"—were delivered from 5:30 to 7:00 P.M. at the university in two moieties, 23–27 April and 14–18 May. They were given under the aegis of two epigraphic statements, Leibniz's disturbing question "Why is there not nothing?" and Nietzsche's astounding affirmation that "art affirms, Job affirms." Nightly Steiner would return to these two points in order to reflect on their bearing on the topic of creativity, whether divine or human. His presentations, considered as performances, were the work of a master reader of those seminal texts that are embedded in European culture and that constitute the bedrock of Western civilization. The opening lecture set forth numerous questions that would echo throughout the entire series.

Thereafter followed a magisterial reading of the Book of Job, particularly the "Speech out of the Whirlwind" (chaps. 38–41), where finally the LORD (YHWH) answers Job's long, dense series of complaints with a set of powerful arguments focused on creation. The essence of the divine speech concerns the structures and techniques of the creation of the world—in relation to which Job's personal problems are put into perspective and thereby diminished, theodicy being an evasion of such issues rather than an answer to them (cf. Tilley 1991, 89–112). Steiner's focus was on the way the Hebrew notion of divine creation functions as the resolution of Job's situation.

Then, in his third lecture, Steiner looked at Plato's notion of divine creation. Here the essence of divine creativity is the geometer's art. Creation as geometry posits a mathematical activity in which the deity as mathematician creates a universe incapable of change because complete and perfect. Plato's *Theaetetus* was the dominant influence in Steiner's presentation here (with the work of Myles Burnyeat perhaps in the background). In a quite brilliant comparative and contrastive way, Steiner made some very fine points about the essential differences between the Hebrew and the Greek ways of representing creation. The Platonic world is fixed and static, it cannot change; whereas the Hebrew God creates in such a fashion that change is possible and creation becomes an ongoing process. Creation becomes future-oriented, and future possibilities for change render the past undeterminative of the future. Here we enter the realm of the messianic (in a Benjaminesque sense), though Steiner did not take that line in his lectures.

The first section of the lectures ended with two evenings devoted to the *Commedia*, especially to Dante's reading of and relation to Virgil. For Steiner, Dante forms one of the two greatest moments or peaks in Western cultural achievement. The other is formed by Proust—the absence of Shakespeare here being indicative of Steiner's "war" with the ultimate artist and his refusal to acknowledge the bard as the equal of Dante or Proust. So his reading of Dante was a very rich one. It was also dense with allusion and exegesis, which must have been lost on many in the audience and driven others back to Dante's text. (However Steiner may ultimately be judged as a contributor to cultural reflection in our time, he must always be credited with the practical achievement of stimulating his listeners and readers to return to the original texts that fund our culture.) This bald account of the first moiety of the lectures does no justice to the range and detail of Steiner's exegetical scrutiny of the European tradition of art and literature. Each lecture was graced by wit and pertinent asides, all superbly controlled by an overarching concern with the central topic of creativity.

In the course of the week we were given striking vignettes of Picasso and Flaubert, Kafka and Tolstoy (among many others). Readers familiar with Steiner's major writings will know exactly what I am describing here. There was a brilliant treatment of Goethe and the invention (discovery?) of time in the late eighteenth century. The emergence of the crowd in the consciousness of writers and the influence of the development of manufacturing processes on artists were also incorporated into the lectures. Examples too numerous to list here were given to illustrate the nature of the complex relations between artists and their creations. Most striking were the points about how Emma Bovary and Anna Karenina escape from and outlive their creators. What is creativity that a "mere" fiction such as Emma Bovary should outlive her creator Flaubert? What is divine creativity that a Picasso should live out his life and do his work in conscious rivalry to that other creator? Steiner raised the questions, but left the audience to reflect on possible answers (if answers there be).

A month later the second moiety of lectures began. Steiner developed the theme of artistic creation more fully, especially focusing on the nature of three-dimensional creation (i.e., sculpture) in relation to Ibsen's *When We Dead Awaken*. The third lecture of this week was a sensitive, and in many ways a scintillating, reading of some of the creative elements in Proust's *A la recherche du temps perdu*. At home in the French, Steiner produced a masterly evocation of moments of that great twentieth-century text and its depiction of the nature of musical creation. The penultimate lecture took up that focus on music and developed it further, with particular reference to Thomas Mann's *Doctor Faustus* and Hermann Hesse's *The Glass-Bead Game (Magister Ludi)*. Steiner offered some fascinating reflections on modern music, especially on rock and acid house. Music was a leitmotif running through all the lectures, because it is the human art form *par excellence*. The final lecture looked at Heidegger, then attempted to pull together all the various themes and strands of the lectures.

Under the general title "Grammars of Creation," the lectures focused on the nature of artistic creativity. Many of the examples scrutinized would have justified a separate lecture series each (e.g., Job, Plato, Virgil, Dante, Proust), so allowance must be made for the shorthand nature of much of what Steiner had to say. The texts cited and the extracts read, the examples given and the illustrations elucidated, were all evocations of the central theme of the lectures: human creativity as analogous to divine creation. Steiner also made much of the distinctions between "creation" and "invention," though there are ranges of human activity in which the two shade into each other and the distinctions lose their differences. But what I never quite got hold of was the sense in which creation may be said to have a grammar, and thus I remain puzzled as to what exactly is grammatical about creation.

Grammar implies deep structures, syntax, rules, and universal norms controlling usage. Does creation correspond to a grammar model? Here I believe Steiner did not address directly the sense (or senses) in which creativity could be said to be rule-bound. Whether God as creator is also bound by rules, so creation follows necessary structures, also remains unclear to me. I did not find the model or trope of grammar to be a helpful one in the discussion of creativity, and I think that further elucidation here would have been most helpful.

In Steiner's defense it must be said that between the lectures as delivered and the lectures as published in book form there will doubtless be enormous differences, as a result of the extensive revision and expansion that remain to be done. The published version may sort out some of these problems, or make clear just what exactly is grammatical about creation. God as a grammarian strikes me as a problematic designation, which threatens to render God subordinate to a prior necessity determining divine actions. It also seems to put us back in the Plato-Socrates debate about the nature of the good and whether it is good because the gods will it or whether it is willed by the gods because it is good. A grammar of creation which preexists the gods will pose insurmountable problems for traditional forms of Western theology.

Throughout the lectures Steiner made numerous allusions to Jewish thinking about God, especially to Talmudic views on the nature of divine creation. These may be developed in the published version and may therefore address the problem of creation as grammar. Perhaps human beings are subjected to such grammatical constraints when creating, these being constraints that do not, however, operate for gods. However, we know so very little about the springs of human creativity that it may be unwise to press the grammar analogy too far. How does a Mozart conceive a symphony, or a Rilke a poem? Is musical composition like playing chess? Can a major composer "see" a composition the way a chess player sees the next fifty moves? Steiner touched on all these issues in his lectures but, true to form, left his audience profoundly moved, yet stuck with many more questions than answers.

The question of God has invariably flitted through Steiner's work, without ever being systematically developed. In his *Real Presences* (1989), the "presence" behind the text—absent from the text?—evokes the question of God more fully than in anything else he has written. But it is God as "transcendence," that is, the undefined, unknown God, rather than the overdetermined, overdefined God of traditional Jewish religion and Christian ecclesiastical creeds. In the lectures the God of traditional theological thought appeared at times to be the object of Steiner's discourse: God as the creator of the world (as specified in Genesis 1), as Job's torturer and interlocutor, and as the Talmudic *En Sof.* At other times in the lectures the term *God* carried no more freight than does an allusion to *transcendence* (i.e., that which is beyond the human). But neither the lectures nor *Real Presences* fully addresses the issue of transcendence with the kind of precision which is required if Steiner's (now famous) "wager on transcendence" is to become an effective evocation of the transcendental.

Perhaps such questions cannot be answered, or should not be answered. Perhaps in their evocation Steiner has done his work. But one still wants him to push open the doors he appears to have unlocked. Do human beings create because there *is* a God or because there *is not* a God? I know Steiner's answer to that question. But one wants argument rather than assertion, warrants rather than wagers. Is the God—I use the upper-case letter but recognize that a lower-case one might be equally appropriate—a creative person believes in necessarily an existent being? Might not belief in God be belief in a rhetorical or fictional god? The poetry of Wallace Stevens forces this issue. Does Steiner think it makes any difference whether the sense of transcendence has a referent?

Other supplementary questions crowd in. Given the fact that so many people believe in God (of some description or other), why is there so little real creativity? Was there really more creativity around in the ages when belief in God was more conventionally acceptable? What is the explanation for van Gogh's art when the abandoning of his religion became the necessary condition for his producing his great art in the first place? In what sense can Picasso or Einstein be said to have believed in God? Did Marcel Proust believe in God or transcendence? Clement Greenberg once asked the question, "What great painter after El Greco was a fundamentally religious man?" (Greenberg 1961, 97) and that makes me wonder whether we are not here in an area of definitions, rather than one of dichotomies between "God" and "not-God." There are perhaps too many questions, but this is always the effect of Steiner's work.

◇ ◇ ◇

George Steiner is a Jew. Hence my first epigraph to this essay adapts the statement in Isaiah 28.16: "Look, I lay (as a foundation) in Zion a stone, a tested stone, a precious cornerstone well founded: the one who believes will not make haste." The verse is not easily translated, especially as the notion of foundation (*ysd*) is used three times in ways that escape precise English translation. Theology has never been a major feature of Jewish religion. The highly theoretical, philosophical constructions that constitute theology are very much at home in Christian thinking, whereas Jewish movements have tended to eschew such speculative constructions in favor of halachic and textualist procedures. There are, of course, exceptions to these generalizations (e.g., the Kabbala tends to be mystical, speculative, and comprehensive), but generally the nature of the theological in Judaism is different from that in Christianity. So to talk about Steiner as a theologian is to use a metaphor to make a point—which must be qualified by the recognition of Steiner's Jewishness.

But though he is a Jew, he is not Orthodox; most Jews are not. Indeed, Steiner is a secular Jew (I use the phrase as Yovel uses it for

Spinoza). But his Jewishness is important, because it reminds us that he stands in a long line of Jewish intellectuals who have been influential in the creation of the modern European intellectual tradition, starting with Spinoza and including Heine, Marx (even if these two did become cultural "Christians"), Freud, Einstein, Kafka, and Benjamin. The Jew in Christian Europe is both insider and outsider, in a certain sense at home in European thought, in another sense quite alien to it. Steiner lives in the Western intellectual tradition and has written significant works on that tradition from Homer and the classical authors to the major writers and poets of the post-Enlightenment period. His Jewishness gives him an outsider's eye and ear for that tradition. As a Jew, he just escaped the destruction of the Shoah, which annihilated European Jewry in this century. He has written significantly on the Shoah: his haunting novel *The Portage to San Cristóbal of A.H.* (1981) was turned into a controversial play in the 1980s; various writings on the death camps appear, like diamonds in coal mines, in his most important collection of essays, *Language and Silence* (1967). He has also written about what it is to be a Jew (see Steiner 1967, 119–35) and the nature of Jewish existence as the experience of Diaspora lived in the homeland of the text ("Our Homeland, the Text").

Orthodox Judaism does not like Steiner. In an interview in the *London Times* with Rabbi Dr. Jonathan Sacks, just after it had been announced that he was to be the new Chief Rabbi of Great Britain, in succession to Rabbi Dr. Jakobovits (this is a curious English institution relating to certain orthodox congregations, which was created in Victorian times), the Chief Rabbi-elect twice took the opportunity to criticize Steiner (Amiel 1990). In a short interview such excessive devotion to Steiner's shortcomings as a Jew indicates a profound hostility toward the kind of Jew he is. His lack of orthodoxy and of Hebrew and Aramaic (necessary for reading the Bible and the Talmud) make him an obvious target for a quasi-fundamentalistic Jewishness that emphasizes a narrow conformism and rejects the intellectual tradition of the West as having anything to do with true religion. Sacks's own brilliant intellectual attainments have been subordinated to his religious calling in a way that highlights the tensions between Orthodox Judaism and the existence of secular Jews such as Steiner. But any account of Steiner the theologian must take cognizance of his Jewishness and the uneasy relationship between him and the adherents of Orthodox Jewish practice. A Steiner in Zion becomes a reminder of some of the tensions inherent in the Hebrew Bible (cf. the "stone of striking" in Isaiah 8.14) and the long history of various kinds of factionalism within the Jewish community.

As a Jew Steiner is perhaps more open to Jewish influences than some theologians may be. Spinoza and Kafka, Buber and Rosenzweig, Scholem and Benjamin are obvious examples of the Jewish presences in Steiner's work. Other Jewish voices can also be heard in his work, especially that of Emmanuel Levinas (an important philosopher whose work has yet to win its deserved influence on Western thought). To these Jewish voices must be added some distinctive Christian ones that contribute to Steiner's theological formation.

Like Spinoza, Steiner openly faces the Christian contribution to the European cultural heritage and appears to be at home in Christian literature. To be engaged in the literature and history of European culture necessitates a deep familiarity with Augustine and Origen, Aquinas and Dante, Milton and Blake, Luther and Calvin, Barth and Bultmann (just to single out a few major figures). Intimacy with Christian mythology is a *sine qua non* for understanding Dante and Milton (to say the least). While a trawl through the writings of Steiner, especially the formidable *After Babel: Aspects of Language and Translation* (1975), would demonstrate the truth of this contention that Steiner is on reading terms with the major Christian theologians and writers (neither Pascal nor Kierkegaard should be forgotten as dominant influences on his thought), it is unnecessary to multiply examples in order to make the point. As a Jew he combines knowledge of things Jewish with an unusual sensitivity to things Christian. Steiner is perhaps not a theologian *manqué*, but just a very acute reader whose ear is open (to use another phrase from the Book of Isaiah [50.4, 5]) to the many voices that constitute the richness of the European cultural tradition.

One Christian voice that is a real presence in and behind Steiner's *Real Presences* is that of the formidable Scots theologian Donald Mac-Kinnon. A long-term friend of Steiner's, MacKinnon has taught him much about the depths and intricacies of classical Christian thought. Both men share a deep and abiding interest in tragedy and have written illuminatingly on it (cf. Steiner 1961; 1990; MacKinnon 1968, 97–104; 1974, 114–45; 1979, 182–95). Both have been Gifford Lecturers (Mac-Kinnon gave the 1965–66 lectures in Edinburgh). Although at times there is a MacKinnonesque timbre to Steiner's voice, it is never an overwhelming influence blotting out that unique Steinerian voice. Steiner has learned from MacKinnon, but has also successfully transmuted that learning into his own most distinctive reading of the tradition. If theology could only free itself from its ecclesiastical captivities, then Steiner's Jewish glossing—does this term that he himself uses of Jeremiah (*After Babel*, 147) understate Steiner's contribution?—of the Christian tradition might well point to a future for cultural theology which would be the transcending (*Aufhebung?*) of what passes today for theology.

It would require an essay much longer than this one to do justice to the theological dimension in Steiner's work and a further essay to explore the significance of the Bible for his thinking. Unlike many other literary critics working in English literature today, Steiner has *not* written a book on the Bible. Even though books on the Bible and/as literature are a growth industry now, Steiner has not transgressed his own strict linguistic code and offered us his repristinations of that iconic book. He has written on the Bible in the course of his many books (see the index to *After Babel*), and he has recently reviewed various books on the Bible (e.g., Steiner 1988; 1991a), but we await his ultimate thoughts on that book. As far as the Bible is concerned, Steiner is a reader, rather than a critic, of it. (That strong opposition of reader to critic is the subject of one of Steiner's best essays [Steiner 1984]). So we shall probably never see such a book. However, in order to conclude this brief exploration of his work, I shall focus on two aspects of the Bible which bear directly on his interests.

In May 1992 Steiner hosted the conference "The Great Tautology" at Robinson College, Cambridge. This was a multi-tradition (i.e., Jewish, Christian, Muslim, and nonbelieving) discussion of the meaning, historical interpretation, and contemporary significance of the great tautology of Exodus 3.14, "I am that I am." Among the main contributors were Steiner, Donald MacKinnon, Miles Burnyeat, Seyyed Hossein Nasr, Alexander Broadie, and David Burrell. It was an exciting event of genuine pluralistic discussion about one of the foundational texts of Western and Middle Eastern religions, and it offered a further expression of Steiner's active commitment to serious thought about matters theological and philosophical.

Exodus 3.14 is a good point at which to break into the hermeneutical circle that is the Bible. The tautology itself illustrates the biblical writers' love of puns and wordplay. Untensed Hebrew plays havoc with Indo-European language systems and enthrones ambiguity at the heart of the theological enterprise. That "I am" of Exodus echoes throughout the Bible, especially in the Fourth Gospel and in everyday speech. Shakespeare and Coleridge mine its deep structures, and Heidegger finds in it a unique account of being. Whether being or presence is the dominant thought behind the text is a question for much debate. Even more difficult to determine is the question of the existence of the one speaking in the burning bush. That question touches all existence today and reflects much of Steiner's deep concern with real presences in his recent writings on our contemporary situation (Steiner 1986a; 1989a). Given the absence of that being (speaking from the midst of the bush) in so many of today's constructions, Steiner sees only "spiritual and existential duplicity" (1986a, 22). Only by wagering on transcendence (a metaphor running through many of his writings, though perhaps most notably in *Real Presences*), by avowing mystery (i.e., that which is *beyond* ourselves, the transcendental), can we restore meaning and value to things. For Steiner transcendence is the key to understanding the experience of the bush. Immanence will not do for him—"The symmetries of immanence are cruel" (1991b, xxi [= 1989b, 43])—hence the encounter at the bush turns Moses (the religion of Moses? the text that tells the story?) into the Shepherd of Being (to use a Heideggerian phrase in a somewhat repristinated fashion). It is at this point in his work that Steiner dons the garb of a theologian and his *oeuvre* becomes an important contribution to the theological enterprise.

The Bible comes to us out of a past other than our own and out of languages other than our own. To master it requires considerable philological fortitude and linguistic skill. Hebrew, Aramaic, and Greek are the languages of the Bible, though the Latin Bible is really the book that contributes to the creation of European culture, Luther's German Bible and the English Authorized Version (the end of a line of Englished Bibles long in the making) considerably contributing to the development of modern German and English literary sensibilities. Theology has always been written in languages other than English: first in Greek, then Latin, and, finally, German. To be a theologian or to do theology is first and foremost to become a linguist or a polyglot. As talk about God (i.e., theology at its lowest level), theology is always translation. God's speech is a trope and has to be translated into human speech. Study of the Bible is a very good way into the realization that theology is always done in somebody else's language. Of course there is theology *in translation,* just as the Bible is in translation for most people, but that is the point so often missed. The translation process is a good metaphor for theology because it underlines the translational nature of the discipline.

Steiner has written at length about translation and is at home in a number of languages (see 1975, 115–18). His feeling for language (*Sprachgefühl*) makes him a good reader of theology and gives him access to the theological enterprise at a level beyond that of many practicing theologians. Hence he can read the Bible in the company of Karl Barth and Rudolf Bultmann (and criticize those who fail to do so yet persist in writing on the Bible). This capacity can make for a certain hauteur in his criticisms of others who read less well than he does himself. His review of *The Literary Guide to the Bible* (1988), edited by Robert Alter and Frank Kermode, is a good example of this. He makes many good points in praise and blame of the various authors, though his criticisms are not always entirely accurate (e.g., the accusation that no reference is made to Karl Barth on Romans is wrong, because Kermode does quote from him). But his essential criticism of the blandness of the book is profoundly theological. In demanding that "the plain question of divine inspiration . . . must be posed, must be faced squarely and unflinchingly," Steiner is injecting, into calm scholarly discussion of the Bible, the radical otherness of the theological. The voices in the Bible come to us from beyond ourselves (i.e., are transcendental). The poet who wrote the Book of Job produced something unique in all world literature. This book is different from all our classical sources, and the true hermeneut's task is to explain, to elucidate that difference. If Steiner cannot conceive of the author of the Book of Job as "dwelling within common existence and parlance," then we must number Steiner among the theologians, rather than among the mere literary critics.

◇ ◇ ◇

I could continue my exploration of the theological dimensions of Steiner's work ad infinitum or, at least, until I had produced a book-length treatment. Space shall not permit that endeavor. In commenting on his books I have put into practice the very vice against which his recent books have inveighed. I have written a commentary on his texts instead of reading them and consenting to be addressed by them. But my comments on his Gifford Lectures are offered not so much as commentary, but rather as a sort of preview of the book that in due course will be published. In the meantime, Steiner's other books are available throughout the West and do themselves afford his readers a large opportunity for the kind of theological engagement that his work consistently seeks to elicit.

Works Cited

Amiel, Barbara. "The Unorthodox Traditionalist," *London Times*, 13 March 1990.
Carroll, Robert P. "Review of George Steiner, *Real Presences*," *Scottish Journal of Theology* 46, no. 1 (1993): 100–103.
Deutscher, Isaac. *The Non-Jewish Jew and Other Essays.* Oxford: Oxford University Press, 1968.
Greenberg, Clement. *Art and Culture: Critical Essays.* Boston: Beacon Press, 1961.
MacKinnon, Donald M. *Borderlands of Theology and Other Essays.* London: Lutterworth Press, 1968.
———. *The Problem of Metaphysics.* Cambridge: Cambridge University Press, 1974.
———. *Explorations in Theology 5.* London: SCM Press, 1979.
Steiner, George. *Tolstoy or Dostoevsky: An Essay in the Old Criticism.* New York: Knopf, 1959.
———. *The Death of Tragedy.* London: Faber and Faber, 1961.
———. *Language and Silence: Essays 1958–1966.* London: Faber and Faber, 1967.
———. *After Babel: Aspects of Language and Translation.* New York: Oxford University Press, 1975.
———. *The Portage to San Cristóbal of A.H.* New York: Simon and Schuster, 1981.
———. "'Critic'/'Reader,'" in *George Steiner: A Reader.* New York: Oxford University Press, 1984.
———. "Our Homeland, the Text," *Salmagundi* 66 (Winter-Spring 1985): 4–25.
———. *A Reading against Shakespeare: The W. P. Ker Lecture.* Glasgow: University of Glasgow, 1986a.
———. *Real Presences: The Leslie Stephen Memorial Lecture.* Cambridge: Cambridge University Press, 1986b.
———. "Review of *The Literary Guide to the Bible*," *New Yorker*, 11 January 1988.
———. "Heidegger, Again," *Salmagundi* 82–83 (Spring-Summer 1989a).
———. *Real Presences: Is There Anything in What We Say?* London: Faber and Faber, 1989b.

————. "Literary Forms: A Note on Absolute Tragedy," *Literature and Theology: An Interdisciplinary Journal of Theory and Criticism* 4, no. 2 (July 1990): 147–56.

————. "Battles of the Book: Revaluations of Scripture from Dante to de Man," *Times Literary Supplement* 4629 (20 December 1991a).

————. *Martin Heidegger: With a New Introduction.* Chicago: Chicago University Press, 1991b.

Stevens, Wallace. *The Collected Poems of Wallace Stevens.* London: Faber and Faber, 1984.

Tilley, Terrence, W. *The Evils of Theodicy.* Washington, D.C.: Georgetown University Press, 1991.

Yovel, Yirmiyahu. *Spinoza and Other Heretics.* 2 vols. Princeton: Princeton University Press, 1990.

A Responsion

◇ ◇ ◇

Responsion (now rare, says the O.E.D.): signifying "a reply" and also
the remittance of a chivalric debt or obligation.

To read these thirteen essays about my work has been demanding.
Criticism and dissent are constantly needed. One grows by them.
Praise monumentalizes and makes one's present an epilogue to an
irreparable past. But diverse as these essays are, each embodies, by its
simple existence and inclusion in this book, an act of radical generosity.
It entails the possibility, beyond friendship or consensus, that there is in
my writings and teaching something worth serious notice and contention. For reasons to which a number of contributors advert, much of
what I have tried to imagine and to argue has been either marginalized
or passed under silence. To many my books have been, in the proper
sense of the term, impertinent; to others, unacceptable. I have no
school and, being as vain as the next man, have been spared the discipline of refusing most honors or professional comforts. It is, in consequence, with a sense of wonder, almost of unease, that I turn to the
considerations in this collection, offered by scholars and critics otherwise heavily engaged and who must know that their investment in
reading me will harvest no general echo from their peers.

The first reply is, therefore, one of thanks. From the opening sentence of my earliest book, *Tolstoy or Dostoevsky*, in which I defined true criticism, true reading as a "debt of love" onward, I have felt our age and climate of spirit to be one of *invidia*, of the sneer. Because of this we come close to lacking the language of thanks, the motions of praise which inhabit gratitude. I have dwelt on these in *Real Presences*, in trying to delineate that *cortesia* and tact of heart without which there cannot be answerability, responsible response to our encounter with "the other," be it in the form of art, music, literature, or systematic thought. Now, aiming at responsion to this gathering, I seek words that are exact, that are scrupulous. I do not know that I will find those that can fully convey my pleasure in obligation, my almost sensory experience of the evidence stated in the ancient play on words and the music of words whereby "to think is to thank." In this instance to thank the begetters and editors and each of those who took time and largesse to accept their invitation.

Correspondingly, I take my task to be that of thinking, briefly, with and, at certain points, against those who have, so prodigally, made me their guest.

The nearing shadow of Hitler made me. Privileged as it was humanly, in respect of schooling, of the natural availability of books and of the arts, my childhood in Paris was wholly on edge. My grimly clairvoyant father knew what was to come. The unrootedness, the assumption of exile and peregrine survival which Mark Krupnick, Robert Boyers, and Ronald Sharp allude to, was in-built. The insight that trees have roots and can be lightning-struck, whereas men have legs with which to advance on the future or take refuge, was hammered home early. Of the Jewish boys and girls in my school class and circle, two have survived (of whom I am one). The unmerited scandal of this survival, the pathological bent toward some immediate sharing of their hideous fate (how would I have behaved, how abject would my fears have been?) is with me always. It is inherent in my sense of lamed self and of my assignment. Which is that of "remembrancer" (another archaic word), of one who learns by heart in order to hand on what would otherwise be ash. As Krupnick points out, I am of "no place." Which is also to attempt to be of "wherever," to enact the beliefs that the homeland of the mind is a table at which one is allowed to write and that no nation, no city, is not worth leaving on grounds of injustice, corruption, philistinism. I take this autistic ubiquity to be the very essence of Judaism in our estate. I believe that it is the determinant function of the Jew as survivor to be a guest among men, to exemplify and articulate the creed according to which we will perish or descend further into bestiality on this grimed planet unless we learn to live as one another's guests. I understand far less of Heidegger than Graham Ward intimates. But I am utterly persuaded by Heidegger's finding that we are guests of Being, transient dwellers in a temporality and "thrownness" entirely beyond our grasp, and that this condition makes of us the custodians of language and of certain values and astonishments in the face of life itself.

These sentiments and the efforts made to exist accordingly—I bridle at those who mouth principles that they do not perform, be they parlor Marxists, lounge Zionists outside Israel, or intellectuals aiming to please and to succeed—have often generated isolation. My (tactless) asides about passports having to be collected like postage stamps, my nausea at chauvinism and at unexamined loyalties, have not made allies. The polis is that structure designed to execute Socrates. Nationalism has "the necessary murder" and warfare as its direct sequel (witness the modulation from the moral autochtony of a Jeremiah to the armed camp that is now Israel, from the messianic internationalism of Marx and of Trotsky to the Gulag). We have entered into an era of homicidal tribalism, of mass murder over bits of colored cloth called flags. A polyglot unhousedness is sharply out of tune.

Worse: this frequently unplanned border-crossing—the Geneva expression is *frontalier*—extends to my interests. The University of Chicago gave me a lasting passion for the sciences. This passion, which my nullity in mathematics renders literally childish, led in turn to the high places of the pure and applied sciences which are the Institute for Advanced Study in Princeton and Churchill College, Cambridge. Had I lived in the quattrocento, I would now and again have sought to have lunch with the painters. To an extent scarcely plumbed by humanists and literati, it has been in this century the scientists who have largely enlisted and voiced the energies of speculative imagining, of questioning wit, of confidence of soul. I have, moreover, not only ranged too widely in literary and philosophic studies (as Nathan Scott gently adduces), writing on Russian fiction and Greek drama, on Homer and Paul Celan, on Heidegger and Dante, but also published a book on chess. There are possible apologias. To the masters in the crafts of reading and of poetics, to Auerbach, Curtius, Jakobson, or Contini, such a range would appear minimal. I remain by their unworried lights a monographer. But it is not, I admit, apologia I incline to.

Specialization has reached moronic vehemence. Learned lives are expended on reiterative minutiae. Academic rewards go to the narrow scholiast, to the blinkered. Men and women in the learned professions proclaim themselves to be experts on one author, in one brief historical period, in one aesthetic medium. They look with contempt (and dank worry) on the "generalist." By definition he or she will perpetrate errata, imprecisions, and judgments tainted by swiftness. The title of my Geneva chair, the oldest in the comparative rubric, is that of *littérature générale*. This tag honors me. Would that it was called, even more exactly, *de lecture*—a chair of reading, for those learning how to read and to read with others. It may be that cows have fields. The geography of consciousness should be that of unfenced *errance*, Montaigne's comely word. At his death, Edmund Wilson, my immediate predecessor on the *New Yorker*, was learning Hungarian.

In the evident absence of genius, such catholicities can not only occasion error and superficiality: the wide ranger fails to press home, to make institutionally serviceable, some of his best findings. When Ruth Padel, in her characteristically penetrating reading, comes to favor the definitions of *The Death of Tragedy* above those put forward in later work, she directs me to what was incomplete and provisional in that early book, to that which ought to have been closely debated and made systematic from the outset. The "working metaphor" of the Judaic blackmail of the ideal, of the pressures on Western consciousness of the exigence of perfection inherent in Mosaic monotheism, in the teachings of Jesus, and in utopian Marxism, *is* developed in subsequent texts. But I have failed to give it a full-scale and sufficiently documented exposition. As a result, it has been widely and too often loosely cited and put to facile polemic use. In respect of *After Babel*, the exploitation (the pilfering) has been pervasive. Dozens of books and a score of articles have fed, usually with no or with minimal acknowledgment, on that comprehensive study. The burgeoning category of translation studies, of the poetics of linguistic transfer, has at numerous points sprung from *After Babel* (a new, thoroughly revised edition of which has recently appeared). Having mapped a complex terrain, I might have done better to remain within and to cultivate it. After *Antigones* it was regularly put to me that the disputed conjecture as to the generic interrelations between myth and syntax required an extensive statement and additional exemplification. I have let others gather this problematic harvest. Now it is for me late afternoon.

Even the authentically stellar run the risk of self-dispersal, of suggesting rather than enforcing. Together with the Authorized Version and with Shakespeare, it is indeed Coleridge I turn to most in English literature. John Bayley's intuition on this point moves and delights me. The difference being, of course, that Coleridge's self-dissemination and fragmentation followed on compactions of genius. Yet nevertheless I venture to think that there is cohesion. The first page of *Tolstoy or Dostoevsky* declares the "Real Presences" that were to come more than thirty years later. *The Death of Tragedy* addresses directly themes that *Antigones* concentrates and deepens. There is very little in my ensuing books and essays which is not announced in *Language and Silence*. As both hostile and sympathetic readers have underlined, *In Bluebeard's Castle* intimately prefigures *The Portage to San Cristóbal of A.H.* The matter of music, which has moved to the resistant center for me, is raised and questioned in the very earliest essays. *After Babel*, in its reflections on the ontology of hope in the discovery of the future tense of the verb, anticipates the dramatization of the grammars of the messianic in *Proofs* (a fiction recently published and therefore outside the view of the contributors of this volume). Nothing is more heartwarming to me than Caryl Emerson's emphasis on the threads that unify and make continuous the external diversity of my publications.

This is of especial pertinence (as Boyers and Sharp so clearly observe) to the interplay between philosophic-critical discourse, acts of reading, and my parables, novellas, and novel. I do not possess the inventive innocence, the somnambular immediacy, of the poet and novelist. (I have, praise be, never gotten over the blinding revelation of the light-years that separate verse, of the sort I wrote and published long ago, from poetry. It is not prose that is the contrary of poetry, it is well-turned verse of the kind schoolboys and young mandarins in the European context were taught to turn out.) My fictions are, in essence, allegories of argument, "stagings" of ideas. Twice, perhaps, I have known "possession" and have experienced the numbing radiance of ungoverned compulsion—in the counterpoint set of the Lieber and the A.H. monologues in *The Portage* and in "Conversation Piece" as it closes *Proofs and Three Parables*. I have known, in Heidegger's "radical intransitivity," Gerald Bruns's enlightening phrase, what it feels like not to write but to "be written." What is, however, plain to see is the instrumental collusion between the genres in my work. In a tribute to Ernst Bloch (republished among my essays), I wondered whether some "Pythagorean form" located at the confluence of philosophic discourse and the imaginary, even of symbolic notation and traditional semantics, might follow on the established novel. It is by no means "fact-fiction" I had in mind, but something of the guise intimated not only in the "lyric intellections" of a Bloch or a Péguy but also in the Heraclitean tenor of Wittgenstein's *Tractatus*. It is at the journeyman level toward the advent of such modes of language under stress of thought that I attempt to serve in my own "counter-factual" narratives. Where it is not arrogant pretense or mere impatience, what passes, quite falsely, for "theory" in the humanities is, in fact, narrative, a storytelling of ideas.

There is, moreover, a "figure in the carpet," which is that of my Judaism, of my search for a homeland in the text. Edith Wyschogrod is admirably lucid on this crux. I suppose there is hardly a paragraph I have written—and this includes the approximately two hundred pieces for the *New Yorker*—wholly abstinent from some element of sensibility or interior citation with reference to Judaism after the Shoah or to the black roots of that catastrophe. I have already indicated the personal background. The dialectic of "Athens/Jerusalem" has been perennial throughout my teaching and published work. Here there is a debt to that major though still hidden thinker, Leon Shestov, which has gone unnoticed in these essays. Of late two topics, that of the contiguities of the deaths by law of Socrates and of Jesus, and that of the enigmatic fatality of the Jewish refusal of Christ's claims to messianic status, have obsessed me. Robert Carroll is acutely aware of the links between these two questions and such recent work as my 1990 Gifford Lectures on "Grammars of Creation" (still to be put into legible order). Inevitably, these concerns have brought with them, most visibly in *Real Presences* and in my almost uninterrupted (interior) exchanges with Walter Benjamin, with Paul Celan, with Donald MacKinnon (I am no reader of Buber), a shift in register, a new coloration that can be perceived as "Christianizing." It is indeed in such motions of vision as those of von Balthasar and MacKinnon that I have found the echo chamber indispensable to my uncertainties. I had not in any way foreseen this modulation, and it troubles me.

No deeps of light—I find no other expression—thrown into the long midnight of our century surpass those given to us by such Jewish visionaries as Kafka, Mandelstam, and Celan. But the legacy of iconoclasm, of juridical rationalism in Judaism inhibits an idiom that endeavors to come nearer the transcendent possibility, the otherness of informing unreason in the arts. In trying to hammer out some perception, however rudimentary, into the paradoxes of real presence as we meet with them in the aesthetic, I found myself resorting to the pulses of metaphor, to the analytics of mystery in the Augustinian, Thomist, and Pascalian semantics and aura. (Neumann senses this clearly.) The tensions between inheritance and underlying syntax, between personal identity and compelled reference, already performative in Benjamin and in Celan's uses of Hölderlin and of Heidegger, have, since the *Antigones*, grown palpable in my conjectures and language. Through them I have begun to glimpse the sickening wellspring of Jewish self-refusal in Simone Weil. This is somber ground.

The "goodly company" here assembled tempts me to try to state as concisely as possible the principal themes with which my work can be identified.

As several contributors emphasize, language has been its pivot. My earliest published essays bore on "The Retreat from the Word," on the substitution of formal codes—logical, mathematical, pictorial—for classical verbal discourse across large tracts of modern communication and information. In "The Hollow Miracle," I argued the destruction of the German language under Nazi use and the duplicities within that language which allowed the deployment of the lexicon and syntax of the inhuman. In analogy, I attempted, in "Night Words," to indicate the voidance of humane speech and the encodings of animality as we find them in pornography and in the more general "pornographies" of kitsch, of advertising, of the pop arts, be they visual or literary (there is much here I would want to debate with my friend in dissent, Guido Almansi). These various forays soon forced on me the central question of the relations between the aesthetic and the barbaric. Posited some forty years ago, my "profile" of the man or woman who reads Rilke in the morning and plays Schubert after dinner though torturing or humiliating living beings during the day has been very widely taken up. Less understood and explored has been my concomitant suggestion that the humanities (literature, art, music) can paradoxically dehumanize, that we listen so ardently to the cry of Cordelia that we fail to hear, or to attach urgency to, the cry in the street. I do not have a satisfactory answer. So much in my writings evokes Blake's "idiot questioner." But I am persuaded that we must find ways of making imagining concrete in and through our study and teaching of the humanities if these are not to be seduced by, to become accomplices to, political and social bestiality (we are accomplices to that which leaves us indifferent).

In respect of language, *After Babel* advances two fundamental theses. I argued that the crazy-quilt multiplicity of human tongues, the development of hundreds of mutually incomprehensible languages in one archipelago, pointed to a radically counter-Darwinian mechanism. It spoke of the need of our consciousness to construe alternative realities, to liberate itself from the determinist uniformities of the biological. Each language opens its own particular window on the sum of being, on the landscapes of denial and of possibility. In a Chomskyan climate, this proposal has been ignored by established linguists but has its subterranean life. Nor have I found much response among linguists or psycho-linguists to the second thesis whereby it is "counter-factuality," that is, the scandalous human discovery of the future tense, of "if" clauses, of optatives which comes very near to underwriting our freedom and our tenacities of hope. We endure because we can "speak tomorrow," because consciousness emancipates itself from the despotism of the fact by virtue of conditional and future constructs in grammar. Of this, I remain convinced.

Following on Ruth Padel, others will, I hope, engage my discrimination between the tragicomic impulse in what passes for "tragedy"—most notably in Shakespeare—and "absolute tragedy." The latter is spelt out in only a handful of texts, such as Euripides' *Bacchae*, Racine's plays, and Büchner's *Wozzeck*. It declares a condition in which men and women are unwelcome guests of life, in which they suffer arbitrary sadism and injustice beyond understanding and theodicy. This may well be a scarcely endurable blueprint, but so are the mere realities of Khmer Rouge massacres, of mass starvation, of the torment of children and animals, of the willful laying waste of the earth which persist, which have accelerated after Auschwitz. Samuel Beckett's theater began in eloquent, prolix clowning; it ended in a dying scream out of blackness. Yes, Ruth, we do need more laughter and better books on comedy (a genre more elusive than tragedy). But what in our late twentieth-century situation would give them substance?

Internal logic led from these questions to the formulation of the notion of "an epilogue," of a cultural-historical context—that of the present—in which older contracts between word and world have been broken. The human word is made Word (or *Logos*) only where these contracts are in general force and observance. I have sought to date their abrogation, very roughly, around the time and work of Rimbaud and Mallarmé. Nietzsche's obituary of God and the secularization of the psyche implicit in Freud are (vast) footnotes to this preceding breach. Our arts, our poetics, "come after" as does a satyr play after high tragedy. Where the ontological query as to the existence or non-existence of God is empty verbiage, where such a query is no longer even worth deconstructing, we enter a new semiology, a new apprehension of whether there is meaning to meaning. I now see clearly that this has been a concern throughout my work, that the transit from words to the Word, from theories of signs to presumptions of substance, has been an inevitable motif. The "real presence" was there from the outset, in my attempts at a reading of Dostoevsky's Stavrogin, in my account of why it is that Tolstoy does not leave anonymous even the most minor of his dramatis personae.

What has come, as it were of itself, is the movement of music toward the center of me. Psychologists instruct us that this is not unusual among the aging, that addicts of language and of reading often turn to music in their decline. This may be, and a listener's passion was already allowed me in childhood. But more could be involved. The effects of music on our psychosomatic states, the "invention" of melody, the nature of the meanings of and in music, seem to me imperative. They challenge our very concepts of intelligibility, intentionality, and reason. The question "What in the world is music like?" has become for me the metaphysical inquiry incarnate. In experiencing the phenomenologies of music, *I know that I do not know what I know*. In close turn, this awkward phrase, this contradiction within tautology, seems to me to conduct us to precisely the frontier between the mundane (in the etymological sense) and the "unworldly," between that in immanence which is subject to the analytic and that which lies just on the other side of metaphor. This intuition—and would that a working musician or composer had been heard in this collection—may be erroneous. From Plato and Augustine to Kierkegaard, to Nietzsche, and to Adorno, the number of those who have had anything adequate to *say* about music is a handful. What I feel certain of is the challenge. A semantics, a narrative of readings (and literary "theory" is nothing else but narrative grown impatient), a program of deconstruction or of psychoanalytic discovery which ignores or evades the fact of music, is vacant at its core. It is, in Lévi-Strauss's arresting formulation, the invention of melody which remains the *mystère suprême des sciences de l'homme*. The bare lineaments of a semantics of music seem to lie beyond our present reach. It is my hope that *Real Presences* may come to be seen as a prologue to a prologue of such a semantics. We must take this arduous path if we hope one day to make better sense of sense.

The last issue I want to touch on is in some ways the most precarious (it is inwoven in Mark Krupnick's treatment, it is the gravamen of my long dialogue with Robert Boyers). The new fiction now being published pivots on it. It is, of course, that of *élitisme* and democratic education, of aesthetic-abstract values and social justice. I have never been able to disguise my faith in Spinoza's equation of excellence and difficulty. I am convinced that nearly everything worth close investment in philosophy, poetics, the arts, demands stringent schooling and, often, a body of knowledge such as was imparted in the education of the privileged and the gifted prior to the present (today, schooling is very largely planned amnesia). I am, I suppose, a Platonic anarchist. I take it to be the primary obligation of the body politic to search out, to safeguard institutionally, the irreducible enigma of individual intellectual and artistic unfolding. Such a community honors the life of the mind, celebrates the arts, and privileges the essential gratuity of thought. It acknowledges unashamedly that for the great mass of us there will be no afterlife, no resonance in time beyond that of the inclusion of our names in mouldering telephone books. There is no democracy to excellence. It so happens that from Periclean Athens to Medicean Florence, from Elizabethan royalty and the *ancien régime* to the frozen night of Stalinism, creation has drawn strengths from oppression and censorship. "Squeeze us," said Joyce, "for we are olives." It so happens that it is in the twilight of diverse totalitarian orderings that a poem, an essay on Hegel, a painting, a symphony, are judged to be supremely dangerous, which is to say supremely important.

In these preceding sentences, my "it so happens" is transparent cant. I am bound to ask my readers and myself whether libertarian democracies, mass-consumption economies, and ecumenical politics of populist education, are naturally concordant with philosophic and aesthetic making of the first rank. It is glaringly obvious that the overwhelming majority of our species will prefer Disneyland to Aeschylus, and Michael Jackson to Bach. It is no less evident—I have stressed this throughout my work—that the price exacted in order to provide the context of peril and subversion which seems to generate certain summits of mind and imagination may, socially, humanely, already have been too steep. How many slaves for one Plato, how many in abjection for one Pushkin or Mandelstam? There are no facile balance sheets. But the possibility that there are organic affinities between inequality and *poiesis*, between constraint and depth of shaping, is a real one. "Censorship is the mother of metaphor" (Borges).

Much in the American paradigm, in that "California" of pre-packaged dreams toward which long-suffering humanity is now rushing, is committed to not posing the question. "Political correctness" (and how long will it take to repair the damage?) is a perfectly natural outcome of the leveling process inherent in pluralistic populism, in a society whose representative "philosopher" proclaims that "anything goes." It is at this vital crux that I differ with some of my American critics and readers. It is here that I persist in finding indispensable certain Old-World ironies and *tristia*. Absolute thought, certain magnitudes in music, come of solitude and of arrogant despair. Would Henry Adams, would Robert Hutchins, in whose Aristotelian university I came of age, disagree?

To end on a question, to make of questions a response to questions, is known to be a Jewish vice. As I read these essays, something more direct is to the point. A vote of thanks. Carried *nem con*. Which is to say: with all my heart.

Books by George Steiner

Tolstoy or Dostoevsky: An Essay in the Old Criticism. New York: Knopf, 1959; reprint, Chicago: University of Chicago Press, 1985.

The Death of Tragedy. New York: Knopf, 1961; reprint, New York: Oxford University Press, 1980.

(Editor, with Robert Fagles) *Homer: A Collection of Critical Essays*. Englewood Cliffs, N.J.: Prentice-Hall, 1962.

Anno Domini: Three Stories. New York: Atheneum, 1964.

(Editor) *The Penguin Book of Modern Verse Translation*. Harmondsworth: Penguin Books, 1966; reprinted as *Poem into Poem: World Poetry in Modern Verse Translation*, 1970.

Language and Silence: Essays on Language, Literature, and the Inhuman. New York: Atheneum, 1967.

Extraterritorial: Papers on Literature and the Language Revolution. New York: Atheneum, 1971.

In Bluebeard's Castle: Some Notes towards the Redefinition of Culture. New Haven: Yale University Press, 1971.

Fields of Force: Fischer and Spassky in Reykjavik. New York: Viking, 1973 (published in England as *The Sporting Scene: White Knights in Reykjavik*, London: Faber and Faber, 1973).

After Babel: Aspects of Language and Translation. New York: Oxford University Press, 1975; 2d and rev. ed., 1992.

On Difficulty and Other Essays. New York: Oxford University Press, 1978.

Martin Heidegger. New York: Viking, 1978 (published in England as *Heidegger*, London: Fontana, 1978).

The Portage to San Cristóbal of A.H. (novel). New York: Simon and Schuster, 1981.

Antigones: How the Antigone Legend Has Endured in Western Literature, Art, and Thought. New York: Oxford University Press, 1984.

George Steiner: A Reader. New York: Oxford University Press, 1984.

A Reading against Shakespeare: The W. P. Ker Lecture. Glasgow: University of Glasgow, 1986.

Real Presences: The Leslie Stephen Memorial Lecture. Cambridge: Cambridge University Press, 1986.

Real Presences. Chicago: University of Chicago Press, 1989.

Proofs and Three Parables (fiction). New York: Granta Books/Penguin, 1993.

Notes on Contributors

GUIDO ALMANSI, formerly Professor of English and Comparative Literature at the University of East Anglia, is the author of *L'estetica dell'osceno* (1974), *The Writer as Liar* (1975), *Amica Ironia* (1984), and, with Claude Beguin, *The Theatre of Sleep* (1986).

JOHN BAYLEY is Warton Professor of English Literature at Oxford University. His books include *The Romantic Survival* (1957), *The Characters of Love* (1962), *Tolstoy and the Novel* (1966), *Pushkin: A Comparative Commentary* (1971), and *Housman's Poems* (1992).

ROBERT BOYERS is Editor of the American quarterly *Salmagundi* and Professor of English at Skidmore College. His most recent books are *Atrocity and Amnesia: The Political Novel since 1945* (1985) and *After the Avant-Garde* (1988).

GERALD L. BRUNS is William P. and Hazel B. White Professor of English at the University of Notre Dame. His books include *Modern Poetry and the Idea of Language* (1974), *Heidegger's Estrangements* (1989), and *Hermeneutics Ancient and Modern* (1992).

ROBERT P. CARROLL is Dean of the Faculty of Divinity at the University of Glasgow, where he also serves as Professor of Biblical Studies. Among his numerous books are *When Prophecy Failed* (1979), *From Chaos to Covenant* (1981), and *Jeremiah: A Commentary* (1986).

CARYL EMERSON is Professor of Slavic Languages and Literatures and of Comparative Literature at Princeton University. Her books include *Boris Godunov: Transpositions of a Russian Theme* (1986) and, with Gary Saul Morson, *Mikhail Bakhtin: Creation of a Prosaics* (1990). She is the translator of Bakhtin's *Problems of Dostoevsky's Poetics* (1984) and, with Michael Holquist, *The Dialogic Imagination* (1981).

MARK KRUPNICK is Professor of Religion and Literature at the University of Chicago Divinity School and the author of *Lionel Trilling and the Fate of Cultural Criticism* (1986). His essays and reviews have appeared in such journals as *Tikkun, Soundings, Contemporary Literature,* and the *New York Review of Books.*

GERHARD NEUMANN is Professor of the History of German Literature at the University of Munich and Editor of the *Hofmannsthal Jahrbuch*. His books include studies and editions of Goethe, Kafka, German aphorisms, and comparative literature.

RUTH PADEL is the author of *In and Out of the Mind: Greek Images of the Tragic Self* (1992); three collections of poems—*Alibi* (1985), *Summer Snow* (1990), and *Angel* (1993); and articles on modern and ancient Greek poetry, on classics and feminism, and on Greek religion and myth. Her book "Whom Gods Destroy: Elements of Greek and Tragic Madness" is forthcoming.

NATHAN A. SCOTT, JR., is William R. Kenan Professor Emeritus of Religious Studies and Professor Emeritus of English at the University of Virginia. Among his numerous books are *Negative Capability* (1969), *The Wild Prayer of Longing: Poetry and the Sacred* (1971), *The Poetics of Belief* (1985), and *The Poetry of Civic Virtue: Eliot, Malraux, Auden* (1976). His most recent book is *Visions of Presence in Modern American Poetry* (1993).

RONALD A. SHARP is John Crowe Ransom Professor of English at Kenyon College and former Editor of the *Kenyon Review*. His books include *Keats, Skepticism, and the Religion of Beauty* (1979), *Friendship and Literature: Spirit and Form* (1986), and, with Eudora Welty, *The Norton Book of Friendship* (1991).

GRAHAM WARD is Assistant Editor of *Literature and Theology* and Chaplain, Fellow, and Tutor in Theology at Exeter College, Oxford University. His essays on theology, philosophy, and aesthetics have appeared in such journals as *Modern Theology, Cambridge Review*, and *London Magazine*. He has recently completed a book on Karl Barth and twentieth-century philosophies of language.

EDITH WYSCHOGROD is J. Newton Rayzor Professor of Philosophy and Religious Thought at Rice University. Her recent books include *Saints and Postmodernism: Revisioning Moral Philosophy* (1990) and *Spirit in Ashes: Hegel, Heidegger and Man-Made Mass Death* (1985).

Library of Congress Cataloging-in-Publication Data

Reading George Steiner / edited by Nathan A. Scott, Jr. and
Ronald A. Sharp.
    p.   cm.
    Includes bibliographical references and index.
    ISBN 0-8018-4832-6 (alk. paper)   ISBN 0-8018-4888-1
(pbk.)
    1. Steiner, George, 1929– . I. Scott, Nathan A.
II. Sharp, Ronald A.
P85.S74R4   1994
809—dc20   93-21013
                                        CIP